THE RETURN OF
HOLY RUSSIA

"*The Return of Holy Russia* gives us perspectives on Russia's spiritual history we sorely need. It helps us understand why the Putin administration has trouble giving up its entanglements with Ukraine, why many Russians will match their claims of 'exceptionalism' against America's, why Russian thinkers reject America's claim to worldwide moral leadership, and why transpersonal psychology is flourishing to a greater degree in Russia than it is in America where it was born. Today, as Russia and the West sink into confrontations that threaten the world with accidental nuclear war, we need the rich understanding of Russia's culture that Lachman's book provides."

MICHAEL MURPHY, COFOUNDER AND CHAIRMAN EMERITUS
OF THE BOARD OF THE ESALEN INSTITUTE

"Gary Lachman is a writer with an elegantly readable style, a passionate interest in aspects of the world that history normally neglects, and a profound understanding of psychology. In *The Return of Holy Russia* he has found his ideal subject. It's an intoxicating examination of the intense and distinctive relationship between Russian culture and religious feeling, of the kind that flowered into exotic cults and occult beliefs in the late nineteenth century, seemed to go underground during the Soviet Union, and may now be emerging again in Vladimir Putin's authoritarian regime. I read it with delight."

PHILIP PULLMAN, AWARD-WINNING AUTHOR OF
THE TRILOGY *HIS DARK MATERIALS*

"Russia is neither the West nor the East. It is both. And it participates in deep Christian mystical, indigenous, esoteric, and occult currents that were mostly lost or forgotten in Western Christianity and actively suppressed in secular modernity. In his new book, Gary Lachman shows us why the return of these esoteric currents via the new (and old) claim of a Holy Russia is so important, why such nationalist theologies cannot really be our answer, and why particular Russian thinkers can point us in the right direction—toward a 'third way' beyond pure reason and past faith toward a new or future gnosis, or knowing within, that all is good. This sounds outrageous to many a modern ear of course. Hence the importance of this book."

Jeffrey J. Kripal, J. Newton Rayzor Chair in
Philosophy and Religious Thought at Rice University and
author of Secret Body

"This book seeks to frame Putin's own political philosophy within that of his self-declared mentors in Russia's pre-Soviet Silver Age of the early twentieth century—and more broadly to the overarching spiritual history of Russia, neglected by mainstream historians but vital to an understanding of that country's destiny in a post-Soviet world. The values of the Silver Age philosophers that Putin misapprehends and distorts, Lachman tells us, are the very ones the rest of the world might well adopt to ensure the future well-being of our planet."

Victoria Nelson, author of The Secret Life of Puppets

"In this unprecedented and gloriously learned book, Gary Lachman explores how Russia, the indestructible nation, is in many regards the historical repository for the mystical traditions of the East and West and, as such, harbors an unforeseen destiny in our world. *The Return of Holy Russia* is a startlingly brave and thrilling work of historicism and political-mystical philosophy. I found it absolutely enthralling."

Mitch Horowitz, PEN Award–winning author of
Occult America and The Miracle Club

"This is Gary Lachman's most profound work so far, and the most topical. Like his admired Colin Wilson, he can convey in one book the harvest from a hundred others. The overview of Russian history here is an example, leading up to the Silver Age when the perennial search for national identity included psychic awareness and spiritual aspiration. Major players, many of them familiar from Gary's other works, are Blavatsky, Steiner, Ouspensky, Roerich, Rasputin, Papus, and the Christian philosophers Berdyaev and Solovyov. The surprise is that a century later, under Vladimir Putin, the philosophies and ideals of that age are being revived and actively promoted. While the leading thinkers of the West deny any meaning to the cosmos or to human history, Russia seems to have taken a philosophical turn well worthy of study and respect."

JOSCELYN GODWIN, AUTHOR OF
THE GREATER AND LESSER WORLDS OF ROBERT FLUDD

"Gary Lachman has that rare ability of the best public intellectual, which is to redact and convey complex ideas without dumbing them down. In his new book, Lachman shows us again what he does best, pointing out the hidden significance of what most scholars have ignored. For nearly a century, Russia was largely cut-off from the rest of the Western world and consequently its spiritual heritage forms a blind spot in the minds of the reading public. What do Greek Orthodox Christianity, ideas of a Third Rome, medieval Russian paganism, 19th-century Russian Romanticism, the Silver Age at St. Petersburg's Stray Dog Café, and Vladimir Putin have in common? Lachman not only tells us but also makes a strong case for why it's important we should know."

DANA SAWYER, PROFESSOR OF RELIGION AND PHILOSOPHY AT THE
MAINE COLLEGE OF ART AND AUTHOR OF *ALDOUS HUXLEY*

"A clear, accurate, comprehensive, and enjoyable exploration of a civilization that many know only through clichés. This may be Gary Lachman's best book yet."

RICHARD SMOLEY, AUTHOR OF *A THEOLOGY OF LOVE*

ALSO BY GARY LACHMAN

Dark Star Rising: Magick and Power in the Age of Trump

Lost Knowledge of the Imagination

Beyond the Robot: The Life and Work of Colin Wilson

The Secret Teachers of the Western World

Revolutionaries of the Soul

*Aleister Crowley: Magick, Rock and Roll, and
the Wickedest Man in the World*

The Caretakers of the Cosmos

Swedenborg: An Introduction to His Life and Ideas

Madame Blavatsky: The Mother of Modern Spirituality

The Quest for Hermes Trismegistus

Jung The Mystic

The Dedalus Book of Literary Suicides: Dead Letters

Politics and the Occult

Rudolf Steiner: An Introduction to His Life and Work

The Dedalus Occult Reader (Ed.)

The Dedalus Book of the Occult: A Dark Muse

In Search of P.D. Ouspensky

A Secret History of Consciousness

*Turn Off Your Mind: The Mystic Sixties and the Dark Side
of the Age of Aquarius*

Two Essays on Colin Wilson

As Gary Valentine

New York Rocker: My Life in the Blank Generation

THE RETURN OF
HOLY RUSSIA

Apocalyptic History, Mystical Awakening, and the Struggle for the Soul of the World

GARY LACHMAN

Inner Traditions
Rochester, Vermont

Inner Traditions
One Park Street
Rochester, Vermont 05767
www.InnerTraditions.com

Text stock is SFI certified

Cataloging-in-Publication Data for this title is available from the Library of Congress

ISBN 978-1-62055-810-2 (print)
ISBN 978-1-62055-811-9 (ebook)

Printed and bound in the United States by Lake Book Manufacturing, Inc.
The text stock is SFI certified. The Sustainable Forestry Initiative® program
promotes sustainable forest management.

10 9 8 7 6 5 4 3 2 1

Text design and layout by Debbie Glogover
This book was typeset in Garamond Premier Pro with Balalaika, Gotham, ITC
Cheltenham and Museo Sans used as display typefaces

To send correspondence to the author of this book, mail a first-class letter to the
author c/o Inner Traditions • Bear & Company, One Park Street, Rochester, VT
05767, and we will forward the communication, or contact the author directly at
garylachman.co.uk.

To Anja Fløde Bjørlo, my guide,
without whom I am lost.

"Ever seen a leaf—a leaf from a tree?"

"Yes."

"I saw one recently—a yellow one, a little green, wilted at the edges. Blown by the wind. When I was a little boy, I used to shut my eyes in winter and imagine a green leaf, with veins on it, and the sun shining. . . ."

"What's this—an allegory?"

"No; why? Not an allegory—a leaf, just a leaf. A leaf is good. Everything's good."

"Everything?"

"Everything. Man's unhappy because he doesn't know he's happy . . . he who finds out will become happy at once, instantly. . . ."

"When did you find out you were so happy?"

"I was walking about the room. I stopped the clock. . . . It was twenty-three minutes to three."

FYODOR DOSTOYEVSKY,
THE DEVILS

Contents

INTRODUCTION

Welcome to the Silver Age (1890–1920)   1
A Time of Magic and Mysticism

1   **Russian Man**   16
Angel and Devil

2   **Motherland**   36
A Country of Extremes

3   **Beauty Will Save the World**   60
The Roots of Iconography

4   **The Lost Kingdom**   85
After the Fall of Kiev

5   **From Mongols to Muscovy**   109
Religious Colonization and the Builders of Russia

6   **A Terrible Time of Troubles**   135
Apocalyptic Expectations

7   **A Window on the West**   164
The Mission to Modernize

8 The Beautiful Soul 193
A Return to Childlike Innocence

9 The New Men 221
The New Reality

10 The Silver Age 251
Seekers, Sages, Saints, and Sinners

11 The End of Holy Russia 285
Power to the People

12 ESP in the USSR 319
Mind and the Masses

13 The Return of Holy Russia? 355
The Occult Revival

EPILOGUE
A Third Way? 385
A Different Way of Knowing

Acknowledgments 394

Notes 395

Bibliography 418

Index 426

About the Author 438

Welcome to the Silver Age (1890–1920)

A Time of Magic and Mysticism

In 1906 the spiritual scientist Rudolf Steiner, then head of the German branch of the Theosophical Society, gave a series of lectures to an audience of mostly Russian and German listeners in the Parisian suburb of Passy. Steiner was originally supposed to have given the lectures in Russia the year before, during a tour organized by his second wife, the Baltic Russian Marie von Sivers. The revolution of 1905 made that impossible, and the tour was canceled.

Many of the radicals who had opposed the tsar left Russia following the revolution and headed to the political-exile capital of Europe, Paris. In summer 1906, Steiner took part in the Theosophical Congress held in Paris that year, and while he and the Russians were in town, it made sense for him to give the canceled lectures there. He did, holding them at first in a private house. Steiner was so popular, however, and his audience grew so large that eventually the French Theosophists, who resented Steiner's celebrity—he was second only to Annie Besant, the leader, in prestige within the Theosophical Society—were forced to offer him the use of a lecture hall.

Although the cofounder of Theosophy, Madame Blavatsky, was

Russian, her emphasis on the Eastern sources of esoteric wisdom—and critical remarks about Christianity—put off many of her countrymen, who felt more at home with Steiner's heavily Christianized version of Theosophy. Russia as we know it had itself come into existence when Prince Vladimir of Kiev accepted Eastern Orthodox Christianity as the official religion of his people in 989 CE. A fusion between the emerging Russian national soul and Orthodox Christianity took place then, and has remained in place ever since. And as Orthodox Christianity has a more mystical character than either Western Catholicism or Protestantism, it allowed an easier absorption of Steiner's Christianized occult science.[1]

Steiner had a remarkable audience for his lectures. Among those seated were some of the cream of the Russian literary and spiritual avant-garde. These included the novelist, historian, and mystical philosopher Dmitri Merezhkovsky, who wrote about Atlantis and the Apocalypse; his wife, the poet Zinaida Gippius, a well-known habitué of St. Petersburg's notorious Stray Dog Café, home to many mystics and artists; and the poets Konstantin Balmont and N. M. Minski, important figures in the Symbolist movement.[2] They and other poets, novelists, philosophers, artists, and musicians were part of a powerful spiritual and cultural renaissance in Russia at that time, a period known as the Silver Age. It was a time of magic and mysticism, which saw a vital resurgence of interest in the occult, and a profound return to spiritual and religious values, along with a creative intensity unlike anything the West had seen since the Renaissance. This was the time of the God-seekers, pilgrims of the soul and explorers of the spirit who sought through art and ideas the salvation of the world.

What Steiner had to say in his lectures appealed to his audience and confirmed much of what they already believed. Steiner spoke of the evolution of the cosmos and of consciousness—for him the two are the same—and of the different civilizations that had appeared on the Earth since the sinking of Atlantis, a planetary catastrophe that took place some ten thousand years ago, at least according to his account. He told his audience that humanity was currently moving toward the end of the fifth post-Atlantean epoch, which was that of Western civilization. Each epoch has a "mission" or "task," related to the evolution of consciousness. The task of the fifth epoch, Steiner said, was to develop the intellect, the individual "I," the ego. This had been accomplished. In fact, it had been achieved too well, and the radically individual Western ego was in danger of completely losing touch with its source in the spiritual powers.

Yet what was beginning to emerge, Steiner told his audience, were signs of the *next* cultural epoch, a new consciousness rising up that will transcend the separateness of the Western "I" and regain its connection to the world. The civilization of the sixth post-Atlantean cultural epoch would not be fully established until 3500 CE, Steiner said. But already there were indications of it, signs and developments that were preparing the way. And many of them, he told his audience, could be found in Russia.

The qualities that the coming new epoch must develop as its task, Steiner said, were a sense of community, an attitude of selflessness, a capacity for patience, and an openness to higher truth. All these, he believed, were in an embryonic state in the Russian people. Within them was the seed of a new age, something that the representatives of the Silver Age believed as well. The Russian character, Steiner said, was a child, "in whose soul lay questions all humanity must answer in order to master the future."[3] The Russian soul was able to contain contradictory ideas and polar opposites in a way that a Western logical mind would find impossible. For example, for Russians, the idea of a "rational mysticism" or a "mystical rationalism" is not contradictory; it is the sign of a higher consciousness.

The feminine East and the masculine West, Steiner said, must come together to produce the child of the new era, a "third way" combining these opposites and going beyond both. "Many characteristics of the sixth epoch of culture will be entirely different from those of our age." People will feel the suffering of others as their own, and will accept others, whoever they may be, as brothers and sisters. The individual's well-being will be dependent on that of the whole, while any truths and belief that he or she holds dear will be the result of his or her own reflection and be rooted in his or her own soul. Any real knowledge in the sixth cultural epoch will have to include the spiritual element in reality.

These potentialities were already present in the Russian people, Steiner said, and it was their task to "bring to definite expression the elementary forces that now lie within them." Their consciousness of their mission and its significance may at present be "extremely hazy and confused," and "understood in the wrong sense," such knowledge "may easily lead to pride and superciliousness, precisely in the East." But Steiner had faith in the Russians. They were "Christ's own people." Their souls were open to the "Christ impulse," and in their aura Christ himself was present.

STEINER'S LECTURES MADE a powerful impression on his audience. Up until the time of the Red Terror, when Vladimir Lenin and his Bolsheviks ruthlessly gained control of the Russian state by brutally wiping out any opposition, Steiner's ideas were an important part of the Russian cultural scene. Another lecture series, in Helsinki, Finland, in 1913, was held specifically for his Russian disciples; in it Steiner* made many of the same remarks about the coming new epoch.[4] But by the 1920s, any seeds of a new cultural evolution had been trampled underfoot by the seemingly unstoppable march of the dictatorship of the proletariat. The irrevocable class war, necessitated by Marxist "historical science," relegated any predictions other than those pronounced by the revolutionary avant-garde to the dustbin of ideas. And the bright lights of the Silver Age, whose visions of a spiritual Russia were incompatible with the new iron regime, were either dead, imprisoned, or in exile,

---

*By this time Steiner had broken with the Theosophical Society over Annie Besant and Charles Leadbeater's promotion of the young Jiddu Krishnamurti as the avatar of the new age.

their hopes for a future world crushed and ignored. For what was left of the century, their work would languish in obscurity, while their homeland would suffer one of the worst tyrannies history has ever known. Whatever signs of a new cultural epoch may have been emerging in the feverish days of the Silver Age, for the next seventy-odd years, they were nowhere to be found.

In recent times this has changed, and there has been renewed interest in the ideas and visions of the sages of the Silver Age and in the questions about the future of Russia that they had tried to answer. Perhaps not surprisingly, this interest comes from Russia itself, and not only from its average readers. Word about whom one should be reading these days has come down from the top.

In 2014, at the annual meeting of United Russia—since 2001 the country's dominant political party—along with the usual rhetoric of party politics, Russian president Vladimir Putin passed on to his regional governors some suggested reading.[5] Putin likes to come across as bookish, and he has not been shy to talk about his favorite writers.[6] But the reading list Putin passed on to his governors did not suggest a brushup on Turgenev or an encouragement to get through Gogol. The books Putin asked his governors to read were works of philosophy. They were books of ideas about Russia.

The three thinkers Putin suggested his governors get to know were Vladimir Solovyov, a friend of the novelist Fyodor Dostoyevsky and, according to the late American Russian scholar James Scanlan, "the greatest and most influential of Russia's philosophical thinkers"; Nikolai Berdyaev, the aristocratic Christian existential "philosopher of freedom"; and Ivan Ilyin, a more political thinker than either Berdyaev or Solovyov, and whose ideas for some form a kind of "Russian fascism."

All three were major figures of the Silver Age, and until the collapse of the Soviet Union in 1991, their work was for the most part unavailable in their homeland. Since then, they and their contemporaries have enjoyed a tremendous revival, along with other literature of a mystical, occult, and spiritual bent that for decades was banned within the Soviet bloc.

The books Putin asked his governors to read—Solovyov's *The Justification of the Good*, Berdyaev's *The Philosophy of Inequality*, and Ilyin's posthumous *Our Tasks*—are not page-turners, unless you like ideas. They are demanding, impassioned, philosophical texts. That a world leader should ask his governors to read works of philosophy seems reason enough to take note, but the reaction from much of the Western press has, perhaps not surprisingly, been less than adulatory. The idea, expressed by Steiner and other prophets of a declining West, that Russia has some unique historical "mission," a special task to accomplish of planetary significance, is shared, in their own way, by Solovyov, Berdyaev, and Ilyin. As might be expected, this did not go down well with many members of the Western critical establishment. For them, these Silver Age thinkers and their thoughts about "the Russian idea," are very badly tarnished.

For David Brooks in the *New York Times,* to read Solovyov, Berdyaev, and Ilyin is to enter a world of "melodrama, mysticism and grandiose eschatological visions" aimed at supporting Russian "exceptionalism," the idea that it is "superior" to other nations on the planet.[7] Maria Snegovaya in the *Washington Post*—whom Brooks quotes—expresses dismay that Putin is reading "a bunch of Russian nationalist philosophers of the early twentieth century" who are concerned solely with "Russia's messianic role in world history."[8] Even Putin's reading of Dostoyevsky, one of his favorite authors, is suspect. For an anonymous writer for the *Harvard Political Review,* Putin's "aggression" can be chalked up to Dostoyevsky's messianic answer to the "Russian Idea," as can the penchant for "imperialist authoritarianism" in the Russian people—which, one assumes, accounts for their recently voting their president in for another six years.[9]

That these and other Western political analysts suspect Putin's motives for giving his governors a reading list is understandable. Politicians rarely do anything for sheer edification, and it stands to reason that the same is true here as well. But that Western critics should characterize these important philosophers and their ideas in such a shallow, superficial way is simply bad journalism and does their readers a disservice. While it is true, as Rudolf Steiner said, that the Russian mind is "exceedingly difficult to understand from the Western European point of view"—he was referring to Solovyov when he said this—he also believed that it was salutary for that point of view to exert itself to do just that, and not dismiss what it finds difficult to understand as incomprehensible. That was sheer mental laziness. The frothy rhetoric churned up by such commentators as Brooks about "Putin's philosophers" only muddles an already murky situation, and makes such laziness easier to fall into.

Steiner and others, including many Russians, whom I will look at in this book—which attempts to take the idea of a "third way" seriously—believed that *something* was germinating in the vast Russian motherland that would have an impact on the future. This may mean nothing at all. Such ideas may be no more than the work of a too-active imagination. And that such beliefs can be used for dubious political purposes is, sadly, only too true. But then perhaps such ideas are something more than "just imagination," and perhaps they can be influential in ways other than informing jingoist rhetoric. If so, it strikes me that it would make sense to try to understand them. This seems a more interesting way to look at Putin's reading suggestions than to cursorily chalk them up solely to material for crude nationalist propaganda.

Brooks and other Western analysts may not take the "Russian idea" seriously, but it was a theme that preoccupied Dostoyevsky, Tolstoy, and practically every major Russian writer in the nineteenth and early twentieth centuries. And the philosophers Putin assigned to his regional governors did take it seriously. And so, it appears, does Putin. We should do the same. What is needed is not to castigate Putin or anyone else for reading these thinkers, but to differentiate between what the sages of the Silver Age thought about the "coming Russia," before the Bolshevik boot came down on them, and what their powerful new reader makes of their ideas.

THAT PUTIN HAS his own ideas about a new Russia should be obvious to anyone who has paid attention to his speeches and policies over the past decade. In my previous book, *Dark Star Rising: Magick and Power in the Age of Trump,* I look at one idea about a new Russia that has kept Putin busy. This is "Eurasia," a version of the "Russian idea" that was developed by anti-Bolshevik Russian émigrés in the 1920s. Believing that the 1917 revolution was a "mystical catharsis" that would bring on the "end of history," these White Russian exiles wanted to be ready with a new vision of Russia with which they could return to their homeland once the Bolshevik "experiment" had collapsed, and which they optimistically believed would happen fairly soon.

Exiled to Europe by the Red Terror, these intellectuals envisioned a new character and identity for their people. If they were not tsarist or Marxist, *what* were they? The answer they decided on was that they were Eurasians, natives of a new, *original* civilization emerging from the vast homeland of the mother of all continents. Russia was not a poor relation of Europe, perpetually trying to keep up with its progressive cousin and never quite getting into step. It was a totally *other* culture, with other values, other beliefs, and, most important, another *destiny,* just coming into its own.

The original Eurasianist dream faded. The Bolshevik experiment did not collapse—or its fall took much longer than the exiles had hoped—and the vision of a new Eurasian civilization, rising up as the West declined, found itself sidelined by the irresistible progress of dialectical materialism. But by the late 1980s, when glasnost and perestroika loosened the grip of the Soviet censor, Eurasia was back, brought into the mainstream of Russian consciousness by the remarkable popularity of the maverick historian and ethnographer Lev Gumilev, son of two poets of the Silver Age, and intellectual martyr of the Stalinist regime.* By the late 1990s, when Russia went from the heady days of the Soviet collapse to the pandemonium of social anarchy and an existential identity crisis, Eurasia emerged as an idea that could bring order and meaning to a people facing economic and political chaos, just as the Eurasianists of the 1920s had intended it to do.

As I show in *Dark Star Rising,* one person who took the Eurasia idea very seriously was the ex-Soviet punk dissident turned establishment geopolitical savant Alexander Dugin. In 1997 Dugin's book *The Foundations of Geopolitics* appeared, and, if accounts of its success are accurate, it was an enormous bestseller. One thing it had going for it was Dugin's vision of a coming planetary Armageddon, a global apocalypse arising from the final and decisive clash between the world's two remaining superpowers: the Atlanticist West, which was determined to turn the world into a borderless marketplace, and the traditional, spiritual civilization of Eurasia, resolved to resist the commercialization of the Earth.

On a less millenarian note, Dugin's blueprint for the rising Eurasian civilization included regaining territories that had been part of the former USSR but had now broken away to form what in Russia is known as the "near abroad." In *Dark Star Rising* I show that there is reason to believe that events in Crimea and Ukraine in 2014 were not a little informed by Dugin's geopolitical prophecies. References to Eurasia can be found throughout Putin's speeches, and the establishment of a Eurasian Economic Union—a kind of answer to the European Union—with many former Soviet territories as members, as well as other Eurasian-friendly organizations, suggests that Putin and others are taking the idea seriously.

ANOTHER IDEA THAT Putin is taking seriously is that of Russia as a nation of "traditional values." It is along these lines that

---

*Nikolai Gumilev (1886–1921) and Anna Akhmatova (1889–1966).

commentators are beginning to speak of a new cold war opening up between Russia and the West. Skirmishes here are not triggered by ideological clashes between capitalism and communism, but by different moral, ethical, and religious worldviews. To think of Russia, home of gangland politics and ostentatious oligarchs, as more morally sensitive than the West may seem counterintuitive. But in Putin's Russia, the extreme liberalism and permissiveness that characterize Western society—its "anything goes" sensibility—smacks of little more than decadence, and our commercialization of practically everything reeks of selfishness and ego gratification, Steiner's independent Western "I" turned into a gluttonous, consuming "me." Nothing seems to resist the spread of the "me" economy, in which everything is yielding and negotiable, even reality. To this Putin's Russia upholds more "traditional" standards, and its attitude toward sex, family, and gender roles seems to the "progressive" West highly conservative, if not repressive.

Putin finds his traditional values in his Orthodox belief, and it is in this role of defender of the true faith that, along with Eurasia and the thinkers of the Silver Age, the idea of Holy Russia seems to be making a comeback. This was an identity that Russia and her "God-bearing people" embraced practically from the start, from their earliest adoption of Orthodox Christianity, to the attempt at a theocratic rule during the Muscovite empire of the late Middle Ages, and to the idea of its being a "Third Rome," after the downfall of the first one and the capture of Constantinople by the Turks in 1453. This was a notion proposed by the Russian monk Philotheus of Pskov in the early sixteenth century. Writing to Grand Prince Vasily III in 1511 he says, "Two Romes have fallen, a third stands, a fourth there shall not be."[10] Rome had fallen to the barbarians and Byzantium to the Turks, and now Moscow remained to take on the mantle of the true Christian teaching. And it is here, perhaps, that we can find the roots of the notion that Russia has a "mission," that special destiny that informs the different versions of the "Russian idea."

ALTHOUGH MANY FINE points of doctrine and dogma separate the Eastern Orthodox Church from Roman Catholicism and Protestantism, one thing that does set Orthodoxy apart from its Western counterparts is its attitude toward the end-time, the Apocalypse and the Second Coming. While these are indeed part of the Western Church, it has generally damped down any millenarian zeal, and focused more on dealing with the crises and challenges of everyday life. "Repent ye sinner for the end is nigh," is left to street-corner prophets and Jehovah's Witnesses. The Western Church has been more *this*-worldly, and its interest in worldly power is one of the criticisms that its eastern counterpart has made against it.

The end days, however, have always been of great importance to the Eastern Church, which has always been more open to mysticism and esoteric knowledge.[11] Its focus has been more eschatological than the West, and this anticipation of the Second Coming and the establishment of the Kingdom of Heaven on Earth was something that the Russian people embraced wholeheartedly when they accepted Eastern Orthodoxy as their religion. They took the idea of rebirth very seriously; this is why Easter is a much more important holy day in the Orthodox calendar than Christmas. Resurrection was of the essence. They did not give lip service to the Apocalypse.

This belief that the world was moving toward some event after which *everything* would be different, became a part of the Russian soul. As Berdyaev said, Russians are either "apocalyptists" or "nihilists," that is, for them it is a case of everything or nothing, either the millennium and Heaven on Earth, or the void.

BUT THE MYSTICAL, spiritual character of the Russian soul seemed to be in place even before its contact with Orthodoxy and its embrace of the true faith. Before the journey of Princess Olga from Kiev to Constantinople in 957—the beauty of which overwhelmed her and made certain her conversion—the Russian people had a rich pagan tradition full of gods and goddesses, elemental forces, and nature spirits. As with other pagan people converted to Christianity—of whom the Russians were one of the last—this tradition did not die out but was maintained alongside the new Christian belief, an arrangement known as *dvoeverie,* "double faith," an example, perhaps, of the ability of the Russian soul to hold contradictory ideas simultaneously, and of the tensions at work in doing so.[12]

This ancient pagan animism found it easy to accommodate the new belief, and, rather than be eradicated by it, entered into it. With the aid of mystically potent icons—"windows on another world" as they were called by Father Pavel Florensky, an important figure of the Silver Age—this native paganism helped the spread of Orthodoxy within Russia. During the centuries of the "Mongol yoke," the influence of shamanism and other magical practices reached the courts of the vassal Russian princes, and when that yoke had been broken, in the days of the Muscovite empire, alchemists, Hermeticists, Kabbalists, and other savants of the occult sciences were welcomed and their counsel sought.

ONE IMPORTANT ESOTERIC influence on Russian history was Freemasonry. Peter the Great, the Westernizing tsar whose eponymous city Petersburg was seen as a window on Europe, was believed to have been initiated into a Masonic lodge during his visit to England in 1698. During the reign of Catherine the Great, Freemasonry spread throughout Russia, and the "progressive" social and religious ideas associated with it prepared the ground for the great artistic and spiritual awakening of the Russian soul in the nineteenth century.

Esoteric ideas even made their way to Tsar Alexander I, the savior of Europe in the Napoleonic wars and leader of the Holy Alliance, who was believed to have faked his own death in order to retire from power to spend his last days in spiritual contemplation. That the last days of the Romanovs were filled with mystical and apocalyptic expectation is well known. Rasputin is the most notorious figure here, but he was not the only mystical character giving advice to the doomed dynasty. And in the years of Soviet rule, ideas of an occult, mystical, and magical character continued to influence the commissars and comrades of the great Bolshevik experiment, with God-seekers becoming God-builders. More than one historian has noted that the millenarian trend in Russia thought made it more receptive to the Marxist vision of a coming classless utopia.

With Putin's interest in notions such as Eurasia, in the philosophers of the Silver Age, and his gestures toward Holy Russia, this Russian interest in things mystical and apocalyptic seems to be continuing.

THIS BOOK WILL look at what we might call the mystical history of Russia, its obsession with apocalypse, and what that might mean for us today. It is a continuation of my study of "occult politics" in the postmodern world that I began with *Dark Star Rising*. Unlike the Western political analysts I've mentioned, I begin with the premise that the notion that Russia has some special "mission" in history is not mere nonsense or simply a mystical excuse for the crudest nationalism. Instead, I see it as an idea that deserves to be taken seriously, in the way that the thinkers associated with it understood it. It strikes me that the kind of brute nationalism and "exceptionalism" that Western critics see in the work of the Silver Age sages would have been the furthest thing from their minds. They were not concerned with furthering Russia's interests at the expense of the rest of the world, but in understanding what Russia could offer to a Western world that seemed in great need of help, and to a Russia that needed it even more.

The central aim of Russian philosophy, that strange hybrid, which appeared in the nineteenth century seemingly without precedent, was to rectify the imbalance that Western thought, with its emphasis on materialism, positivism, and utilitarianism, had created, through its rejection of inner, spiritual reality. When Rudolf Steiner said that, for

Westerners, the Russian mind is difficult to understand, he wasn't exaggerating. This is not because Russian thinkers are inherently any more difficult than Western ones, but because they begin with premises that logical Western thinking doesn't accept. The kinds of questions that obsessed Russian thought in the nineteenth and early twentieth centuries, such as the "meaning" of history, seem to the Western positivist mind nonsensical. Yet it was precisely because the West rejected any notion of meaning—something that the East possessed, while lacking Western science—that the idea of Russia being able to offer a "third way," partaking of both East and West, came about.

With their insistence on the importance of meaning, the Russian philosophers of the Silver Age anticipated in many ways the existentialism to come. But where existentialism at best offered a stoic endurance of the meaninglessness of existence, while turning a scornful eye on the Western science that led to it, the sages of the Silver Age had their sights on something more positive. Their response was more creative, and offered more to be gained, and in many ways addressed concerns that form the focus of much of the "alternative" or "spiritual" philosophy of our own day.[13] The collapse of faith in the criteria of truth and fact that have been ours since the Enlightenment, and which has given rise to our "post-truth," "alternative fact," postmodern world, was anticipated by the Russian thinkers of the Silver Age, who tried to offer a way out of this cul-de-sac.[14] By the end of this book I hope to show that insights into the evolution of consciousness that can help us past our present hurdles can be found in the ideas and visions of the thinkers of that time.* Anyone who makes the effort to try to understand what the sages of the Silver Age had to say will see there is still much in it that we can learn from today. That is the point of this book. In my look at the roots of Holy Russia and

---

*This was recognized by the Esalen Institute and Lindisfarne Press who in the 1990s collaborated in reprinting English translations of works by Nikolai Berdyaev, Vladimir Solovyov, and other important figures from the Silver Age in their Library of Russian Philosophy series.

its meaning in the past, I am interested in what its return today can signify for the crisis at our doorstep.

But before we begin our journey through the turbulent history of the Russian idea, we should first become acquainted with the hero of our tale, that unpredictable and contradictory character known as "Russian man."

1

Russian Man

Angel and Devil

In 1919 the German novelist Hermann Hesse published a short book titled *Blick ins Chaos* (A Glimpse into Chaos). It consisted, for the most part, of two essays on the Russian novelist Fyodor Dostoyevsky, and focused mainly on his novels *The Brothers Karamazov* and *The Idiot*. But the subtitle of one essay gives us an idea of what was on Hesse's mind. It read: "Or the Decline of Europe." Europe was in decline, Hesse believed, and had been so for some time. There was something in Dostoyevsky's books that made this unavoidably clear, Hesse felt, and that was why they were enormously popular with the young in his country. But what was even more important, Hesse believed, was that there was also something in them that offered a hope of renewal and the promise of rebirth.

That Europe was in decline was not a new idea. The philosopher Nietzsche had said so some years earlier, before he went irrevocably mad; sadly, it was Nietzsche's fate to be taken seriously only after he had gone insane. And in 1892 the Austrian Zionist, physician, and social critic Max Nordau published a book, *Degeneration,* which argued that practically all of modern culture was rife with disease, decadence, and dissolution. The fact that Nietzsche, then languishing in syphilitic madness in Weimar—where his sister dressed him in a toga and displayed him to important guests—was one of Nordau's targets might suggest he had a point. And that Europe was still emerging from the aftermath of the most destructive war yet waged on its blood-soaked soil surely helped Hesse's thesis. In fact a book that made Hesse's point in elaborate, poetic, and metaphysical detail, not to mention great length—Oswald Spengler's *The Decline of the West*—had appeared in 1918 at the end of World War I and had become an international bestseller.

Hesse knew of Spengler's work—it would have been impossible for him not to—and wrote well of it, and their views had much in common. I should perhaps also mention that one reader of Hesse's essays, the poet T. S. Eliot, was so moved by them that he journeyed to Switzerland and visited Hesse in his home in Montagnola to pay his respects. Hesse's influence can be found in Eliot's most famous poem, *The Waste Land,* which was published in 1922 and depicts the bleak, nihilistic landscape that stretched across the European continent in the dark years *entre-deux-guerres.*

BUT IF ALL Hesse had said was that Europe was going downhill, his essays would not have had the impact they had, nor would they stand out from the mass of writing about decadence and degeneration, which made up much of the rhetoric of the fin de siècle, and the years that followed it. What was important in Hesse's essays was that he saw something on its way, a light coming over the horizon, a dawn breaking over eastern Europe that offered the possibility of new life and new ways to replace what had grown stale and stagnant. If Europe could grab hold of this lifeline, Hesse believed, what was worth saving in it could be saved.

The decline that most concerned Hesse was not an economic or military one, although, to be sure, the Germany that he—shattered by the war and the collapse of his first marriage—had only recently left to resettle in Switzerland was on its knees on both accounts. Nor was it a physical one, like that felt by the British during the

Second Boer War (1889–92), when more than half of the recruits had
failed military fitness exams; one result of this was Robert Baden-
Powell's founding of the Boy Scouts in 1910. The decline that most
troubled Hesse was a spiritual one. Europe's soul was dying, or was
perhaps already dead, a victim of the materialism, positivism, atheism,
utilitarianism, and all the other forces of the modern West that seemed
determined to turn life into a global factory-production line.

But a chance of resuscitation seemed on hand, coming from the
direction of the morning sun. Hesse turned his gaze that way. This
would not be the first time, he knew, that the West sought *ex oriente lux,*
light out of the East, to illuminate its darkness, nor would it be the last.
But if it ever needed it, it did then.

Yet the light that Hesse saw rising over the eastern horizon was not
that of the peace and tranquillity that many who seek enlightenment
hope to get from the East. Far from it. It was more like the sudden flares
and flashes thrown up by some great conflagration, with many strange
shadows and much thick smoke accompanying the flames. Here was
blinding bright light, torrid heat, and turbid darkness. After all, Hesse
had not fixed his gaze upon the imperturbable figure of the Buddha, the
image of serenity incarnate. No. What he had looked into was chaos.

What did he see?

WHAT HESSE SAW in his glimpse into chaos was "Russian man," the
"coming and imminent man of the European crisis," whom Hesse
believed had already arrived and whose influence could be felt.[1] Who or
what is "Russian man?" He is "the ideal of the Karamazovs, a primeval,
occult, Asiatic ideal," that Hesse believed was beginning to take over
Europe. Through this ideal Europe is "turning back to Asia . . . to the
mother, the Faustian 'Mothers,'" the primal source of all life in Goethe's
great drama.[2]

Europeans of the old stamp feel the approach of Russian man as
a threat, Hesse tells us, and it is in his approach that we can chart

Europe's decline. This is the dwindling of the inspiration of the Enlightenment, with its clarity, reason, and logic, the individual "I" set apart from and mastering its world, that Rudolf Steiner argued it was the task of European man to develop. Russian man ignores such distinctions. He is "struggling to escape from the opposites, from characteristics," and reaches "beyond the principle of individuation" back to the "primal stuff, the unformed material of souls."[3] Such dissolution is precisely what Dr. Nordau had diagnosed in his book, and to him it was not a good sign. But Hesse believed that to those open to this influence, it offers the possibility of new life. To be sure, there were no guarantees. But as the poet Hölderlin, whose poetry Hesse loved, said, "Where there is danger, deliverance lies also."

THE DANGER, HOWEVER, was real, and Hesse well knew it.[4] It came in the form of an abandonment of all distinction between one thing and another, in an openness to *all* experience, no matter how questionable, dark, or absurd. It meant a "turning away from every fixed morality and ethic in favor of a universal understanding, a universal validation," what Hesse called a "new dangerous, terrifying sanctity." Russian man is "beyond good and evil" and any other opposites. He is an indiscriminate yea-sayer, who can "perceive the divine, the necessary . . . even in what is most wicked and ugly. . . ." Russian man cannot be adequately described as a hysteric, a drunkard, a criminal, a poet, a sinner, or a saint, but only as "the simultaneous combination of all these characteristics." He is murderer and judge, egoist and altruist, angel and devil. We cannot, Hesse says, "get at him from a fixed, moralistic, ethical, dogmatic—in a word, a European standpoint."[5] He is good and evil, God and Devil, inside and out, all at once.

BECAUSE OF THIS antinomian, unfixed character, unlike Western man, who is on his way out or at best will become a museum piece, Russian man presents the "unshaped material of the future."[6] He is the chaos out of which what is to come will appear; the promise of a new beginning, bringing with it all the uncertainty and apprehension that accompanies the unknown.

This was something that Oswald Spengler also saw. In *The Decline of the West,* he speaks of the "immeasurable difference between the Faustian"—his term for Western man—"and the Russian soul," and believed that as the West was going under—the literal meaning of the title of his book in the original German* says as much—Russia was beginning to stir, and would awaken to full consciousness sometime soon.[7]

"WESTERN MAN LOOKS up," Spengler tells us, and points to the soaring medieval Gothic church spires as proof.[8] These are the architectural equivalent of the Western "I," the individual ego, striving toward heaven. But Russians know nothing of this, Spengler says. They look *out,* horizontally, across the immense, endless steppes around them, and this limitless expanse leads them to think of "we," the indiscriminate embrace of brothers and sisters. The Russian does not think of a father God, at home somewhere in the sky, but of a "fraternal love, radiating in all directions," and finds the Faustian fretting over an individual self "incomprehensible."[9] Spengler speaks of a religious "style that will awaken when the real Russian religion awakens."[10] "What sort of Christianity," he asks, "will come forth one day from this world-feeling?"[11] "What have we to expect of the Russia that is to come?"[12]

With Hesse, Spengler sees Dostoyevsky as the prophet of the ominously approaching Russia. Dostoyevsky's "passionate power of living is comprehensive enough to embrace all things," Spengler tells us.[13]

---

*The title in German, *Das Untergang des Abendlands,* translates as "The going under of the evening lands."

"Such a soul as his can look beyond everything that we call social, for the things of this world seem to it so unimportant as not to be worth improving"—an attitude that led to Dostoyevsky being called a reactionary in his lifetime and that during the Soviet period led to his demonization and to some of his work being banned. Nevertheless, "to Dostoevsky's Christianity the next thousand years will belong." He is *"the coming Russia."*[14]

Exactly what Dostoyevsky's Christianity would be like and how it would differ from its Western variants are questions we will look at further on. But Hesse and Spengler were not the only ones predicting important futures for Russia. Walter Schubart is a little-known German philosopher. In 1933 he escaped the Nazis by fleeing to Latvia, where he managed to live and work for a few years. But in 1940 he was arrested by the Soviets—who then occupied the country—and by most accounts died in a concentration camp in Kazakhstan in 1941. In 1938 he published an essay, "Europe and the Soul of the East." In it he agreed with Spengler that Europe was in decline. But he disagreed with him that it was inevitable, and with Hesse Schubart believed that the West could experience a rebirth if it could integrate its "Promethean" character—its scientific and technological mastery—with the mystical, religious character of "Messianic Russia." "The Russian mission," Schubart believed, "is to liberate the world from the contagion of the Late West . . . to liberate Europe from its own terminal Western hubris, to redeem the West or to 'replace' it." In 1950 Schubart's book *Russia and Western Man* was published in an English translation. In it he also spoke of a new religious consciousness arising in the East.

This hoped-for union of the mystical East with the scientific West is a common theme in much writing about Russia, and in Russia itself the opposition between these two polarities has produced enormous tensions over the centuries that at times have torn the country apart. Placed between the materialist West and the spiritual East, Russia is thought to partake of both opposites and to offer the promise of some future creative synthesis, as Schubart argued, a "third way," that would transcend the polarities and bring into existence something new. Much about this "third way" has been written in a vaguely spiritual manner. But some prophets speak of this needed rapprochement in very specific terms.

IN 1932, THE American "sleeping prophet" Edgar Cayce was asked while in a trance what the "attitude" of "capitalist nations" should be toward Russia, then in the grip of Stalin's paranoid tyranny. Cayce replied that, "On Russia's religious development will come the great hope of the world."[15] When asked to be more specific, Cayce replied that, "there is to come . . . an entire change in the attitude of both nations as powers in the financial and economic world." Russia, he said, had enormous reserves of natural resources, something that remains true today, but it lacks the wherewithal to profit by these. The United States has the ability to develop these resources, so a cooperation between the two nations, the prophet declared, would make them "powers," a détente that many still hope for. And in 1944, when the Allies had turned the war in their favor, and Russia was about to invade Germany, Cayce repeated that, "in Russia comes the hope of the world." Not the "Communistic" hope but that of a "freedom" in which "each man will live for his fellow man," the brotherhood and embrace of *all,* that Spengler had seen was on its way.[16]

It was in a similar vein that in 1949, the theosophist Alice Bailey, in communication with her spiritual master, Djwhal Khul, "the Tibetan," remarked that Russia's task is to link the East and the West. Russia had to synthesize these and other opposites in a way that makes Bailey's reading of the Russian mission echo much of Hesse's remarks about Russian man. The Russian to come will bring together "the world of desire and of spiritual aspiration," the "fanaticism which produces cruelty and the understanding that produces love," materialism and holiness, selfishness and unselfishness, all "in a most pronounced and peculiar manner."[17] "A great spiritual conflict" is taking place in Russia, Bailey tells us, which will produce a "new and magical religion." This will be a "great and spiritual religion, which will justify the crucifixion of a great nation." She also speaks of a "vital Russian exponent of true religion . . . for whom many Russians have been looking and who will be the justification of a most ancient prophecy."[18]

About who this "vital Russian exponent of true religion" and ful-filler of prophecy may be, we can speculate, and indeed many have. But before we turn our focus to such details, let us get a better look at our subject in the abstract.

As COLIN WILSON writes in his study of the Siberian healer and holy man Grigori Rasputin, whose influence on Tsarina Alexandra many argue led to the downfall of the Romanovs, "the Russian is a creature of contradictions."[19] He is not an inhabitant of the middle ground; he blows scorching hot or icy cold but is rarely lukewarm. Russians are a people of extremes; as Berdyaev said, with them it is either all or noth-ing, the millennium or the abyss. In them slavery and revolt, cruelty and kindness, the individual and the collective, the national and the uni-versal, faith and disbelief are inseparable.[20] It is either one or the other; absolute freedom or total control, and the alternations between the two mark the abrupt discontinuities of Russian history.

This tendency to avoid bourgeois compromise is visible in the behavior of the Russian people. Lethargy and bovine docility go hand in hand with eruptions of mania and revolt. Much of Russian history is like this: utter doldrums and then a tidal wave. For years things may be at a slow simmer with no sign of trouble; then, suddenly, the pressure cooker explodes and mayhem is let loose. The violence that erupts with tragic regularity in Russian history, Wilson suggests, is a result of a frustrated will to make things happen, running into the wall of the Russian "immovable object."[21] The immobility of the mass seems at times to require extreme measures; hence the long history of Russian autocratic rule, and the tendency of the Russian people to return to it.

The Russians themselves know this, and a part of them rebels against it. The conflict lies deep in their being. As George M. Young writes in his account of the Cosmist thinkers of the early twentieth century, for Russians the question is not "What is true?" but "What must we do about it?" a concern whose urgency sets them apart from their Western counterparts.[22] More than one tract concerned with the fate of Russia was titled *Chto délat'?* usually translated as *What Is To Be Done?*, the title of an influential novel by the populist radical thinker Nikolay Chernyshevsky. It was a mantra that echoed throughout the Russian nineteenth century.

Russian laziness is archetypal.* Unlike the Westerner, who is always in a hurry and feels an urgent need to "get things done," there has always been a sedentary character to the Russian, an acceptance and contentment with what is, that makes him or her quite comfortable with doing nothing at all. This brooding, somnolent character of the Russian soul, its "vagueness and sluggishness," Wilson writes, stems from an inherent lack of purpose, a complacency traditionally rooted in the Russian character's inheritance of an Asiatic past.[23] It shares something with the diffidence that T. E. Lawrence ("of Arabia") met with in his dealings with the Arabs, a people who, like the Russians, can be moved by an idea, but whose "less taut wills flagged before mine," Lawrence wrote, because they lacked his western European "energy of motive."[24]

This static character is portrayed throughout Russian literature. There is even a word for it, *byt,* a "deeply rooted, petrified routine life."[25] Nikolai Gogol gave it its national stamp, in his novel *Dead Souls* (1842), which set the mold for numerous stories depicting the numbing,

---

*I apologize to readers who may find these comments about "the Russian character" or "soul" offensive and outdated, given our current concern with avoiding racial or national stereotypes. I personally do not find this danger so serious, and my outline of the characteristics of "Russian man"—and "Russian woman" too—are based on wide reading and multiple sources.

stagnant atmosphere of Russian provincial towns. Fyodor Sologub took the mood to schizophrenic lengths in his insightfully decadent novel *The Petty Demon* (1905) in which provincial ennui leads to a catalog of perversions. In Ivan Goncharov's *Oblomov* (1859), the eponymous hero takes fifty pages to get out of bed. He is a "superfluous man"; much of the novel depicts his inability to *do* anything, because, as is the case with many figures in Russian literature, they see no reason to do one thing rather than another, a dilemma that Dostoyevsky took to existential extremes with the character of Stavrogin in *The Devils* (1872).*

The stagnancy of the Russian soul even reached the immortality of English humor. In "The Clicking of Cuthbert" (1921), P. G. Wodehouse, not usually concerned with existential dilemmas, remarks on "Vladimir Brusiloff," the "famous Russian novelist" who "specialized in grey studies of hopeless misery, where nothing happened till page three hundred and eighty, when the muzhik decided to commit suicide."[26] I suspect that Wodehouse's Brusiloff is based on the Russian Symbolist poet and novelist Valery Briussov, whose work, along with that of other Russian writers from the Silver Age, was having a brief popularity in England at the time.[27]

While more disciplined nationalities, like the Germans, may find Russian inertia exasperating—a thought that came to the Austrian poet Rilke, during a visit to Russia—the "eternal patience" of these people is not wholly reprehensible.[28] As more than one commentator has noted, their patient endurance is evidence of a great strength. As Berdyaev in his study of Russian history, *The Russian Idea,* remarks, "the Russian has a greater capacity for enduring suffering than the man of the West."[29] A look at Russian history shows that the Russian people have had ample opportunity to prove this; if one were insensitive, one could say that suffering seems like the Russian national pastime. Famines, massacres, wars, revolutions, persecutions, invasions, dictators, tyrants, and other

---

*Curiously, both Goncharov's and Sologub's novels gave birth to personality profiles and behaviors associated with their antiheroes. In Goncharov's case it was Oblomovism; with Sologub it was Peredonovism, based on his sadomasochistic character.

seismic disturbances that would wreck another people, have found in the Russian character a stamina able to absorb these catastrophes, to recover from them, and to carry on.

"There is a strength to endure everything," the cynical Ivan Karamazov tells his mystical brother Alyosha, in Dostoyevsky's master-piece.[30] That strength is shown throughout the novel, and it was just as well that Dostoyevsky and his readers had it, because for no other people—except perhaps the Jews—has it been so sorely needed or tested. The Russian capacity to endure suffering is matched by their sensitivity to it. No people seem as aware of the inequities, injustices, and inadequacies of the world—again perhaps except the Jews. When Dostoyevsky's novels were first translated into English, in the now-classic renditions by Constance Garnett, many readers found it impossible to finish his books, so acute was his perception of life's suffering. Even authors of the top rank were not up to it. In *Tolstoy or Dostoevsky,* George Steiner records that while Henry James admitted that he couldn't finish *Crime and Punishment,* Robert Louis Stevenson confessed that it almost "finished" him—meaning the reality depicted was almost too much for him.[31] Stevenson of course was no stranger to human evil and the complexities of the psyche, as *The Strange Case of Dr. Jekyll and Mr. Hyde* shows. But even for this poet of man's darker double, Dostoyevsky's revelations proved almost too great.

YET WHILE RUSSIANS may seem the most patient people in the world—for Rilke "Russia was reality," but a reality that is "distant" and "coming infinitely slowly to those who have patience"—they are also no strangers to sudden inexplicable acts, abrupt unpremeditated displays of often bizarre behavior, the irruption of which is a common event in Russian literature. This could be the *muzhik** blowing his brains out, Dostoyevsky's Stavrogin inexplicably biting the

---

*serf

ear of an elderly gentleman, or the inhabitants of the perfect state in Briussov's early dystopia "The Republic of the Southern Cross" (1905).[32] The citizens of this republic become so weary of perfection that, as Dostoyevsky's "underground man" suggests, they go insane on purpose, and, infected with a virulent "contradiction-mania," bring the utopia crashing down.

I don't know if anyone has proposed it—at least I haven't seen it in anything I've read—but I wonder if we can root this penchant for sudden manic behavior in the Viking side of the Russian family? The western part of the Russian East-West mix came from the north, from Scandinavia. These were Vikings invited to act as protectors of the local Slavic people along the Dnieper, who had a thriving business in trade. If Russian inertia can be attributed to its Asian past, can the sudden outbursts of anarchy and chaos traditionally recognized as part of the Russian character have their roots in the old Nordic blood, which carried memories of their berserker ancestors?

WHEN SPEAKING OF the Russian character in his lectures to his Russian audience, like Hermann Hesse, Rudolf Steiner spoke of "Russian man." But when he had to give an example, it was a Russian woman whom he chose. Helena Petrovna Blavatsky was, as mentioned, the cofounder of the Theosophical Society. As accounts of her life show, Madame Blavatsky, or HPB as she liked to be called, embodied everything Russian man did, and then some. She was born in 1831 in Ekaterinoslav (now Dnipropetrovsk) in Ukraine, which was then part of Russia (and indeed, exactly who Ukraine belongs to is a central question in Russian history, as it is today).[33] Steiner spoke of Blavatsky as an "electrically charged Leyden jar" from whom "sparks"—occult truths—could be produced. She was a "cheeky creature" who showed a "lack of consistency in external behaviour," an understatement that only the abstemious Dr. Steiner, sobriety itself, could make.[34] For him Blavatsky was a perfect example of a truth about Russians that more than one commentator has observed: that they possess power, an elemental force, at the expense of form, the "primal, Asiatic ideal" that troubled Hesse. For Colin Wilson, writing in *The Occult*, Blavatsky was an "explosive madcap." Peter Washington, author of *Madame Blavatsky's Baboon*, saw her as a "badly wrapped and glittering Christmas parcel" who "rarely said exactly the same thing twice"—a character trait certainly not limited to Russians.

For a spiritual teacher, Blavatsky had a warrior spirit, and accounts of her life put her on the barricades with Mazzini's forces battling the papal troops at Mentana. It was precisely her Garibaldi blouse, a memento of her military service, and equally blousy manner that captivated the upright Colonel Henry Steel Olcott and led to the formation of the Theosophical Society. She smoked like a chimney, cared nothing for ceremony, and had a colorful vocabulary. She was known for sudden and inexplicable explosions of devastating anger or overwhelming self-sacrifice, and was possessed of an indomitable sense of humor. Not surprisingly she had an electrifying effect on practically everyone around her. Her aim, to create a true brotherhood of man, regardless of race, sex, creed, or color—an initiative rooted in her Masonic pedigree (her great-grandfather, as we will see, was an important figure in Russian Freemasonry)—corroborated Spengler's later insight that Russians think in terms of "we." She was, we might say, the prototype of the "crazy guru," whose bizarre but spiritually educative behavior is beyond the comprehension of the uninitiated, and who isn't above some chicanery if it is in the service of a good cause.

While Blavatsky's reputation as an esoteric charlatan, a phony medium, and pious fraud—much of it based on hearsay and biased reports—puts her in the ranks of Russian men, she also meets the qualifications for what is known in Russia as a "holy fool." *Yurodstvo* means "being a fool for Christ's sake," and while Blavatsky may not have played this role in the name of Christ—as mentioned, her remarks about Christianity made her few friends in Russia—she certainly took to the role with gusto. According to Berdyaev, "being a fool for Christ's sake" means to accept "humiliations at the hand of other people," and to acquiesce "in the mockery of the world," which is really a way of "throwing out a challenge to it."[35] In the Sufi tradition this is known as the "way of blame." It was a road Blavatsky walked, and there were other Russians on it too.

IT WAS HER intense devotion to spiritual truth—"No Religion Higher than Truth" is the motto of the Theosophical Society—that sustained Blavatsky against the calumny she attracted. This obsession with the spirit is a common trait of the Russian soul. No people are more God obsessed. Berdyaev tells the story of the Russians who spent all night in a café in deep conversation. When the proprietor said he would like to close up and go home, they replied, "We can't go home yet. We haven't decided whether God exists or not," and carried on. Although the question of God's existence troubles contemporary atheists, who go to great lengths to dissuade people from thinking about it, their anxiety rarely reaches this intensity.[36] It was this urgency, this primal "need to know," to pose and answer ultimate questions, which stunned Western consciousness when the simmering volcano of Russian literature erupted in the nineteenth century.

Mention of Madame Blavatsky reminds us that, unlike any other nation, Russia has produced a remarkable brood of religious, spiritual, and mystical characters, men and women who have given themselves, body and soul, to the inner life. "Russia has always been full of mystical and prophetic sects," Berdyaev tells us, "and among them there has always been a thirst for the transfiguration of life."[37] It is this word, "transfiguration," which is at the heart of the "Russia idea." Although the lazy side of the Russian soul is content, like Oblomov, to sit near his stove all day—and needs an Ivan the Terrible to get him moving—it is this animal contentment that repels its spiritual side and leads to a profound world rejection. This is in anticipation of the world to come. Russians are often anxious to get there and see the intervening historical process as at best a nuisance, at worst a barrier, impeding the arrival of the last days.

THIS OBSESSION WITH the spirit has led to Russia producing a peculiar kind of character, in Colin Wilson's words, powerful "mages—men and women who impress by their spiritual authority."[38] While Germany produces astrologers, France alchemists, Ireland seers, and the British have more haunted houses per square mile than anywhere else, Russia breeds individuals of unique spiritual strength.

G. I. Gurdjieff was not Russian. He came from a Greek and Armenian background. But during the possible times of his birth—an exact date remains inconclusive*—his parents' home was in either Turkish or Russian possession.[39] Yet he surfaced as a spiritual teacher in Russia during the Silver Age, after years spent in Egypt, the Holy Land, and central Asia, searching out esoteric knowledge with a band of fellow travelers known as the Seekers of Truth.[40] Like Madame Blavatsky, Gurdjieff was something of a crazy guru, and his inexplicable and often inconvenient behavior kept his students on their toes—which he often stepped on. He made inordinate demands on his followers and created difficult situations. The writer Fritz Peters's account of a train journey with Gurdjieff in which he caused lengthy delays, kept everyone awake, ate foul-smelling foods, demanded special treatment, and in general was a royal pain, reads like the "slow burn" in an old comedy film.[41] This was, like Blavatsky's Marx Brothers antics, a teaching strategy, aimed at shaking his followers awake, disturbing their "sleep," and forcing them to push past their mechanical limits and achieve real consciousness.

It did not always work. The man responsible for presenting Gurdjieff to the world was P. D. Ouspensky, a well-known figure on the occult and esoteric Silver Age scenes. Ouspensky, a popular writer on metaphysical themes and habitué of the Stray Dog Café—his lectures were attended by Berdyaev—met Gurdjieff in Moscow after a disappointing "search for the miraculous" in Egypt, India, and the Near East, which left him no better than when he started out. His account

---

*Years given are 1866, 1872, and 1877.

of his years with Gurdjieff, *In Search of the Miraculous* (1949), provides in microcosm what we can see as the backdrop to "mystic Russia": the search for spiritual truth against the chaos of history. The First World War, the Bolshevik revolution, and the Russian Civil War propelled Gurdjieff, Ouspensky, and their colleagues across an exploding country and deposited them at the gates of an unwelcoming eastern Europe—much as many involuntary immigrants find themselves today.

By this time Gurdjieff's inconsistent behavior began to grate on the disciplined, scientific Ouspensky—a thoroughly Westernized Russian—and his crazy-guru antics proved too much. While Ouspensky's writing is clarity itself, and his approach to Gurdjieff's ideas as systematic as Euclid, Gurdjieff is something different, as his disruptive tactics show. Gurdjieff's mammoth masterpiece of parenthetical remarks and dependent clauses, *Beelzebub's Tales to His Grandson* (1951), may suggest that when Rudolf Steiner said that Russia had great power but poor form, he was on to something—even acknowledging again that Gurdjieff himself wasn't Russian. Yet there are many similarities between Gurdjieff and Blavatsky, whose own tomes *Isis Unveiled* (1877) and *The Secret Doctrine* (1888) often seem, like Gurdjieff's, to be bursting at the seams. Both benefited by having a Western mind—in Blavatsky's case Olcott's—bringing some logic and order to their Dionysian, protean personalities.

All three of these seekers combined an intensity of spiritual pursuit with a physical attempt to satisfy it, a geographical and not only symbolic "search for the miraculous." If we accept her claims, Blavatsky traveled in Tibet—or got as near to it as possible—at a time when European men were not allowed admission. Gurdjieff claims to have penetrated the secret monastery of the Sarmoung Brotherhood, somewhere in the fastness of central Asia. Ouspensky met with teachers of "schools," in ashrams and dervish tekkes, in his quest for forgotten knowledge. This kind of pilgrimage is unique to the Russian, who does not wait for God to come to him, but goes out of his door to track him down.

One such seeker was Rasputin, who seems to fit the Russian man *identikit* to a tee. His tag as the Holy Devil, made popular by a sensational and mostly unreliable biography by René Fülöp-Miller, an Austrian writer and journalist, says as much.[42] Rasputin was a drunkard and saint, a mystic and sensualist, an ascetic and satyr, a penitent and sinner, a peasant who humbled aristocracy and a heretic who had the gift of healing. His spiritual obsession and religious devotion were as intense as any we've seen, and he was as holy a fool as he was a devil. At fourteen, after being publically whipped for robbing an old man, Rasputin suffered "a fit of mysticism." He started attending church, talking with priests, and visiting monasteries. People in his village often saw him sitting by the roadside scourging himself with thistles, praying incessantly. They thought he was inspired and tossed coins to him.[43]

Rasputin began visiting the monastery at Verkhoturye in a neighboring province. He traveled there from his home village of Pokrovskoe, in western Siberia, on foot, a distance of more than four hundred miles. Because the young Rasputin radiated "a passion for spiritual knowledge," the monks were happy to speak with him about God and his intentions and how best he could serve them. After witnessing a visitation of the Blessed Virgin, Rasputin was told by his counselor, the hermit Makary at Verkhoturye, that he must go to the monastery at Mount Athos in Greece, in order to strengthen his devotion and make himself worthy of the miracle. Having walked the four hundred plus miles to see his mentor, Rasputin and a friend began their journey to Greece the same way, a trek of more than two thousand miles.[44] Unfortunately Rasputin was disappointed in Mount Athos; he found the homosexual practices of the monks repulsive and, leaving his friend, who had taken vows, he abandoned the "filth and vermin" of the monastery for a side trip to the Holy Land, a mere extra eight hundred and fifty miles. I should mention that all of these distances are only one-way.

Like Blavatsky, Rasputin walked the "way of blame," and practiced *yurodstvo;* he was indeed a fool for Christ. In Rasputin's case this led to more than accusations of charlatanry; the "humiliation at the hands of other people" that he had to accept ultimately included his assassination at the hands of Prince Yussupov and his accomplices in 1916, an event he predicted.[45] But if nothing else, his extraordinary travels in search of spiritual knowledge make clear that, as Berdyaev tells us, the Russians are "pilgrims," perpetual seekers "in search of divine truth and justice." "Pilgrims refuse obedience to the powers that be," Berdyaev tells us, himself an exile from his homeland for many years.[46] The pilgrimage through this earthly life, which characterizes the Russian experience, constitutes a refusal to accept the limitations of the world and a determination to reach one's holy destination, the Kingdom of Heaven to come.

It should be no surprise then that one of the most popular Russian devotional works of the nineteenth and early twentieth centuries—and which since the 1990s has become popular again—is the anonymous *The Way of a Pilgrim* (1884). This is the account of a mendicant monk who travels throughout Ukraine, Russia, and Siberia, inwardly intoning the "Jesus prayer"—"Lord Jesus have mercy on me"—"without ceasing," an example, perhaps, of Russian man's excessiveness. The Jesus prayer, a kind of Christian mantra, was part of the Hesychast revival in the nineteenth century, a contemplative, meditative religious practice that followed the *via negativa,* the apophatic roots of Orthodoxy in the "negative theology" of the early church fathers.[47]

Apophatic means "empty," "without content," and is based on the recognition that God transcends any attribute we can impute to him; a similar insight informs the *sunyata* of Mahayana Buddhism and the *neti-neti*—"not this, not that"—of Hinduism. We know God best by emptying ourselves of any preconceptions about him and allowing his presence to enter our hearts. That is the purpose of the Jesus prayer.

A spiritual practice based on eliminating any human conception about the Divine, and so preventing it from staining his pure radiance, seems not too distant from an apocalyptic sense of history and the eagerness with which the Russian soul sought to fulfill it. But an inner apocalypse was also available. By retreating into his interior world, and focusing his consciousness on the one goal, the pilgrim transcends the mere earthly world and achieves communion with God.

The anonymous mendicant of *The Way of a Pilgrim* begins his pilgrimage by visiting a *starets* (pl. *startsy*), a spiritual guide. These startsy were elders of the church who were seen as spiritual teachers, charismatic figures whose authority was based on their own personal power. They are the men and women who, as Colin Wilson said, "impress by their spiritual authority." Probably the most well-known example of a starets is a fictional one, although the figure of Father Zossima in *The Brothers Karamazov* is said to have been based on Saint Ambrose, the fourth-century bishop of Milan and an important influence on Saint Augustine and Elder Leonid of the famous Optina Pustyn monastery, an early nineteenth-century starets. Like the startsy in real life, Zossima is a wanderer. Like Buddhist monks, startsy took to the road and brought their message to the land, subsisting on the alms and offerings of the village folk they met. They were wanderers of the spirit, bringing the glad tidings of Christ's message to his God-bearing people.

As Spengler said, the Russian does not look up, but out, into the horizon, across vast tracts of space that lie before, not above him. His soul reaches out to them. His arms open to embrace those he meets. The road beckons. Praying without ceasing the pilgrim follows on. As James H. Billington writes, "the relentlessly horizontal plain" intensified the "longing to find a . . . link with God and some higher plane of reality."[48]

This sense of the open space around one, of infinite forward direction—one's "horizontality," to steal a word from geology—must, I imagine, also influence one's sense of time. Can we see this as another factor informing the sense of history peculiar to the Russian mind? Did the pilgrim on the road, heading toward his holy destination, give to the Russian soul a feeling that history must be a similar road that all humanity is walking? And were the stages along the way, the eruptions and catastrophes that marked the destiny of the Russian people, like the signposts telling the pilgrim that he was nearing his destination? Roads go somewhere. We follow them to their end—at least the most determined pilgrims do. And one path at least that we are all on, that of life, will take each of us to our own final destinations. Will it have taken us somewhere? That was a question that Russian man felt he had to answer. We can say that his attempts to do so make up the very meaning of history that he wants to understand.

2

Motherland

A Country of Extremes

When exactly Russian history begins is a question that runs throughout much of Russian history. It is closely related to the Russian quest for identity. The search for what it means to be Russian is usually undertaken by trying to answer the questions, "Where have we come from?" and "Where are we going to?" Russians have been asking themselves those questions very seriously at least since the early eighteenth century, and some of the greatest literature—and music—ever written is a product of their attempts to answer them. Both questions have elicited a variety of responses. Myths and traditions about the origins of the Russian people are not scarce, and as we've seen, ideas, visions, and uncertainties about their future are also not difficult to find.

This later concern came to a head in the Silver Age, and was abruptly aborted by the rise of the Bolsheviks, who had their own ideas about the future of Russia—and the rest of the world—under the dictatorship of the proletariat. With that dictatorship grinding to a halt in the early 1990s, the question of Russia's future, the "classic question of Russian identity," again took center stage.[1] Yet in many ways the people asking it were still faced with the same challenge that the Russian genius of the nineteenth century left unanswered. At the end of *Dead*

Souls, his masterpiece, Nikolai Gogol—whose attempts to answer the Russian question led to a rejection of his art in the name of God and a long, slow suicide through asceticism—sees Russia as a *troika,* the traditional sleigh pulled by three horses, racing out, faster and faster, under the starry night and onto the endless steppes. "Russia, where are you flying to?" Gogol asks, as the horses speed on. She doesn't answer, but "everything is flying past, and, looking askance, other nations and states draw aside and make way for her."[2]

Other nations may not be drawing aside to make way for Russia—indeed, that they are not has been a sore point in recent times. But that Russia still seems to be hurtling into some unknown future is not an uncommon feeling.

IT SEEMS GENERALLY agreed that Russian history, up until the collapse of the USSR, can be broken down into four empires or, from a less imperial perspective, five periods. The empires are Kievan Rus' (850–1240), the Muscovite empire (1400–1605), the Romanov empire (1613–1917), and the Soviet empire (1918–1991).[3] What the present still-inchoate character of post-Soviet Russia will eventually metamorphose into remains to be seen.

If we look at this sequence as periods we can add to it the time of the "Tartar yoke" (1240–1400), the centuries of subjugation to the Mongols of the Golden Horde, which left a seemingly ineradicable mark on the Russian psyche. Much in the character of Russian political and social organization has been attributed to the autocratic, hierarchical, "traditional" ways of the Mongols, and much of it informed the Muscovite empire that emerged when their yoke had been thrown off. As more than one historian suggests, the tendency toward despotic rule and a submissive, almost masochistic fatalism among the people are most likely an inheritance from the Tartars, and both informed the quasi-oriental court of the Muscovite tsars.

The Muscovite period, according to Nikolai Berdyaev, was the worst in Russian history; he called it the "most stifling," precisely because of this "Asiatic and Tartar" influence.[4] Others, like the Slavophiles of the nineteenth century, looked to the Muscovite empire as a past glory to be regained, while modern Eurasianists, such as Lev Gumilev, see the Tartars as heaven sent, "saving" Russia from domination by the Catholic West.[5] This is a revisioning of Russian history that Gumilev's followers, like Alexander Dugin, carry on today.

Berdyaev makes the point that, contrary to the romantic ideas of the nineteenth-century Slavophiles—who envisioned a Pan-Slavic nation and whose ideas informed some of Dostoyevsky's less liberal views— Russian history has never been "organic." Instead it has consisted of a series of "interruptions," a somewhat sedate word for the cataclysmic character of the shifts Berdyaev speaks of. It may be one of those interruptions that Russia is experiencing now, which will end with a new order being established. Berdyaev, who died in 1948, did not see the end of the Bolshevik experiment, but like a good Silver Age sage, he believed that the Soviet Union was not a final destination and that "it is quite possible that there will be yet another new Russia."[6]

As we have seen—and will see again as we go along—he was not the only one with this expectation.

IT'S NOT UNCOMMON for accounts of Russian history, or of any nation's in fact, to begin with a dramatic event. In our case this could be the Viking Rurik's arrival in Novgorod in 862, Queen Olga's visit to Constantinople in 955, or a sixteen-year-old Ivan IV—soon to be nicknamed "the Terrible"—being crowned as tsar of all of Russia in 1547. But as Philip Longworth points out in his fascinating history of Russia's empires, what was there and remained and was at the heart of it all was the land. It, and the arrival of Orthodox Christianity in the tenth century, made the Russians who they are—with certain admixtures of Western influences whose importance still remains a debated question. And as James H. Billington writes, the one seems to have prepared the nascent Russian people for the other. The "particularly difficult material conditions in Russia," Billington tells us, produced in the people "an unusually intense spirituality."[7] When Prince Vladimir was baptized into the Byzantine faith in 991 at Cherson in Crimea on the shores of the Black Sea—today a place of pilgrimage—the people of Kievan Rus' found a focus for that intensity.[8]

But before this there was the land, "Damp Mother Earth," and her children, the Slavic people. Familial metaphors seem to suit the Russian experience more than they do other nations; if the tsar was "Little Father," the land was the Great Mother, the source of all. There was the "black earth," the rich, fertile soil of the "motherland" in Ukraine; the vast tracts of the steppes stretching into Siberia; the mountains of the Caucasus; the rivers and endless forests; the inhospitable tundra; and above all the climate. All gave to the people who migrated to these lands as the last Ice Age receded, a character that set them apart from others. That Russian man is full of contradictions and drawn to excess can be rooted in no small part in the fact that the world in which he found himself required him to be this way. It was a land of extremes that "does not like doing things by halves," and it demanded that same commitment from its inhabitants.[9]

The earliest ones of these—that we know of—can be dated back to before the Ice Age. In a grave in Sungir, near the city of Vladimir in central Russia, bones of children, a boy and a girl, were found dating back to 26,000 years ago.[10] They had been buried in their garments, and their remains had been decorated with shells. Ivory bracelets, spears made from mammoth tusks, some stone tools, and some antler rods were found at the site. Who these children were and how they came to be there we will most likely never know. The people who inhabited this area did not survive the approaching cold and with the Ice Age they were gone.

The people who came after them—some 10,000 years later—moved into the area of what is today Ukraine from the northwest, which means Europe. Contrary to what Slavophiles and modern-day

Eurasianists believe, Russians are European by descent; this at least was the conclusion reached by a major study carried out in 2000. It found that, genetically, Russians are descended from people who, to escape the approaching glaciers, migrated south from Europe to what we know as Ukraine.[11] An answer to the question of whether Ukraine "belongs" to Russia or to Europe—in the sense of the European Union—a controversial one today, may be rooted in the vast migrations of people from a frigid west to a more hospitable east.

The people who made that journey found themselves at the end of it in a huge area of land to the north and west of the Black Sea. The earth there was rich, the wildlife plentiful, and both could sustain them. The terrain beyond these limits was for the most part little else but vast tracts of marshland. It was uninhabitable, and much of its bleak environment could not support even the simplest forms of life. It would take millennia for Damp Mother Earth, awakening as the ice sheets receded, to transform this uninviting landscape into a place suitable for humans.

Yet eventually the great freeze thawed, and life returned to the somnolent land. The people started to move north into unexplored regions. They followed wildlife into these areas, which time and nature had transformed from a desolate wasteland into the great forests of Russia: seas of aspen, pine, larch, hazel, willow, and birch. These early people fed on wild pig, horse, and deer, domesticated some animals, and understood the rudiments of cultivation, which they carried with them as they slowly followed the herds to the north.

As they penetrated further into this strange new world it slowly had an effect on them. Having to adapt to less sunlight and colder air, over generations their hair gradually lightened and turned blond, their skin became fair, and their noses lengthened and narrowed. It was during these long excursions into the colder north that the people who would become Russians began to acquire the characteristics that we associate today with their modern descendants: a hardy toughness, an ability to endure cold, an indifference to privation, and a capacity for suffering that reached from their Neolithic roots to the masterpieces of their literature. Aptly enough it was the cold that produced in the people a "compensating warmth in communal, human relations": the "we" huddling together have a better chance of enduring subzero conditions than do independent "me's," shivering on their own.[12] The harsh conditions make the logic of pooling resources and working together unavoidable and anchored a preference for the collective over the individual in the Russian character. It may also be from the unpredictable character of the Russian climate—sudden temperature shifts being one example—that the often inexplicable behavior of Russian man descends.

THE DEMANDING CONDITIONS in which these proto-Russians lived—a holiday compared to the Ice Age but to more temperate climes certainly not a picnic—made the migrations difficult and sporadic. One help was the rivers, like the Dnieper and the Don, which would eventually lead to the creation of the land that would be called Russia. It was the terrain too, that fractured and separated the original Slavic-speaking people into their different branches and gave rise to different languages, the mountains, marshes, and bogs producing and maintaining distinct linguistic differences. Longworth even suggests that the long animosity between the Russians and the Poles, and which makes up a great deal of the history of these people, has its roots in geography, an idea that would meet, I suspect, with the approval of today's devotees of geopolitics.[13]

As in other places on the planet, by 4000 BCE, settlements of differing size appeared in Ukraine, mostly near the rivers; one of the largest, Talianki, about 150 miles south of Kiev, is thought to have supported 10,000 people.[14] Civilization was taking hold in other parts of the land too. In the north, in what would become Finland and the Baltic states, a burial ground dating from about 5000 BCE was discovered. These people made tools—knives, hooks, even harpoons—and

hunted beaver, seals, and elk. Yet not all their industry was for utilitarian purposes; much jewelry, made of ivory and amber, and even
musical instruments—bells and pipes—were found among their
remains. It seems that early Russians, like their modern counterparts,
liked music, and we can assume they also liked to dance. They also
seemed to have practiced animal sacrifice, which tells us they had a
religious sense. And that they buried their dead with offerings to the
spirits, figures of their gods, and also items that the deceased could
use or liked—much as ancient Egyptians did—suggests they believed
in an afterlife. Many of the bodies were buried facing east and were
decorated with red ochre, a burial adornment that goes back to
Neanderthal man.[15]

That the bodies were buried facing east suggests that these people
were sun worshipers. What we know of the ancient beliefs of the pagan
tribes who would eventually metamorphose into the "God-bearing"
people of Holy Russia is fragmentary, and comes down to us from
sources* already steeped in Orthodoxy. Yet we've seen that the ability
of Russian man to hold contradictory views was an asset here. Through
the magic of *dvoeverie* or "dual belief," he was able to satisfy both the
"intense spirituality" that the rigors of the land generated, with its
powerful sense of *another* world awaiting him in eternity, and also the
deep connection that he felt with his roots right here in Damp Mother
Earth. This meant that the gods of the ancient land were not cast out,
but remained in power, side by side with the new pantheon, the two
often being worshiped simultaneously.[16]

For the early Russians this connection to the trees and fields and
rivers around them took the form of an animism that gave a character
and even a peculiar *personality* to the forces of nature. They spoke to
them. These people "saw the agency of nonhuman beings in every situation that could arise, in rivers, fields, and forests, in the home and in

---

*Such as the *Russian Primary Chronicle* of the early twelfth century and the *Novgorod
First Chronicle* composed between the ninth and thirteenth century.

the sky."[17] It is this personified nature that informs the world of Russian fairy tales, with stories of the mythical firebird and of magic geese and falcons. It was a world alive and inhabited by spiritual beings who could be helpful if respected, but who more often than not posed a threat, a reflection, perhaps of the unforgiving character of the Russian land, itself full of dangers.

There were higher gods, who seemed to embody a polarity of forces that kept the universe in existence. An all-powerful creator god, Rod, manifested in a polarity of light and dark, of clean and unclean spirits. The first pair of opposites he produced was a white god and a black god, Belobog, who was masculine, and Chernobog, who was feminine: *bog* being the Slavic term for god. Hence the "God-seekers" of the Silver Age were called *bogoiskateli*.

This duality may have roots in Zoroastrianism, which sees reality as involved in a great cosmic war between the powers of light and darkness. Manichaeism, another dualistic religion with many similarities to Zoroastrianism—although there are also significant differences— is thought to have reached the Slavs by the third century CE. What connection, if any, this may have with the ancient beliefs of the Slavs remains unclear. The Bogomils, a heretical Christian sect that in the tenth to twelfth centuries spread across Europe from the Balkans to France—the Cathars were their last members—were so called because they believed themselves to be "dear to God." Their dualist beliefs also link them with the Manichaeans.[18]

What seems interesting in the context of our aim of understanding Russia as in some way the source of a "third way," beyond that of either the materialist West or the mystical East, is that a similar pattern of what we might call "polarity and transcendence" seems to have been in place in the earliest beliefs of her people. The universe for them was the result of a constant tension between opposing forces, between masculine powers and feminine ones, between the waxing and waning of light, between a creative, energizing spirit and a receptive, generating one.

But the lesser gods were closer to the people and could be found in the nature around them. Some of the important pre-Christian deities were Perun, the thunder god, who is related to the Norse god Thor. There was Dazhbog, the sun god, and Jutrobog, the god of the moon. The moon was very important in the ancient Slavic religion. It bestowed abundance and health and was even seen as the creator of mankind. Up into the nineteenth century the moon god was still worshiped by peasants in parts of Ukraine, in the form of circle dances.* There was Kupala, the goddess of water, important in a land where rivers were a central source of food and transportation. But there were dangers here also, like the *rusalki,* mermaids who tempted the unwary into the cold, dark depths, where they would join the spirits of other drowned men. The *leshie* were wood sprites, relations of the spirit Kikamora, the genius loci of the forests and steppes. The *polyovyk* inhabited the fields, and the *domovyk* were the deities of the household, whom it was wise to propitiate, if you wanted a quiet home.

The *mora* were generic demons whose business was to torment mankind. One very dangerous spirit to emerge from these myths and who would become a popular figure in Slavic folklore was Baba Yaga, a feminine demon whose name alone could frighten children, and not a few adults. Another important ancient deity was Mokosh, the feminine goddess of the moist, wet earth—Damp Mother Earth—who, through the alchemy of *dvoeverie,* became for western Slavs the Black Madonna, and who can be seen today in many Catholic churches.

As William Anderson suggests in his book *The Face of Glory,* the Black Madonna found in many churches in Europe may be a lingering expression of an earlier pre-Christian fertility religion. As Anderson points out, many Christian churches were built on the grounds of ancient pagan sites.[20] Even the magnificent rose window of Chartres Cathedral's north transept has a Virgin with a black face at its

---

*Oddly enough, Alexander Dugin is apparently very interested in the revival of such dances.[19]

center. Other decorations found on old churches—chevrons, spirals, lozenges—also seem to refer back to an ancient pagan worship of the Great Mother.

That statuettes of pregnant women were found at many of the prehistoric graves discovered in what would become Russia suggests that these people worshiped the feminine generative power. It also suggests that they may have lived under a matriarchy—which, like the red ochre found in the graves in Finland, is also something associated with Neanderthal man, who may also have worshiped a mother deity.[21] Whatever may be the truth here, we can assume that it was echoes of the Great Mother, in her form as Damp Mother Earth, who in the Russian Orthodox Church led to Mary being worshiped more as the actual mother of God—with everything that this entails—than as the recipient of the miracle of a virgin birth.[22]

BETWEEN THAT MIRACLE and our ancient Russians lay a great deal of history. And we can assume, fairly safely I think, that these people were ignorant of it. Unlike today, when news travels so quickly that it is no longer news by the time we hear it, the ancient world had no such media. News, if it traveled at all, did so very slowly. It may be difficult for us to grasp, but while the great civilizations of the ancient world rose and fell—the Egyptians, the Babylonians, the Persians— little word of their achievements reached these people, if any did at all. Parts of Russia were practically still in the Stone Age, and the people were still hunters and gatherers. The great civilizations of China and India were unknown to them. And Rome, to whom more than one Russian tsar or emperor looked for legitimacy—the tradition of Russian rule being rooted in the Roman Empire is a tenacious one— had, by the time Russia came into existence, disappeared, fallen to the barbarians that, ironically enough, would play a central role in the rise of Russia itself.

A millennium before Christ, tribes of nomads from the southern steppes charged up from the Black Sea and entered Ukraine. The Cimmerians, the Scythians, and the Sarmatians were horsemen, warriors, and herdsmen who moved out from central Asia into the lands bordering on areas the pre-Christian Slavs were cultivating. In successive waves each horde swept across the vast plains toward the west, conquering everything in their path. For ages these lands gave themselves up to plunder, pillage, and battle, with precious little respite and with whole peoples disappearing into the endless horizon without a trace.

In the *Odyssey* Homer speaks of the Cimmerians as living on the opposite side of Oceanus, the mythical river god who encircles the Earth. There is no sun in that land and it is at the gates of Hades. In fact, the Cimmerians, who were of Iranian descent, inhabited the steppes to the north of the Black Sea, in the area between the Danube and Don Rivers.[23] At least they did until the Scythians arrived and moved them out, which seems to have happened sometime around 700 BCE. About the Scythians the Greek historian Herodotus—the venerable "father of history"—wrote some hair-raising reports. Intrigued by stories of their brutality, Herodotus made a special trip to investigate for himself. These savages, he discovered, skinned their enemies (and often made garments of the skin), used their skulls as goblets, on occasion drank blood—which, being an emetic, must have been unpleasant—and thought it good practice to take at least one life a year.[24]

The Sarmatians, who conquered the Scythians in the third century BCE, were, like them, a warrior race and also of Iranian descent. They too were master horsemen. They were also brilliant metalworkers and effective military strategists, and their technical innovations, like the metal stirrup and spur, influenced the Romans—against whom they fought, alongside German tribes, in the first century CE. There is a suggestion that their social structure, like that perhaps of the prehistoric Russians, may have been matriarchal; the fact that unmarried Sarmatian women fought alongside men may be the origin of Greek legends of the Amazons. Yet little remains from these romantic, nomadic peoples, who entered history dramatically but left it practically without notice, except these contributions, and the famous "Scythian gold," which is actually Sarmatian miniature jewelry, housed today in the Hermitage Museum in St. Petersburg. But perhaps that is not all. According to one historian, what they also offer is the "recurring temptation" for some Russians "to think of themselves as a uniquely 'Eurasian' people."[25] The Russians in question here are the Eurasianists that fled the Bolshevik revolution and their twenty-first-century counterparts at work in Russia today.[26]

Here they figure as participants in a long process of historical demolition, whose overarching theme we can characterize as the "fall of Rome." Rome was not built in a day, nor did it collapse overnight. Its decline took place over centuries; its death throes lasted for years. As the Cimmerians fell to the Scythians, and the Scythians to the Sarmatians, these conquerors too were eventually overrun by the Goths in what was then Dacia—Romania today—in the third century CE. Some of the Sarmatians joined the Goths and went on to invade western Europe.

The Sarmatians' end came when the Huns, another tribe of horsemen warriors, this time from Mongolia, invaded southern Russia toward the end of the fourth century CE. These people were fiercer still, and their name today is still a byword for cruelty and destruction. Those Sarmatians who were not wiped out were assimilated, and as a separate people they were no more.

The advance of the Huns forced the people in the lands they invaded to move west, triggering the series of barbarian incursions that led to the fall of Rome.[27] The Huns themselves, led by their most notorious leader Attila, after ransacking eastern Europe, were pushed back by the Romans but had to be bribed by one of their last emperors, Valentinian III, in order to spare the Eternal City—which, as would soon be made clear, was perhaps not as eternal as its people believed. In 455 the Vandals, another barbarian tribe whose passion for mayhem has given us our word *vandalize,* attacked the city, and this "sack of

Rome"—the third of four—spelled the start of the actual end. Twenty-one years later, in 476, Romulus Augustulus, the last emperor of the Western Empire, was deposed by Odoacer, a German warrior, who crowned himself the first king of Italy. The Eastern Empire, however, remained intact, untroubled by the fall of its Western counterpart, an important point for our story.

Among the many peoples who picked and hacked at what was left of Rome, and at the Europe that was left unprotected with its demise, were raiders from the north. It was these people who were eventually known as the Vikings. If the Scythians were a violent crew—and if what we've heard from Herodotus is anything to go by, they were—the Vikings were a match for them, and may even have gone beyond the Scythians a notch or two. The Vikings were the most devastating raiders the West had seen since the Huns. Swift, savage, and merciless, in battle they were like madmen, the "berserkers" mentioned earlier. Their violence was so extreme that some historians suspect they took some kind of drug before battle.[28] Among some of their more gruesome practices was a particular gory form of human sacrifice known as "the blood eagle." A prisoner was held down while his ribs were sawn out; then, while he was still alive, his lungs were torn out and laid "spread eagle" beside him, his organs made to resemble the bird's wings. As Colin Wilson remarks, the Vikings "seemed to have no mercy or conscience," which seems, perhaps, something of an understatement.[29]

The Vikings burned and pillaged in lightning "smash and grab" raids on coastal towns and monasteries in what is now northern France, the Low Countries, and England, getting away with their loot in the fast, narrow boats for which they are famous, before the army could arrive. They burned the English city of York to the ground. It is said that Charlemagne, the first Holy Roman emperor, cried when he saw the black sails of the Vikings in the English Channel. If so, he had good cause. Being inland was not necessarily a protection. The Vikings sailed up the Seine and raided Paris. Often they were offered bribes to leave without attacking. Usually they took the money—it was known as "Danegeld," as these Vikings were mostly Danish—and rampaged anyway. It was good business. If a town paid the bribe, the Vikings might not attack. They might, but there was a chance they wouldn't. If the bribe wasn't paid, then a raid was certain. A bribe was no guarantee, but it was the best offer.

This shrewdness helped in activities that are less popularly known about the Vikings than their taste for plunder and rapine. They were also successful traders, and raids on unprotected settlements could turn into an exchange of goods, without the carnage and with as much profit. Over time the logic of this reached them, and the berserkers saw that there was better career advancement ahead of them as merchants and mercenaries, than as criminals.

BY THE TIME Swedish Vikings made their way into northern Russia, navigating the rivers in search of trade routes to the rich markets of the south—such as Constantinople, the second Rome—the indigenous Slavs had established settlements and were themselves trading well in a variety of goods, such as honey, wax, furs, and slaves, a staple item.[30] Clusters of villages had grown up. As these clusters grew larger they became centers for important activities, such as religious rites, which required a temple for rituals and smiths for the increasing demand for metalwork. Simple protection from hostile neighbors or marauding bands was often reason enough for creating fortified settlements, usually at the confluence of rivers.

It was through the rivers that primitive Russia encountered emissaries from the outer world. These were traders. Arabs are known to have traded with Russians as early as the seventh century; coins of Arab silver dating from that time have been found at settlement sites. As the need to grow increased, the surrounding forests were cleared, and the towns expanded, as did the population. As it did, the need to find and cultivate new areas of land did as well. This led to the dispersal of the original Slavs into different tribes that would come to speak different languages, rooted in old Slavonic. The descendants of these people eventually settled in what are now Russia, Ukraine, and Belarus. Whether these different tribes and languages represent superficial distinctions among what is really one people—the Russians—or true differences amounting to separate nations is a question that has generated an enormous amount of debate and not a little political and cultural strife.

Outsiders brought trade and increased the locals' prosperity, but they also brought something else. Although some contemporary historians, working from the perspective of establishing a "purely Russian" origin for Russia, maintain the idea that the Russians come from an unadulterated stock, most of the evidence suggests otherwise.[31] Contact with the outer world invariably leads to cross-marriages between tribes, and this was as true for the indigenous peoples of this primitive Russia as it was for anyone else. The most important contact in this regard came to Russia from the north.

Scandinavians, hearing of the rich markets of Byzantium, grew eager to make their way south. They were tired of raiding western Europe and were looking for new territories to exploit. They were also hungry for items not easily found in the West, the rare spices and silks the market for which drove much later exploration. Along with being ruthless killers, the Vikings were also known to be equally ruthless at business. According to the tenth-century Arab traveler Ibn Rusta, the Vikings were so greedy that "even the man who has only modest wealth is envied by his brother, who would not hesitate to do away with him in order to steal it."[32] We might see such covetousness as a source of some of the troubles that will face the early Russians—and perhaps some more recent ones too.

THE VIKINGS KNEW that the market routes to the second Rome were controlled by the Khazars. The Khazars were a Turkic-speaking people from central Asia who settled in the south Russian steppes in the early seventh century. Caught between the Christians and the Muslims, with both of whom they traded very lucratively, in 740 CE the Khazar ruler, the *khagan*, and his ruling elite converted to Judaism.

As Arthur Koestler points out in *The Thirteenth Tribe* (1976), his book about the Khazars, this was absolutely unprecedented, and remains an event yet to be satisfactorily accounted for by historians. Tradition accounts for it with the story that the *khagan* made the decision to convert after an angel came to him in a dream and advised him to do so. His conversion was supposed to signal a universal conversion to Judaism that would presage the end of history. If it turned out to be something of a damp squib, it was nevertheless a fascinating one. As Koestler writes, a few years after turning back the Arabs from overrunning eastern Europe—and saving the Byzantine Empire from a possible early collapse—in 740 CE, the Khazar "King, his court and the military ruling class embraced the Jewish faith, and Judaism became the state religion of the Khazars."[33]

"No doubt," Koestler continues, "their contemporaries were as astonished by this decision as modern scholars were," when evidence for this remarkable development was found in Arab, Byzantine, Russian, and Hebrew sources. It was remarkable, if for no other reason, because, while Christianity and Islam had powerful support in the Byzantine and Arab world (and converting to either one would make this available to the converted) Judaism had no support whatsoever and was a religion of the persecuted.[34] The thesis of Koestler's controversial book is that after the end of the Khazar empire in the eleventh century—precipitated by their defeat at the hands of the Russian Svyatoslav I in the tenth century—what was left of the people migrated into eastern Europe—Russia and Poland—where "at the dawn of the Modern Age, the greatest concentration of Jews was found."[35]

This suggested to Koestler and other historians that the Jews of eastern Europe—and hence a great deal of the rest of the world—may have been of Khazar rather than Semitic origin. Needless to say,

Koestler's book did not go down well with many Jewish readers, even though Koestler himself came from a Jewish background.*[36] One factor that might prove a hurdle for Koestler's thesis is that, while the elite of Khazar society had converted to Judaism, the larger populace apparently remained pagan, or what we might call "multi-faith," embracing Christianity and Islam as well as the state religion.[37] If so, then not all the Khazars immigrating to eastern Europe may have been of the Jewish faith—although by the time they did, paganism would no longer have been a serious contender.

But before they fell, the Khazars maintained a very profitable commercial state running from Russia to the eastern Mediterranean. And through them the Slavs were able to do business as far as Baghdad; hence the stores of Arab silver discovered on some sites. Their main centers were the cities of Itil, along the river Volga, and Sarkel, both destroyed by Svyatoslav I and left in ruins.[38] But it was reports of the riches, luxuries, and exotic goods that passed through the Khazar's hands that reached the Vikings who began to make their way from the southern shores of Finland to these growing Russian settlements.

The earliest Viking settlements in Russia date to around 750 CE. These appeared near Lake Ladoga, near where Peter the Great would bring St. Petersburg into existence a millennium later. The Vikings could easily reach the lake, leaving their settlements on the Finnish coast, and crossing the narrowest part of the gulf, with which Lake Ladoga connects. Through here they could enter the Russian waterways, navigable rivers, and easy portages that could bring them far to the south.[39] They established themselves first at Staraja Ladoga—"old Ladoga"—on the lake. This was near the site of what would become Novgorod, or "new town" in Old Church Slavonic. Russia itself came to be known as the country of "towns" to the Vikings who made their way into it. With them they brought honey, weapons, furs, and slaves,

*As Ian Hamilton in *Koestler: A Biography* remarks, "It was a thesis greeted with less than universal enthusiasm."

to trade for the exotic goods coming out of Constantinople, such as silk, spices, and precious stones.

But as the traditional account of the founding of the first Russia state has it, they also brought something else.

THE EARLY RUSSIANS were apparently a quarrelsome lot, at least this is the impression given by the story of how they came to have their first political identity. Before the Vikings arrived, feuding among the different tribes had been going on for some time. The Krivichie in the west, the Slovenic and Viatichi in the north and east, the Derevlians—known as the "old settlers"—the Soveriane, Poliane, Chud, and Ves were fighting among themselves constantly. When this became too much, the tribal leaders looked outside for someone to bring some law and order to the land. As the *Russian Primary Chronicle,* the earliest account of Russian history, tells it, in 862 the elders called on Swedish Vikings known as the Varangians to do the job. They said, "our land is vast and abundant, but there is no order in it. Come and reign as princes and have authority over us." The Varangians, who knew a good deal when they saw one, accepted. Their leader, a Jutlander known as Rurik, who had already made a name for himself as a fierce warrior, became their prince, and two other Varangians, his brothers, ruled with him. Each had a base in a different town. Rurik ruled from Novgorod, Sineus in Beloozero, and Truvor in Izborsk. When Sineus and Truvor died soon after establishing their rule, Rurik ruled alone from Novgorod.

The Varangians must have been good warriors, as many of them who came to Russia continued south from Novgorod to Constantinople, where they became part of the elite Byzantine imperial guard, a prestigious, well-paid position.[40] The name, which is Greek, may come from an Old Norse word *vár,* meaning a "pledge" or "oath."[41] The Varangians were warriors who were pledged to support and defend each other— they had, as it were, each other's back.

We can imagine Rurik and his band deciding that it would probably mean a quieter and perhaps longer life, if they acted as policemen for the local Slavs, with a good salary and excellent living conditions, rather than continue their hit-and-run raiding—although they most likely continued with some raiding, but in a different neighborhood. Novgorod, where Rurik took charge—it was known as Holmgarðr to the Vikings—was already a thriving trading settlement. There is some uncertainty whether Rurik started at Novgorod to begin with or came there after first establishing himself at Staraja Ladoga, the original Viking settlement on Lake Ladoga. Some accounts have Rurik founding Novgorod himself.

Exactly when the Varangians began to rule and whether they were in Novgorod earlier than their invitation to do so, remain points of debate among academic archaeologists and historians. For our purposes it is enough to show that with this invitation we find an early example of what many historians and political analysts see as an example of the "vagueness and sluggishness," the lack of purpose and discipline of the Russian people—in short, their chaos—and their need for a strong ruler to bring order to them and the land.

Or it would be if this account were considered authentic.

Many historians believe that Rurik and his brothers were at the very least semilegendary, meaning that while they may have existed, much of what is said about or attributed to them is at best less than verifiable. Some historians consider them completely mythical. The current dominant opinion seems to be that the account of Rurik's invitation to rule in the *Russian Primary Chronicle* was got up to legitimize the Rurik Dynasty, the descendants of Rurik—or the supposed ones—in order to establish their right to rule. If this has not absolutely demolished the idea that the *Primary Chronicle* provides an accurate if incomplete account, it does make it difficult to uphold it against the weight of academic opinion.

That an account of an unruly people reaching out to a strong leader to bring *stability* to them—a word that has not been absent in recent discussions about politics in post-Soviet Russia—was upheld as the very foundation of rule in Russia, would not have been a handicap for future autocratic rulers who wanted to get their message across. That post-Soviet Russian historians of a liberal persuasion, wary of the propaganda value of this foundation myth for politicians who find themselves on the opposite side, should seek to undermine it is understandable. They argue that not only is the invitation to come and rule a chaotic collection of feuding tribes a concoction, but the idea that the Russian people are so feckless and lazy that they need a strong man to make anything out of them, is only a means of subjugating these people. Telling your subjects they are children is a good way to make them accept that they need supervision.

This may be so, and no doubt much political mileage has been gotten from this idea, for good or ill. But it is still a matter of historical fact that throughout Russian history—with a few exceptions, such as Novgorod itself, as we shall see—autocracy, or rule by a strong leader, has been the dominant style and character of Russian political life. Enormous efforts have been made to change this, and attempts to Westernize (i.e., make more liberal) Russian political life have had varying success, most of them hitting a very solid wall of resistance. Indeed, how far Western influences have "taken" in Russia, and what it meant when they have, are questions that inform the overarching question of Russian identity.

THAT RURIK AND his clan accepted the Slavs' offer did not stop other Varangians from carrying on in the old ways. If Novgorod was the first stop on the waterways into Russia, there were destinations further south that seemed very attractive to others. One of these was Kiev.

As James H. Billington writes, Russian history can be understood as a tale of three cities: Kiev, Moscow, and St. Petersburg.[42] The origins of the first of these remain obscure, but the *Russian Primary Chronicle* tells us that around the same time that Rurik accepted the job of bringing order to the Slavs, circa 860, two other Varangians decided that they would like to rule a city too. The one they picked was Kiev, which was then under Khazar control. Like Novgorod and Smolensk, another early Slav settlement, Kiev was a fortified trading town along the river Dnieper. It was in fact an important trading hub, with connections to western cities, such as Kraków, Prague, and Breslau, and water routes to the Baltic and Black Seas. Excavations carried out in the oldest part of the city discovered the remains of a pre-Viking pagan temple, which suggests that Kiev was a thriving establishment before the Vikings arrived. Other finds suggest that trade had been going on between Kiev and the Vikings for some time.

Kiev's prosperity was most likely an inducement for two Varangian adventurers, Askold and Dir, to seize it from the Khazars. By this time the Scandinavians who settled in these Slavic lands had come to be known as the Rus, a term that may originate in the Finnish name for the Swedes, *Ruotsi*.[43] The Rus were a warrior elite, in service to the Slavs—at least to the ones who paid them. The ones who didn't usually received encouragement to do so.

ASKOLD AND DIR were not satisfied with their capture of Kiev and had designs on the legendary city of Constantinople, capital of the Eastern Roman Empire, which, unlike its western cousin, was still intact and formidable. Not formidable enough, however, to dissuade the two Varangian adventurers from mounting a raid on Constantinople's riches. It is ironic that a nation that would soon find an identity through Orthodox Christianity had its first contact with that tradition through the agency of a marauding attack. But that is how the Rus and the Byzantine civilization they would inherit came together.

An army of some 8,000 warriors in some 200 ships made the difficult and dangerous journey from Kiev, through the river Dnieper's rapids and across lands roaming with bandit tribes like the Pechenegs, to the Black Sea. From there, the black sails of the Vikings approached the holy city of Byzantium. The Byzantine Christians were caught off guard; by the time the Vikings were at the gates it was too late.

The attack was so savage, the Vikings so fierce, that many Christians thought the raid was divine punishment for their sins. They had never seen anything like them. As the historian Judith Herrin writes, with their "red hair, wild clothes, and fierce, incomprehensible shouts," the northerners terrified them.[44] What added insult to injury is that the Byzantines saw the Rus as an "obscure people" of "no account," rather as if a major league team had lost the pennant to some nobody bush-leaguers. They were little more than savages. But it was in this way, as Philip Longworth writes, that the "Rus leaped to the front of the political stage and the history books."[45]

What exactly led to the next development is unclear, but in 882, nine years after the death of Rurik, his grandson, Oleg, gained control of Kiev from Askold and Dir, whom he called "renegades," and both of whom he killed. Most likely Oleg wanted to establish good relations with both the Khazars and the Byzantines, as they would be needed in order to stay in business. Kiev was still under Khazar protection, but Oleg had gained control over a huge area of land, which provided goods with which he could trade with Constantinople. Furs, honey, swords, and slaves, male and female, made their way from the Viking posts to Baghdad and beyond. Yet relations with both the Khazars and Constantinople were not the best. Oleg led an attack on the holy city himself in 907, which led the Byzantines to make a deal with him. The Rus were given tribute, and their merchants room and board in Constantinople at the city's expense. With the Khazars, Oleg, who had set himself up as *khagan* of Kiev, arranged a kind of tacit agreement. The Khazars were the ostensible rulers of Kiev, but they were to stay out of his way, and for a time the question of who actually was in charge was unsettled. Local tribespeople often had to pay tribute to both Oleg's Rus and the Khazars.

When Oleg died, power in Kiev moved to Igor, Oleg's foster son who, like many Russian men to come, proved as covetous as the Varangians observed by the Arab traveler Ibn Fusta. Such voraciousness led to his downfall. When Igor increased the tribute he demanded from the "old settlers," the Derevlians, and then demanded even more, they decided that they had had enough, and killed him. Igor's widow, Olga, retaliated by raising an army of warriors. She attacked the Derevlian town of Ikorosan, destroyed it, and killed or captured the rebels and massacred the townsfolk. Olga did this in the name of her infant son, Svyatoslav, who would later rule the Rus. This was the same Olga who would soon lead the Rus to their spiritual destiny.

Her older son, Prince Igor, would bring that destiny a bit closer too. In 941 he launched another attack on Constantinople; exactly why is unclear. But it was not successful. One reason it failed is that this time the Byzantines were ready for the Rus and had some surprises of their own. One such was "Greek fire." This was the invention of a Syrian architect of the seventh century called Callinicus who came to live in Constantinople. He discovered that when sulphur, quicklime, saltpeter, bitumen, and naphtha are mixed, they produce a flame that is almost impossible to put out. (The historian Edward Gibbon suggested that urine could do the trick, but this seems a hypothesis difficult to prove.[46])

The exact recipe is lost to us, but to the ancient world Greek fire was as effective a weapon as napalm, and the Byzantines protected its recipe in the same way that nations today keep their military secrets under lock and key. It had saved Constantinople in the past from the Arabs. Now it performed the same service with the Rus. Catapults hurled flaming balls of flax saturated with the chemicals onto the Rus ships, setting them ablaze. Unmanned sailboats aflame with the fire were sent sailing into them, or it was poured down long tubes and spread upon the water, which only made the fire worse. Men who sought to escape the clinging flames by leaping into the harbor only found themselves burning even more, or drowning instead, brought down by their armor.[47]

After this it seems that both the Rus and the Byzantines decided that it would be better all around if they could reach some agreement. As is often the case, business helped them arrive at an effective and equitable reconciliation. Among other things, Constantinople needed slaves, and the Rus could provide a steady supply of them. Smash-and-grab raids and a lucrative slave trade may not seem the best auspices for a fledgling nation on its way to accepting its holy mission. But history works in strange ways, and through expedients as unlikely as the voyage to Byzantium was difficult, that was exactly what was about to happen.

3

Beauty Will Save the World

The Roots of Iconography

The third century CE was not a particularly good time for the Roman Empire. For one thing, the turnover of emperors had become rather swift, with seventy of them coming and going in as many years. As the empire was now effectively ruled by the military, and had been for some time, if there was an emperor the generals didn't like, they simply got rid of him. There were other worries too. The Goths threatened from the north, the Sassanids, a new Persian dynasty, did the same from the east, and other parts of the empire were crumbling through revolt, plague, and famine. As in other times of crisis, a strong man appeared to bring things to order. In this case it was the emperor Diocletian, who seized power in 284 CE and took extreme measures to keep the empire from disintegrating. He also was responsible for the last major persecution of the Christians. This religious sect had grown from a small band of disciples of a Jewish fanatic who had been ignominiously executed two centuries earlier, to a cult that had become strong enough to rival the Roman gods themselves.

After bringing order to the failing empire, through draconian edicts and high taxes, Diocletian, who was something of a contemplative, decided that things had grown too big for one man to manage alone. He decided to appoint a co-emperor. This other caesar was one of Diocletian's most trusted generals, Maximian, who would rule from Milan, while Diocletian would do the same from Nicomedia. This was a Greek city on the east side of the Bosporus, the narrow strait separating Europe from Asia in what we now call Turkey.

Diocletian then thought that even two men were not enough to run the empire, which now stretched from Britain in the north, to Spain, Egypt, and North Africa in the south, and to the Black Sea in the east. He then appointed two other sub-emperors attached to himself and Maximian. Technically, Diocletian and Maximian held the title of "Augustus," while these others did not. One sub-emperor was Diocletian's son-in-law Galerius, who ruled the Balkans. The other was Constantius I Chlorus, who would rule Gaul. Of the four, it's Constantius I Chlorus who concerns us.

In 305 Diocletian abdicated the throne and for his last years turned his attention to religious pursuits; he had already identified himself with the Roman god Jove or Jupiter—like the Greek Zeus, the most important of the gods—and to some degree his reign can be seen as a kind of theocracy. This divine rule, however, did not last long. The forces of disintegration that Diocletian had kept at bay during his reign soon returned, and almost immediately upon his abdication the struggle to succeed him began to tear the empire apart. The contenders here were Galerius, Maximian's son Maxentius, and Constantius I Chlorus.

Constantius I was nicknamed "Chlorus," because his face was apparently a pale shade of green. He had success in putting down a usurper named Carausius in Britain; part of his campaign included sailing up the Thames to Londinium (present-day London) to lay waste to the remnants of the rebels' army. When Maximian followed Diocletian's lead and abdicated too, Constantius I Chlorus was left as the senior caesar of the tetrarchy, the rule of four emperors. When Constantius I Chlorus died in 306, while defeating the Picts, his troops declared his son, Constantine, as emperor. This did not go down well with Maxentius who, not surprisingly, challenged Constantine's right to rule.

On the day before the decisive battle between Constantine and Maxentius at the Milvian Bridge—which took place on October 28, 312— Constantine is said to have had a vision. He saw a cross of light in the sky above the sun and the words *In hoc signo vinces,* "in this sign you shall conquer," emblazoned in the air. That night he had a dream in which Christ told him that if he had the cross painted on his soldiers' shields, he would be victorious. (Some accounts say it was the chi-rho sign, the first two letters of the Greek word *christos;* it looks something like a capital *P,* with an elongated bottom passing through the center of a capital *X.*) Constantine took the advice and won the battle, famously tossing the body of the defeated Maxentius into the river Tiber.

Constantine had some sympathy toward the Christians. His mother was Christian and would make a pilgrimage to the Holy Land—perhaps to atone for some of her son's sins. While there she said she had located the cross on which Jesus had been crucified. As we will see, Constantine played an important part in the history of Christianity. But his vision, while granting him victory, did not lead to his conversion, at least not immediately. And the fact that when the mood struck him, Constantine could be just as cruel and vicious as the worst of the previous caesars suggests that he had yet to absorb much of the Christian teachings about mercy and love. For example, he once "steamed" his wife Fausta to death by locking her in the baths and increasing the heat, and had his eldest son Crispus executed because of suspected improper relations between the two (she was Crispus's stepmother).[1]

After years of civil war, Constantine eventually defeated his final challenger, Licinius, and in 324 became sole ruler of the empire, the first single emperor since Diocletian seized power forty years earlier. In gratitude for the vision that had given him victory, Constantine gave Christianity a "favored" status among the religions in the empire. In 313 he had already produced the Edict of Milan, which called for the toleration of the Christians, ending the ages of persecution and martyrs. In 380, with the Edict of Thessalonica, Emperor Theodosius I, Constantine's successor, made Christianity the state religion of the empire. Soon after this, paganism was outlawed and pagans persecuted. We can mark the end of the pagan world by the closing of the Neoplatonic Academy, or "School of Athens," by Justinian I in 529 CE.

Three centuries after Roman soldiers played dice for the robe of the crucified king of the Jews, his religion of slaves, prostitutes, and other social misfits was now the official creed of the empire that had persecuted them. Yet Constantine himself was not baptized into the new state religion until he was on his deathbed in 337.

Why he remained a pagan until just before his death remains something of a mystery. One suggestion is that he may have waited until the end so that, once baptized, he would have no opportunity to sin, apparently a not uncommon practice at the time, and which smacks to some degree of hedging one's bets.[2] But there may have been more than religious reasons for his making Christianity the official religion of Rome. Accepting that Constantine may very well have seen his vision and had his dream, we can also see that, as would happen with a fledgling Russia, having a single strong faith is a very good means of binding a people together. Christians throughout the empire would be grateful to Constantine, which meant that he had bases of support wherever they were. As H. G. Wells remarks in *A Short History of the World,* Constantine may have used Christianity as "a means of using and controlling the wills of men." For Wells, no lover of religion, Constantine's reign was one of "war, the bitterest theology, and the usual vices of mankind."[3]

But it may also be the case, as Colin Wilson points out, that Constantine might have thought it fitting for a newly victorious emperor to begin his reign with a bang, as it were, and saw declaring Christianity the new state creed as a dramatic enough gesture. He was a serious student of the religion and took an interest in theological debate. He sided against the Donatists, Christians who condemned other Christians who had "collaborated" with the pagans during the persecutions, in favor of a unified church. And in 325 he called for the Council of Nicaea to end the squabbling over the Arian heresy.

Arius was an Alexandrian priest who taught that Jesus was not of the same divine nature as God. He viewed the Holy Trinity from a Neoplatonic perspective, one going back to the early church patriarchs, in which the Father is of a completely "other" character, beyond attributes, and the Son somewhat more human, a reasonable enough opinion. This was declared heresy by the council and Arius was excommunicated and sentenced to exile. Constantine's sister, Constantia, however, succeeding in having him return to Constantinople. But fate was not with him, and as he made his way to sign a compromise agreement that would allow him back into the church, Arius dropped dead in the street.

Constantine's seriousness about Christianity can be seen in other ways as well. During a visit to Rome he offended city officials by refusing to participate in a pagan ritual. He never returned to the Eternal City, which he now left to its own devices. This was no loss. He already had his eye on a new location for the capital of his empire.

CONSTANTINE'S OTHER SHOCK move and equally dramatic gesture of celebration was to transfer his seat of power to a Greek city on the other side of the Bosporus from Diocletian's Nicomedia. This was Byzantium, a port first settled in the seventh century BCE by a Greek named Byzas who, according to legend, hailed from Megara and captured it from Thracian tribes around 657 BCE. The town was rebuilt in 196 CE by the Roman emperor Septimus Severus after he had razed it to the ground for opposing him in a civil war. It had been controlled and fought over by the Persians, Athenians, Spartans, and Macedonians. Lying on a peninsula bordered by the Golden Horn, the Bosporus, and the Sea of Marmara, its natural harbor was a perfect port, and its location, at the meeting place of East and West, gave it strategic military and economic importance. When Constantine declared his eponymous city open in May 330, he called it the "New Rome." He then set to work making sure that it lived up to the title.

Just as Alexander the Great wanted his eponymous city, Alexandria, to stun those who visited it, Constantinople—Constantine's New Rome—would leave those who came through its gates awestruck and dazed. Its only land approach, to the west, would be protected by enormous walls. Within these, Constantine did his best to re-create the Eternal City. As in Rome, the chariot races at the Hippodrome, with statues of the gods, mythological heroes, and great rulers like Alexander and Julius Caesar looking on, became the center of the city's life. The public baths, made of marble from the far corners of the Roman world, were equally splendid. Constantine had sculptures and architectural flourishes from all across the empire brought to his New Rome: an obelisk from Karnak in Egypt and the famous Serpent Column celebrating the Greek victory over the Persians in 479 from Delphi were among the many wonders he had brought to adorn his new capital. Its markets were full of rare delicacies and delights, with amber, furs, precious metals, exotic oils, spices, grains, dyes, papyrus, and other specialty goods on display. Royal splendor seemed to run through the streets, where a medley of tongues could be heard in this most cosmopolitan of cities. For more than a thousand years, life among the Byzantines of the New Rome was rich, sumptuous, and dazzling.

According to James H. Billington, Byzantium was "Greek in speech but Oriental in magnificence."[4] It was Roman in rule and Christian in religion—Constantine had banned all pagan rituals—but there was an exotic splendor to Constantinople that rightly earned it a reputation for beauty surpassing anywhere else at the time and, it has to be said, also for decadence. That beauty was part of a total unity embracing the entire Byzantine world, and the memory of this complete perfection, involving everything about the culture, would haunt poets and other romantics for centuries.

One of these, W. B. Yeats, in his poem "Sailing to Byzantium," sang the praises of the city's "monuments of unaging intellect."[5] For Yeats, "in early Byzantium . . . religious, aesthetic, and practical life were one. . . ." Its "painters, mosaic workers, gold and silver smiths, scribes" were all "absorbed in . . . the vision of a whole people."[6] As the poet and Yeats scholar Kathleen Raine put it, for Yeats, Byzantium represented "perhaps the most perfect embodiment of the spiritual order which has existed upon earth." And at the center of this order was "the magical and compelling beauty of the numinous."[7]

Perhaps nothing was more numinous in Constantinople than Hagia Sophia, the Church of the Holy Wisdom. It was built by the emperor Justinian in 537, and today stands in Istanbul (the former Constantinople) as a museum, after serving as a mosque from 1453 to 1935. Earlier versions of this basilica church were built by Constantius II, Constantine's son, in 360, and then again in 415, when it was rebuilt by Emperor Theodosius II after a fire. It was a fire again that led to its last and most lasting version.

In 532 the two main groups involved in the chariot races at the Hippodrome, the Greens and the Blues, normally rivals, found common cause in their dissatisfaction with Justinian's rule. They threw their support behind a pretender to the throne named Hypatius. With crowds cheering him on, Hypatius was robed in imperial purple in the Hippodrome and his claim to the throne declared. The crowds chanted "Nika," which means "conquer," and the riots that followed are known as the Nika Rebellion.

To make their point, the rebels set fire to the city center and the rebuilt Church of the Holy Wisdom was caught up in the flames. Justinian, who seems to have been a weak character, was ready to flee the city; boats were waiting for him in the harbor. His wife Theodora, however, who began her career as a prostitute, was made of sterner stuff, at least according to the account that has come down to us by the historian Procopius of Caesarea. When faced with the idea of flight, she is said to have replied, "Purple makes a fine shroud"— meaning she would rather die as a queen in her imperial purple than live in exile—and to have shamed Justinian into action.[8] Rather than escape or even bargain with the rebels, he immediately sent troops into the Hippodrome, who promptly slaughtered anyone there and quickly restored order.

Rather than rebuild on the same scale of the church that had been destroyed, Justinian had bigger plans. What they led to was one of the largest buildings in the world and one of the most stunning churches in Christendom. The result, a work of "unparalleled magnificence," was an architectural showpiece celebrating the sheer size and strength of the Eastern Roman Empire.[9] Just as Constantine had materials brought from all corners of the empire to build his city, so too did Justinian gather different materials from all the lands in his domain for his new Church of the Holy Wisdom.

Purple marble from Egypt, speckled marble from Phrygia, green marble from Thessaly, white marble from quarries near the Sea of Marmara, these and other rare materials, such as onyx, silver, gold, crystal, ivory, and enamel, reached Justinian's builders from all points on the empire's compass. Eight porphyry columns came from the Temple of the Sun in Rome. Eight columns of green marble came from ancient Ephesus on the Ionian coast.[10] Mosaics of archangels done in red, green, blue, and gold tesserae, from different artists in the realm, looked down from the high vaulted arches.

Rome, left to its own devices by Constantine I, had by this time fallen to the barbarians. While Justinian was completing the construction of Hagia Sophia, Rome was undergoing a siege by the Ostrogoths. The Eternal City was no longer what it had been, but Constantinople now had more than enough splendor to make up for the loss. When Justinian contemplated what he had accomplished, after work on the building was complete, he is said to have remarked, "Solomon, I have surpassed thee." Many who visited the Church of the Holy Wisdom, I suspect, may have agreed.

The most immediately stunning feature of Hagia Sophia was its dome. Although there had been some domed structures prior to it, such as the Pantheon in Rome, they were nothing like Hagia Sophia in scale. At more than a hundred feet in diameter, and rising to one hundred-eighty feet from its multicolored marble floor, like some other sacred structures, there seemed to be more space within it than without.* Looking up at the light streaming through forty windows ringing the dome's circumference, with gold mosaics and icons lit by innumerable lamps, and huge angels hovering overhead, visitors were amazed that it was at all possible for the huge ceiling to be supported. Procopius tells us that for him it seemed to be floating, carried aloft by the light itself. The space below it was cavernous and shot through with, as Oswald Spengler says, an "unreal, fairy-tale light," which "for Northerners" is "always . . . seductive."[11] How true Spengler's assessment is will soon become clear.

Unlike the Gothic impulse, which strives upward in order to pierce the heavens and reach the divine, the Magian soul, according to Spengler, and of which Hagia Sophia is a supreme example, creates "eternal vaults," a vast enclosed space that it populates with symbols of the spiritual beings of an interior universe.

If the dome of Hagia Sophia is impressive from within its walls, "sparkling" with "golden mosaics and arabesques," it is equally striking from without.[12] Visitors approaching from the sea watch the great dome rise up over the city and dominate the landscape. Today the minarets put in place after the fall of New Rome to the Turks mark the true end of the Roman Empire. But it is still the dome that speaks of a lost kingdom that once ruled the world.

IT WOULD HAVE been the dome that first struck Princess Olga of Kiev when in 955 she approached New Rome from the Black Sea. As Yeats did in his imagination—having never visited Constantinople in the flesh—she had "sailed the seas and come / To the holy city of Byzantium."[13] And like others who had done the same, she was impressed.

---

*In 1996 I had an opportunity to test this thesis during a visit to Hagia Sophia. Some years earlier a "mini search for the miraculous" had me in Chartres Cathedral in France, among other places. A similar sense of an enclosed but nevertheless infinite space was a central feature of that visit too.

Like Constantine, Olga was sympathetic to Christianity, and there is some suspicion that her conversion had something to do with atoning for the sins of her past life. Her revenge against the murderers of her husband, Prince Igor, had been brutal and thorough. Feigning gestures of reconciliation, she accepted a group of nobles from the offending tribe into her camp where, rather than enjoy a banquet, they were buried alive. More ambassadors came. This delegation was locked in the bathhouses and burned alive. At a ritual celebration at her husband's grave, when members of the offending tribe had drunk themselves into a stupor, Olga's warriors, who remained sober, hacked them to pieces. It was only after this that she attacked Ikorosan, the main city of the Derevlians, and burned it to the ground.

Yet her voyage to Byzantium had political motivations too. After raiding Constantinople and then setting up trade agreements with it, the Rus began to see the advantage of the institutions that had made it a powerful state. The Rus, tired of the squabbles that invariably arose when the succession of power was not clearly laid out—as was often the case with them—decided it was time to learn how the Romans did it. Princess Olga was sent to see for herself. On the Byzantine side, it was clear to them that having the Rus as trading partners would be better than having them as a possible constant threat. For one party, the meeting between the two was a good and necessary bit of diplomacy. For the other it meant, according to some views, the beginning of their historical destiny.

Olga was given the royal treatment; the red carpet was rolled out and she was received with the highest dignity. For Emperor Constantine VII Porphyrogenitus—"born in purple," that is, of imperial blood—this visit by a Rus queen was one diplomatic visit among many; as more than one historian has pointed out, the Byzantines considered the Rus little more than savages. For Olga, however, it was something that would remain with her for the rest of her life. She was shown the great walls that defended the city, was taken to the huge cistern that held water for its inhabitants, was walked around the Hippodrome and, like other visitors, she gazed up at the column surmounted by the golden head of Constantine I that towered over the central market, where every good imaginable was in plentiful supply and on offer. A special visit with the empress was arranged for her in her private quarters where a "women only" dinner was laid out.[14]

The golden table on which Olga ate rare and delicious foods—and where she was introduced to the use of a knife and fork; before this she, like her people, tore her meat with her hands—the elaborate court proceedings, and the magnificent displays of wealth and luxury were overwhelming. So were the fantastic mechanical devices that the emperor had installed in the imperial palace, to which, as an honored dignitary, Olga had gained access. Yeats had written of "forms" that "Grecian goldsmiths make / Of hammered gold and gold enamelling / To keep a drowsy emperor awake," but it seems that Constantine VII had his own ideas about home entertainment.[15]

Constantine VII was a man of wide learning and eager intellectual curiosity; it is through his prolific writings that much of what we know about Byzantium has come down to us. One area that fascinated him was mechanics and engineering. Like other visitors, Olga was amazed at Constantine's mechanical songbirds, tweeting from the branches of a jeweled tree, and the equally mechanical roaring lions that rolled their eyes as an accompaniment. Constantine had had these made for his amusement, but also to create an air of mystery and the supernatural about his court. Probably his most impressive conjuring trick was his hydraulic throne, which shot him thirty feet up above his guests, who marveled at his magnificence, as he regarded them from on high.

Such devices may strike us as like something out of *The Wizard of Oz*, flashy shows of magic and power to awe an audience and distract it from what's really happening, whatever that might be. Or simply smoke and mirrors to stun heathen dignitaries into conversion. But as Timothy Ware, a scholar of Orthodoxy, suggests, these displays of mechanical magic were necessary to "make clear the emperor's status as vice regent of God."[16] He was "God's representative on earth." Byzantium, Ware tells us, was an "icon of the heavenly Jerusalem," a representation on Earth of the Kingdom of Heaven. Constantine VII himself justified his special effects by seeing them as a means of illustrating the macro-microcosmical relationship between that kingdom and this one. "By such means" as his magical devices, he wrote, "we figure forth the harmonious movement of God the creator around this universe, while the imperial power is preserved in proportion and order."[17]

The emperor held a unique place in Byzantine Orthodoxy, unlike that of any Western emperor. He was the earthly embodiment of a spiritual realm, which had its correspondence in the city of Constantine, a "living image of God's government in heaven."[18] In Byzantium, there was no separation of church and state. Life there was a "unified whole," with no clear demarcation between the religious and the secular. They formed two parts of a "single organism."[19]

Religion so permeated every aspect of life in Byzantium that even commercial contracts and agreements were marked with a cross.[20] Religious arguments and discussion obsessed the Byzantines in a way they would the God-seekers of the Silver Age. Gregory of Nyssa, bishop and later saint, who visited Constantinople around 381, complained that when he asked about the price of bread, he received a theological disquisition for an answer.[21] This was the unity that moved Yeats and for which, in what seemed to him an increasingly fracturing world, he yearned: that "perfect embodiment of the spiritual order," which he believed could be found in every reflection of Byzantine life, from the smallest trivial item, to the great dome of Hagia Sophia.

It was this effect, of having entered not only a city—even a "Great City," Micklagaard, as the Rus called it—but an entirely different world, that struck Olga as it had struck others before her and would strike those to come. New trade agreements with the Byzantines and importing institutions and other practical ideas from them to use at home were, of course, important. But this sense of another world, unlike anything she had ever seen or even dreamed of—*that* was what hit home most powerfully.

Here too, Constantine VII and his predecessors, like Justinian, had decided to spare no effort or expense. Along with architectural delights and rare materials, Hagia Sophia had benefited by the collection of relics from throughout Christendom that had been brought to her. Among the most important were Jesus's swaddling clothes, the table at which he and his disciples had the Last Supper, and the True Cross, or at least part of it. These were concrete links to the reality of the Savior, or so Olga believed, and as such they helped create a sense of the numinous. The chanting of the monks, the incense, the innumerable lamps throwing their flickering light on the glittering golden mosaics, the mementoes of Christ's life, the cavernous dome sparkled with illuminated icons, the golden altar encrusted with jewels and other precious stones, the mysterious ritual and service in a language—Greek—she didn't understand: to Olga, used to more humble atmospheres, even though she was royalty, everything conspired to create the effect of heaven on earth.

And it worked. Olga experienced what other ambassadors of the Rus did when they encountered the mystical beauty of the Byzantine church. A later group sent on a reconnaissance mission by Olga's grandson, Vladimir, reported that they "knew not whether we were in heaven or on earth. For on earth there is no such splendour or such beauty."[22] In *The Idiot,* his attempt to portray a truly "good" soul in the character of the epileptic Christlike prince Myshkin, Fyodor Dostoyevsky tells us that "beauty will save the world." If so, that work of salvation may have started here.

It is likely that Olga had already been baptized into the Orthodox Church before her voyage to Byzantium. By the time she visited Constantinople, Orthodox missionaries had established themselves in Kiev. Yet we can imagine that while there she would have wanted to take the sacrament again, now in a setting of appropriate splendor and mystery, and also as a sign of her commitment to bring the faith back with her to her people. On this second baptism, the emperor himself served as her godfather, and she was also given a new name: Helen. This was the name of the mother of Constantine the Great, the first Christian emperor. Olga's christening forged a link to the empire that future rulers would seek to reestablish.

Olga's conversion, we can assume, was the indirect result of the energetic missionary work of two Greek monks from Thessalonica, the brothers Cyril (826–869) and Methodius (815–885). Cyril—who was called Constantine before taking vows—was a scholar, fluent in many languages, and Methodius was an effective administrator.

At around the same time as Rurik was settling in at Novgorod, Cyril and Methodius were spreading the glad tidings to the Khazars, or at least were trying to; as the Khazars remained Jewish, they were apparently not very successful. Undeterred, in 863 the brothers were asked by Prince Rostislav of Moravia (an area in the present day Czech Republic) to prepare services to be performed in Slavonic for his people. This meant that the brothers would have to translate Greek into Slavonic. In order to do this they first had to create a Slavonic alphabet. They knew a Slavonic dialect from their childhood in Macedonia, and it was from this that the Cyrillic alphabet eventually emerged.

One difference between the Eastern and Western Churches was that while the Western Church used only Latin in its services—which meant for the most part that their congregations did not understand them—in the Eastern Church services and the Gospel would be given in the local language, something that didn't happen in the Western Church on any wide scale until Martin Luther kicked up a stir. This put Orthodox missionaries at an advantage over Catholic ones, a situation that led to much animosity from the German missionaries competing with them. Although Cyril and Methodius's Moravian mission was eventually not successful—Moravia became Roman Catholic—their work in translation and creating an alphabet meant that Slavs in other places would hear the good word: they did in Bulgaria and they did in Serbia and they did in Russia too.

In 869 an Orthodox bishop had been sent to Kiev, but his work was cut short by Oleg who, we remember, captured the city in 882. Yet by 945 there was a church in Kiev. Ten years later Olga, who had brought a priest with her in her entourage, was making her way back from New Rome laden with ideas about how to transform her pagan people into a Christian nation. She was full of the memory of the beauty she had seen and the mystery she had experienced, and was determined to import some of the marvels and wonders that had amazed her in Byzantium, "the city of the world's desire," to her own city of Kiev.[23]

OLGA'S CONVERSION CAME at a good time, especially when considering the possibility that beauty could, indeed, save the world. One of the most important means of spreading knowledge of the Orthodox Church was through icons, the strikingly illuminated representations of Jesus, Mary, the saints, and other holy figures, that became a central part of Russian spirituality. A little more than a century before Olga's trip to Byzantium, the second of two outbreaks of *iconoclasm*— literally the "smashing of images"—had been brought to an end by the empress Theodora. In 726 Leo III began an attack on the use of images in worship, accusing them of spreading idolatry, the worship of idols; this lasted until 780. In 815 Leo V the Armenian began another purge, which ended in 843, when the empress Theodora made icons a permanent part of Orthodox worship.

Iconoclasm hit the West in Florence, Italy, in the late fifteenth century in the form of Savonarola and his "bonfire of the vanities." It broke out again in cities such as Zurich, Copenhagen, and Geneva during the Protestant Reformation that soon followed. This ban on images can be traced back to Judaism, and it is something that it shares with Islam, another "religion of the book." It is the ban on "graven images" from the Ten Commandments. Neoplatonic "negative theology," which we will return to further on, also contributes to it. But while the use of images and representations has been part of Western worship, it has never been as powerful and central an element in it as it was in the Eastern Church.

For Russians, an icon is something more than a representation or image: it is the promise of another world and often the means of entering it.

What happened when Orthodoxy began to enter the consciousness of the Rus was not that they simply began to worship a new god; that could have happened with a pagan deity. It was that this new god and religion were part of a package deal that also included art and beauty. Going by Olga's reaction—who, after all, was a princess—they seem to have had little experience of these before this. It was through the beautiful that the true and the good came to the Rus. This meant that for the Russian soul, the idea of an "art for art's sake" is completely foreign. Art is for the sake of our souls. As James H. Billington points out, this is why Russians do not seek "satisfaction" in art, as Westerners do, but "salvation."[24] For them beauty must save the world; otherwise there is no reason for it. This is an idea that would inform the Symbolists of the Silver Age, and which made the work of Tolstoy and Dostoyevsky radically different from contemporaries like Flaubert for whom art serves no such purpose. It would even lead Tolstoy to finally renounce art in favor of the Gospel, something that Gogol had already done some years before him.

THE ROOTS OF iconography go back, it seems, to the ancient Egyptians. When the pharaoh's body was mummified it was placed in a sarcophagus; the final touch of which was the mask placed over the face. Here the sacred artist would paint an idealized portrait of the deceased, the face with which he would enter eternity. After Egypt was conquered by Alexander the Great in 331 BCE, this practiced died out, but not completely. The new rulers, equally desirous of an eternal life in the beyond, began to practice a variant of it. They too were mummified, but the masks they wore in death were flattened out, unlike those of the ancient pharaohs. They were also executed in a more "realistic" manner, the style we know as "classical."[25]

The technique used in these funerary paintings is known as

encaustic; this is a means of fixing bright colors on wooden panels using egg-based tempera paint and burnt wax. It seems that this technique was picked up by some early Christians who had fled persecution and retreated to the desert. Many of these death masks from this time were found at the Fayum oasis in Egypt, on the left bank of the Nile, sixty-five miles south of Cairo.[26] It's thought that Christians fleeing the cities found themselves here and took over the practice of painting a portrait of their dead.

This practice, and that of "holy pictures" in general, increased after Constantine's conversion and Christianity's subsequent triumph over paganism. (There was a brief return to paganism under the rule of Julian the Apostate, but after his short term as emperor [361–363] it was finished.) Icons—Greek for pictures—helped spread Christianity throughout the empire much better than words. Not all of Constantine's subjects knew Greek, but all of them could understand an image.

Today we use the word *iconic* thoughtlessly, referring to some easily recognizable product of popular culture, or see *icons* as handy tools on our computers, an indication of the deterioration of our vocabulary. But the true icon was more than a sign, or a kind of wordless religious comic strip, simply teaching the lessons or history of the church. They were, as Timothy Ware writes, "dynamic manifestations of man's spiritual power to redeem creation through beauty and art."[27] They were not merely an aid in catechism, but an example of the power inherent in the spirit to *transform* reality, to take the "triviality of everydayness"—in the philosopher Heidegger's phrase—and redeem it; that is, show it in its *transfigured truth,* the truth that art alone could reveal.

Iconoclasm arose over a misunderstanding. Iconoclasts believed that by prostrating and praying before an icon, one was worshiping the icon itself, the thing, *not* what it represented, the golden calf of the biblical story. This was idolatry. But as Father Pavel Florensky said, icons are "windows on another world." They are not magical totems, but small glimpses of the transfigured world and a "pledge of the coming victory of the redeemed creation over the fallen one."[28] Salvation, for Russians, is not simply personal, but involves the entire universe. Everything, from the smallest atom to the largest sun, must be saved—a project that the Cosmists of the twentieth century took very literally. This belief in the power of art to transform reality was another central theme among the Symbolist poets and artists of the Silver Age. Through esoteric philosophers such as P. D. Ouspensky, it reached important figures—such as Kasimir Malevich—in the modernism that superseded them. Indeed, more than a few elements of Malevich's aggressively nonrepresentational art arguably have roots in ancient iconography.[29]

By the time Olga returned to Kiev on her mission to convert the Rus, icons were an established part of Orthodox worship and remained so until their suppression under the Bolsheviks. Their use highlights a difference between the Eastern and Western Churches. As those differences will play a part in our story, it is perhaps best that I briefly spell them out here. Geography, language, invasions, and politics, among other things, helped bifurcate the once Catholic—meaning universal—Church into two different and often opposing traditions. But theological issues and different approaches to worship played a large part in the split too.

In 451 the emperor Marcian convened the Fourth Ecumenical Council of the Christian Church, known as the Council of Chalcedon, because of where it was held (now Kadiköy in modern Turkey). Among other items, what was important about this council is that it established five patriarchates, the office or residence—or see—of a father of the church, a bishop. These were Rome, Constantinople, Alexandria, Antioch, and Jerusalem. Although the bishop of Rome—the pope—was given primacy of honor as "first among equals," he was not a monarch or autocrat, and major decisions about theological or other disputes had to be arrived at through a council, and agreed to by the other bishops. Gradually, though, this understanding began to be challenged, and increasingly the Western Church saw itself as loyal to one bishop and one authority, the pope in Rome. This arrangement never took hold in the Eastern Church. To this day, there is no equivalent of the pope in the Eastern Church, and major decisions are still arrived at through debates held in councils of church leaders.

The barbarian invasions of the fifth century made communication between the eastern and western halves of the empire difficult, if not impossible, and with this came the decline in learning. Latin was no longer the universal language of the empire and was limited to the lands that its remnants held against the Goths and other tribes. Greek had always been the language of choice of Byzantium. This difference in language informed the different "styles"—for sake of a better word—of the Eastern and Western Churches. Latin is a more practical language than Greek, which is of a more philosophical character. This distinction can be seen in Spengler's remark that Rome gave us little in the way of philosophy, but much in the way of practical pursuits, like engineering and jurisprudence.*[30] To which Heidegger might have replied that it is only in Greek—and German—that one can really think.[31]

Now, fewer and fewer Latin speakers knew Greek and vice versa; loss of Greek was precisely one of the reasons for the so-called Dark Ages, which, if they were not as dark as we used to believe, were certainly rather dim. With the rise of Islam, Constantinople became even more isolated from the West. And in 800, when on Christmas Day, Pope Leo III crowned Charlemagne emperor of the Holy Roman Empire, the Eastern Church took this as a slight, given that they were not consulted. In 1054 this antagonism was heightened by a contretemps, which came to be known as the Great Schism—although relations between the two churches still continued after this and were really not over until the Council of Florence and Ferrara of 1438–45 failed to bring about their proposed reunification.

The source of the schism, which was really a gradual estrangement, is

---

*"One Roman law weighed more than all the lyrics and school metaphysics of the time together."

what is known as the *filioque,* an addition to the Nicene Creed introduced by the Church of Spain at the Council of Toledo in 589. In the original creed, a statement of Christian belief adopted in 325 at the Council of Nicaea, it states that the Holy Spirit—perhaps the most mysterious member of the Holy Trinity—"proceeds from the Father," that is, from God. The *filioque* is a slight amendment that adds "and the Son." So with the *filioque,* the Holy Spirit proceeds from the Father *and* the Son.

The idea was that without this addition, Jesus, the Son, would seem less than God, which he wasn't, or at least wasn't supposed to be. It was the same idea that had got Arius into trouble. The Eastern Church argued that the West had no right to add anything to the creed without consulting *all* the bishops and refused to adopt the addition. It continued to maintain that the Holy Spirit proceeded from the Father, period. How exactly this diminishes Jesus's status is unclear, and what difference it made to the Holy Spirit is not spelled out. Nevertheless, much ink and anathematizing has gone into the at times violent disputes aroused by this hairsplitting over the years. At bottom, however, there is a metaphysical reason for all the fighting, and it is one that informs the iconoclasm of which it is a part.

It goes back to the earliest days of Christian theology and the work of an unknown person, whom we refer to for sheer convenience as Dionysius the Areopagite, or, less generously, Pseudo-Dionysius. He was born in Syria, lived in the early sixth century, and was a Christian student of Damascius (458–538), the last teacher of the Neoplatonic Academy, made redundant by Justinian I. He has been confused with two other people,* but what makes him important here is that he brought together Neoplatonism and Christianity and created the angelic hierarchies of the Christian universe.

Neoplatonism is a mystical approach to the philosophy of Plato that arose in the third century CE in Alexandria through the agency of its

---

*He was confused with the Athenian converted by the apostle Paul, mentioned in Acts 17:34, and with Saint Dionysius (Latin for Denis), the patron saint of France. We don't know who he really was.

most eloquent expositor, the philosopher Plotinus (204–270). Briefly put, Plotinus believed that the true reality resided in the One, or the Absolute, a condition of utter perfection and self-sufficiency, which existed in some non-manifest way, beyond the realm of the senses or even the intellect—rather like the God of the Christians and the Jews. From it proceeded two emanations, what Plotinus called Mind or Nous, which he regarded as the Platonic Forms or Ideas—the blueprints, as it were, of reality—and the Anima Mundi, or World Soul, a kind of inner life animating everything and linking it with everything else, what he called "the sympathy of all things." It is through the Forms and the World Soul that nature and the physical world come into existence. The philosopher's job, Plotinus believed, was to reunite with the One, through a series of mental operations that revealed it to consciousness.

Later Neoplatonists, such as Porphyry (233–305), Plotinus's student, softened Plotinus's austere approach by bringing in the Greek myths, which were read as symbolic accounts of the soul's journey. By the time of Iamblichus (245–325), Neoplatonism had transformed itself into a kind of ritual magic; the path to the One now lay through arcane ceremony. Iamblichus had introduced more intermediate spheres of reality between ourselves and the Absolute and had peopled them with a variety of spiritual beings, who would respond to certain "mysterious acts" performed by the philosopher, who had by now become something of a mage. This baroque esoteric universe was transformed into a complex, complicated, and at times confusing system by the last great Neoplatonist, Proclus (412–485), who lived to see the last days of paganism and its persecution by the Christians.

It is somewhat ironic that the person who would salvage the Neoplatonic ladder of reality was a believer in the very faith in the name of which Neoplatonic philosophers were being persecuted—witness the sad fate of the philosopher Hypatia (370–415), who was beaten to death and had the flesh scraped from her bones by a mob of Alexandrian Christians. But like the early church fathers Clement of Alexandria (150–215) and Origen (185–252)—important figures in the

Eastern Church—Dionysius the Areopagite, whoever he was, saw the value in Greek ideas and wanted to preserve them from his less insightful colleagues. This was an aim and effort that would find many adherents within the church in the centuries that followed.

What Dionysius did was to take Proclus's complex system of intermediary worlds between ours and the Absolute, and use this as a model with which to bring order and coherence to Christian theology, which was still fluid and what we might call a "work in progress." The result was the "celestial hierarchy" spelled out in Dionysius's writings, such as *The Mystical Theology* and *The Divine Names.* These are the seraphim, cherubim, thrones, dominions, virtues, powers, principalities, archangels, and angels that make up the Christian spiritual universe.

Although Dionysius's work was known to the Eastern Church from early on, because of the loss of Greek it was not known in the West until the ninth century, when John Scotus Eriugena, an Irish monk and scholar, translated it into Latin in 862. As I point out in *The Secret Teachers of the Western World,* Dionysius's "theology of light" had an enormous influence on the rise of the Gothic, and if there is one person we can thank for stained-glass windows, such as we find in masterpieces like Chartres Cathedral, it is him.[32] But it was the Neoplatonic notion of "emanation" that caused trouble, of the kind we saw with Arius.

For Plotinus and his followers, the One or Absolute does not decide to create the world ex nihilo, out of nothing, by divine fiat. It can't help but create it. As the sun's light and warmth emanate from it, so too do the Forms, the World Soul, and eventually, ourselves emanate from the One. Without its light and warmth the sun would not be a sun. So too are the One's emanations inseparable from it being itself.

For Christian theology this raises some problems. Unlike the Neoplatonic trinity of Absolute, Ideas, and World Soul, which descends one from the other, the members of the Holy Trinity are to be understood as existing simultaneously: three in one and one in three—not one, two, three. In the Neoplatonic view Jesus would have second place; still exalted, certainly, but not coterminous with the Father, and the

Holy Spirit would have even lesser rank. This, we saw, was the wall Arius hit.

Another problem is that an emanationist view suggests that God *had* to create the world—or at least that he couldn't not create it, even if he wanted to. The sun does not choose to shine; if it didn't, it wouldn't be a sun. Such considerations seem to place a limit on God, who is not supposed to have any limitations. In what we can call the "creationist" view—not to be confused with creationism—God did not have to create the world. There was no pressure on him to do so or not; that is, the creation of the world was not necessary. It was a free act of God's will. He could just as well not have made it. A Neoplatonic image of this could be a cold, dark sun suspended in a dark, empty space that suddenly decides to shine.

The question of how a God who is utterly beyond human comprehension can in any way relate to his faithful is linked to the questions about Jesus's nature that would plague the church for centuries and produce an enormous number of split hairs and heads. The riddle of how much of Jesus's nature was human, how much divine, and how the two interacted, kept many a theologian awake at night, and cost some people their lives. For our purposes we can see this conundrum in terms of a distinction that originates with Dionysius and which centers around the debate between whether the spirit—for sake of a better term—is "immanent" or "transcendent," whether, that is, it partakes of this world or is utterly beyond it.

An absolute break between the divine world and this one preserves the purity and sanctity of the divine and undermines human hubris, but it also lowers human standing and makes the world a place of sin. A divine that partakes of this world allows humans to partake of it, but opens the door to human deification and lowers the divine's stature. With this in mind, two different ways of worship and paths to union with the divine opened up, what are known as the *via negativa* and the *via positiva,* the way of negation and the way of affirmation.

The way of negation is that of the "negative theology" for which

Dionysius argued in his writings. Recognizing that anything we could say about God would only limit his perfection, Dionysius proposed approaching God through what he is not. This is the apophatic tradition, an inner emptying or *kenosis* that will play an important part in the monastic movement of the fourteenth century. This was rooted in the Hesychast practice, the "inner stillness," that became influential at the monastery of Mount Athos in Greece, although its roots go back much further.

We will return to the Hesychasts further on. What concerns us here is the other path, the way of affirmation, the *via positiva*. It was through this path that Olga tried to bring the Word to her people.

SADLY, SHE WAS not successful. It would take a generation before the Rus accepted Orthodoxy, and even then the pagan traditions would strongly resist the advance of Byzantium, in some places for centuries. We've already seen the advantages of *dvoeverie,* or "double belief." Olga brought missionaries back with her, and if their efforts were not at first a total success, they did begin a flow of Byzantine influence into the lands of the "wild people" of the north. Among the new developments prompted by Olga's voyage was a desire among many Rus to learn the alphabet. What there was to read in it was the Gospels; so in a sense we can say that for the recipients of the new literacy, the medium certainly helped spread the message.

Yet Olga's mission, for all its personal significance, was also unsuccessful diplomatically. She had asked for a metropolitan see to be established in Kiev, but this was denied; a metropolitan is a local church leader, of lesser rank than a patriarch. She had also tried to secure a dynastic marriage between her son, Svyatoslav I, and the emperor's daughter, who was the *porphyrogenitus,* that is "born in purple," but was denied this too.

This rejection may have had something to do with Svyatoslav's rejection of Orthodoxy. When pressed by his mother to convert, he refused, saying that he would look silly to his fellow warriors if he accepted this religion of love and gentleness. He was a devotee of Perun the thunder god, and he intended to remain one. Svyatoslav was something of an impulsive character, and he did not like to be thwarted. During a campaign against the Bulgarian city of Philippopolis (present-day Plovdiv), when the people finally surrendered after putting up a brave resistance, he had 20,000 of them impaled.[33] His mother had some influence on him, but as most of the soldiers in Svyatoslav's command were pagans, they were able to diminish this until in the end her headstrong son did what he wanted—and that was not to become Christian.

This must have been heartbreaking to Olga. She knew a single faith was needed to unite her people, who still bickered and fought in pointless feuds. She had used some of the wealth she had created through her efficient collection and administration of the tribal tribute paid to Kiev to build churches there (she had, it seems, established the first system of taxation for the Rus). One was the Church of the Wisdom of God, built on the burial site of Askold, one of the Varangians who captured the city from the Khazars. She also built a Church of Saint Sophia and converted many Rus to the new faith. But many of the Kievan elite remained pagan and resented her efforts at raising churches and making converts. Svyatoslav himself took to killing Christians and destroying churches, some that Olga herself had raised. Shamans dressed in colorful robes hung with tinkling bells were also not convinced that the black-hooded monks chanting their orisons were really more powerful than the spirits they knew and communed with through the forests and fields.

But slowly the new faith entered the life of the Rus. The priests spoke to them in their own language and told them of Christ's miracles. Even more persuasive were the icons that spoke in the universal language of color and form. These showed, more than any sermon could, the beauty of truth and the truth of beauty. And with the icons came the bells that would become as much a carrier of the Word as the icons were, although they spoke in sound and the other in imagery. If beauty could save the world, it seemed to be making a good start.

4

The Lost Kingdom

After the Fall of Kiev

When Svyatoslav I the pagan was not killing Christians or destroying churches, his aggressive tendencies were put to expedient use by the Byzantines. He had already eliminated the Khazars, driving them out of Itil on the Volga and then razing it to the ground. This opened up the lucrative commercial empire that the Khazars had controlled in the south, and the new trade opportunities helped an already prospering Kiev. When Bulgar tribes in the Balkans troubled Constantinople, Svyatoslav offered his assistance to the emperor, who accepted it. It was during this campaign that, as mentioned, he had 20,000 inhabitants of a rebel city impaled. Such excesses would soon lead to his downfall.

Svyatoslav I coveted control of the Danube, an essential trade route to the west, and he sought to establish a capital in the delta for what he hoped to be the start of an empire. Although he was at first helpful to Constantinople in dealing with pests, the emperor soon recognized that with Svyatoslav I in place instead of the Bulgars, he had only traded one problem for another. A worse one in fact, as Syvatoslav I's hunger to expand and dominate the area was clear. At one point, when he had gone too far, the imperial army stepped in and Syvatoslav I's dream of an empire was aborted. An account of a meeting between the pagan warrior and Emperor John Tzimiskes—himself a general—in 971 gives an idea of what the first Russian prince with a Slavic name was like. He was of strong build and medium height, with a shaved head except for a single lock of hair that marked his nobility. He wore golden armor and earrings, and was of a dark, savage disposition.[1] He was also apparently insufficiently humble before the emperor, which was a mistake. It led to Syvatoslav I's being ambushed and killed by the Pechenegs, a Turkic-speaking nomadic tribe of central Asia, an efficient expression of realpolitik Byzantine emperors were not loath to employ.

Not surprisingly, with Svyatoslav I's death, a struggle for power broke out among his three sons, who ruled Novgorod, Kiev, and Derevliana. At the end, one remained, Vladimir. Like his father he was pagan, and after first fleeing from his Christian brother Iaropolk to Sweden, he then achieved victory over him, with the help of some mercenaries he had brought back with him on his return. By this time, the original Varangian or Nordic strain of the Rus had been completely assimilated into the indigenous Slavs. From this point on, all Russian leaders would have Slavic names.

Vladimir continued to defend paganism against the spread of Orthodoxy—as his father did, he worshiped Perun, the god of thunder—but as his grandmother Olga had, he saw that a single faith would be the best way to fuse the different tribes of the Rus together and end the squabbling and bickering that had kept them divided and weak. (There is some suggestion that he had already tried to do this with his pagan beliefs.) Olga herself, before committing wholly to Orthodoxy, had investigated Roman Catholicism, meeting with German priests and missionaries, of the same order that drove Cyril and Methodius out of Moravia. Her gestures of interest were politically motivated, intended to let the Byzantines know that other powers were also interested in having her join them. But she was also an educated consumer, who liked to shop around.

As did his grandmother, Vladimir also decided to investigate his options. In the *Primary Chronicle* it is recounted how Vladimir sent out emissaries to learn of Islam and the Western Church. They did, and they were unimpressed. They found the worship of Islam "frenzied" and that of Catholicism without "glory."[2] (Vladimir also rejected Islam because of its ban on alcohol, drinking being a favorite pastime of his and the other Rus.) But as Goldilocks would in the fairy tale, they found their third option "just right." It was these emissaries who, on attending a mass in Hagia Sophia, wrote that they "knew not whether they were in heaven or on earth." What they did know was that "God dwells there"—in Byzantium—"among men," and that the service was "fairer than the ceremonies of other nations."

It would seem that the world-rejecting romanticism and eschatological hunger that is at the heart of Russian spirituality begins here. Vladimir's emissaries hit the nail on the esoteric head when one of them wrote that "every man, after tasting something sweet, is afterward unwilling to accept that which is bitter."[3] Like the elusive "blue flower" of German Romanticism, the sweetness they tasted in Hagia Sophia spoiled Vladimir's emissaries for anything lesser.* The beauty of Byzantium, once seen, cannot be forgotten. After that, one has two choices: either patiently endure the time here on Earth until the Kingdom of Heaven has come and we are raised up in its glory—which, if what the priests said was true, would not be that long in coming— or try to create some of that glory here and now. The Rus exposed to Byzantium's wonders took option number two. If beauty could save the world they would help it along.

The chance to do this came when Emperor Basil II needed Vladimir's help in putting down a rebellion. Vladimir, most likely recalling a similar distress signal sent to his father, was determined to negotiate the best terms for his service. The central demand—the deal breaker, we could say—was the imperial connection that was denied Svyatoslav I. In exchange for unleashing a 6,000-man-strong army of battle-hardened Rus warriors against the emperor's enemies, Vladimir requested an imperial bride—the emperor's sister Anna.

---

*The mystical "blue flower" makes its most well-known appearance in the unfinished novel *Heinrich von Ofterdingen* by Novalis.

This was no small bargaining chip. Marrying off someone of por-phyrogenite status to a foreigner was simply not done; like the recipe for Greek fire, it was one of the most highly guarded treasures of Byzantium, not to be given at a trifle. Constantine VII Porphyrogenitus, Vladimir's grandmother's own godfather, had argued against it emphatically. The imperial blood must stay Roman. But realpolitik won out, and Basil II accepted Vladimir's terms, on one condition: that he convert to Orthodoxy.

Vladimir agreed. How convinced he was of the truth of Orthodoxy, or how motivated by seeking atonement for past sins—as his grandmother may have been—is unclear. Certainly prior to his canon-izing, Vladimir was no saint, in more ways than one. He was a slave trader, as many Rus were. He already had three wives and a harem of some several hundred concubines, and his career, like that of the other Rus princes, was stained with blood—awash in it, we might say. He was also a politically astute tactician, who was most likely motivated more by expediency than by religious passion. Yet, unless accounts of his post-pagan rule are inaccurate or misinformed, he took his conver-sion seriously. However he felt about it, it was, as the cliché has it, a defining moment for him and the Rus. If not for himself, then certainly for his people, his baptism turned out to be "the most fateful religious ceremony in Russian history."[4]

In the summer of 989, after having earlier that year crushed the rebellion against his soon-to-be new in-laws, Vladimir reminded Emperor Basil II of his agreement. Earlier reminders had gone unac-knowledged and without effect, so this time Vladimir decided to make a point of it by seizing control of Cherson in Crimea, an ancient city and important Byzantine trading port on a peninsula on the Black Sea—a move that his present-day Russian namesake seems to have echoed in 2014. Vladimir added pressure by mentioning that if the wedding did not proceed tout de suite, he might have to seize control of Constantinople too. With his 6,000 Varangians twiddling their thumbs in Micklagaard, this would not be impossible.

Vladimir's impatience no doubt worried Basil, but his reluctance to fulfill his part of the bargain is understandable. To give a *porphyrogenita* to a foreigner in marriage was unheard of. It had never been done. Requests from royalty of other nations had already been turned down. And, as the historian John Julius Norwich points out, not only was Vladimir a foreigner, he was a pagan and killer who had slain his own brother to secure his rule and may have taken part in rituals of human sacrifice.[5] (Was the "blood eagle" still being performed?) We have already mentioned the harem and multiple wives. Aside from crushing the rebellion, we can say that Vladimir did not come with particularly good references.

Other concerns had also occupied Basil's mind—he had, after all, just dealt with an uprising—but Vladimir's reminder did the trick, and his royal sister Anna was soon off with her imperial entourage, crossing the Black Sea to Cherson for the wedding. The site where Vladimir's baptism and the wedding were supposed to have taken place is now a ruin, visited by devout tourists who mingle with holiday bathers. These, according to the historian Neal Ascherson, are more interested in the nearby transparent waters than in the "sacramental moment" that turned an "irritable tyrant" into a saint and gave the Russian soul a collective blue flower by pointing its imagination "for a thousand years toward . . . the city of Constantinople."[6]

After his baptism and wedding, Vladimir returned control of Cherson to Basil, as the traditional gift to the bride's brother. Then he and his new wife returned to Kiev, accompanied by members of the clergy, who did not wait to begin their work of spreading the Word. Almost as soon as they reached the city, missionaries headed out to the countryside, converting whole towns and villages. Although they were successful, there was resistance, and Christians had been and were still being persecuted by the pagan faithful, some even put to death. And while the missionaries began the work of Christianizing the Rus, Vladimir kept his part of the bargain and began to dethrone the pagan gods to whom until then he had shown fealty.

Along with Perun, Vladimir had worshiped other pagan deities, setting up shrines and statues of them and making dutiful offerings. But all this changed with his baptism. The story is that a tall statue of Perun with a golden head and silver moustaches that Vladimir had erected on a hill overlooking Kiev was pulled down. It and the other heathen idols—of Mokosh, the goddess of nature, Dazhbog, the sun god, and Jutrobog, the god of the moon—were then ritually flogged and finally tossed into the Dnieper. Other symbols of the old gods soon received similar humiliating treatment. Mass baptisms of Vladimir's warriors then took place in the Dnieper, which were followed by the baptism of all of Kiev's citizens.

Vladimir then closed down his harem, setting his concubines free—one hopes his warriors were able to make honest women of them—and broke his marriages with his other wives. He then set his mind to overseeing the work of the missionaries. He officiated at baptisms and was occasionally a godfather. He built churches in Kiev and throughout the Rus land, where priests from Constantinople would proclaim the Word. The graven images of fallen idols were now replaced with the shimmering transcendental beauty of icons, which were accompanied by sacred relics and other emblems of the new faith.

Vladimir also seems to have taken the social side of Orthodoxy seriously. According to Timothy Ware, on feast days he distributed food to the poor, a policy he enforced throughout the land and that was adopted by later rulers. And in what seems a reversal of his savage ways, it appears he was moved by Christian forgiveness or perhaps was convinced to be so by his imperial wife.

Along with Orthodoxy, the Rus also imported the Byzantine code of law, which Vladimir set to reforming. In Kiev and throughout the Rus land, the death penalty was abolished, as was torture. Also forbidden was punishment by mutilation, a form of deterrent that was peculiarly popular in Constantinople, not only for criminals, but for political opponents, who could be blinded or castrated.[7] For example, at the same time as Emperor John Tzimiskes was dealing with Svyatoslav I, he also had to deal with a revolt raised against him by a general, Leo Phokas. Leo's punishment for his rebellion was to be blinded. He could not then lead another army into battle, a necessary practice then in order to secure authority. A similar pragmatism informed other punitive acts. A castrated enemy could leave no heirs. Cruel and unusual by our standards, in those brutal times these measures made a gruesome sense.

Against this, a moving expression of the new Christian ethic of nonviolence was found in the voluntary deaths of Vladimir's youngest sons Boris and Gleb, who in 1015 allowed themselves to be slaughtered, rather than take up arms against their elder brother, Svyatopolk, who eliminated them in a bid for power following Vladimir's death; this act earned him the title "the Accursed." With the early Christians killed by pagans, the innocents Boris and Gleb made up the first martyrs for the Word in the Rus lands.

VLADIMIR'S GRANDMOTHER OLGA, who died in 969, would have been proud. What she had tried to accomplish was now coming to pass. But Vladimir's baptism did not mean only that the Rus had become Christian or were in the process of becoming so. It also meant that they were forming the first Russian state. Here was the beginning of Kievan Rus'—a fairy-tale-like medieval Russia that has remained as a kind of archetype in the Russian psyche. It is rather like the Arthurian legend for the British, with tales of a wonderful, magical golden age of heroes and princesses and saints that, "like the golden days of childhood, was never dimmed in the memory of the Russian nation."[8] The fact that this magical age, in historical terms, lasted just a short time—a mere two centuries—and was wiped out practically without a trace only adds to its mystery and allure. It is truly a "lost kingdom." But it is here that, more or less, Russia as we know it began to rise out of tribal squabbles and become a unified nation, however briefly, with the help of Orthodox Christianity.

Given this, it is not surprising that for a Russia that is yet again reforming itself after a "time of troubles"—if it has not already solidified—looking back to Kievan Rus' for inspiration in creating a future, and securing the legitimacy to pursue it, has become popular. It is also no surprise that a current strong man, credited with pulling his country out of chaos, would want to secure the geopolitical heart of the Russian state—Kiev—in the same way that the tales of Kievan Rus' occupy the heart of the Russian soul.

As Serhii Plokhy points out in *Lost Kingdom,* a history of Russian nationalism, the sixty-foot statue of Prince Vladimir the Great, erected by his namesake Vladimir Putin outside the Kremlin in 2015, is an unmistakable sign that Putin identifies himself with the founder of the Russian state. It also makes clear that he is aware of the "importance of Kievan Rus' for the historical identity of contemporary Russia." As Plokhy tells us, the foundation stone of the statue was taken from Cherson, the site of Vladimir's baptism, and was laid in 2015 not long after Putin's annexation of Crimea.[9] The stone itself was brought back to Moscow during the Russian incursions into Ukraine in 2014—or, as the Russian media described it, the spontaneous uprising of ethnic Russians against their Ukrainian oppressors.

That Archimandrite Tikhon, thought to be Putin's confessor, was directly involved in the campaign to erect the statue, suggests that the strong bond between the early Russian church and the early Russian state is something that the current Vladimir would like to reestablish. Such a desire seemed clear from Putin's speech at the statue's unveiling, which took place on November 4, 2016, the Day of National Unity, a mandatory public holiday reintroduced by Putin in 2005. It had been initiated in 1613 by the tsar Michael Romanov, the first of the Romanov dynasty, to commemorate the end of that period's "time of trouble." After 1917 the Bolsheviks had replaced it with a commemoration of the revolution.

In his speech Putin praised Vladimir as a "gatherer and protector of the Russian lands" who "laid the foundation of a strong, united, centralized state" and said that his adoption of Orthodoxy laid "the foundations of the morals and values that define our life even to the present day."[10] The twenty-first-century Vladimir may not yet have called it Holy Russia, but that he thought it was seems clear.

AND IT IS indeed with Kievan Rus' that Holy Russia begins to take form. What was different about converting to Orthodoxy rather than to the Church of Rome is that the Rus were able to adopt a belief that had already passed through its doctrinal difficulties and absorb it lock, stock, and barrel, with the "uncritical enthusiasm of the new convert."[11] Everything had been worked out, the true faith had been revealed, and what was left for the Rus to do was not to debate or discuss theological niceties, but to proclaim the Word with passion and devotion. There was also a sense that they had converted just in time, as the apocalyptic atmosphere of Orthodoxy and its powerful historical intuition of a coming cosmic denouement took hold. As James H. Billington remarked, for the early Christian Rus, "Man's function was not to analyse that which had been resolved or to explain that which is mysterious, but lovingly and humbly to embellish the inherited forms of praise and worship."[12] So they did.

A desire to duplicate the beauty of Constantinople took hold in Kiev, and within a few decades evidence of this and its success began to appear. Cathedrals modeled on Hagia Sophia, like that of Santa Sophia, erected by Vladimir's son, Yaroslav the Wise, in 1037, rose up. It was started in 1017, and masons, architects, artists, and engineers from Byzantium were imported to do the work, filling the cavernous spaces with mosaics, icons, angels, and the glittering images of the saints. It has thirteen domes, one for Jesus and each of the apostles. An earlier, oaken Santa Sophia in Novgorod may have been the model, but the size and grandeur of the cathedral in Kiev hearkens back to Constantinople.

Another architectural wonder echoing Byzantium was the famous Golden Gate of Kiev, familiar to fans of Modest Mussorgsky's *Pictures at an Exhibition*. It was erected around the same time as Santa Sophia and like it was designed to replicate the glory of Constantinople and the splendid Golden Gate dating back to the fifth century. It was part of the general fortification of the city that Yaroslav undertook against nomadic invaders, who were always a threat. Exactly why the gate was called golden is not known. It may have been because of a small Church of the Annunciation that crowned it, whose dome, like that of Santa Sophia, was golden. Sadly, unlike Santa Sophia, the Golden Gate did not survive. After being partially destroyed by the Mongol invasion of 1240—to which we shall return—it was in use for centuries until gradually it crumbled, and was left to ruin. By the late eighteenth century it was covered in earth. A partial excavation and reconstruction of what remained was undertaken in the nineteenth century. In 1982 a reconstruction of the gate was completed by the Soviets, but as there are no images of the original, it is unclear how close this attempt is to what Yaroslav had in mind. Understandably, opinion on the result is divided.

Nevertheless, there on a hill overlooking the Dnieper, with the wild steppes on the horizon and far from the Black Sea's shores, a kind of Byzantium II was rising up, that would come to be known as "the mother of Russian cities."

WHILE THE OUTER signs of Orthodoxy were replacing those of paganism, the inner world of the Russian soul was also being altered. Monasticism had been a part of Christianity since the early days of the desert fathers when, sickened with the decadence of the cities, they had left them to seek solitude and God in the wasteland. The monastic urge had struck very powerfully in the Eastern Church, and now that movement had entered Kiev. The Petchersky Lavra, or Monastery of the Caves, in Kiev—*lavra* is an ancient word for monastery—was one of the most important monastic sites in early Russia. It was founded by Saint Antony (983–1073), a Russian monk who had gone to Mount Athos and lived in a cave practicing "inner stillness" until he was given the mission to return to Kiev to spread the monastic idea. He did, and took up residence in another cave, this one overlooking the Dnieper, where disciples soon gathered around him. One of these, Theodius (d. eleventh century), organized the monks along the monastic rule of Theodore, a monk from Constantinople. Part of Theodius's regime was the kind of social work that Vladimir had introduced, giving food, shelter, and aid to the needy.

Theodius took the kenotic vow of poverty seriously, emptying himself not only of inner furbishing but also of outer things. The Hesychast practice that had dominated Mount Athos had now been transferred to Kiev. Theodius's determination to live humbly, as Christ did, started early. He came from a noble family, but rather than wear the silks and finery of his privileged class, he clothed himself in the rags and tatters of the poor. As Christ did, he accepted the insults and humiliation given him, as he joined the slaves in their work, gladly taking on the role of the *yurodstvo,* the "holy fool," a part that other intensely spiritual Russians would also play. He remained humble even when he became abbot of the monastery, and his piety earned him the respect of those who knew him, from noble to peasant.

The cave system that ran beneath the central hill of Kiev, in which Saint Antony and Saint Theodius had founded their monastery, became the birthplace of Russian icon painting. Here, in the extensive catacombs, the monks who had passed on were mummified and set to rest in alcoves that lined the walls, a holy picture placed by them, a promise of the life to come. As in Egypt, it was as funerary art that the first Russian icons were made. The earliest Russian icon painter was Alypius of the Caves who died in 1114. He had studied the icon painters of Constantinople and dedicated his life to bringing their art to his people. Like Theodius, Alypius lived a life of poverty and humility. He did not seek fame and painted his icons for God alone. He often worked without charge, repairing icons in churches if he saw that they had become worn. If he did accept a fee, he kept some money for his materials, some to live on, and gave the rest to the poor. He was thought to have miraculous powers and is said to have cured a man of leprosy by anointing his limbs with the paint used for his icons.

Angels and God himself, Alypius said, often helped him in his work. This may account for the miracles associated with his icons. A story tells how a man who built a church wanted Alypius to paint icons for it. He met two monks who accepted his money and said they would tell Alypius of his wishes. They kept the money and didn't breathe a word about the job to Alypius. When the man complained to Alypius that he hadn't yet painted the icons and asked to be repaid, Alypius explained that this was the first he had heard of it. But when he went to retrieve the boards the man had provided for the job, he discovered that the icons had miraculously been painted. Later, when the church suffered a fire, the same icons miraculously were spared.[13]

One icon to survive from this time, Alypius's "Mother of God" (Theotokos or "God-bearing"), an image of the Virgin and Child, was itself supposed to have performed a miracle, curing Prince Roman of Chernigov—of the Rurik line—of blindness in 1288. The prince was so moved that he had a monastery built in gratitude.[14] When Alypius himself died, he was found with his right hand on his chest, making the sign of the cross, a last gesture of faith said to have been echoed by the holy devil Rasputin, when his body was fished out of the frozen Neva River in St. Petersburg some centuries later.

The Theotokos, or image of Mary, the Mother of God, became a perhaps even more popular holy picture than those of her son or the saints. We can account for this preference by recalling the importance of Damp Mother Earth for the Slavs, the primal connection the Russian soul has with the soil and the source of life. The abstract God the Father, existing in some immaterial, unrepresentable realm beyond human comprehension, was little comfort to anyone outside of theologians. But the icons of Mary and her suffering son were an expression of the need the Russian soul has for what we can call a "concrete spirituality." It was the beauty of Byzantium that captured the soul and senses of Olga and Vladimir's emissaries, not the logic of Orthodox dogma. This hunger for a holiness that could be grasped as one could the fruit of the earth informed a spirituality that could be seen and felt in all of

Kiev, a city alight with holy icons, and filled with songs of praise and the fragrance of incense, as its first native metropolitan, Ilarion, said of it.[15] And no image of the holy had such a hold on the Kievan soul as that of the Virgin Mother.

In 431 the Council of Ephesus established that Mary was indeed "God-bearing" and not, as the bishop of Constantinople Nestorius had maintained, only "Christ-bearing," a distinction arising from the disputes over the "true" nature of Christ, mentioned earlier. Nestorius's position was deemed heretical, and it gave rise to Nestorianism, some remnants of which remain active today.* Henceforth, Mary was to be called *Theotokos* and not, as Nestorius had insisted, only *Christokos*.

The fine-tunings and hairsplitting of these theological niceties were no doubt lost on most of the Rus who looked to the icon of the Mother for what they needed: comfort and protection in a difficult world and intercession with a distant Father. In the churches that rose up in the wake of the missionaries, the glittering interiors were filled with images of the Pantokrator, Christ as the creator of the universe, enthroned like a Byzantine emperor, but also with those of the Theotokos, Mary, the God-bearer. It was to her that most of the people prayed, and it was her image that for many guaranteed protection.

The Theotokos was believed to have miraculous powers. Icons of the Virgin Mother were known to heal the sick, bring sight to the blind, make the lame walk, and even stop epidemics. Her protective powers were most remarkably shown in her defense of her cities. The famous Vladimir Mother of God, named for the city it was moved to from Kiev in the thirteenth century, after being taken to Kiev from Constantinople, was believed to have warded off the Mongols on several occasions. Another Mother of God, from Smolensk, together with one from Kazan, was thought to have helped defeat Napoleon.[16]

Lesser icons were also believed to have miraculous powers. In his account of his travels in Russia in the early seventeenth century, the

---

*In the Assyrian Church of the East and the Church of the East and Abroad.

German scholar and geographer Adam Olearius remarked on the strange practices many of the people performed with their icons. For them they seemed more like magical talismans than figures of veneration. Olearius remarked that the Russians "attribute a power to the pictures as though they could help to bring about something particular."[17] He tells of a brewer dipping an icon into his beer, in order to improve its quality, and remarks that when Russians want to "pursue the pleasures of the flesh" they make sure to cover the icon.[18] (One wonders if Rasputin took such precautions.) Icons were even believed to be able to extinguish a fire, although their success rate seems to have been poor, considering the number of fires that ravaged many early Russian cities, given that their houses were made of wood.

These examples of how the icons themselves, and not necessarily the holy individual they represented, were believed to be magically efficacious, suggest that the iconoclasts of the eighth and ninth century might have had some cause to be concerned about the abuses of idolatry. But then, the church has always defended the power of sacred relics, and the origin of icons itself is rooted, at least in tradition, in one such miraculous item.

A legend of the sixth century tells of Christ sending an image of himself on a cloth to King Abgar V of Edessa, in order to cure him of an illness. This cloth became known as the Mandylion—from the Arabic *mandil* for "cloth"—and it was eventually stolen from Constantinople by the crusaders who sacked the city in 1204. Today it resides in the Vatican. Like the Turin shroud and the veil of Saint Veronica, both of which are believed to carry the image of Christ *acheiropoietos,* "not made by human hands" but miraculously, the Mandylion was used by the iconodules— those on the *via positiva* who were in favor of icons—to argue that if Jesus himself was happy to present his likeness to one in need, then icon painters and those who venerate their work are only following in his footsteps. Unlike those on the *via negativa,* who rejected imagery in favor of an inner emptiness, the lovers of icons rejoiced in a spirituality that allowed them to see and touch the object of their worship.

Why was this important? Because it meant that the icon was a promise. It told the faithful that the incarnation was true, that spirit could inhabit the flesh and be transformed, that the human and the divine could meet, as Mary's miracle professed. But the icon also affirmed that the work of transformation was not over and was to be carried on. Like the God who created us in his image, we too are creative and through art can transform the world, an idea that Nikolai Berdyaev would make a central theme of his work. As the follower and friend of the philosopher Vladimir Solovyof, Prince Eugene Trubetskoy, wrote, the work of spiritual art is "the transformation of the entire universe into a temple of God."

The icon "points to a supernatural and eternal reality" that is, paradoxically, available "here and now."[19] For Trubetskoy, and for others, icons were "meditations in color," anticipatory glimpses and visions of that transformed world, which, for the early Russians, seemed to be a not-too-distant destination. For what the icons told in their glimmering light was a story whose end had yet to come about but which, by all accounts, would reach its conclusion soon.

ALONG WITH BEAUTY, Orthodoxy brought to the Rus something else: history. Unlike the pagan beliefs, which followed the eternal return of the seasons, the unchanging cycles of Damp Mother Earth, Christ's Incarnation and Crucifixion were singular events, unrepeatable one-offs happening at particular points in time. They were part of a narrative, a linear drama that was expected to reach its conclusion in the more or less near future. Along with images of Christ Pantokrator and the Theotokos and those of the angels Gabriel and Michael, worshipers at the early Russian churches would have also seen mosaics depicting the Last Judgment, Christ's Second Coming, and the end days. These were not ancient events commemorated in gold and sparkling colors, or the depiction of myths and legends. They were prophecies and visions of a coming climax in which the faithful in Christ would be participants and toward which they were surely moving.

THE JEWS SEEMED to be the people to have introduced the idea that time, history, was moving toward something, that it had a destination, a goal, although Zoroastrianism too looked forward to a final, decisive battle between Ahura Mazda and Ahriman, the principles of light and of darkness. For the pagan world, history in the "profane" sense, allotted it by Mircea Eliade, is nonexistent. There is no progress, no future, nothing that time or history is heading toward. It is static or cyclical, ages turning one into the other in the way that the stars turn round their eternal courses. To be sure, there is a progressive decline as the cycle moves from a Golden Age, through ages of Silver and Bronze, until the age of Iron—the Hindu Kali Yuga—arrives, which some speculate to be on us at present. But then the cycle starts again and repeats ad infinitum. Like a circle, it does not *arrive* anywhere, except at itself.

This changed with the Jews, who came to believe that they had a *mission,* that they were chosen by God to perform a unique task that had a beginning and an end, as did Creation. As Genesis says, "In the beginning . . ." When the Jews were conquered and lost their nation, they looked to a future savior who would free them from captivity and return them to their land. Jews that had accepted Christ believed that that historical narrative had been completed: the Messiah had come, although what Jesus brought—a new covenant—was not exactly what many had expected. But Christ's Crucifixion and Ascension started the clock all over again, this time ticking toward another deadline: the Second Coming or Parousia, which was to arrive in roughly a thousand years, although exactly how this was calculated and according to what calendar led to some complications. Nevertheless, it was this finale that the Russians who had accepted the Word now contemplated and which set them apart from the other people of the steppe.

It was also this profound historical sense that would motivate the expansion of monasteries in the coming centuries and which, practically more than anything else, would lead to a Russian empire. It would also inform the resurgence of icon painting in the fourteenth and fifteenth centuries. And, practically a millennium from when it was first introduced to the Russian people, it would inform a revolutionary creed that rejected all religion, but which adopted the belief in some future heavenly kingdom, through the courtesy of Marxist dialectics.

The new religion impressed on its awed adherents that an event of catastrophic proportions was fast approaching. Christ would descend from the heavens to judge the living and the dead; the faithful would be saved, the wicked punished. The sky would open and hell's fires would burst forth.

The early worshipers gazing on these fantastic scenes of death and resurrection, destruction and renewal, would not know that before this spiritual apocalypse would come to pass, a scourge of a more human kind would lay waste to their golden city.

IT SEEMS IT was for good reason that Yaroslav was nicknamed the Wise. From most accounts he seems to have been a good ruler, and it is during his time that the legends of Kievan Rus', still alive in contemporary Russians, come down to us. He is responsible for the first Russian code of laws, which laid the foundation for what became known as *Russkaya pravda,* "Russian justice." He issued coinage in his image; before this the Rus used what money came to hand through trading. He had respect for learning and had many books translated from Greek to Slavonic. And his rule was recognized by European powers. He had married the daughter of the king of Sweden. His own daughters married kings of France, Hungary, and Norway, and his son, Vsevolod, married into the Byzantine imperial family. He was also an effective military leader, defending Kiev from the Poles, Pechenegs, Lithuanians, Estonians, and Finns, and extending its territories in the Baltic. We can say that with Yaroslav, Kievan Rus' was on the medieval political map. Sadly, it would not stay there for long.

Yaroslav came to power in 1019, after defeating his older brother Syvatopolk who, we remember, is called "the Accursed" for murdering their younger brothers Boris and Gleb. It was to stop the kind of brotherly slaughter that followed the death of his father Vladimir that Yaroslav sought to unify the Rus' through the church, which, as we've seen, he promoted vigorously. One means of doing this was by establishing a feast day in commemoration of his murdered brothers. Their martyrdom became a model of Christian love and faith and their memory was celebrated several times a year. It also linked Yaroslav's rule with the new religion, an echo of the fusion of church and state that reigned in Byzantium, and which Yaroslav wanted to establish at home.

This point was emphasized in a treatise on "Law and Grace" that Ilarion, appointed Metropolitian of Kiev by Yaroslav in 1051, delivered on Easter two years earlier, to mark the completion of the walls Yaroslav had built to defend the city. In it he praised Yaroslav for transforming Kiev into a New Jerusalem. His evidence for this is the "great and holy temple of Divine Wisdom"—Santa Sophia—that he has built in this "city of glory, Kiev," just as David, son of Solomon, had done in the past. Ilarion calls on Vladimir to rise up from the dead to see what his son has accomplished. Vladimir himself is compared to Constantine the Great; he is equally wise and equally devoted to God, and so, Ilarion reasons, is deserving of equal respect and obedience from his people and their church.

Given that Vladimir was no longer there to receive this respect—even allowing for Ilarion's call for his resurrection—it naturally should go to his heir, Yaroslav. And just as Vladimir brought the true faith to the Rus' and expelled the pagan idols, so too shall Yaroslav lead the Rus' in their mission to spread the Word.[20] Ilarion's point was clear. The Rus' were now the new chosen people.

Yaroslav did lead them, but once his rule was over, not surprisingly, things began to fall apart. In 1054, on his deathbed, Yaroslav called his sons together and bade them promise that they abide by what he had written in what has come to be known as his "Testament." He had divided his empire into five regions, one for each of his sons, and he asked the four younger sons to respect and obey Iziaslav, the eldest, who would become grand prince of Kiev, a title that would soon lose much of its prestige. All should come to the aid of the others, and if one brother should claim the territory of another, the other brothers should defend the injured brother's rights. The five listened respectfully as dutiful sons should and assured their father that they would abide by his wishes. But as soon as Yaroslav died, the fighting started, and it continued for the next sixty years.

The problem was that Yaroslav had not set out a rule of succession that would avoid the covetousness and squabbling that characterized the early Varangians, and which had been halted with Vladimir but had now returned. With nothing to inhibit them but their own Christian consciences and their dead father's appeal to their better natures, sons who felt slighted by what was known as the "appanage" system soon sought to grab a bigger slice of the pie. Briefly, this was a way of "lateral" rather than "vertical" succession, designed to grant some land and authority to younger sons who, in the system of primogeniture—everything going to the eldest son—would get nothing.

Kievan Rus' operated with this system. It was generous and at first worked in the sense that everyone was a "winner." But soon the system spread out too wide, the branches of the family tree becoming heavy with dissatisfied descendants who felt their dignity and rights were slighted. In a small tribe, family ties made for loyalty, a principle not foreign to organizations like the Mafia. But as this grew, why a distant cousin received more than you—who were clearly deserving of more—would soon become a nagging concern. So now, just as Vladimir's sons had turned against each other, so too did Yaroslav's. This plunged Kievan Rus' into a series of family feuds that spelled the beginning of the end for the lost kingdom.

That a nomadic tribe, the Polovtsians—whose dances form a popular part of Alexander Borodin's opera *Prince Igor*—were making trouble for the Rus' did not help. When they defeated a Russian army sent to scatter them, a revolt against Grand Prince Iziaslav rose up. The Polovtsians were defeated by Iziaslav's brother Svyatoslav—Borodin's opera is about his victory—and no sooner had he beaten them than he joined forces with his other brothers to eject Iziaslav. When Svyatoslav died in 1077, Iziaslav returned. He was killed in 1078. Kiev then went to Vsevolod, Yaroslav's last surviving son. But when he died in 1094 criteria to decide who shall rule went into freefall. Dividing the empire into regions ruled by jealous and dissatisfied descendants turned the kingdom of the Holy Rus' into a jumble of bickering principalities engaged in pointless internecine warfare.

The chaos was halted for a time when Vladimir II Monomakh came to power in 1113. He was the son of Grand Prince Vsevolod I Yaroslavich and Irina, daughter of the Byzantine emperor Constantine XI Monomachus, who had himself come to power through marriage, when the empress Zoe, of the Macedonian dynasty, took him as her third husband. This link to the Byzantines would, like Vladimir's marriage to Anna, be proclaimed later, when ties to the Roman Empire were an important argument for legitimizing rule. As Prince of Chernigov, Vladimir II had the respect of his fellow princes, and he took the lead in the councils convened to stop the interfamily killing. When Grand Prince Svyatopolk II died, the *veche*—council—named Vladimir II as his successor.

He managed to unite the feuding tribes by directing their aggressions against a common enemy, the Polovtsians, who had continued to raid in Kievan territories. Although no longer fighting among themselves, however briefly, the Rus were almost constantly at war. In his "Testament," one of the earliest examples of Old Russian lay writing, Vladimir II recounts that he had been involved in eighty-three campaigns and had himself killed two hundred of the enemy. Like another Vladimir, he was not modest about his toughness and courage. He writes of being gored, thrown, trampled, bitten, and otherwise mangled by wild horses, bison, elk, boar, bear, not to mention the many other fractures and bruises occasioned by his rough life. When he died in 1125 his son Oleg came to power, but the fractures now were in Kiev, and they would not heal. Any sense of unity, familial or holy, was fast deteriorating.

Other changes affected the golden city. Years of feuds had taken their toll on trade and gradually new trading centers rose up, like the city of Vladimir, which took business away from Kiev. Already established centers like Novgorod, which had taken a different path than the princely one of Kiev and had not been as affected by the tribal wars, were prospering and would continue to do so while Kiev declined. By 1157 Grand Prince Andrej Bogoliubsky transferred the seat of power from Kiev to Vladimir. He did this after accompanying his father, Yury Dolgoruky, the founder of Moscow, on his conquest of Kiev in 1155. By this time the golden city had fallen in and out of a dizzying number of hands, and it would continue to do so with war, assassination, plunder, and chaos accelerating the speed of transfer.

In 1175 Andrej Bogoliubsky, who styled himself as a Byzantine autocrat and whom the church thought on a par with Solomon, was assassinated. When his successor, Vsevolod III, his brother, died in 1212, predictably his sons quarreled. War returned. Although by now only a nominal prize, possession of Kiev pushed the ambitious, greedy, aggressive, and shortsighted heirs of the Rurik line—of whom there were many—to disastrous ends. And by 1222 a new power was making itself felt in the Kievan territories that would finally put a stop to the squabbling, at least for a while.

THE MONGOL CONQUEROR Temujin, better known as Genghis Khan (1167–1227), did not have an easy start in life. His father Yesugei, another great warrior, was betrayed and murdered when he was arranging the boy Temujin's marriage. Temujin—who was nine years old—and his mother and his siblings were then cast out of the tribe and forced to live on their own on the steppes. The difficult conditions of living in the wild hardened Temujin. They also made him quite ruthless. As a teenager he killed one of his brothers in a murderous rage over a fish. He was then captured by his former tribe and held under brutal conditions until he managed to escape. These challenges led him to become a cunning and efficient killer. By 1206 he was the ruler of a kingdom that would eventually stretch from southeastern Asia to the borders of eastern Europe and comprise the largest land empire in history.

By 1222, the Mongols had already conquered China and central Asia and were pushing west. An expeditionary force led by Jebe, one of Genghis Khan's great generals, and Subtai the Valiant, his greatest, encountered the army of a coalition of Russian principalities at the Kalka River, in what is now the Donetsk region of Ukraine. Although the Russians were easily defeated, and Kievan Rus' lay unprotected, the Mongols withdrew. But a decade later they were back. Had the Rus' princes buried their respective hatchets in the earth instead of each other, they might have been able to pull together and offer more resistance to the flood tide of horsemen that engulfed their land. As it was, they proved relatively easy picking for the savage warriors who quickly overwhelmed them.

In 1236 Subtai returned. Jebe had died in 1223 and this time Subtai came with Batu Khan, the grandson of Genghis Khan, who had died in 1227, his last orders being to exterminate the inhabitants of Ning-hsia, the capital of the Tangut people whom he was already engaged in annihilating. Batu Khan was commander of the western empire; like the Roman Empire, the Mongol Empire too had become too big for one man to manage. Batu Khan was also the founder of the Golden Horde, a semi-independent khanate within the Mongol Empire. With him he brought an army of some 130,000 riding bowmen. His mission, given him by the great khan Ögedei, was to conquer the West. He did, starting with Kievan Rus'.

When Batu demanded allegiance from Yuri II of Vladimir-Suzdal—a principality that had risen to prominence as Kiev had declined—he refused. Batu then laid waste to the city of Ryazan. Forces sent to hold him back were defeated, and soon the city of Kolomna and then a fledgling Moscow were burned. Then the capital was also burned, the royal family with it, except for the prince, who escaped to form another army. This too was defeated, his forces annihilated. Other cities likewise fell.

One place that managed to escape the devastation was the Invisible City of Kitezh, the subject of Nikolai Rimsky-Korsakov's opera *The Legend of the Invisible City of Kitezh and the Maiden Fevroniya*. The story is that as Batu Khan approached the city with his army, they were astounded to find that it had no fortifications. They heard the people inside praying to God for deliverance. Assured of an easy victory, and resentful at the people's pusillanimous response, Batu's army advanced. But suddenly, as they did, fountains of water miraculously shot up through the ground, and as the soldiers drew back, the entire city sank into Lake Svetloyar. They watched as the golden dome of the cathedral sank beneath the waters, as in Edgar Allan Poe's poem "The City in the Sea." To this day it is said that only the pure of heart can find their way to the sunken city, and that voices in prayer can still be heard, coming from what has been called a kind of "Russian Atlantis."

One city that was not so lucky was Kiev. Batu Khan had reached it in 1240, leaving a trail of destruction behind him. By then Kiev was part of the principality of Halych-Volhynia, whose ruler, Danylo of Halych, was away, trying to raise an army. The city was defended by his military commander, Voivode Dmytro, who had about 1,000 men.

When Batu sent his cousin Möngke, who would become another great conqueror, to offer terms of surrender, he is said to have been moved by the beauty of the city, and to have encouraged his envoys to convince the Rus that there was no need for its destruction. Möngke's envoys, however, were killed, and Kiev's fate was sealed. Beauty may save the world, but it didn't save Kiev, although its annihilators did hesitate long enough to breathe a sigh of regret. By this time the rest of the Mongol army had arrived and outnumbered the Rus' ten to one. On November 28 the Mongols brought their catapults to within range of Yaroslav's walls and began their bombardment. The Golden Gate received a pummeling. For more than a week projectiles rained hard and unrelenting upon the mother of Russian cities. On December 6 the defenses collapsed, and the invaders swarmed in.

As did the Byzantines when faced with the savage fury of the

Varangians, the faithful of Kiev believed that God had sent a scourge among them because of their sins. Many people took shelter in the Church of the Tithes (also known as the Church of the Dormition* of the Virgin), the first stone church in Kiev, erected by Vladimir at the start of the golden age. On the day after the walls were breached, the balcony of the church collapsed under the weight of the people on it. Many were killed. The Mongols made short work of those who weren't. Most of Kiev's inhabitants were slaughtered; of fifty thousand, only two thousand survived. The city was plundered, then burned, and little was left after the smoke cleared; only a few buildings remained standing. Batu then turned his sights toward Poland and the Mongol wave surged on. It was only the death of the great khan Ögedei in 1241 that saved western Europe from devastation. Receiving news of his uncle's demise, Batu Khan was obliged to return to Karakorum, the Mongol capital, to take part in the council to decide on his successor.

Western Europe was saved, but the lost kingdom was lost. For the next two centuries, the Mongols ruled in Russia.

---

*Dormition, or "sleep" in Orthodoxy, serves the same purpose as the Assumption in the Catholic Church: both signify that Mary did not suffer the corruption of death but was taken up into heaven.

5

From Mongols to Muscovy

Religious Colonization and the Builders of Russia

Exactly how much of an influence the years of the "Tartar yoke" had on the future Russia remains a point of contention. We've seen that Berdyaev saw these years as Russia's worst. For him they were the "most stifling," precisely because of this "Asiatic and Tartar" influence. For the Eurasianists—like Berdyaev, exiled in Europe by the Bolsheviks—the roughly two and a half centuries of Mongol rule were a source to mine for their vision of a new Russia, rooted in its Asiatic past. Lev Gumilev, who enjoyed a remarkable if brief celebrity in the late 1980s and early '90s, wrote thrilling accounts of the Huns, Mongols, and Tartars sweeping across the infinite plains. If these did not always meet the requirements of academic verifiability, they certainly instilled in his readers a sense of the grandeur and adventure of these ancient nomads, and gave them reason to be proud of this romantic past—if indeed it was theirs.

More pedestrian assessments of what Russia inherited from the Mongols are sadly less exciting. And I should point out that while it was the Mongol Empire that had conquered Kievan Rus', its immediate agents in the matter were the Tartars, a Turkic-speaking people who had been absorbed into the Mongolian hordes. When speaking of this time, the yoke may be called Mongol or Tartar, but it amounts to the same thing.

Recent revising of medieval history suggests that the Mongols may not have been quite the bloodthirsty savages previous accounts have painted them as, or at least not only that. For one thing, for a people with no qualms about decimating entire cities and their inhabitants, they were surprisingly tolerant when it came to matters of religion. Genghis Khan himself took an interest in Islam and accepted the advice of Muslim jurists on civic administration. Although Genghis was a devotee of a shamanistic tradition called Tengriism, he was also interested in Taoism and spent much time in conversation with a Taoist monk from whom, among other things, he hoped to learn the alchemical trick of prolonging life.[1]

Yet it seems the general view among most scholars is that the Mongols made little if any intellectual or artistic contribution to Russian culture.* They encouraged the art and culture of the tribes they conquered, but had little of their own to pass on—a common drawback, it is assumed, of a nomadic people. In the case of Russia, some words for money and weapons, some military and administrative institutions and a peculiarly abasing expression of submission to authority— *chelobitnaia*, "beating the forehead" on the ground as a petitioner lay prostrate before a prince—seem to make up most of the recognizably Mongol ways that percolated down into everyday Russian life.

The psychological or spiritual effect on the Russian psyche of the years of the Tartar yoke are, however, harder matters to assess. One general view is that if nothing else, the Mongol masters provided a common enemy against which the subdued principalities could unify. Their overthrow was a goal to which the Russian people could look forward, even if that liberation took some time to arrive. In the meantime, their subjugation was, like the difficult conditions of their land, another burden that they had to carry, another portion of suffering they had to endure.

Their greatest aid in this was of course the church. Although like

---

*"Too often the cultural level of nomads is thought to have been invariably low, and their part in the development of modern society is frequently represented as a purely negative one. Such generalizations are, of course, misleading."[2]

the great khan, most of the Mongols at this time were Tengriists, they made no effort to convert the conquered Russians to their creed. As did the Romans, at least in their pre-Christian period, they realized that forcing a conquered people to give up their religion would only foment rebellion, while allowing them to continue their worship, as long as they paid tribute to their masters, would help keep the peace. (Christians offered the chance to avoid martyrdom by burning incense to Jupiter or another pagan god, paying them a kind of spiritual lip service, decided to make a point of it.)

In any case, the pagan beliefs of the Mongols would not have been that different from those of the pre-Christian Rus. And in many cases, the Rus who encountered their new masters were still as pagan as they were. And the opposite was also true; many Mongols were actually Christian. They could also have been Buddhists or Manichaeans.

Tengri is the name of the supreme deity in the animistic religion of the Mongols. This included ancestor worship along with belief in a variety of nature spirits, and sub-gods and goddesses, lower in rank than Tengri. The central focus of worship was the Blue Mighty Eternal Heaven, the great sky overhead. Like the God of negative theology, Tengri's true nature is unknowable. He is beyond human comprehension, timeless and infinite. Tengri shamans put themselves into trance states and communicated with the spirits, healed the sick, and prophesized about the future of the tribe. Astrology, weather magic, and ecstatic states brought on by drumming and dancing were part of Tengri worship. Genghis Khan himself was declared a supreme shaman after he had a rival shaman, Teb Tengi, executed. While decimating Kievan Rus', Batu Khan had a council of shamans advising him on his strategy.

And just as God had chosen the Hebrews—and, according to some accounts, the Russians after them—to be his favored people and to carry out his will, so too did Tengri choose the Mongols to go forth and conquer. Yet unlike other conquering religions—say, Islam—the warriors of Tengri did not demand that their subjects adopt the beliefs of their conquerors. As we've seen, the exact opposite happened, and not only with rank-and-file Mongols. Many Mongol princes took Nestorian Christian wives, and the great khan Ögedei, son of Genghis Khan, took a Christian wife from the Keraites, a tribe that had converted to Nestorianism. The khans took an interest in promoting discussion and debate among the religions of their empire, and during Ögedei's rule, many churches and temples were built that enjoyed special privileges, among them, being exempt from taxes.

Ironically, this liberal attitude toward religion eventually played a part in fracturing the Mongol Empire. The dictates of the religion of a region grew to carry more importance than the civic law. Eventually this led to the region becoming a separate entity, and with this the Mongol Empire disintegrated from within. By the mid-fourteenth century, as a unified power it was no more, having broken up into rival kingdoms.

Some cities of Kievan Rus' hardly felt the impact of the Mongols and rather than be invaded, came to a workable agreement with them. One such was Novgorod, which continued to prosper as Kiev declined. It had escaped the Mongol onslaught because it was surrounded by marshlands; the horsemen could not reach it easily, and so concentrated on the south and east of the country. Much of the Russian north profited from this collateral benefit, a prerequisite of the terrain, which helped to make the north the region of the Russian revival, in the mid-fifteenth century. Novgorod had also gone a different route politically than Kiev. For one thing, there was more pagan resistance there, and the people had to be forcibly baptized by Vladimir soon after he had converted Kiev.

Yet they took to the new religion and, as mentioned earlier, a wooden Church of the Holy Wisdom built by Joachim the Korsunian (of Cherson) around 989 may have been the model for Kiev's own Church of the Holy Wisdom. In 1045 Vladimir of Novgorod, son of Yaroslav the Wise, built the stone Santa Sophia, which still stands today. Although like its sister church in Kiev, Novgorod's Santa Sophia is modeled on Constantinople's Hagia Sophia, certain refinements and alterations in the design give it a peculiarly "Russian" look and feel—think onion dome and tent roof—that distinguishes it from its Byzantine ancestry.

Joachim, the first bishop of Novgorod, was sent to the city to spread the word from Cherson. And like Vladimir, he did so with a splash—literally. As Vladimir did, he toppled a statue of the pagan god Perun and threw it into the Volkhov River. Where the statue had stood he started a monastery. The first Church of the Holy Wisdom was built on the site of a pagan graveyard. When Vladimir erected the stone church, he had a library installed, which held books collected by Yaroslav. And in later years the church became the home of Our Lady of the Sign, an icon that is said to have miraculously saved Novgorod from being sacked by Prince Andrej Bogoliubsky when he besieged the city in 1170 with a coalition of other princes.

As the Novgorodian saga tells it, while the people were cowering behind the city walls, Ioann the bishop heard a voice telling him to retrieve the icon and to show it to the armies besieging them. Ioann got the icon, and when he saw that the image of the Virgin had tears running from her eyes, he showed it to the enemy. This apparently so unhinged them that they became mad and started fighting among themselves. When they saw this, the Novgorod defenders charged out and quickly dispatched them. It appears that icons were very partial to their local worshipers.

Yaroslav was called the Wise not only because of his bibliophilia. He had good political savvy and understood when it was expedient to allow a neighbor some independence. He granted Novgorod self-government. Novgorod was an important trading center for eastern Europe, with links to Constantinople, but it had also made good relations with the West, and through its presence in the Baltic had made contact with the Hanseatic League, the trading confederation that would dominate northeastern Europe until the mid-fifteenth century. Novgorod would later become one of the major centers of the league's activities.

Novgorod did not go down the same princely route as Kiev and the other principalities. Instead it developed a system of rule by council, or *veche,* a public assembly, although exactly who assembled and how and for what purposes are not precisely clear. In some cases the *veche* is reported to have been something like a town meeting; in others it seems more like something taking place behind closed doors.

The nature and character of the *veche,* like much else, remains a matter of scholarly debate. It is often compared to the Nordic *thing,* an assembly of free men, who gathered to make decisions about important matters. From what we know the *veche* was responsible for choosing a mayor and the head of the militia. It also had a say in choosing the archbishop and with appointments at the monasteries, and had a hand in settling legal disputes and other civic matters. The *veche,* which took place in other cities but which became particularly identified with Novgorod, is often cited as an example of how Russian political and social life has a history of democracy, as well as of autocratic rule, something that opponents of President Putin are at pains to point out. Yet some historians argue that the democratic character and authority of the *veche* is exaggerated and that while assemblies took place and positions were granted, they were ultimately vetted by the oligarchy, the wealthy trading boyar (noble) families, who were the real power in Novgorod—a situation not unfamiliar to many Russian people today, who have their own oligarchies to contend with.

Yet however the *veche* operated, it remained the city's governing body until it lost its sovereignty in 1478, when it came under Moscow's complete control. Oddly, it was another Russian force and not the Mongols or the West that ended Novgorod's independence. It was in fact in order to save Novgorod from Western invaders that its greatest hero made a bargain with the Mongols, which placed it under their rule, but allowed it to remain its essential self.

IN 1237, JUST as the Mongols were descending on Kiev, Alexander, son of Yaroslav II Vsevolodovich, Grand Prince of Vladimir, was made Prince of Novgorod, a title that actually meant he was the city's military defender. He was still in his teens. In 1240 he defeated the Swedes, who had attacked Novgorod because of its incursions into Finnish territory, in a battle at the confluence of the Izhora and Neva Rivers. Because of his decisive victory, Alexander was nicknamed "Nevsky," "of the Neva." So was born Alexander Nevsky, saint and national hero.

Yet Alexander was apparently ambitious, and when he began to take too much of an interest in the city's running, the people he had just saved sent him away. Two years later they called him back. In 1242 Pope Gregory IX was intent on Christianizing the Baltic, and he regarded the Orthodox Russians as little more than heretics. In 1204, under the order of Pope Innocent III, crusaders had pillaged the holy city of Byzantium, filling their pockets at the expense of the "schismatics," and desecrating holy relics while at it. Now, Gregory IX charged the Teutonic Knights, a religious order of spiritual warriors rather like the Knights Templar, with the task of what we might call "religious cleansing." Basically, the Russians had the choice of converting to Catholicism or being slaughtered.

Alexander refused to submit to Rome, but he knew that he could not fight the Germans and the Mongols at the same time. He chose to submit to Mongol rule so that he could concentrate his forces on defeating the Teutonic Knights. He did this because of something we have looked at already: the Mongol tolerance of religious plurality. They were open to what we might call being multi-faith, while the Teutonic Knights had one thing in mind: convert or die.

Rather than forsake the true Word of Holy Rus', Alexander made a deal with one invader in order to beat back another. Proof that this was a good decision came in the famous "battle on the ice." On April 5, 1242, Alexander saved Novgorod by defeating the Teutonic Knights and their crusader army on frozen Lake Peipus, on the border between present-day Estonia and Russia. The battle was immortalized and made into anti-German nationalist propaganda in Sergei Eisenstein's film *Alexander Nevsky* (1938)—with a score by Sergei Prokofiev—which had the Teutonic Knights sporting Kaiser Wilhelm helmets and their bishop's mitre bearing swastikas. When Stalin recognized that his people needed something more than the ideal of "international communism" to spur them to resistance, he declared Alexander Nevsky a national hero. During what came to be known as the Great Patriotic War, Stalin reinstated the Order of Alexander Nevsky, a military honor that had been established by Catherine I in 1725, following a war with Sweden, and which had dropped out of fashion following the revolution.

During the years of the Molotov-Ribbentrop nonaggression pact between Russia and Germany (1939–40) the film was taken out of circulation; Eisenstein himself was out of favor at the time. But in 1941, when Hitler decided to invade Russia (without, it seems, checking the weather forecast, a mistake Napoleon had already made), it was released again and used to stir the long-enduring Russian people to come to the defense of Mother Russia. It was not the tenets of dialectical materialism or the inescapable conflict of the class war that would get Russians in Stalingrad and other cities defending their country with tooth and nail, and often with little else. It was their love of Damp Mother Earth. Stalin knew this, and it saved Russia from the Germans. Sadly, it did not save them from Stalin.

Alexander Nevsky was made a saint and is Russia's great national hero. But he owed allegiance to the Tartars and on more than one occasion took up arms against his fellow Russians to uphold Tartar rule. In 1246, when Grand Prince Yaroslav died from poisoning administered by Törgene, the great khan's mother, during a visit to the great khan Guyuk in Mongolia, the usual battle for succession took place among the other princes. When Alexander and his younger brother Andrew asked Guyuk for help in restoring order, he appointed Andrew Grand Prince of Vladimir and made Alexander Grand Prince of Kiev.

Alexander wasn't happy about the snub—Kiev was no longer the seat of power—but he accepted the decision. But when he discovered that Andrew was planning a rebellion against the Tartars, with the help of some Western forces, Alexander brought word of this to Batu Khan, who sent an army, deposed Andrew, and put Alexander on the throne. Alexander installed his son, Vasily, to rule in Novgorod. When the city turned him out in favor of an anti-Mongol ruler, Alexander promptly arrived with his army and reinstalled his son. And when a revolt broke out in Novgorod because of a census the Tartars had enforced in order to secure more tax, Alexander, worried that the uprising would unleash Mongol reprisals on all of Russia, helped put down the revolt and ensured that his people paid the tax.

ALEXANDER'S ROLE MAY seem an exception, but he was one of several Russian princes who began to take on some of the authority and fulfill some of the duties of the *baskaks*, Mongol deputies who were placed in cities to ensure that the Russians toed the line. As the princes began to ensure order and obedience, the baskaks disappeared. Gradually, in this way, the Russians began to acquire some small power. Eventually they would have enough to challenge their rulers and to depose them. By the time they did, the new Russia to appear would do so from the north.

Yet the Russia to come would learn from its masters, and in some ways its years of tutelage were, in the long run, to its advantage. Although the princes still quarreled and fought among themselves— they seemed constitutionally unable to maintain a peace—and were by turns domineering to their subjects and subservient to their masters (a schizophrenic arrangement that may have contributed to the manic/depressive, ecstatic/lethargic duality of the Russian psyche) some drift toward a kind of unity seemed to be happening, with a growing Moscow becoming the center of gravity. The princes themselves adopted some of the character of the Mongol hierarchy in their own courts. Systems of tax collection and economic administration established by the Mongols were absorbed into Russian life. These borrowings were handy as, once they had recovered from the initial shock of the Mongol invasion, trade and commerce were restored and began to flourish. The population grew, and, as is inevitable, it spread out into new territories. These provided more goods to sell, like furs, and land to develop. Their Tartar masters may have received the lion's share of this new bounty, but their vassal princes got a good portion too, and with it were slowly able to accumulate wealth of their own.

THE SHIFT OF significance from Kiev in the south to the cities of the north, like Novgorod, Vladimir, and eventually Moscow, was motivated by trade, population, and the advantages of easy portage in the Volga basin. Yet another factor, perhaps more important than any of these, was at work.

One of the developments under the Mongol yoke was that the church took on an even greater role in providing some sense of identity for her flock. They may have lost their former glory and have been ruled by a foreign invader, but Russians knew who they were every time they gazed at an icon or prayed to a saint. But along with the inner security the church provided, it also helped to organize civic life, feast days, and other holy dates on the calendar, thus maintaining a continuity amid frequent chaos. At a time when as a political entity it no longer existed, what held the remnants of Kievan Rus' together was religion. *Sobornost,* a term that the nineteenth-century Slavophiles, as well as Berdyaev, will use to suggest a community of like-minded people, stems from the Russian *sobor,** which means "cathedral," but also "gathering." The church was where the people gathered, and the people gathered in the church.[3]

And as the princes became wealthier, the church reaped the benefit of this wealth. Donations aimed at securing a good seat in heaven—motivated by the desire to make amends for past transgressions—went to establishing more securely the church's place in this world. They also

---

*One literal expression of the twin meaning of *sobor* as "church" and "gathering" were the "one-day churches," *obydennyi khram,* places of worship built in a single day from virgin forests. This was usually done as an offering to stop the spread of plague. Accounts from 1467 and 1654 say as much.

helped to increase the scope of that place, pushing its frontiers out into the deep forest of the north.

One of the most important agents of Russian northern expansion was monasticism. A pattern of what we could call "accidental colonization" became established, that went something like this: Monks, seeking solitude in order to gain the "inner stillness" needed for the knowledge of God, would enter the dark forest and establish a hermitage. Gradually they acquired disciples, followers who wished to imitate their lives, and around them would rise up a monastery. The monastery would draw visitors and more aspirants to the monastic life. It would expand until gradually a town would grow up around it. As this became larger, monks seeking more solitude than they could get in the new town, went deeper into the forest and started the cycle over again.[4] Gradually, in this way, vast areas of woodland were cleared and cultivated. And so, in one of history's ironies, the desire to enter a purely inner life led to the expansion of the outer one.

Missionary work continued under the Mongols. As we've seen, Mongol princes married Christian women, and the church enjoyed many privileges under their rule and protection. Priests and bishops were often welcomed at the Mongol capital and allowed to petition for new favors. Paganism was still alive in the north, and missionaries sent there to spread the Word met with resistance. Gradually, the church established itself and formed bases from which it could spread deeper into the ancient forests.

One of the heroes of this adventure was Saint Stephen of Perm (1340–1396). After thirteen years spent in a monastery, he set out to bring the Orthodox message to the pagans of the Ural Mountains, the Komi or Zyrian people. Like Cyril and Methodius, he translated the Gospels into the tongue of the locals, inventing an alphabet based on runes. He was a painter and through icons spread the glad tidings that beauty and truth were one. His adventures and encounters with pagan shamans—in which he invariably comes out the victor—are recounted in "The Life of Stephen of Perm" and have become part of Russian religious folklore.

The most famous "pioneer monk" of this time was Saint Sergius of Radonezh (1314–1392), Russia's national saint. He was considered a *podvizhnik,* a "heroic mover" or "frontier hero." As one scholar remarks, he seemed to be a "combination of Saint Francis and Paul Bunyan."[5] He was called Bartholomew until he was tonsured and took vows, and was born in Rostov, a city under the dominance of a growing Moscow. He arrived at a difficult time. The city was open to frequent attacks by rival princes and Tartar raiders, food was scarce, and it had seen the black plague. Ivan I, Grand Prince of Moscow, was offering a tax break on any families who volunteered to relocate to a desolate area north of the city. Sergius's father took him up on the offer, and the family moved to Radonezh, which at the time was somewhere in the back of beyond. Sergius was seven. When his father died some years later, Sergius and his brother Stefan, who was already a monk, decided to leave the city and live as hermits in the forest.

At first they lived in primitive conditions, only the simplest of shelters. Then they built a small church. But Stefan, who had already spent many years in a monastery, did not care for the hermit's life and soon left. In Moscow he joined another monastery. As was traditionally the case, the Monastery of the Apparition—the one he joined—was near the city, not in the wilderness. But this was soon to change.

Sergius remained in the forest, living a life of abstinence, hard labor, and prayer. He continued this solitary practice for some time, but gradually word of the hermit reached town and people began to visit him, bringing gifts and seeking blessings. A few visitors remained and took up the hermit's life. The cells Sergius built for them and for the others who followed began to multiply, and eventually he agreed to establish his hermitage as an official monastery, with himself as its abbot—a reluctant one, according to reports. As Theodius had in Kiev at the Monastery of the Caves, Sergius ran the monastery according to the system set down by Saint Theodore. The Monastery of the Holy Trinity in Zagorsk, founded in 1337, quickly became a site of pilgrimage and is today the most important center for Russian Orthodox spirituality.

One of the differences between the Monastery of the Caves and Sergius's Monastery of the Holy Trinity is that while the first was within the city's limits, the latter is set out in the middle of nowhere. This meant that a monk's life there was harder than one in the city. Conditions were harsher, the work more demanding, and the solitude required greater discipline and a stronger sense of purpose. Something else that gave Sergius's monastery a special character was an important factor in providing that purpose.

Many of the monks who came to Sergius's monastery or to the many others that sprang up in the century that followed its founding—some 150 in total, and also in the wilderness—were followers of the Hesychast tradition. Hesychast, we remember, is a tradition of prayer and meditation that became dominant on Mount Athos. *Hesychia* is a Greek word meaning "inner calm," and it was through achieving this that the monks who followed this tradition believed that they could come to know God, to feel his presence directly.

Certain conditions and physical exercises aided this.* The monks fasted and sat in darkness, slowing their breath, and sinking their chins down to their chests, fixing their vision on the heart. Repetition of the Jesus prayer—"Lord Jesus Christ, Son of God, have mercy on me"— served as a kind of Orthodox mantra, with the repetition gradually becoming inaudible and maintained solely inwardly. Some monks even began to find the prayer itself, like other parts of scripture, more of a barrier to achieving the "inner calm" than an aid. Even icons became a distraction. Their desire to achieve a direct link to the divine and their confidence in their ability to do this through their own efforts—and not solely through God's grace—filled them with the sense of purpose needed to endure the conditions of their life in the wilderness. It also led to what is known as the Hesychast controversy.

Although anchored in church fathers like Clement of Alexandria

---

*A collection of texts, *The Philokalia*, written between the fourth and fifteenth centuries and first published in Greek in 1782, sets out the basic principles and practices of *Hesychia*. It would later be an influence on the psychological system of P. D. Ouspensky.

and Origen, and codified by Dionysius the Areopagite, by the fourteenth century the negative theology these mystics promoted began to raise difficult questions for theologians. The doctrine of a divinity so beyond human thought that even to say it is incomprehensible commits the sin one wishes to avoid—that of making any positive statements about God—does not suggest itself as one prone to facilitate contact between the human and the holy. But what Origen and Dionysius and others on the apophatic path maintain is that it is precisely by the act of *kenosis*—inner emptying—that a place is made in the human soul ready to be filled with the Divine spirit. The rejection of all predicates attributable to God creates a kind of inner vessel, which can receive his Presence. It is precisely the recognition that God is beyond anything we can think that does the trick. In a sense, it is rather like the sudden "click" that precedes *satori,* the illumination of the sheer "is-ness" of things, that is the aim of Zen Buddhism.

The form the holy presence took for the Hesychasts was that of "uncreated light," the light that the apostles saw on Mount Tabor when Jesus was "transfigured," wrapped in the holy radiance of God. The apostles with Jesus on the mountain saw him shine with an inner refulgence. The practitioners of the Hesychast tradition said that their meditations revealed the same light and opened them to the same illumination.

Some theologians disagreed, and their reservations were rooted in the same kinds of questions about God's nature—insofar as we can say he has one—and that of Jesus that we have encountered before. Fundamentally it is the question once again of immanence or transcendence. It was also one of authority. If a Hesychast monk finds even the Jesus prayer a distraction from his perception of the "uncreated light," what point is there of a religious order, whose task it is to guide him along the safe path to salvation?

Such possibilities seemed dangerous. For some it was the height of human hubris to think that through some physical and mental exercises one could *know* God. How could one know the unknowable? And what did holding one's breath have to do with it? "Which of you by taking thought can add a cubit unto his stature?" asks Matthew in the Gospel. No one can, the theologians said. For them the Hesychast way smacked of the Pelagian heresy, whereby man is thought capable of ridding himself of sin through his own efforts.* Surely this was arrogance and nothing more.

The argument reached a climax in 1337 when Barlaam the Calabrian, an Italian theologian, dismissed the Hesychasts' claims as a form of medieval navel-gazing. He called the Hesychasts *"omphalopsychoi,"* people with their souls in their stomach, and argued that holding one's breath and focusing the attention on the heart were useless. In fact, they were worse than useless, as they actively took attention away from one's sinfulness. How can one's body help in one's prayers? The body is made of gross matter, low and sinful, full of carnal passions, while God, the object of our prayers, is far beyond such fleshly realities.

Saint Gregory of Palamas, the archbishop of Thessalonica, took up the Hesychast banner and refuted Barlaam. First he argued that there is nothing wrong in using the body to intensify our prayers. God made us—body and soul—and we should pray to him with the whole of ourselves. The Jesus prayer was also known as the "prayer of the heart," and it was aimed at bringing the whole person and not just his or her mind into his or her prayer. It was, we can say, a version of what the alchemist and Egyptologist René Schwaller de Lubicz would later call "the intelligence of the heart," which also wants to go beyond the mere "granular" cerebral consciousness of the intellect.[6] Jesus incarnated fully into a human body. We should give him praise in the same way.

Gregory also argued that while it is true that we cannot know God's essence (*ousia*) directly, we can know his energies (*energeia*). That is what the apostles experienced on Mount Tabor. The "uncreated light" they saw was not sensual, physical light, but a divine illumination, a

---

*Pelagius was a Christian theologian of the fourth and fifth century who argued against the doctrine of original sin and in favor of man's free will and ability to improve himself through his own efforts.

kind of glow given off by the divine in the same way that the sunlight is given off by the sun. We cannot look at the sun directly, but nevertheless we see its light. Dionysius the Areopagite said that the closest we come to experiencing God on earth is through light, which is the closest approximation in our dense world to his being. Gregory's arguments were persuasive, and through a series of councils held between 1341 and 1351 the Hesychast tradition was accepted as part of the Orthodox practice of faith.*

The uncreated light the Hesychast monks perceived was not limited to the cells of their monasteries. As they understood it, it was a foretaste of how all of creation will be seen, how all of it will be radiant, when Christ returns. It was a glimpse of the world to come, when the entire cosmos, and not only sinful man, will be redeemed. It was a promise of the coming transfiguration, when the light of God, his energies, will shine forth and, from the smallest speck of dust to the farthest star, fill the entire universe.

Such a vision of a spiritually redeemed world was not that different from the pantheistic appreciation of a living nature, animated by spirits and informed by the vital energy of gods, that was at the heart of the old pagan beliefs. The Easter holy day, with its promise of resurrection and rebirth, fit well with the pagan celebration of the return of spring. That the monks themselves went "back to nature," leaving the cities for the deep forests—in the way that their spiritual ancestors had headed to the desert—helped spread the message that God was everywhere and in everything. Icons often depicted Saint Sergius speaking with the animals of the forest, preaching to the plants and trees, like Saint Francis of Assisi, who preached to his "sisters, the birds" and whose blessing calmed savage beasts. For the Hesychasts, every living thing was a mirror of divine light.

---

*A similar practice in the West to emerge from negative theology was the *Gelassenheit* or "letting go" of Meister Eckhart (1260–1328) and the anonymous author of *The Cloud of Unknowing* (circa 1350). Their attempts to know God directly were seen as heretical and were not assimilated into the Western Church.

It is not surprising that a people who endured humiliation and whose lives were for the most part made up of the necessity of dealing with the difficulties of a harsh environment would find the idea of a coming transformation that would change all of this forever very appealing.

THE MONASTIC MOVEMENT in Russia of the fourteenth and fifteenth centuries was one of the most remarkable examples of what we might call "religious colonization" in history. In the century following Sergius's death, it reached as far as the Arctic, with the monastery of Saint Cyril on the White Lake and that of Saint Savva and Saint Zosima on Solovetsky Island in the White Sea. Miraculous powers were attributed to the remains of the monks who founded these rest stops on the way to the Apocalypse, and legends about miracles and wonders drew seekers to these desolate locations. As they came, these settlements grew. In this way these monks and their followers were, like Saint Sergius, the "builders of Russia."

As more than one historian has pointed out, this was a rare example of a spiritual thrust pushing out across boundaries well in advance of a military, political, or economic one. It was not war or invasion or the search for more profitable trade that motivated these rugged pioneers, for that is what they were. They opened the dark forests to the uncreated light, clearing woodland with an ax in one hand and an icon in the other, and establishing townships in the process. What drove them on was the search for Godhead and the gradual divinization of the human, a process known as *theosis,* whereby we become more and more like God, just as he became like us.

Theosis occupied the sages of the Silver Age. For them the distinction between the God-man, or the human who becomes more like God, a central theme of Solovyov, and the man-God, the divinization of the "only human," enthroning man *as he is,* unredeemed, in the seat of the deity, was crucial and too easily misunderstood. Whether we grasp it any better today is debatable.

One path to *theosis* led by way of the icons. Indeed, it was by prayer and contemplating the icon—"meditating in colors"—that monks could achieve the kind of radiance associated with the uncreated light. As they sat in prayer, bathing in the inner light, they accumulated spiritual energies that could be felt by those near them. The Russian word for saint is *sviatoi,* which means "light," and those on the saintly path were thought to give off a spiritual glow. The devout aspirant would become what was called *prepodobny,* meaning that he or she was "very like" the ethereal images of the icons. Thus, the *via positiva* provided not only a means of achieving *theosis* but also a model to gauge your progress. If the icon depicted a glimpse of the transfigured life, the more one approximated its spiritual beauty, the more one shared in that life. And it was during what we can call the "monastic explosion" that Russia's greatest icon painter lived and worked.

WE KNOW NEXT to nothing about the early life of Andrei Rublev (1360–1427?).[7] What we do know is that he was a monk "who appears to have spent almost all of his life" doing little else but "painting holy pictures," a characterization that comes through in Andrei Tarkovsky's monumental film about him, the eponymous *Andrei Rublev* (1966).[8] He is assumed to have lived in Saint Sergius's Monastery of the Holy Trinity and there to have studied with the icon master Theophanes the Greek. We know he worked on the decorations for the Cathedral of the Annunciation in Moscow's Kremlin and also for the Assumption Cathedral in Vladimir and the Trinity Cathedral in Saint Sergius's Monastery of the Holy Trinity in Zagorsk. He was a colleague of Daniel Cherni, known as "the Black," another monk and icon painter.

What sets Rublev's work apart from that of others is a purity of intent, an austerity of aim that one finds echoed half a millennium later in the nonrepresentational hypermodernist work of Kazimir Malevich.[9] Nothing extraneous enters the frame. In Rublev's "Holy Trinity," painted around 1411, all narrative elements are excised, and the painting is reduced to three angels, seated at a table at the center of which is a chalice. There is a necessity at work here that is at once intense and soothing. This icon was used for the iconostasis—a screen covered with icons separating the nave from the sanctuary in Orthodox churches—for the main church in Serguis's Holy Trinity monastery.[10]

One of Rublev's most haunting works, called simply *Spas,* Russian for "savior," depicts a slightly elongated portrait of Christ, whose human character seems to have relaxed the more often angular features familiar to icons. This is a human Christ, but one who also looks into another world and whose gaze leads us to see it too. This work, originally created for the iconostasis of the Cathedral of the Assumption in Zvenigorod, was almost lost to humanity—as most of Rublev's work was; only a few pieces remain—and was only saved by an observant participant in the Bolshevik revolution. It had been relegated to firewood to help keep Lenin's new Russians warm, when a young proletarian realized it burned with a light of its own. He pulled it from the woodpile, and it now resides in the Tretyakov Museum in Moscow. Yet although this one work of spiritual genius was saved from the flames, many more and those who venerated them were not so well treated by the agents of the Red Terror and the persecution of Orthodoxy under Stalin. Since the collapse of the USSR and the end of that dark time, icon painting and veneration have enjoyed a tremendous revival, a sign that, at least on the popular front, Holy Russia has indeed returned.[11]

IN 1349 STEPHEN of Novgorod went on a group tour with others of his native town to visit the holy city of Byzantium. As a good Orthodox Christian, he was duly impressed with what he saw. Santa Sophia, of course, with its icons, mosaics, and enormous dome was a marvel. The great column with the statue of Justinian atop it and that of Constantine were wonders. But what occupied Stephen the most, it seems, were the holy relics.[12] Those of Saint Arsenius, Saint Anne, Saint John Chrysostom, Saint Basil, Saint Bacchus, and others received his kisses and veneration, and he seemed to track down sacred remains with the eagerness that a kid today might chase after Pokémon Go icons. In a way, we can see this as a fitting symbol for Byzantium itself. Although it could still awe a visitor from the cold north, Constantine's city had become something of a holy relic, and in gazing at its wonders, visitors in Stephen's time were gleaning some fading radiations from a glory that was past.

Byzantium had never recovered from the sack of 1204, when, during its "darkest hour," the soldiers of Christ from the Fourth Crusade entered into an "orgy of brutality and vandalism" in which irreplaceable works of beauty and craftsmanship were destroyed and holy images profaned, in a mad frenzy of ruin and plunder.[13] It lingered on in various states of war, invasion, and revolt and for a time was ruled by its rival, Rome. And although it could still send a holy shiver down the spine of a pilgrim, by the time of Stephen of Novgorod's visit, it was "accepted throughout Christendom that Byzantium was on the verge of collapse."[14] The only questions were: When would it fall and into whose hands? Even the dome of Santa Sophia that Stephen had gazed up at had been repaired with funds coming from the Russian churches. The Turk was at the gate and would not be detained for long. The Second Rome was in its last days and everyone knew it. It would hold on for another century or so and make desperate attempts to resist the inevitable, but its end was in sight.

That message had reached the Russian north. Not long after Stephen's visit to the holy city, the Turks had charged into Serbia on their sweep into the Balkans, and in 1389 at the Battle of Kosovo defeated the Serbian prince Lazar Hrebeljanović. Although it was a Pyrrhic victory—by the end of the battle both armies were decimated—enough of the Turks remained to carry on their thrust. In 1393 they reached the Bulgarian capital of Trnovo, which they captured, after a three-month siege. After a heroic resistance, the city's patriarch, who led the defense, conceded defeat. Later, when the city's boyars were executed—tricked into an assembly and then summarily slaughtered—the patriarch was supposed to have been miraculously saved. No such miracle arrived for the Balkans. By the end of the fourteenth century the region was in the control of the infidel who threatened to advance farther into the West.[15]

Both Serbia and Bulgaria had sought to fill Byzantium's shoes, proposing themselves as candidates for the position of capital of Orthodoxy when the inevitable happened and Constantinople fell.[16] Their plans fell through as both kingdoms fell to the Turks. It was then that the hopes of the Orthodox Russians, and those of other Slavs, turned to a city that had until then played a less than central role in the destiny of the Rus'. For it was at this time that Moscow began its ascension to the status of a Third Rome.

THIS WAS A significance that, in its earliest time, no one would have thought applicable to Moscow. Founded in 1147 by Prince Yuri Dolgorukiy, son of Vladimir Monomakh, scholarly opinion has it that as of 1200 Moscow was "hardly heard of" and would have been considered "one of the least likely candidates for future greatness."[17] These estimates do not seem unreasonable. At the time, Moscow was a small, wooden settlement, established along a tributary of the Volga River, and when the Mongols came it did not benefit by having a forbidding terrain as did Novgorod, which it would soon rival. As he did with Kiev and other cities of the south, Batu Khan attacked Moscow, burned it to the ground, and slaughtered its inhabitants. It began its resurrection in the mid-1260s, when Daniel Alexandrovich, the son of Alexander Nevsky, inherited what was left: a timber fort along the Moskva River. Daniel ruled Moscow until 1303, building it up from practically nothing to a growing, prosperous city. During his reign he established Moscow's first monastery, starting with a wooden church. This later became the Danilov Monastery, where Daniel is buried, having become a monk before he died at the age of forty-two.

Moscow began its struggle for prominence over the other Russian principalities with the career of Prince Ivan I, nicknamed "Kalita," or "money bags," because of his skill at collecting funds and thrift in retaining them. He was born in 1288 and was a grandson of Alexander Nevsky. (He was indeed Daniel Alexandrovich's son.) Like his grandfather, Ivan I knew he had to play by the Mongol rules, and also like him, on more than one occasion he had to take up arms against his fellow Russians and in defense of the Tartar yoke. At one point he commanded an army of 50,000 Tartars, sent to quell an uprising in the city of Tver. By most accounts, Ivan I was no hero and was most likely motivated by what seems a prudent concern for his wealth and for the patrimony he would leave behind. He kept himself in the Tartar good books, was a friend to the church, and did what was expected of him. He became Grand Prince of Vladimir and Prince of Moscow in 1325.

It was not until a few years later that he was made a Grand Prince of All Russia, an appointment that marks the first step on the path to the end of Tartar rule. Ivan I had been disappointed more than once in his ambitions, but time was on his side, and his patience bore fruit. Uzbek Khan, ruler of the Golden Horde—the remnant of the Mongol Empire that still controlled Russia—had kept Ivan I from achieving his aim, recognizing that Moscow had grown to great power and needed a tight rein. While under the Tartar yoke, all succession was decided by the khan, and twice already Uzbek Khan had passed Ivan I over. He was a good vassal prince, obedient and effective, and he had no complaints. Yet to entrust him with still more power by appointing him grand prince might prove dangerous.

It did, eventually. But this concern was soon countered by another, and Uzbek Khan's hand was forced.

A new threat to Tartar rule had risen up in the West in the form of the Grand Duchy of Lithuania. Pagan Lithuania, a Baltic people, had become Catholic under the ministrations of the Teutonic Knights and their offshoot, the Livonian Order. Following the Mongol invasion, lands of the former Kievan Rus' fractured into separate territories, which would become Ukraine and Belarus, later known as "Little Russia" and "White Russia." The growing Grand Duchy of Lithuania had absorbed some of this land and was encroaching on Novgorod and other Russian cities. Now, a strong Moscow, able to call its fellow princes together in defense of their land and their faith—as well as the Tartar interests—seemed a good idea.

Ivan I agreed, and he took advantage of the situation to have himself made chief tax collector for the tribute due the khan. The princes would collect the tribute—taking over the duties of the *baskaks*—and they would give it to him. He would then present it to the khan. What this amounted to was Moscow's dominance over the other cities, as it would be Moscow's responsibility to see that the tribute was paid. In this way the Tartar yoke gradually loosened, but it would still be some time before it completely fell away.

Ivan I's crafty patience wasn't alone in helping Moscow rise to prominence. He knew the importance of the church in establishing authority among the Russian people. And the church itself seemed aware that a shift was taking place. In 1325 Ivan I invited Petr, metropolitan of Kiev, to move his seat to Moscow. If nothing else signaled the growing importance of the north, this surely did. The original home of Holy Russia was left behind, and to ensure that the move into the new neighborhood would be smooth, Ivan I had a new place of worship built, just for the occasion. This was the Cathedral of the Dormition, which resides within the walls of the city's interior fortress, the Kremlin. Starting out as a fortified settlement, this inner citadel had grown in size and strength, its wooden walls soon giving way to stone. By the next century, it would become the heart of the new Russian Empire.

That the move from Kiev to Moscow coincided with Moscow's rise to prominence, and the subtle but felt shift in the weight of the Tartar yoke, symbolizes the renewed unity seen between the fate of the church and that of Russia. And following the death of Ivan I, it was the church that kept the easily fractured Russians together. The adhesive here came in the form of Petr's successor to the metropolitan seat, Aleksei, abbot of the Monastery of the Apparition in Moscow that Saint Sergius's brother Stefan left the wilderness to join. (And we remember that it was Ivan I's tax break for relocation that led to Sergius becoming a saint in the first place.)

Among the victims of the Black Death were Ivan I's sons. All, except for one, Ivan II, fell to it. Ivan II, known as "the Meek," lacked any of his father's qualities, as self-serving and cautious as they were, and the business of running a principality that was beginning to gather itself and others together in order to remove its oppressor fell to Aleksei. He had served under Daniel Alexandrovich and had gained respect among the Tartars. Known as the "wonderworker of all Russia," in 1357 Aleksei was summoned to the court of Jani Beg, ruler at the time of the Golden Horde. Aleksei was known as a healer, and Jani Beg had summoned him so that he could cure his wife Taidulla of blindness (some accounts say it was his mother).

Aleksei said such miracles were beyond him, but that they were not beyond God. Aleksei sprinkled her eyes with holy water and prayed; Taidulla's sight was restored. The Chudov Monastery in the Kremlin, founded in 1358, was an expression of Jani Beg's gratitude. Other monasteries arose because of Aleksei's miraculous powers. Returning to Moscow from Constantinople, he calmed a storm in the Black Sea by vowing to build a temple if the ship touched land safely. The Monastery of the Icon Acheiropoietos ("not made by hands") in Moscow was founded in 1361 in fulfillment of that vow. Monasteries that had fallen into disrepair were rebuilt under Aleksei's administration, and many monks who joined Sergius and the other "builders of Russia" were sent out into the wilderness with his blessings.

Aleksei brokered peace treaties between rival principalities, argued eloquently for the need to gather behind Moscow, and maintained good relations with the Tartars, doing his best to keep the fragile unity Ivan I had achieved from separating into its fractious parts. He was also tutor, mentor, and surrogate father to Dmitry II Ivanovich, Ivan II's son, who would strike the first blow against Tartar rule. When Ivan II died in 1359, Dmitry was still a boy, and for the first years of his reign, Aleksei was the real power. When Dmitry came to the throne, one of the first things he did was to replace the Kremlin's wooden fortifications with those of stone. This soon served Moscow in good stead when it repelled attacks by the Lithuanians, who were supporting Dmitry's rival, Mikhail II of Tver, who was making a bid for supremacy. With the ambitions of Tver subdued, Dmitry turned his attentions to the real enemy.

As INNER STRIFE and tribal jealousies continued to undermine the strength of the Golden Horde, Dmitry began to reach out further and further beyond the limits of the Tartar yoke, testing how loose it had become. He and the other princes began to withhold their tribute, and as they did the khan took note and soon decided that enough was enough. In 1378 the Mongol warlord Mamai sent an army to punish Moscow for insubordination. If Mamai expected an easy victory, he was surprised. Dmitry defeated Mamai's army at the battle of the Vozha River, and for the first time since 1240, when Batu Khan laid waste to Kiev, the Tartars were sent packing. Determined to show Dmitry who was boss, two years later Mamai returned, this time leading an army himself. It did not help. In 1380 Dmitry's army defeated Mamai's at the battle of Kulikovo, near the Don River.

The battle was seen as a turning point in Russia's history and a confirmation of its historic destiny and sacred duty as bearer of the Word. A measure of the battle's importance can be seen in the fact that before the engagement Dmitry made a special visit to Sergius so that he could receive his blessing. Sergius even sent monks back with Dmitry to lead his troops to meet the enemy. They were not fighting for Moscow or Russia but for the true faith. And as Alexander Nevsky earned his nickname through a battle near a river, so too did Dmitry Donsky, or "Dmitry of the Don," earn his own sobriquet. Holy Russia had triumphed and thrown off its oppressor—at least for a while.

The freedom, unfortunately, did not last. Shamed by his defeat, Mamai was relieved of his command when a rival warlord, Tokhtamysh, took control of his army, killing Mamai in the process. Tokhtamysh then set out to do what Mamai had failed to accomplish. In 1382 Tokhtamysh attacked Moscow, but was beaten back; accounts of that battle record the first time that firearms were used by the Russians. Tokhtamysh had made an ally of the principality of Suzdal—a rival of Moscow—and two days later, when two of its dukes, brothers-in-law of Dmitry, assured the Muscovites that if they opened the city's gates, no harm would come to them, they agreed.

It was a mistake. No sooner had they opened the gates than the Tartars swarmed in, massacreing the townspeople and destroying the city. Dmitry had been able to raise a large army to defeat the Tartars at Kulikovo—soldiers had come from across the land—but it was not to be this time. He had to admit defeat and accept Mongol rule. The Tartar yoke was back in place; Dmitry had to allow his son to be taken hostage to make sure it was harnessed tight. But the Russians knew that the Tartars were not invincible, and soon enough their yoke would be gone for good.

6

A Terrible Time of Troubles

Apocalyptic Expectations

When the Russians eventually did throw off the Tartar yoke, it was something of an anticlimax. We could even say that the yoke fell off practically of its own accord. There was no final battle, such as at Kulikovo, and in the end it was the Tartars themselves who saved the Russians the trouble of putting up a fight. It was one of their own who did away with Khan Ahmed of the Great Horde, the remnant of the Golden Horde that still expected tribute from Moscow. When Ivak, khan of the Nogary Horde, a rival power, killed Ahmed in 1481 and absorbed his army, the Russians no longer had to worry about the Tartar yoke. The new master to arise in the land was Muscovy itself, something that the other principalities had by that time come to understand.

The man responsible for this was Ivan III (1440–1505), known as "the Great" and "the gatherer of the lands." It was he who, in 1480, faced off against the Tartars on one side of the Ugra River, about 150 miles from Moscow, while Khan Ahmed and his army cooled their heels on the other. They did this for several weeks, neither one eager or confident enough to do more than rattle their sabres and shout abuse. Word is that Ivan himself needed a pep talk from the bishop of Rostov before he even brought his army to the river's banks.

In the history books this shouting match is known as the "great stand on the Ugra River," but from its descriptions it sounds like the two armies, neither of whom really wanted to fight, got into respective panics, had mutual nervous breakdowns, and abruptly left the scene of the aborted battle. An example, perhaps, of a major change in history that turned on a dud.

A few years earlier, in 1476, Ivan had already refused to pay tribute to the khan, emboldened by some successful skirmishes against the Tartars a year or so before. Hence Ahmed's attempt now to bring him to heel. But after scowling fearfully across the water at his renegade vassal for some weeks, Ahmed decided to back down and retreat onto the steppes. The fact that reinforcements from Prince Casimir, ruler of Poland and Lithuania, with whom Ahmed had entered into an agreement, and who had coveted Muscovy possessions, failed to materialize surely had something to do with his decision.[1]

Ahmed had planned to return the next year with a larger army, but Khan Ivak, who had designs on Ahmed's territory, boldly made a claim for them and killed Ahmed in the process. The "great stand on the Ugra River" was the last attempt by the Tartars to collect tribute from the Russians. By the time Ahmed was dead the Great Horde was collapsing in on itself, and the Tartars no longer concerned themselves with Russia. Ivan spent the rest of his reign securing Moscow's dominance and establishing it as a major player on the European stage.

Ivan had arrived, as many characters in this history have, in the midst of a civil war, one of the family squabbles that decimated the Russian princes and kept them under Tartar rule. His father was Vasilii II, grandson of Dmitry of the Don. He was known as "the Blind" (or "the Dark") because he had had his eyes plucked out by his cousin, Dmitri Shemiaka, in revenge for his own blinding of Dmitri's brother, Vasilii Kosoi, during a struggle for power with Vasilii's uncle Iurii. Apparently the proscription against mutilation that Vladimir I had initiated back in the golden days of Kievan Rus' was no longer respected.

When Vasilii I died, Vasilii II was only ten years old, and so a council of regents was created to rule until he came of age. Vasilii's uncle Iurii, however, had been left out of the plan, and he claimed a right to the throne based on the old appanage system. Eventually, with the help of an army, he was able to secure it briefly. Civil war broke out, and in the process Vasilii II captured one of Iurii's sons and blinded him. When Vasilii II fell into his cousin Dmitri's hands, he did the same to him. Yet Vasilii the Blind was able to gather support from the people, and in the end it was he who won, Dmitri eventually passing out of the proceedings by being poisoned in Novgorod.

While much of this was taking place, Ivan III was kept safe, hidden in a monastery. Perhaps having a father blinded by his relatives fixed in the young Ivan's mind the idea that securing control over his rivals was paramount above all other concerns. If so, it was a powerful reminder that a strong hand was necessary for a secure rule. At the age of twelve he had been given nominal command over the force assigned to finish off what was left of his father's opponents. At eighteen he was fighting on his eastern border against the Kazan Tartars, part of the Golden Horde who had no yoke on Russia. In 1462, Vasilii II died, and the title of grand prince went to Ivan III.

As a child, Ivan had been betrothed to the daughter of the Grand Prince of Tver, but in 1467 Maria of Tver died suddenly—as was often the case, poison was suspected, but exactly who may have administered it remains unclear. Maria had one son, aptly named Ivan the Young, and his father was concerned that a single offspring was not enough to secure a succession of rule, a point upon which his brothers no doubt wished to capitalize. Clearly, Ivan needed another wife. Oddly enough, an answer to his dilemma came from an unlikely source.

A message from Rome came from Cardinal Bessarion, offering Ivan the hand of his ward, Zoë Palaeologus, who was the niece of Constantine XI, the last emperor of Byzantium. The last emperor of Byzantium? Yes. In 1453, when Ivan III was around thirteen, the inevitable had finally occurred: Constantinople had fallen to the Turks.

THE END WAS long in coming, but by the mid-fifteenth century the inexorable march of Islam had finally reached the holy city of Byzantium. Thessalonica had fallen in 1430, and reports of the atrocities and desecration carried out on the city sent a shiver of despair through the collective Orthodox consciousness. A faint hope of salvation came from the West. In 1438–1445 the Council of Ferrara and Florence was convened in order to iron out differences between the Catholic and Orthodox Churches, in the hope that in return for official recognition of Latin rule, the West would send aid to save Constantinople. Cardinal Bessarion was one of the many clerics attending the council and urging the union, but from the point of view of esoteric history, the most important attendee was George Gemistos Plethon (1355–1452).

Gemistos was a Byzantine philosopher, a master of Plato, and of what came to be known as the *prisca theologia,* or "primal theology," the "perennial philosophy" bestowed upon mankind in the ancient past and handed down through the ages from sage to sage. Much more of pagan philosophy had survived in the Eastern Empire than in the West, and Gemistos had it at his fingertips. He was nicknamed "Plethon," because his knowledge made him a second Plato. But while Gemistos's knowledge of his namesake was unrivaled, he held another source of wisdom in as high esteem as the father of philosophy, perhaps even higher. These were the Chaldean Oracles, prophetic writings attributed to the Persian sage Zoroaster, but which subsequent scholarship placed at the door of the Juliani, a Roman family of the second century CE, who practiced magic and prophecy and engaged in what today we would call "channeling." For Gemistos, Zoroaster was at the head of the "golden chain of adepts" reaching back into the primal past, great sages and philosophers who proclaimed the ancient wisdom and passed it on to their disciples, who went on to do the same, down the centuries.

Gemistos had little interest in theological disputes, and when he was not called upon to elucidate a neat logical point, he entertained himself and others at the council by discoursing on the primal wisdom of the ancients. Along with Cardinal Bessarion, another who was taken with Gemistos's oratory was Cosimo de' Medici, Florence's great power broker. Cosimo was a learned man, and he was impressed with Gemistos's account of the *prisca theologia* and his eloquent exposition of Plato, who, we must remember, was still little known and less read in the West at this time; the Dim Ages had seen to that. Cosimo was so impressed with what he heard from Gemistos that he decided to open his own Platonic academy, picking up where the Neoplatonic Academy had left off when Justinian I had shut it down in 529.

Ironically, it was precisely the fall of Constantinople that enabled Cosimo to fulfill his dream. Just before the holy city fell, many of its scholars and monks fled, taking with them their libraries, which they sold to fuel their flight. These were eagerly picked up by book scouts, one of whom, a monk named Leonardo de Pistoia, worked for Cosimo. In 1463, via escape routes from the Turks, works by Plato and others, as well as the fabled *Corpus Hermeticum,* believed to be written by the great sage Hermes Trismegistus, came into the hands of Marsilio Ficino, whom Cosimo had set up as translator and scholar in his new Platonic academy. Thus it was as refugees from war that the writings that would trigger the Hermetic Renaissance of the fifteenth century—and inform much of the artistic Renaissance itself—came out of the darkness and into the light.[2]

But if the Council of Ferrara and Florence was something of an esoteric success, it was less so for the Orthodox Church. Although an agreement had been reached in which the Orthodox delegates accepted the use of the *filioque,* submitted to papal authority, and modified their views on Purgatory so that they were in line with the West, when they heard of it, the Byzantines themselves rejected the idea. To submit to the spiritual authority of the West was to them worse than submitting to their imminent slaughter by the Turks. A similar loyalty to the true faith had made Alexander Nevsky submit to the Mongols rather than to the Teutonic Knights. Now the people of the holy city shunned the clerics who had sold their souls in order to protect their skins—or such at least seems how many inhabitants of Constantinople regarded the forced reunion of the churches.

In the end the West did not come to the aid of its eastern sister. Aside from the Venetians who were already in the city and a contingent of Genoese led by Giovanni Giustiniani, the Byzantines were on their own. The capitulation to the pope did not bring the desired aid, and when the disaster fell, many believed that it was because of this unholy misalliance that retribution had come to them. They had lost the true faith, and God was punishing them.

If so, he meted out his punishment through the eager hands of Mehmed II, a twenty-one-year-old sultan who was carrying on the work of his father, Murad II. Known as Mehmed the Conqueror, in April 1453 the young sultan subjected the ancient walls of Constantinople to a sustained bombardment by the giant cannon he had forged for precisely this siege. He had at his disposal an army of some 100,000 men, trained crack troops and fierce irregulars. Constantine XI, posthumous in-law of Ivan III, had roughly 8,000 people to defend the city. Much of his army was made up of women, children, and elders. They resisted the siege for weeks, repairing breaches in the walls as soon as they were made, but eventually the sheer number of Mehmed II's forces overcame them. When a fifth-century wall was finally shattered by Mehmed II's monster cannon, the Turks rushed in and the slaughter began.

Constantine XI himself had refused to leave the city, and when the enemy surged in he threw off his royal robes and with his great sword leaped into the thickest part of the melee. His body was never found. For weeks the inhabitants of the holy city had carried their icons through the streets, chanting orisons for salvation. Signs and portents had foretold the worst. A lunar eclipse had not boded well; that a holy icon fell from its place confirmed the people's fears. A thunderstorm stopped a procession in its tracks, and a strange glow over Hagia Sophia meant for many that the spirit had abandoned them.

Nevertheless, in the end the people huddled in the Church of the Holy Wisdom, calling for mercy and forgiveness. They were cut down in their prayers, and the priests at the altar were slaughtered where they stood. The pillage, carnage, and desecration were as to be expected, although some accounts report that after one day of plunder and rape, the city was exhausted of any booty, and the soldiers themselves so fatigued by the destruction, that no one complained when the sultan cut the traditional three-day frenzy short. Mehmed II showed humility before Hagia Sophia, although his soldiers showed less of this before the piles of icons that went up in smoke or the ecclesiastic garments with which they robed themselves and, if some reports are correct, shared with stray dogs. When his senior imam proclaimed the name of Allah from the pulpit of the Church of the Holy Wisdom, Mehmed II bowed. Hagia Sophia had become a mosque, and the Byzantine Empire was no more.

WHILE THE LOSS of the holy city was of course a great blow to the true faith and triggered apocalyptic expectations, it was in other ways propitious for Moscow. It had already begun to be seen by the devout as the real home of the true church.[3] Constantinople had lost its authority by breaking bread with Rome, which to the Orthodox was equivalent to supping with Satan or at least with the Antichrist, and it was no mystery why devastation had come to her. The Russian church had already disavowed itself from any part of the Council of Florence and Ferrara. Metropolitan Isidore, who had approved of the decisions of the council, had been forced into exile. Now events had proved the Russians right. Byzantium was no more. It was Muscovy's time as seat and sole authority of the true religion.

And while Moscow inherited the religious mantle of the holy city, it also found a place to shoulder the responsibility of its fallen political power. That Ivan III was now locked in holy matrimony with a niece of the last Byzantine emperor, was one of several pieces of evidence offered as certain proof that Moscow was now not only the Third Rome, but also the new Byzantium.[4] If it was not yet this in sheer beauty, the many churches Ivan had built and the reconstruction of Moscow and the Kremlin carried out by the Italian architects Ivan had imported would soon put it in the running. But it surely was Byzantine in power and imperial descent. With a wife of imperial blood and the ambition that goes with it, Ivan III was ready to extend the process of consolidating his control that led to him being called "the gatherer of the lands." Because gather is precisely what he did.

Ivan and Zoë were married in the Dormition Cathedral in Moscow in 1472. The union was not welcome by the church, which was already repelled by any dealings with the West, nor was Zöe immediately accepted by the people; as a ward of the pope, she had been obliged to convert. Bessarion, her guardian, who had accompanied her from Rome, had been party to the detested Council of Florence and Ferrara, and no doubt some idea of fulfilling the letter of that unholy agreement lay behind their offering. Yet whatever designs Pope Paul II had in mind—for apparently he was the one who first had the idea of the marriage—things did not go according to plan.

Cardinal Bessarion had hoped that Zoë would convert Ivan to the Western faith. But his expectations were stunted when she reverted to Orthodoxy. She also took a new name, Sophia, indicating her Greek roots. She also urged Ivan to claim imperial status and it was at this time that he began to use the double-headed eagle, symbol of the Roman Empire, as his standard. Zoë also introduced the elaborate ceremony and ritual etiquette familiar to her from her Byzantine heritage. And it was more than likely she who had urged Ivan to stop debasing himself before his Tartar masters, offended at the kowtowing he was obliged to do before them. If in nothing else, Zoë shows herself here in true Byzantine tradition, rather as Theodora did with Justinian the Great.

She also liked the idea of Moscow, her new home, as the Third Rome, now that the second one was gone. It was an idea that Ivan liked as well. It was given an official Orthodox sanction in 1492 by Zosimus, metropolitan of Moscow, in a tract called the *Exposition of the Easter Cycle,* a work made necessary when the end of the world expected for that year didn't arrive, and new calculations and a new calendar were needed.[5] Zosimus hailed Muscovy as the new Byzantium, and the Muscovite tsar as the new emperor. God himself had placed Ivan III on the throne as the new "Tsar Constantine for the new city of Constantine, sovereign of Moscow and the whole Rus' land." Moscow was the new Constantinople, as that city itself had been the new Rome.[6] This was an idea that would gather more momentum and the evidence to legitimize it as the years went on.

BY THE TIME of his marriage Ivan III had already begun the process of "gathering the lands" that would lead to Moscow's dominance and the rise of the Muscovite empire. He was a determined man, tall, thin, and with a slight stoop. Women were said to faint under his gaze. His main target was Novgorod. Against Ivan's bid to grab the title of grand prince, it had sought support from Casimir IV, grand duke of Lithuania and king of Poland—the two states had formed a union in 1385—and now Ivan used that as a reason to finally bring his rival to heel. Casimir's help was more moral than military, and with a Tartar cavalry to lead the way—he had not yet thrown off their yoke—Ivan easily defeated Novgorod's defenders. So savage was his attack that mutilated soldiers, their lips and noses sliced off, were sent ahead of Ivan's army, to show the inhabitants of the city what they could expect.[7]

Ivan claimed that he had attacked Novgorod and subjugated it to his command because it had rebelled against his ancient right to rule.* This, he said, went back to Prince Vladimir and the Rurik clan. He claimed Novgorod as his patrimony. The city's refusal to recognize this and its claim of independence were insults to his ancestors—although one might have pointed out that Yaroslav the Wise had granted Novgorod self-government back in the days of Kievan Rus'. But as Serhii Plokhy points out, what was important here is that Ivan looked to the ancient

---

*It would not lose complete autonomy until 1478.

Rurik line as proof of his legitimacy to rule.[8] This had not been done during the Mongol years; legitimacy then was granted by the khan. Ivan no longer looked to them for support or permission. The new empire had begun.

As the Tartar yoke slipped off and Ivan inexorably gained control over other principalities, treating them much as he did Novgorod, and basing his claims on his Rurik descent, he also established himself as an independent power among other European rulers. He had ambassadors sent to the Holy Roman emperor, the courts of Denmark, Poland, Venice, and other Western lands. His diplomatic efforts paid off; Ivan put backward, isolated Muscovy on the European map. Yet he was not satisfied with mere acknowledgment. He was determined to show his contemporaries that Muscovy was no mere principality. When, in 1488, Frederick III, the Holy Roman emperor, tried to assuage Ivan's ambitions by offering him the title of king, Ivan was enraged and told the emperor's ambassador that he, Ivan, was invested in his authority by God himself, as had been his ancestors, and was in no need of any title granted to him by anyone else.[9] He considered himself the emperor's equal and demanded respect accordingly.

Yet while the finery, comportment, and self-esteem of the Byzantines may have reached Ivan through his wife, they did not immediately trickle down to his emissaries. As Philip Longworth points out, the Russians sent out into the wider world were often seen as barbarians, whatever imperial pedigree their ruler claimed.[10] Some people of learning and culture reached his court through Zoë, and some had served in fallen Byzantium itself. But as Ivan's eminence grew and his royal network stretched out, he was reliant more and more on local talent. This was not always up to the mark. Not only did most Muscovites lack a foreign language, they were also short of "sophistication and self-discipline."[11] Drinking was a common concern, and the emissary from a "boorish society with a tendency to anarchy" was admonished to "drink modestly and not to the point of drunkenness."[12]

BY THE TIME of his death in 1505, the "gathering of the lands" that Ivan III had initiated was, if not complete, certainly off to an impressive start. He had brought Novgorod and Tver under his rule by force, and other lands he had either purchased outright or had convinced their rulers of the right of his authority. By doing so Ivan had tripled the territory of Muscovy's influence. He had even sent expeditions into the Arctic. The idea was to eliminate the old system of a prince's ancestral right and replace it with the new subordination to what effectively Ivan had become, a tsar, or caesar, although it was left to his eponymous grandson, Ivan IV, known as "the Terrible," to make the title official. Ivan's long-term aim was to regain the land of the original Rus', Kiev, which had long been under the rule of Lithuania and Poland, an ambition that may be entertained by Russia's current ruler. This led to a struggle with the Grand Duchy of Lithuania that lasted for half a century and which, in a different form, we might say goes on today.

Ivan was succeeded by his son Vasilii III. He had arrived on the throne via a circuitous route, involving alleged plots against Ivan and against the church. This last was part of what was known as the "Judaizing" heresy, although the only thing Jewish about it was an unhealthy—from the point of view of the conservative clerics—use of critical reasoning in regard to some theological issues, mostly involving the Trinity, and a perceived return to Old Testament interpretations. The heresy was believed to have been started in Novgorod by Skhariya the Jew, a scholar from Kiev brought there by nobles from Lithuania, who, we remember, supported Novgorod in its struggle with Moscow. Eventually it led to Skhariya's execution, the expulsion of Metropolitan Zosimus from Moscow, the arrest of Zoë, who was accused of being part of a plot against her husband, and one of Ivan's closest advisers being burned to death. Vasilii himself had been in and out of favor. For a time Ivan's grandson Dmitry—from his first son, Ivan the Younger—ruled with him. A coup attempt by Vasilii and his supporters was uncovered, and many close to Ivan were arrested. Then in 1499 Vasilii was back in Ivan's good books, although the threat of an armed insurrection led by him prompted Ivan, who was ailing, to come to some understanding with him. Dmitri, his grandson, was arrested; he eventually died in prison.

It was during Vasilii III's reign that the idea of Moscow as the Third Rome began to take on a definite shape. We've seen that it was in a letter to Vasilii around 1511 from the monk Philotheus that the identification of Moscow with the Eternal City was made explicit. Another source of the identification of Moscow with Rome was the legend of the white cowl. This too is attributed to Philotheus, and it is dated to around the same time as his letter to Vasilii III.

There are different versions of the legend but in essence it relates that in the mid-fourteenth century, Philotheus, the patriarch of Constantinople—not the sixteenth-century monk—a man of great spirituality and devotion, had a vision. In it, a young man told him that in ages past, Constantine the Great had given a gift to Pope Sylvester I. It was a white cowl, the kind of hood associated with a monk's cassock. Constantine told the pope that he was to wear it for the glory of the church. It signified the supremacy of spiritual power over the secular world.

The cowl had been for many years in the safe keeping of the West, but now it had come to Philotheus; how exactly it had got to him is a bit obscure. The young man in his vision told Philotheus that the Western Church would try to get the cowl back, but that he was to refuse all requests for its return. And although Philotheus understandably wanted to keep the cowl in the holy city, the young man warned that he must take it to Novgorod or it would be lost. Philotheus needed to bring the cowl to Novgorod, where it would be safe. Even then the threat of the Turk seemed unavoidable.

Some accounts have the cowl getting to Novgorod in Philotheus's day; others have it arriving there a century later, as the holy city fell. In some accounts it was in 1054, the time of the "great schism" between the Eastern and Western Churches, that the cowl came to Constantinople, and it was Pope Sylvester I that comes to Philotheus in his vision and urges him to bring the cowl to Novgorod for safe keeping. Putting aside the political aspects of a challenge to Moscow's spiritual supremacy by its old political and economic rival, what the legend amounts to is the idea that the symbol of Christian purity, associated with the apostle Peter, the founder of the church itself, was now in the safe hands of the rising Muscovite empire, given that Novgorod itself was in those hands too. The white cowl had found a home in the Third Rome.

Another link with Rome was forged in a tract produced in Moscow in 1520 called *Tale of the Princes of Vladimir.* This was a work of what some see as "creative genealogy," that is, an attempt to legitimize Muscovy rule by anchoring it in the past through an invented heritage.[13] In the *Tale of the Princes of Vladimir* the holders of power in the Kremlin are shown to be direct descendants of the great Roman emperors. This connection is made through a legendary character called Prus, who was claimed to be the brother of Augustus, the first emperor of the Roman Empire.

The story is that when parceling out overseers to help him maintain the empire, after appointing other relatives to their tasks, Augustus had given his brother Prus dominion over the lands of the north. These lands were subsequently known as Prussia, and with a little creative geography, Prussia became Scandinavia. At least it is from Prussia that Prince Rurik and his warriors come, according to the *Tale of the Princes of Vladimir.* On his deathbed, an elder of Novgorod tells his people that they must ask the people of that land for a leader. When they do, Rurik of Prus obliges.

One other link to a desired if debatable Roman past was asserted in the *Tale,* this one with a bit more history behind it.* The Muscovy princes were descended from Prince Vladimir Monomakh, who, we remember, briefly held Kievan Rus' together in the twelfth century, during what many see as its last days of glory; his name is remembered

---

*Even if the story of Prus and the Rurik clan is true, which seems doubtful, it secures a very weak link to the Romans. It suggests that practically anyone coming from somewhere within the empire was sufficient contact to establish a connection.

today in the form of the Vladimir Monomakh ballistic-missile submarine.[14] Vladimir got his last name from his mother, Anastasia of Byzantium, who was related to the Byzantine emperor Constantine XI Monomachos. Constantine XI Monomachos *was* related to Emperor Augustus. So at least in this case, there was some actual link to the Roman past that the Muscovy princes were now trying to revive, one less tenuous than the supposed mythical Prus out of whose land the Rurik clan were supposed to appear, when called to rule the undisciplined Novgorodians.[15]

Like Philotheus the monk, Vladimir Monomakh also passed on an article of clothing to subsequent Rurik princes, though one less elusive than Constantine's mystical white cowl. As the *Tale* relates, Constantine had given to Vladimir his emperor's attire, and the most important part of this was what is known as Monomakh's cap, which served the same function as a crown. Most accounts suggest that the gold filigree skullcap known as Monomakh's cap actually came from the khan of the Golden Horde, and may have been more of a symbol of submission to the Tartar yoke than one of power and authority. If so, it would be one more example of history's sense of irony, through which emblems of one status or character, via some strange metamorphosis, are transformed into their opposite.

THE STORIES OF the white cowl and other tales designed to fix Moscow's status as the legitimate inheritor of Byzantium's spiritual and secular power appeared at a time when the expectations of the apocalypse, never far from the surface of Russian consciousness, now ran peculiarly high. The fall of Constantinople and the transfer of the seat of Orthodox spiritual power to Moscow contributed to this. As mentioned, another agent of the apocalyptic atmosphere was the church calendar. The old calendar stopped at the year 1492; at that point, the millennia allotted since the beginning of time until the return of Christ seem to have been used up. And while the discovery of America by

Christopher Columbus did in fact open the way to a New World, it was not quite what the church historians had in mind when they thought of the last days, if indeed they had even heard of it.

The Judaizers had pointed out that the end of times specified by the Orthodox calendar had evidently not arrived. They had reached this conclusion through consulting an astrological text known as "The Six Wings," or *Shestokryl'*.[16] This suggested to them that, not only the calendar, but the whole idea of the Second Coming needed rethinking. To the devout Orthodox who resisted the Judaizing influence, however, it suggested that these wiseacres were in league with the devil, or at least the Antichrist, as their use of magic seemed to prove.

Yet the Muscovy of this time was rampant with alchemical, astrological, divinatory, and other occult preoccupations, and translations of magical and Hermetic texts from the West proved a lucrative business. Later, Russians sent to England to study sought out the knowledge of Dr. John Dee, Queen Elizabeth's astrologer. What Russia had inherited from the Renaissance was not the sober humanism we associate with it, but the Hermetic influence that informed savants like Giordano Bruno. It was this taste for the "inner secrets of the universe" that later made Russia open to the influence of alchemical philosophers such as Jacob Boehme and the Romantic metaphysics of Schelling. One less obscure result from its alchemical obsession was vodka, which arrived in Russia as a by-product of *aqua vitae,* the alchemical elixir of life.[17] One notes that for many Russians, it is precisely that. For many, history seemed to be drawing to a close, but as James H. Billington points out, it was not clear whether the signs and portents boded good or evil for the immediate future. Were they seeing the overture to Christ's return and the Day of Judgment? Or were the indications pointing to the reign of the Antichrist, who would get the proceedings underway and start the countdown to the final transfiguration? It was difficult to tell and, as Billington writes, "this uncertainty as to whether disaster or deliverance was at hand became characteristic of Russian prophetic writings."[18] "Anticipation and fear, exultation and depression" alternated in those who felt that "great things were about to happen in Russia," an ambivalence that remains among Russians today.[19]

We might recall that earlier in this book, when talking about Hermann Hesse's notion of "Russian man," I quoted from Friedrich Hölderlin, one of Hesse's favorite poets, the line that "Where there is danger deliverance lies also." One of the problems of an apocalyptic temperament is being able to tell one from the other, if indeed the two can be pried apart.

AS MIGHT BE expected, these apocalyptic excitations were expressed in extreme ways within the religious communities of the time. Strangely enough this took the form of polar opposites. These were the "pillar-like immobility" of some monks, whose static poses rivaled those of yogis of the East, and the perpetual wandering of the *yurodstvo,* the "holy fools" or "fools for Christ." The one could remain fixed to one place and position for decades, the other was in constant movement.

As in Eastern practices, the static poses adopted by monks were alleged to bring them a special spiritual status and to inspire them to prophecy. The practice went back to the ancient Stylites, ascetics who believed that by mortifying the body one exalts the soul. Stylites were so named because they climbed a pillar—*stylos* in Greek—and remained atop it, motionless and meditating, for years. The practice was popular during the early years of Byzantium. The most famous Stylite was Simeon the Elder who, in 423, climbed a pillar near Aleppo in Syria and remained there until his death in 459. In Russian mythology the practice of "pillar-like immobility" was related to the tales of Ilya Muromets, a fabled warrior of the Kievan Rus' of Vladimir I. After an illness had kept him immobile for thirty years, Ilya was miraculously cured. With a magic horse he then traveled to Kiev, where he dazzled Vladimir's court with his displays of strength and bravery.[20]

The holy fools took another route to sanctity. Like the immobile ascetics, they renounced the flesh and mortified the body, but they did this while moving among the people, taking to the road like Buddhist monks and relying on the generosity and piety of the populace for food and shelter. They spoke with the angels and saints and also with God, and their prophecies, which often sounded like madness, were informed with the holy wisdom of the sacred. Saint Paul had said that the message of the Cross appears as foolishness to the worldly wise, and the church father Tertullian (160–220) had said that the sheer foolishness of Christian teaching ensured its truth.[21] Famously Tertullian said that he believed in the resurrection of the body *because* it is absurd, an existential reasoning the Russian philosopher Lev Shestov followed through a tortuous dialectic in his book *Athens and Jerusalem* (1937). Its title was inspired by Tertullian's rhetorical question, "What has Athens to do with Jerusalem?" that is, what does reason have to do with faith?*

Wandering through the land, the holy fools prophesied dark times ahead and warned that the people must repent and do penance for their sins. One of the most famous of holy fools was Nil Sorsky, although judging by his large body of writings, there was little of the fool about his foolishness.

Nil Sorsky was born in 1443. Little is known of his early life, and there is some debate as to whether he came from a noble or humble background. What is known is that at some point he joined the monastery of Saint Cyril on the White Lake and from there traveled to Mount Athos and the Holy Land and later Constantinople, after its fall. At Mount Athos Nil adopted the Hesychast practice that he would continue for the rest of his life. He was repelled by life in the large monasteries and would later become involved in the controversy over the amount of land they owned. The solitary hermit's life was not for Nil either, and so he found a middle way in what became known as the *skit* style of monastic life. These were small communities of monks, generally of no more than twelve members, in which the mutual aid provided

---

*This was a question asked by the Danish philosopher and "father of existentialism," Søren Kierkegaard, who spoke of the need of a "leap of faith" in order to grasp the truth of Christianity.

by the larger monasteries was available without the loss of solitude.

Like other monks of the Hesychast tradition, Nil practiced the kenotic life, living in poverty and in closeness to nature reminiscent of Saint Francis of Assisi. In the *skit* community, rules, regulations, and rituals were at a minimum. The emphasis was on the inner life and one's personal experience of the sacred. Like other practitioners of the Hesychast teaching, Nil believed that the attempt to have a direct experience of God was more important than maintaining the strict rule of Orthodox ritual. Such ideas, combined with his criticism of the increasing amount of property owned by the monasteries, led to Nil's involvement in the clash between the "possessors" and the "non-possessors," those who believed the monasteries should own land and those who felt they should not. That Nil believed that the church, like its Western counterpart, had grown too fond of worldly power, gives us an idea of which side of this debate he was on.

His opponent here was Joseph Volotsky, or Joseph of Volokolamsk, like Nil a revered saint in the Orthodox tradition. Their clash is reminiscent of that between the Benedictines and Franciscans in the thirteenth century, between the great wealth of the monasteries and Saint Francis's desire to wed Lady Poverty. For Berdyaev it symbolized the struggle between "the twofold nature of the Russian messianic consciousness."[22]

Joseph Voltsky was born in 1439 to a family of landowners. When he was seven he was sent to the monastery at Volokolamsk to be educated. He showed powerful devotion and took to the monastic life immediately. He was hungry for discipline and became something of a stickler for rules. He later left one monastery because the rules were not kept strictly enough; in fact, the monasteries at that time were often veritable dens of iniquity, with homosexuality and alcoholism being quite common within them, something that Rasputin found still to be the case a few centuries later.[23] Eventually Joseph was disillusioned with all the monasteries he visited and decided to found his own, what would become the Joseph-Volokolamsk Monastery, one of the wealthiest in Russia.

Joseph Volotsky was a strong-willed individual, one of the frontier saints who had extended Russia's borders with an icon in one hand and an ax in the other. He was an ascetic and authoritarian and demanded strict adherence to rules of ritual, dress, even of gesture and movement; as Billington describes it, his micromanagement of all activity seemed based on a kind of behaviorist theory of personality: as you act so shall you be.[24] His Christianity was, according to Berdyaev, "harsh almost to the point of sadism."[25] Nil Sorsky's Hesychast ways and kenotic poverty were the exact opposite of this, as was his attitude toward the punishment of heretics. Sorsky was against execution and for forgiveness; Volotsky was less lenient and argued in favor of heretics facing death. The particular heretics he had in mind were the Judaizers, and he devoted considerable thought to the arguments in favor of their execution.

Ivan III was in favor of secularizing the monastic land, but at the council of 1503 that debated the issue, the "possessors" won the day. And with Ivan III's death and Nil Sorsky's soon after—followed by the persecution of his followers—the "symphony" between church and state that would soon produce a theocracy had begun.

THIS "SYMPHONY" OF the spiritual and the secular powers would achieve its greatest performance through the figure of the enigmatic first tsar of all Russia, Ivan IV, better known as "the Terrible." By the time he was crowned tsar of Russia at the age of seventeen in 1547, with all the pomp and glory of lost Byzantium, the fusion between the power of the monasteries and that of the state that had begun with the victory of Jospeh Voltsky and the "possessors" was complete. When Ivan came to the throne, the orchestra needed for such a symphony had been gathered, and the players were all well rehearsed and familiar with the score.

Ivan IV is one of those historical figures around whom a thick, almost impenetrable coating of legend and myth has gathered. There is something of the Grand Guignol about him, a darkness that comes through in Sergei Eisenstein's film *Ivan the Terrible* (1944).* But even after we allow for exaggerated and even invented tales of atrocities by contemporaries wanting to blacken his name—the sixteenth-century equivalent of "fake news" and "alternative facts"—enough evidence remains to recognize that he is not exactly the victim of a smear campaign, even if it is true that his sobriquet, "the Terrible," is a mistranslation of the Russia *groznyi,* which means "the Dreaded."

Ivan IV was sufficiently cruel and ruthless in maintaining his authority and dominance to qualify as one of Colin Wilson's "Right Men." These are individuals—there are Right Women too—who under no circumstances will admit to being wrong and who, if their authority is challenged, will wreak, to them, a perfectly justifiable holy vengeance on those who oppose their will.[26] Russia, sadly, has been subjected to more than one of these characters. As an example in Ivan IV's case, Wilson points to his decimation of the population of Novgorod in 1570, when his paranoia led to him building a wall around the city and spending five weeks torturing its inhabitants. In the end sixty-four thousand people were killed,† to assuage his suspicion that the city was planning a revolt (it wasn't).[27] He may have been known as "the Dreaded," because of his zeal in meting out punishment. But insanity of this sort certainly qualifies as terrible.

Ivan IV came to power in 1533 when his father, Vasilii III, for whom Moscow was the Third Rome, died of an infected abscess; he had been confirmed as a monk shortly before his death. Ivan, who was born in 1530, was three years old, and for the next four years his mother, Elena Glinskaia, ruled as regent in his stead. Elena had Tartar heritage and was a descendant of Mamai, the chief of the Golden Horde that Dmitry of

---

*He is also one of the figures of evil in Paul Leni's German Expressionist horror film *Waxworks* (1924); http://filmdirtblog.blogspot.com/2016/04/waxworks-1924 -paul-lenis-early-horror.html.

†It is true that some recent research suggests that the death toll in what is known as "the massacre of Novgorod" may have been less than what was previously thought. Still, the ferocity and viciousness of Ivan's "punishment" was, even in those brutal times, sufficient to warrant note.

the Don had beaten off in 1380. This may account to some degree for Ivan's despotic character and sudden rages, personality traits that would appear as he got older. Then, when he was seven, Ivan's mother died; she was most likely poisoned. Prince Vasilii Shuisky, from one of the powerful boyar families, who was most likely behind her death, took power.

The Shuiskys were arrogant and haughty and considered themselves of a higher nobility than Ivan's family. During this time Ivan and his brother were subjected to ill treatment and humiliation; Ivan's letters—of which he wrote many—speak of these years with anger and resentment. Yet Prince Vasilii did not enjoy his position for long. He died soon after gaining power, and *his* brother Ivan took over. He too was soon deposed by a rival, who was himself quickly ousted from power by another. This freefall in secular authority was paralleled by a similar crisis in the church, with its leadership seeing the same kind of rapid turnover.[28] Such conditions tend to require and to produce a strong leader to bring things back to order. Ivan IV was ready for the job.

In 1543, on the occasion of his thirteenth birthday, members of Ivan's mother's family staged a coup that eliminated the Shuiskys for good—although with Vasilii IV, during the "Time of Troubles," one did briefly rule as tsar. Ivan himself gave the command for Prince Andrei Shuisky, who was then acting regent and who had subjected Ivan to much abuse—including first beating and then banishing his closest friend—to meet his end. He was tossed to the dogs, who lost no time in tearing him to pieces, such sport not uncommon in those times.[29]

Four years later, on January 16, 1547, in the Dormition Cathedral in the Kremlin, Ivan was crowned Tsar of All Rus'. Although his grandfather, Ivan III, had referred to himself as "tsar" in his letters—and use of the title goes back as far as Yaroslav the Wise—Ivan IV was the first official tsar, having received permission to receive this title from the patriarch of Constantinople, the head of the Orthodox Christian Church.*

---

*As Longworth notes, it is ironic that at the time, the patriarch of Constantinople was a subject of the Ottoman Empire, the Turks allowing the church to retain its independence while under Muslim rule.[30]

That Ivan IV was recognized as tsar, which meant caesar, or emperor, meant more than that he had acquired a peculiarly high status. As the Byzantine emperors had been, he was now God's representative on Earth. During the years of his reign—the longest, so far, in Russian history—the Muscovite empire resembled nothing so much as a theocracy, with Ivan IV a kind of abbot, overseeing with a paranoid and often deadly fastidiousness, the activities of a gigantic monastery.

IVAN HAD BEEN tutored by monks according to the ideas of the Josephite or "possessors" movement, which had striven to fuse the sacred and secular powers together into a holy union, a "symphony," in which the tsar was the chief conductor. As this happened, a similar cohesion took place between the everyday life of the people and the monastic one.[31] More and more applicants from the villages came to the monasteries, which grew larger and wealthier, while everyday life itself took on a religious character, the kind of totality that a poet like Yeats may have admired in Byzantium, but which to a modern reader sounds like a kind of universal revivalist camp.

Fasts were assiduously kept, the number of holy days were increased, vigils were observed, prayers spoken, pilgrimages made, processions followed, all in an atmosphere of often hysterical religiosity and apocalyptic expectation. As Joseph Volotsky had been a meticulous adherent to the rules of monastic life, so now everyday life in Muscovy became similarly astringent. (Oddly, as abstinence increased in the home, profligacy was on the rise among the monks.) The central aim of all of this was to maintain *tradition,* to remember faithfully the rites and beliefs handed down from the past and to keep them pure and intact.* They were sacred and holy and entrusted to the Russian people's care. It is not for nothing that the chant "Memory Eternal!" makes up part of the Orthodox memorial service.[32]

---

*Parallels with Judaism seem clear.

As the everyday life of the people came more and more to resemble life in one of the large and wealthy *lavras,* the tsar, as God's representative on Earth, came to be invested with more and more power, his absolute autocratic rule informed with both Byzantine and Mongol authority; he was both emperor and despot. A word against the tsar was a word against God, and any such insubordinate action was to be reported to the authorities immediately and dealt with summarily.

That his authority and infallibility were sanctioned by God must have added considerable strength to the already supreme self-confidence and megalomania of this Right Man. After all, Metropolitan Makarii himself had conferred divine power on him.[33] Such individuals as Ivan IV are plagued with an inability to control their rage and a facility for justifying their actions through the misdeeds of others. As Ivan IV rose to power, he had no hesitation in meting out holy justice to any who stood in his way, whether they were important figures in the church, or members of his own family.

By most accounts, the early years of Ivan IV's rule were relatively normal. He had found a wife in Anastasia Romanov—a name that will feature largely in later Russian history—picking her out from among several hundred candidates collected at the Kremlin for his perusal.* Ivan was known for his sensuality—apparently his sexual appetite was insatiable, enjoying droit du seigneur with the wives and daughters of the boyars; he himself had seven successive wives—and his cruel streak showed early on. A favorite "sport" of his at the time was hunting merchants through the woods with his dogs. This was not out of the ordinary by contemporary standards, if by ours it seems inhuman.

Ivan introduced some reforms, sought good counsel, and, in celebration of his victory over the Kazans in 1553, built Saint Basil's Cathedral, known as the Kazan Cathedral, in Moscow's Red Square; its mushrooming onion domes, looking like red flames reaching to the sky, are

---

*Some accounts say up to 2,000 possible brides were assembled for Ivan IV's choosing; others put the number at 500 to 1,500.

a Moscow landmark. But in 1560 Anastasia died, and Ivan IV changed. As Colin Wilson writes, "it is charitable to believe that he went insane" at this time.[34] A time of troubles seemed to have come over the land; drought, famine, an unsuccessful war with Poland and Lithuania, and raids by the Crimean Tartars all hit at once. It was at this time that the sobriquet Groznyi begins to adhere to Ivan, although, even allowing for mistranslation, "the Terrible" still seems apt enough.

Ivan IV believed Anastasia had been poisoned by the boyars, just as his mother had been. He swiftly took revenge by having several boyars arrested, tortured, and executed.* Resentment against the boyars, mistrust of those around him, and his enormous sense of his own importance led to the typical Right Man response. Ivan IV demanded absolute and immediate obedience to his command, a tactic that will appear more than once in Russia's future history. The slightest questioning of his orders or hesitation in carrying them out was an affront to God himself and was dealt with accordingly. Hitherto trusted advisers were sent packing and were glad to go. Others, like his friend Prince Andrey Kurbsky, left voluntarily, recognizing that the tsar had passed beyond reasoning and saw everyone as a threat.[35] When a messenger arrived with Kurbsky's letter, explaining to Ivan IV why he left Moscow and went over to the Lithuanians—with whom Muscovy was at war—Ivan thrust a spear through the courier's foot, fixing him, like one of the "immobiles," to the spot. Then, having delivered his "Dear Tsar" letter, the poor man was tortured to death as Ivan looked on.

Ivan seems to have suffered the contradictions of character that we associate with Russian Man. He was cultured, a fine writer and composer, and interested in the arts; during his reign the first printing press was established in Moscow, and he encouraged education among the people. Yet he had a raw sensual appetite that was little short of lascivious, and he took a righteous pleasure in the suffering of others. Accounts leave no doubt that he enjoyed watching the torture and executions of

---

*Subsequent research suggested his suspicions may have been justified.

his victims, procedures he himself would often plan with great attention to detail. But he also had what appears to have been a true religious devotion. He learned his lessons at the monasteries well, and he went on many pilgrimages in his childhood and adult life.[36] On at least one occasion he walked nearly forty miles in bare feet from Moscow to the monastery of Saint Sergius. This religiosity, bordering on fanaticism, comes through in the strange incident in December 1564, when Ivan suddenly abandoned Moscow and headed out of the city on a pilgrimage, with no apparent destination.

After traveling for days he eventually stopped at Alexandrova, a village some hundred miles away. Along with his large entourage he had brought with him the treasury and many precious icons and holy objects from the churches, indicating that he had the power of both the state and the church in his hands.[37] Ivan stayed there for weeks, with no communication with Moscow, while the court grew increasingly anxious, and the business of running the empire ground to a halt. Finally he sent letters saying he had abdicated. He accused the boyars of embezzling funds and the church of protecting traitors, but he told the Russian people that he had no grievance against them. The inference was that he was going to enter a monastery, something he had spoken about frequently.

It was a power play to bring the last resistance to his absolutism in line. The boyars knew they could not rule on their own, and the people of Moscow were clamouring for their tsar. Crowds had followed him to Alexandrova. Finally, a delegation was sent to beg him to return—a man who had ordered the torture and death of thousands.

He agreed, but on one condition. He was to have immediate absolute, unquestioned rule. Every action of his was to have the consent of the church and the boyars. He could mete out punishment of any kind when, where, and to whom it pleased him to do so. With an entire organic religious sociopolitical world about to collapse, and an anxious populace calling for their tsar, the delegation had no choice but to accept. Thus was ushered in one of the darkest periods in all of Russian history, in which Ivan's paranoia, greed, and lasciviousness had the sanction of church and state. A Right Man had found himself in the right place at the right time.

Immediately upon returning to Moscow, Ivan initiated what many see as the first police state. At the center of this was the Oprichnina, a kind of state within a state, and within which Ivan had as despotic a rule as can be imagined.* Here Ivan had his own secret police, the Oprichniki, black-robed and hooded agents of terror who carried brooms and dog's heads on their saddles, and who seem a combination of Spanish Inquisition and Gestapo. They were there to "bite" the disloyal and to sweep the rubbish out of Muscovy—hence the dog heads and brooms—and have been described as a kind of militant "church order" or sacred secret society, a kind of medieval SS. At the height of their power they numbered several thousand. In a presage of purges to come, Ivan unloosed his Oprichniki on anyone whom he perceived as a threat. As his paranoia increased this could mean anyone, although his special targets were the boyars. The Oprichniki operated with carte blanche, accountable to no one but Ivan himself, who indeed was accountable only to God.

One victim of the Oprichniki was Philip II, a monk from Solovetsk whom Ivan had made metropolitan of Moscow. Philip knew Ivan in childhood and had decided to become a monk at the age of thirty, when, during a church service, the words, "No man can serve two masters," moved him profoundly; until then he had had a life at court. Philip was an industrious monk, overseeing many projects, such as constructing cathedrals and building canals, and Ivan invited him to Moscow. Philip had a mind of his own, though, and although Ivan had made him metropolitan, he spoke critically of Ivan's violence, and especially against the Oprichniki, which Philip urged Ivan to dissolve. When Philip refused to bless Ivan's siege of Novgorod, Ivan had him arrested

---

*Ivan effectively divided Russia into two states. The Oprichnina—known as "the widow's share," or greater portion—was his. The rest, the Zemschina, belonged to the boyars.

on trumped-up charges of sorcery and black magic; but not before decapitating his cousin and sending him his head. (Ivan himself often consulted magicians, soothsayers, and astrologers.) The Oprichniki burst into the church during service, stripped Philip of his ecclesiastical robes, dressed him in sackcloth, and brought him to a small, dark cell in a monastery, where he was chained, ill-treated, and starved. In 1569, two days before Christmas, when he still refused to bless Ivan's slaughter, he was strangled, under orders from the tsar, by Mayuta Skuratov, one of the Oprichnina's darkest agents.

Yet by 1572 the Oprichniki had begun to self-destruct, as usually happens with paranoid attempts to enforce loyalty. As happened in the French Revolution and the Stalin purges, the need to supress all resistance began to turn on itself, and by its last days, members of the Oprichniki upper echelon—who had voiced some reservations about the massacre of Novgorod—found themselves accused of laxity of purpose. Not surprisingly, they came to a bad end. Yet these in-house purges—pursued by new recruits among the lower classes, eager to make a reputation—only helped bring on the end. When the Oprichniki fared badly against the Crimean Tartars—who had burnt Moscow in 1571—Ivan saw that their usefulness was at an end and dissolved them.* We can say that his brown shirts had served their purpose and that Ivan had the savvy to sweep his dogs out before they could turn on him.

Yet the end of the Oprichniki did not usher in a new time of peace and stability. The conflict with the Crimean Tartars was costly, and the ongoing war with Poland and Lithuania was going badly. The Swedes, too, had forced Ivan out of the Baltic.[38] Plagues and famine struck the land. His torturing and slaughter continued. And family woes were no better. In 1581 Ivan was most likely responsible for his daughter-in-law suffering a miscarriage. She was dressed immodestly, in his opinion, and he beat her for it. When his second son, Ivan Ivanovich, her husband,

---

*Vladimir Sorokin, one of Russia's best-known contemporary writers, projected a return of the Oprichnina in his dystopian novel *Day of the Oprichnik*.

heard of this, he quarreled with his father. The story is that, in a sudden rage, Ivan hit his son with the iron staff he carried. It was said to have been encrusted with precious stones, whose occult qualities were known to Ivan, and he was said to have impaled courtiers who displeased him with it.[39] The blow killed his son. The work *Ivan the Terrible Killing His Son* by the nineteenth-century Russian painter Ilya Repin depicts this tragic scene; it shows a distraught Right Man, holding his fallen son, aware of what he has done. Many Russians might have hoped that such insight would have reached him earlier.

Ivan himself did not have long to live. By his early fifties he had become impotent, weary, and ill. He is said to have gathered his astrologers and soothsayers and asked them when he would die. They agreed that March 18, 1584, seemed the most likely day. He told them that if he did not die on the day, they would be roasted alive. When the day came and he still lived, he reminded his prophets of his promise. They pointed out that the day was not done until the sun set. Later, while playing chess, Ivan's king fell over repeatedly. Then the tsar himself did too. The soothsayers were right. By sundown on March 18, Ivan the Terrible was dead.

Universal mourning greeted the news of the tsar's passing, a fact that has often provided evidence for the contention that the Russians simply love a tyrant, or at least a strong, paternal figure. In recent years a statue has been erected to him in his hometown—the first ever—and there is even a movement today that wants him canonized as a saint.[40] (He is in some good company; Rasputin, in no way an evil character, is in the running too.[41]) But the passing of this Right Man brought Russia to the same chaos from which he had arisen. Ivan's remaining son, Feodor, was feebleminded and ruled only briefly. He was replaced by Boris Godunov, a man of Tartar descent and of some character, as he was one of the few who could stand up to Ivan and survive.[42] He was, in fact, playing chess with Ivan when he died, and he had even tried to protect his son Ivan from his father's rage, receiving blows from his staff in the process. He had been an Oprichniki and was one of the few "old school" members* who survived their purges.[43]

Boris Godunov was suspected of murdering Prince Dmitry, Ivan's son from his last marriage and by some considered the rightful heir to the throne.† He died in 1591 at the age of ten in the town of Uglich. This story forms the plot of Pushkin's play *Boris Godunov,* upon which Mussorgsky's opera is based. Controversy remains over whether Dmitry was murdered or died by a self-inflicted knife wound during an epileptic fit. A third theory is that his death was faked and he escaped and was ready to return to reclaim the throne. This was an idea that fed the "time of troubles" that followed Boris Godunov's sudden and early death in 1605 at fifty-four, the same age as Ivan.

Once again Russia was in freefall. The first to claim the throne was a pretender claiming to be the lost Dmitry. He was murdered by a mob, urged on by Vasilii IV, one of the Shuiskys who managed to secure the throne briefly. Vasilii IV was soon deposed, and he was followed by two more pretenders. A slave named Ivan Bolotnikov raised the first "class war," slaughtering landowners, but his viciousness was too great after decades of Ivan and he quickly lost support. A character known as the Thief arose but was murdered by one of his own. The chaos was so great that by 1608, the Russians asked the Poles, their perennial enemy, for help, much as the indigenous Slavs called in the Varangians long ago. The Polish king sent his son to rule, and while the Poles occupied Moscow, Sweden moved into Novgorod. At the same time another pretender raised a storm in Pskov.

Confusion reigned, as it often did. Then a family appeared to bring things to order. And for the next three hundred years they did. They were the Romanovs.

---

*He too, like many at the time, had an interest in alchemy and the occult sciences. In 1586 Godunov offered the English magician John Dee a house and a £2,000 yearly salary to work for him. Dee did not, but his son, Arthur, who was also an alchemist, did take up a position in Moscow.

†Yet while the church allowed Ivan to marry his seventh wife, Dmitry's mother, it only officially recognized his first three. Hence Dmitry's claim to the throne would have been dubious at best.

A Window on the West

The Mission to Modernize

When the assembly of the land, the *zemskiy sobor*, met in Moscow in February 1613, in order to elect Michael Romanov as tsar, they may have thought that they were ending Muscovy's "time of troubles." In the sense of bringing some political stability to a highly unstable court, they would have been right. But the empire that Michael had been called to rule was ailing badly. Parts of the country were in ruins. The people had fled the fighting, and the fields lay fallow. Foreign armies, the Poles and Swedes, occupied much of the land. Insurrections flared up. Moscow itself was in such bad shape that for several weeks no decent accommodation could be found for the new tsar. And Russia's standing with other European powers had suffered. Muscovy had become insular, walling itself off from the rest of the world, especially the West, desperately trying to maintain its lifeline of tradition. So while a particular time of troubles had, for the moment, settled down, the chaos that seems to lie just below the surface in Russian history had not vanished; it was still there, bubbling away, and would make an appearance soon enough.

Michael's own reign, it is true, was relatively successful, although he himself was not entirely responsible for this. It saw the largest territorial expansion in Russian history, achieved through his conquests in

Siberia, which were helped along by the Cossacks and the Stroganoffs, a powerful merchant family. And he wisely stayed out of the Thirty Years War,* which wreaked havoc across Europe and gave rise, among other things, to the Rosicrucian diaspora.[1] But Michael himself was not a strong ruler and did not really want the job; with a few exceptions, this was not an uncommon characteristic of the Romanovs. His son Alexis, another gentle but ineffective ruler, would witness a fracture in the Russian nation that would run through practically all its subsequent history. It was a struggle between church and state, spiritual and secular power that saw the symphony each had contributed to end in the dominance of one over the other.

Michael was not the first choice for tsar. But after the other possibilities were rejected, he seemed the country's best bet. Michael's grandfather, Nikita Romanov, was the brother of Ivan IV's first wife and also one of his advisers. Michael was also the nephew of Feodor I, Ivan's son, the last of the Rurikid line. His family had fallen under suspicion during Boris Godunov's rule; he and his mother had been forced into exile at Beloozero, and his father was accused of treason. But now the need to establish some tangible link to the Muscovy past was strong, and the Romanov line was it.

For the first years of his rule, Michael's mother's family was the real power. Michael's education was limited, and he felt no real desire to be a sovereign. He left the decisions to his relatives and while they often took advantage of their positon for personal gain, they did bring peace to the land, settling the conflicts with Poland and Sweden. It was out of this that the true ruler of Muscovy in this time appeared.

Michael's father, Feodor Romanov, had been forced to enter a monastery in the far north by Boris Godunov, just as his wife had been forced to enter a convent. (A reader of Russian history soon discovers that convents and monasteries were regularly used as religious

---

*Had he entered it he would have sided with the Protestants against the Catholics, who were giving him trouble in Poland and Lithuania.

prison camps in this time, rather as mental institutions were during the Soviet era.) There he took the name Philaret. He was later returned to Moscow by the first false Dmitry, who took power after Godunov's death. The second false Dmitry made Philaret patriarch of all Russia, although his actual authority was limited, as was the pretender's itself. In 1610 Philaret was taken prisoner by the Poles when, sent as an emissary to their camp, he refused to recognize their king, Sigismund III, as tsar. With the peace agreed by his in-laws, Philaret was released in 1619.

He then became the de facto ruler of Muscovy until his death in 1633. Although technically he and his son were co-rulers, it was Philaret, the patriarch, who was the real power. And this was as it should be. Philaret believed that the state should be subordinate to the church, an issue that would reach crisis levels during the reign of his grandson Alexis.

Like Joseph of Volokolamsk, Philaret was a stickler for rules, and he set about to reform the practice of Orthodoxy with a certain zeal, beginning the work of correcting liturgical texts that would be carried on after his death. He also insisted on raising the educational level of the clerics, many of whom remained unlettered and unread. He instigated other reforms too, in the military and among the serfs. These, sadly, were not in their favor and only increased the power of the landowners. It was Philaret who turned the serfs from peasants in the employ of a noble to being more or less part of the land he owned—a theme that would form the heart of Gogol's *Dead Souls* and that gives a peculiarly literal understanding of being "close to the soil."

Boris Godunov had, it's true, introduced statutes that tied the peasants to their owner's estate, but this was only in extreme circumstances, and there was a time limit. After five years the serf was free. But many serfs had run from their estates—as slaves in the American South would—and many found themselves in the south of Russia, where they were joining the Cossacks. This, Philaret believed, would only lead to trouble. As it turned out, he was right.

Philaret had made the serfs as much a fixture of the owner's land as its fields. If they left they were literally "stolen property." We can say that the problem that would eventually destroy Russia—at least the Russia of the Romanovs—started here. It was the plight of the serfs that drove the eruption of Russian consciousness in the nineteenth century. More immediately though, it was the issue of religious reform that brought dissonance to the spiritual-secular symphony and would in the end bring its performance to a close.

AFTER PHILARET'S DEATH the indecisive Michael again allowed his relatives to rule. Michael died in 1645 and power passed to his son Alexis. Like his father, Alexis was just sixteen when he came to power, and like his father he was neither well educated nor inclined to rule. Early on in his reign he was dominated by his tutor, Boris Morozov, the most powerful boyar at the time. Alexis remained under Morozov's sway until his tutor's abuse of his position, and increasing taxation of the people and boyars, led, in 1648, to a riot in Moscow. The crowd called for the tsar to execute Morozov. He didn't, but many officials in Morozov's pay were lynched, and Morozov himself was sent into exile.

Like his father, Alexis was a weak character and easily influenced. The next figure to dominate him would lead Muscovy into a crisis from which it is still not clear whether its descendants have recovered.

Nikita Minin was born to a peasant family of Finnish background in 1605 in the village of Veldemanovo, near Nizhny Novgorod. He was treated badly at home and left it to enter a monastery. He later returned home, married, and entered the clergy. At a small parish church his eloquence impressed visitors from Moscow, who invited him to come to the capital. Here they secured him a position at a popular church. Nikita remained there for ten years, a very popular priest, known for his lively sermons. Then, in 1635, disaster struck. His three children died, and Nikita took this as a sign. He convinced his wife to enter a convent. He then left to live at a hermitage on an island in the White Sea. It was at this point that, on becoming a monk, he took the name Nikon.

Nikon, like Joseph of Volokolamsk and Ivan the Terrible, was something of a Right Man. He had an authoritarian streak, was impatient, and had a temper. When a quarrel arose between himself and an elder of the hermitage, Nikon left in a small boat. When a storm broke out Nikon prayed for deliverance, and his fragile boat was cast upon a small island. He later built a monastery there.* After spending some years at another monastery near Novgorod, he became the abbot. Again, like Joseph of Volokolamsk, Nikon was a "can-do" kind of monk.

In 1646 Nikon returned to Moscow on monastic business. While there, he paid his respects to the tsar, as was customary. Alexis was still under the sway of Morozov, but he was powerfully impressed by Nikon's piety and devotion. The asceticism and seriousness of this six-foot-six monk moved the young tsar who, like many Romanovs to follow him, had a true religious sentiment.[2] He began to meet regularly with this monk from the north. He then made Nikon head of the Novospassky (New Savior) Monastery in Moscow, which had a long association with the Romanovs.

In 1649 Patriarch Paissius of Jerusalem visited Moscow. He too was impressed by Nikon, so much so that he helped him get appointed metropolitan of Novgorod, a seat he soon accepted. In Novgorod Nikon had an opportunity to put into practice on a greater, secular scale, the austere authoritarian rule he had exercised in the monasteries. He also indulged in the pomp and splendor of his ecclesiastical power. Not everyone was happy with this. At one point a riot broke out, and Nikon was beaten, but his piety and sincerity won the rioters over and the trouble ended peacefully. As did many of the "possessors," we can say that Nikon tended to abuse the role of the *via positiva* in spiritual life, emphasizing the need for spiritual leaders to *show* their authority in very ostentatious ways. Nikon, we can say, took the *via gloriosa.*

---

*The story is that he planted a wooden cross to thank God for saving him from the storm. Twenty years later he visited the island again and saw that the cross was still standing. He was then patriarch of Russia and ordered that a monastery be built. In 1656 the Monastery of the True Cross was founded.

Alexis had come more and more to rely on Patriarch Joseph of Moscow for spiritual and moral support. (He was also obsessed with astrology and had horoscopes cast frequently.³) The possibility of a new "time of troubles" loomed over him, and when the patriarch died, Alexis felt the need for a new strong character to help him maintain order. He had already begun to see Nikon as a "great sun," a kind of spiritual star.⁴ When Nikon returned from the Solovetsk Monastery—the same one he had left years ago in a huff—where he had been sent to retrieve the remains of Metropolitan Philip, murdered by Ivan the Terrible, Alexis lost no time in appointing him Joseph's successor. Nikon did not accept at first; he knew he had enemies at court and played hard to get. He finally agreed, but on one condition: he demanded full obedience to him from the tsar and all Russians. Alexis consented. At this point Nikon became the true power in Russia. From 1652 until Nikon's downfall in 1666, Muscovy was a theocracy with the monk, not the tsar, on the throne.

Nikon's campaign was twofold: to increase the power of the church, and to reform its liturgy and practice so that it conformed with current Greek criteria. "I am a Russian," he said, "but my faith is Greek."⁵ Both projects emerged from the Josephite movement of the previous century. When Nikon was at the Novospassky Monastery in Moscow, he became acquainted with monks who were carrying on Philaret's liturgical reforms. They were known as the "zealots of piety." The most important and powerful of these was Avvakum Petrovitch, a monk of equal mettle to Nikon. The chaos of the "time of troubles" led many to believe that once again, God was punishing the Russians for the laxity of their religious devotion. Avvakum was one of the many monks who took it upon themselves to put things right.

Avvakum and the other zealots worked hard to make sure that fasts were kept, that the bells were rung at the proper times, that singing in church should be done with fervor, and that the priests preached with a passion and commitment just short of fanaticism. As had Joseph of Volokolamsk, they wanted to justify the idea of Holy Russia, and visitors to Moscow at this time were impressed, not always favorably, with the results. Masses often went on for hours; a stern earnestness was the order of the day. "No mirth, laughter, or jokes" were allowed, and transgressions were severely punished.[6] Music outside of church was prohibited. As Savonarola had done in the fifteenth century, musical instruments often went up in flames in a bonfire of the vanities.

For Nikon, however, Avvakum and his fellow "zealots of piety" were moving too slowly. This impatient Right Man wasn't happy with the incremental changes these so-called zealots were introducing. Error, sloppiness, indolence—a familiar Russian trait—were still rife. Drunkenness, among both shepherd and flock, was common. Other moral faults were only too apparent. The zealots had made some progress, but much more remained to be done, and Nikon couldn't wait. His attempt to make the Russian church Greek overnight led to what is known as the Raskol, or Great Schism, that split Russia and left a fracture in it that has never quite been repaired. That Dostoyevsky would later name the hero of *Crime and Punishment* Raskolnikov is not without meaning.

Nikon's faith may have been Greek, but for other Russians it was Russian. Moscow was the Third Rome, and although many had respect for lost Byzantium, the cozying up to Rome that it had sunk to in fear of the Turk was something that many Muscovites could not forgive or forget. They had kept the tradition. Its mantle had been handed down to them. They had kept the memory of it eternal, and saw no reason to slavishly copy what the Greeks under the Turk did now. So they refused.

Those who refused to accept Nikon's reforms were known as the Old Believers.* Yet it was not so much belief that was at stake here; old

---

*One of the reasons Old Believers rejected Nikon was that he used Greek scholars from Kiev, then under the control of the Poles and Lithuanians. Many of these were priests in the Uniate Church, a combination of Orthodoxy and Catholicism that emerged from the Council of Brest (1596). The Uniate Church was loyal to Rome, however, and was seen by many Russians as a way of drawing believers to the West. This new form of *dvoeverie*—"dual belief"—triggered the reforming response of Philaret and his followers.

believers and new believed pretty much the same things. But the outward signs, the rituals that expressed that belief, they were important.[7] Russians, we remember, put great value on the embodiment of the spirit, its actual presence in the physical, fleshy world. The central symbol here is the number of fingers used in making the sign of the cross. Nikon insisted that worshipers now use three fingers to do so, as the Greeks did, instead of two, as was traditional. The Old Believers insisted on using two and were insistent enough about this to burn themselves to death on occasion in self-inflicted Inquisition-style autos da fé,[8] rather than conform to the change.*

Avvakum, their leader, suffered greatly. He declared that Nikon was the Antichrist, or at least was in league with him, as was Alexis. (He once told the tsar that he was Russian and should speak Russian, not Greek.[9]) He was branded a heretic and endured twenty-two years in prison, twelve of these in an underground cell, before he was burned at the stake in 1682, a martyr for the cause. The autobiography he wrote during his years of imprisonment is considered one of the classics of Russian literature.

The Old Believers fled the cities and Nikon's pogroms, heading to the far north. Eventually they themselves split into two groups: those, like the Protestants in Europe, who wanted to establish their own church, and those who preferred a less hierarchical, more independent style of worship.[10] As Nil Sorsky's way of worship had to do, these radical Old Believers went underground—as the city of Kitezh did at the approach of the Tartars—and fragmented into different sects, who were hunted and persecuted.

IN 1657 TSAR Alexis gave Nikon sovereign power, while he went off to fight the Poles. Nikon used it and continued to garner more and more secular power. He began to remove icons from people's homes, declaring

---

*Vasily Surikov's painting *Boyaryna Morozova* (1881–1887), in the Tretyakov Gallery in Moscow, depicts an Old Believer being hauled off to prison, while a holy fool blesses her in the ancient, traditional way.

the figures were painted incorrectly. Some he publicly ridiculed, vandal-
izing them in the streets, acting like an iconoclast of old.[11] He insisted on
the parishioners singing three hallelujahs instead of two. Processions that
moved clockwise now must be reversed. Churches would be built according to Byzantine models; onion domes and tent roofs were out. Those
who resisted these changes were hauled off to prison; some were executed.

It may seem that, as has happened frequently enough in the West,
blood was spilled and lives were lost over fundamentally trivial matters. Yet, as Berdyaev says, it is a mistake to suppose that the schism
arose simply out of the differences between using two fingers or three
or other such surface phenomena. For him it was of much "greater significance for the whole of Russian history" than is usually assumed.
It was the start of a "deep-seated" division that was to last until his,
Berdyaev's, own time and in many ways still persists today. It was the
clash between what Berdyaev sees as the taste for an authoritarian worship, the "reverence for rites and ceremonies," coming into conflict with
the Russian's inherent "quest for divine truth," which led to pilgrimages
and the apocalyptic perspective.[12]

What was at issue here was sacred history. If the Russian people
had been entrusted with the true faith and the responsibility of preserving its forms of worship—much, say, as the Jews were—then any
changes made to these forms by man, signaled, it seemed, the end-
times, because the forms were to be preserved until the last days arrived.
To the Old Believers, the heretics, it seemed they had. With Nikon's
reforms, Muscovy was no longer the Third Rome; indeed, according
to Avvakum, it had gone over to the other side. And as Philotheus the
monk had pointed out, once the Third Rome was gone, there would
not be another. The reign of the Antichrist had begun.

To THESE ESCHATOLOGICAL concerns Nikon's increasing megalomania
seemed to give unmistakable form. He had by this time adopted the
title "Great Lord," one reserved for the tsar alone. Obeisance to him

should be made accordingly. As Philaret had before him, he had become the de facto ruler of Russia. But where Philaret was much more of an éminence grise, sharing power with his son, or at least keeping up the appearance of doing do, Nikon lacked any such tact. His program of subordinating increasing amounts of secular authority under that of the church was overt. It was a brazen flaunting of power. And it was this that eventually brought him down.

By 1658 Alexis realized that Nikon had gotten out of hand and had to be stopped. He had become a kind of tyrant, or at least an Orthodox pope, claiming infallibility.[13] His insistence on the superiority of spiritual power over temporal had to be opposed. Alexis used Nikon's own enormous self-regard against him. When Nikon was publically insulted, Alexis refused to punish the culprit, and he failed to appear at two of Nikon's services, something he had never missed before. These were clear signs that the patriarch had fallen out of the tsar's favor. It was just short of an outright rebuke, and Nikon could not let it pass.

In a dramatic power play, Nikon publicly stripped himself of his patriarchal vestments—as Philip, whose relics he had gathered, had been forcibly stripped—and left Moscow for the New Jerusalem Monastery, which he had founded. He did not, however, resign as patriarch, and for the next eight years left things in limbo, neither resigning from the position nor fulfilling its responsibilities. Nikon counted on the tsar's lack of resolution and assumed he would call him back. But Alexis had by this time acquired some backbone and stood his ground. Eventually, in 1666—note the date—a council was convened that stripped Nikon of his power and sent him into exile. He died in 1681. Yet while the council rejected Nikon himself, it accepted his reforms. Small wonder that for the Old Believers 1666 marked the beginning of the reign of the Antichrist in Russia.

SUBSEQUENT EVENTS MOST likely confirmed this belief. One was the revolt led by the Cossack Stenka Razin that lasted from 1667 to 1671.

Serfs escaping from the new laws fixing them to the land, found themselves in the south, with little there to support them and no chance
of getting any land of their own. Razin formed a band of these disaffected outcasts and began to raid towns along the Volga, rather like
a seventeenth-century Spartacus.* (Philaret's concern about absconding
serfs, mentioned earlier, proved warranted.) His success prompted further raids, during which his peasant and Cossack revolt grew. Increasing
in number, his army indulged in orgies of violence, rapine, and plunder,
aimed at the nobility and the new bureaucracy that had risen up under
Alexis's rule. The atrocities they carried out were considered excessive,
even for the time.

At one point Razin's rebel army had swelled to some 20,000 men,
and he had succeeded in capturing Astrakhan and Saratov. It was then
that Alexis sent a force to stop the revolt. Alexis had instituted reforms
in the military, and his well-trained troops easily defeated Razin's rag-
tag rebellion. In April 1671 Stenka Razin was captured and brought to
Moscow. There in June, in Red Square, he was tortured and quartered.
His dismembered limbs and head were then impaled on five stakes, a
warning to all.

But rebellion, it seems, was in the air, as it always seemed to be, and
a new "time of troubles" was felt to be on its way. When Alexis died in
1676 he was succeeded by his son Feodor III, who seems a refreshing
change from most of the tsars. He was well educated, intelligent, and of
a reforming disposition. A liberal, he softened many of the harsher penalties for lawbreaking, promoted learning, and had an openness to the
West, a direction in which other heads were also turning. Feodor, however, suffered from an illness that disfigured him—possibly scurvy—
and in 1682 he died at the age of twenty, having produced no heir.†

This presented a problem. Ivan V, Alexis's son from his first marriage,

---

*The Thracian gladiator who led a band of ex-slaves against the Romans in the century
before Christ. He was eventually captured and crucified.
†His first wife died in childbirth, her son with Feodor soon after. Feodor died three
months after his marriage to his second wife.

was mentally and physically handicapped. Peter, his son by his second wife, was only eight years old. However, he was healthy and intelligent. The church and the Naryshkins, Peter's mother's family, pressed for him to take the throne; the nobles agreed, and he was even declared tsar.[14] The Miloslavskys, Ivan's family, however, did not agree with this. Rumors started, most likely by Ivan's family, that both Feodor and Ivan had been killed by the Naryshkins. These rumors triggered an uprising in Moscow, led by the *streltsy*, the troops that carried firearms and formed a social class of their own. They already had a grievance against some of the reforms that had been imposed on the military. They stormed the Kremlin and killed many boyars. The people took to the streets and looting was rife. Then the streltsy stormed the royal residence and killed many of Peter's supporters, including two of his uncles, before his eyes.

The mayhem only stopped when Ivan V was shown to the crowds, alive and well. After this, he and his half brother Peter jointly ruled, with Sophia, Ivan's sister and Peter's half sister acting as regent. This, however, did not stop the machinations of Prince Ivan Khovansky, who had instigated the uprising and wanted to usurp power from the Romanovs, who were leaning too much to the West. Khovansky sided with the Old Believers and wanted Nikon's reforms repealed. Eventually he and leaders of the Old Believers were executed.*

When Ivan died in 1696, he had left behind daughters but no son. For many this was a relief; at least there would be no struggle for succession. Thus the way was made clear for the man who would make enormous efforts to drag Muscovy into the increasingly modern world. One such effort was to move the capital out of Moscow itself, something that would mark the end of the Muscovite empire.

PETER, LATER KNOWN as "the Great," arrived on the throne after being kept in the background and out of Moscow throughout most

---

*Mussorgsky based his unfinished opera *Khovanshchina* (1881) on this incident.

of his half sister Sophia's regency. But when in 1689 a second *streltsy* rebellion broke out, to which the Miloslavskys were party, he had an opportunity to nullify that family's influence and get Sophia out of the way. Peter crushed the rebellion brutally; he executed many of the *streltsy*—he would eventually disband them—and sent Sophia to a convent. When Ivan died there was no longer any opposition to Peter's rule. And unlike many of the Romanov clan, Peter was eager to take up the responsibility and had the intelligence and talent to do so. Whatever one may think of his attempt to force Russia into the modern age—and many still consider it an enormous mistake—his tremendous efforts warrant his nickname.

Peter, like Joseph of Volokolamsk and Nikon, was a "can-do" character. But his drive, determination, and efficiency exceeded even theirs and was not tainted with so many of their Right Man traits. He was authoritarian, to be sure, an autocrat who brooked no nonsense. He was known to beat courtiers who annoyed him—not difficult to do—and he even had his own son tortured and executed when he opposed him.* But his violence was motivated more by an urgent need to "get things done" than by any affront to his ego. The inertia facing him was enormous. Peter saw that his country was backward; it was still living in the Middle Ages. Most Russians saw the world in exactly the same way as people in the time of Vladimir I saw it. They were unaware of the great developments taking place in Europe, the achievements of Copernicus, Kepler, Galileo, and Newton. Their discoveries had altered men's vision of the universe. In order to survive, Russia had to leave the Dark Ages. If Peter had his way, it would not remain in them much longer.

---

*Alexis, Peter's son by his first wife Eudoxia—whom he had sent to a convent—grew up hating his father. He embraced reactionary causes and refused to be groomed to inherit the throne. When ordered to submit or enter a monastery, he fled to Austria. Later, forced to return to Russia, he was arrested. Accused of plotting to overthrow his father, he was tortured and confessed. He is thought to have died in prison from injuries suffered while undergoing interrogation, but there is some suspicion that he may have been strangled.

Peter's childhood outside the hothouse environment of the Muscovite court led to an openness and a curiosity that left him free of the paralyzing constraints of etiquette and manners. He grew up in a milieu in which Western Enlightenment ideas were openly discussed and appreciated, the furthest thing from the Byzantine religious hysteria of the capital.[15] He came into contact with Dutch engineers who lived in a German suburb of Moscow. From them he learned about shipbuilding and shipping. His favorite pastime as a boy was playing soldier. He loved anything to do with forts, sailing, and navigation, and enjoyed mathematics. He did not stand on ceremony. While tsar he was known to enjoy drinking beer with sailors and dock men, people from whom he could *learn* something. (He was also known to enjoy drinking, period.) That was his central motivation: knowledge and its practical application, the essence of Western consciousness. We can see him as a kind of anti-Oblomov, rather like the pragmatic-minded "modern" heroes of many of Bernard Shaw's plays: unsentimental, efficient, driven, and eager for concrete results.* In Russia, we know, that is often difficult. Peter's mission to modernize his country forcibly widened the split in the Russian psyche that had been opened by Nikon's reforms.

One of the first things Peter wanted to get done was to provide Russia with a seaport. He had inherited an empire that covered an enormous territory—the colossal land mass stretching into Siberia later Eurasianists would call "the heartland"—but it had no entry to the seas, except at Archangel on the White Sea, which was frozen in winter and difficult to reach. The necessity of such access and a modern navy to make use of it was clear to Peter. It was this that had made the European nations powerful. The need for a seaport drove Peter into war in the south, where he had success in capturing the Turkish fort of Azov on the river Don, and into what was known as the Great Northern War, that lasted from 1700 to 1721, and that involved Russia, Lithuania, and Denmark-Norway against Sweden.[16]

---

*For example, John Tanner in *Man and Superman*.

At the end of this long war, Sweden was reduced to a second-class power,* and Russia established itself as the new dominant force in the region. And it was on land captured from the Swedes that Peter would make his greatest mark on the world.

Peter's success stemmed in great part from what he learned during his journey to the West, the "Grand Embassy" he embarked on in 1697–98. In doing so he became the first Russian ruler to visit western Europe.[17] Traveling in disguise, he spent a year in Holland and England, where he studied shipbuilding. He visited factories, arsenals, schools, libraries, museums, and learned as many hands-on crafts as he could. He was the kind of person who was happy to roll up his sleeves and join in the work, if it would help get it done quicker and more efficiently. In fact, he would positively relish doing it. He was physically strong and, like Nikon, exceptionally tall—his height often made his disguise ineffective—and did not mind getting his hands dirty. It was this conscientiousness and demand for good work that he brought back to Russia and imposed on his people, most of whom were reluctant to accept it.

Something else Peter is supposed to have encountered during his journey to the West is Freemasonry, which he is said to have introduced to Russia. Many historians say the story is a myth, but there is a persistent idea that he joined a Masonic lodge during his stay in England.[18] Some accounts have him being initiated by the architect Sir Christopher Wren, although Wren's Masonic membership itself is as debatable as Peter's.[19] Critics point out that the Grand Lodge in Britain hadn't yet been formed in 1698; it wasn't founded until 1717, well after Peter's visit. But others suggest it was highly possible that he met Masons while

---

*Oddly enough—or perhaps not—one of the participants in the war, strictly in an engineering capacity, was the Swedish scientist and religious thinker Emanuel Swedenborg. In 1718 Swedenborg was given the task of moving King Charles XII's navy fifteen miles across land in order for it to engage in the Siege of Fredrickshall. Swedenborg was opposed to war; he believed it was ruining Sweden. But he was a loyal subject and managed the job. His opposition to the war proved correct. Charles XII himself was killed by a stray bullet during it, and Sweden lost the war.

in London. Peter, they say, may have joined a lodge of admitted Masons that existed before the Grand Lodge was founded; according to one historian, these were "flourishing in the years after the Revolution of 1688."[20] If so, we shouldn't be surprised. Freemasonry emerged out of the guilds of cathedral builders of the Middle Ages. The engineering skill needed to make stones "upright" and "four square"—and its transfer to the human medium—would have appealed to Peter, as would the Enlightenment values Freemasonry professed.

When Peter returned to Russia, he is said to have instructed his minister, François Lefort, to initiate a Masonic lodge in St. Petersburg, which Peter was about to build.[21] If true, Masonic values would fit in well with Peter's aim of injecting Western Enlightenment ideas into the long-suffering inert mass of the Russian people and of diminishing the hold that the church had upon them. People in Peter's circle, such as the scientist Count James Bruce and the Scottish mercenary Patrick Gordon, had interests that traveled well with Freemasonry.[22] They, too, were supposedly involved in establishing lodges in Russia.[23]

Bruce, Russia's first astronomer, was of Scottish descent and had links to the Jacobite conspiracy. He was a naturalist who practiced alchemy, and he was known in Moscow as a magician. His observatory, the first in Russia, was in the Sukharev Tower in Moscow, which Peter had built to commemorate his victory over the Miloslavskys. Here meetings of a mysterious "Neptune Society," to which Peter belonged, and over which Bruce presided, were held.[24] Legend has it that among Bruce's library—which later became the basis for the Russian Academy of Science—was a book of spells, a "black grimoire" that Peter wished to read but which Bruce refused to give him. He is said to have bricked the book up in the walls of the tower. Catherine the Great is said to have searched for it as did the Soviets, supposedly, when they demolished the tower in 1935. Whatever the truth of this, Freemasonry would become an issue under Catherine, and later Freemasons would claim Peter as their founder when petitioning the government not to ban their activities.

PETER MADE MANY changes in practically all areas of Russian life in order to wrench the country out of the past and into the modern world. In many ways he echoed in a secular way the spiritual micromanagement we've seen with Joseph of Volokolamsk. Appearances were important. He demanded that men shave their beards; boyars who refused had to pay a hefty tax to keep their facial hair. (One sign of the Old Believers was a refusal to shave.) He also insisted on a Western dress code. The long kaftan coat—a Tartar word—worn for centuries was banned, and shorter, European styles were in. Men who refused to change had their kaftans summarily cut on the spot—and also often their beards. Peter's own choice of dress was what we would call "casual." He rejected the Byzantine pomp of his predecessors and opted for much simpler attire; often he dressed as a workman. With him the tsar was no longer a religious figure to be worshiped, but a head of state to be obeyed; the kind of spectacle designed to produce a sense of awe was irrelevant.

Peter also changed the requirements for becoming a monk. Men under thirty were not allowed to enter the monasteries and would instead be put to work; it was a waste of manpower having them sitting in cells; later the age was raised to forty. And at a stroke in 1721—the same year he was crowned emperor in celebration of victory in the Great Northern War—Peter emasculated the church as a political power by abolishing the position of patriarch in Moscow and replacing it with a council known as the Holy Synod. This was made up of priests Peter had under his control and who would rubber-stamp his decisions. Any ideas of a symphony of power performed by the tsar and the patriarch were now long gone. Peter was religious, as were other tsars, but he had no faith in the church hierarchy and would grant it no possibility of obstructing his rule.

PROBABLY THE GREATEST change effected by Peter, which raised questions of Russian identity, was the creation of St. Petersburg, a city that was made both of stone and of dreams. In fact, at the time of its construction, 1703, it was the only place in Russia where a building could be made of stone. All other stone constructions were banned while it was being built, and any stone available for building had to be sent to the site, something that smacks of the pharaohs and the pyramids. As for dreams, like London and Paris, St. Petersburg is a city that has created an imagination all its own; there is the London of Dickens and the Paris of Balzac, and there is the St. Petersburg of Gogol and Dostoyevsky, of Andre Bely and the poets of the Silver Age. As Gogol writes in his prose poem "Nevsky Prospect"—St. Petersburg's grand boulevard—"All is deception, all is a dream, all is not what it seems," a perception Bely would echo in his Anthroposophically informed novel *Petersburg*.[25] Yet for a city that would become a hallucinatory symbol of the quest for Russian identity—was it European, Russian, or some blend of both?—it started out much more like a geometric grid than any sort of poet's dream.

Peter decided to build what he christened Sankt Pieter Burkh on marshlands near Lake Ladoga that he had won from the Swedes. The name was Dutch as was the design; it was modeled on Amsterdam, a city made up of interlocking canals and broad boulevards and which was built on commerce, not religion. No permanent settlement had been raised on the site before, and for good reason. As W. Bruce Lincoln writes in *Sunlight at Midnight: St. Petersburg and the Rise of Modern Russia*, "climate, comfort, and convenience" were not on Peter's mind in choosing the spot.[26] It was not far from the Arctic Circle—a mere five hundred miles, nearby for Russia, and the reason for its famous "white nights"—and was subject to floods. But its nearness to the Neva River, which emptied into the Gulf of Finland, made it the seaport Peter wanted. So, as Alexander and Constantine had done before him, Peter raised a city out of nothing.

It did not grow organically as had Moscow, but was impressed upon the soggy, formless soil by imperial order and laid out with a ruler. It was not named after Peter, but his saint, as was the Saint Peter and Paul fortress, the first structure he laid down, but it had his mark all over it. Made of straight lines and efficiency, and based on the principle of *regulyarnaya*—being "regular" and "regulated"—St. Petersburg rose out of the marsh, a monument to reason and rational order, an archetypal modern city made by fiat and at the price of much human suffering— again, we think of the pyramids.[27] It marked the power of the human mind to control irrational nature. Kiev had its day, as had Moscow. Now it was the age of the third city of Russia.

Peter, however, like Alexander, would not see much of his city. The Great Northern War took up most of his time. Peter was as hands on a militarist as he was a mechanic; he often led his armies into battle. He died before much of anything that survives from his day was built; the grand palaces and aristocratic splendor that made St. Petersburg a rival to Paris would not arise until the reign of his successors, Anna, Elizabeth, and Catherine, each of whom brought a "woman's touch" to the austere orderliness of Peter's Western window. He did not, however, die in battle. He is said to have died from a urinary and bladder ailment that was exacerbated by an act of heroism. Inspecting iron works along the Finnish Gulf, Peter is said to have seen some sailors in distress and to have jumped in the freezing water to save them. Not long after, the uremia he is thought to have suffered from turned worse. On the morning of February 8, 1725, he died. He was fifty-two. The titanic efforts he had made to pull his country out of its doldrums, his predilection for work, and his distaste of rest had taken their toll. But there was no going back. The window on the West was open and the modern world was coming through.

THE NEXT RULER of Russia who would invite the West across her threshold in the way that Peter did shared with him a nickname. But to reach Catherine the Great (1729–1796) we must wade through the usual catastrophes that make up Russian history.

When Peter died, power went to his second wife, a Baltic peasant woman named Yekaterina Alekseyevna, who became Peter's lover and whom he later married. On becoming empress consort, she took the name Catherine I. Catherine had no interest in ruling and ceded power to a council. When she died in 1727, power went to Peter's grandson, Peter II, who was crowned tsar at the age of eleven. He came first under the sway of the Menshikov family, but they were soon eclipsed by the Dolgorukys, one of whose future distant relatives would be Madame Blavatsky.[28] The Dolgorukys tried to set the clock back by moving the capital back to Moscow. But their influence ended in 1730, when Peter II died of smallpox on the day he was supposed to marry into the family.

Power then went to Peter's niece, Anna Ivanova, or "Bloody Anna," as she is often called because of the "spiderlike quality" of her cruelty.[29] She was regent of the Duchy of Courland, in the Baltic countries. Her husband, Fredrik William, the Duke of Courland, had died on their wedding journey to her new home, and she had decided to stay on. When Peter II died, the council ruling in Moscow asked her to take the throne. She accepted. Immediately upon arrival Anna instituted an autocracy the central aim of which was her own entertainment. Anna had little interest in ruling and left state affairs to one of her lovers, the German Ernst Johann Biron, and his advisers. Most of her reign was taken up with wars with Poland and Turkey and with the lavish parties and crude entertainments Anna was partial to. On one occasion, after forcing a noble prince to become her court jester, she compelled him to marry an unattractive Kalmyk woman. In the dead of winter she insisted they spend their wedding night making love in an "ice palace" she had made for them, complete with chairs, windows, beds, and even a fireplace and firewood made of ice.

Anna had named Ivan, the newborn son of her niece Anna Pepoldovna, as heir. She died in 1740. But before the infant tsar knew it, he had been overthrown by Elizabeth, the daughter of Peter and Catherine I. With the support of the people and the army Elizabeth instigated a coup, arresting the two-month-old Ivan and his parents and putting them in prison. Ivan VI never left his jail. In 1764 at the age of twenty-four, during Catherine the Great's reign, he was murdered by his keepers during a bungled attempt at freeing him.

Anna had begun the beautification campaign that would turn St. Petersburg into one of the most spectacular capitals of the world, inviting the Italian architect Bartolomeo Rastrelli to build Tsarskoe Selo, the imperial residence just south of the city. But it was Elizabeth, who also had a love of splendor and finery, who "gave free reign to Rastrelli" to make St. Petersburg the baroque extravaganza that still thrills visitors today.[30] Now, however, it was the court and palace rather than the cathedral and monastery that motivated the embodiment of beauty. The transcendental beauty of the icon was obscured by the humanistic, even pagan beauty of classical mythology.[31] If the icon was a window on another world, so were the paintings that now began to take their place, at least among the aristocracy. But the other world they opened to was just across the border.

Like her father, Elizabeth had a love of the West and wanted to inject its values into her country. She established Russia's first university—in Moscow—and in St. Petersburg founded the Academy of Arts (in 1755 and 1757, respectively). Probably the most well known of her projects was the final version of the Winter Palace, which Rastrelli brought to glorious perfection during her reign. Unfortunately Elizabeth died before she could enjoy Rastrelli's masterwork, suffering a stroke on Christmas Eve 1761 and dying on Christmas Day.

Elizabeth was succeeded by Peter III, her nephew, who was something of an eccentric, even for a Russian nobleman. He was feeble-minded and neurotic, an argumentative, bullying individual of German descent, insanely obsessed with Prussia.* (He was also possibly alcoholic and impotent.) He could barely speak Russian and was a fanatical admirer of Frederick the Great, the "enlightened" German ruler. So great was his admiration that in 1762, almost immediately upon

---

*I should point out that some contemporary historians question this received view of Peter III and recognize a progressive direction in some of his policies.

accepting the throne, Peter III withdrew Russia from the Seven Years' War and formed an alliance with Prussia (Russia had been fighting against Prussia until then).[32] He had married Sophie Friederike Auguste von Anhalt-Zerbst, the daughter of a minor prince, in 1745, when she was fourteen. Sophie, who took the name Catherine, quickly discovered what being married to Peter was like. In 1762, soon into her husband's reign as tsar, she decided to do something about it.

Peter III's exorbitant pro-Prussia sentiments had alienated him from the populace, the military, and practically everyone else. He had been alienated from Catherine for some time, and she believed that he had plans to remove her. She decided to beat him to the punch. With one of her lovers, Grigory Orlov, a military officer, she planned a coup that would relieve her of her husband and free Russia of its pro-German ruler. In July 1762, with the help of the guard, the council, the church, and the educated "enlightened" figures among the aristocracy, Catherine was crowned Catherine II, empress of Russia. Peter III was quickly arrested and soon after murdered, most likely by Orlov.

Catherine was an intelligent, inquisitive, and talented woman; like Peter the Great she had a hunger for knowledge and respected learning. She held liberal, Western views and was known to her circle as a progressive character. While married to Peter III she spent most of her time reading—Rousseau and Montesquieu were favorites—and envisioning how things would be when she became empress. She was ambitious, patient, and cautious, and slowly put a plan together that would secure for her the throne. She also had several lovers, one of whom, Sergei Saltykov, is a likely candidate for being the father of her son Paul, who would inherit it. This has led more than one historian to remark that the tsars to follow may have been Romanov in name only.

Like Peter the Great, Catherine had a great passion for Western ideas. She was a friend of Voltaire and Diderot, corresponded with many of the philosophes of the time, and wanted to create a court that would rival Versailles. But when she tried to manifest her enlightened outlook in the form of state policy, she discovered that it was easier to do this in theory than in practice. The kind of liberal reforms her enlightened mentors inspired were difficult enough to enact in Europe. In a Russia that was barely pulling itself out of the Middle Ages—if at all—she saw they would be well nigh impossible.

A document she drafted, known as the Instruction of Catherine the Great, offered her court a general admonition to use liberal, humanitarian ideals as a guide when drafting laws and making reforms. This was presented to a special commission she had convened in 1767 in order to discover the true wishes of the people. The commission, made up of representatives from different walks of Russian life—except, predictably, the serfs—met and debated for months and got nowhere, getting bogged down in a typical Russian muddle. Catherine's Instruction led to nothing. It was considered too liberal even to be published and was quietly ignored.

In the end precisely the opposite of her intentions happened. Originally Catherine had planned to emancipate the serfs. She soon saw, however, that the landowners would rebel at this and that the country would be thrown into chaos. In order to secure the landowners' support, Catherine actually strengthened their hold on the serfs. According to some estimates, by the end of her reign, virtually all of the serfs in Russian were for all intents and purposes slaves. Thus the scene was set for the eruptions of the following century.

THAT THE RUSSIAN people were not yet ready for the freedoms she herself believed in most likely came home to Catherine through the Pugachev rebellion, a peasant and Cossack uprising along the Volga steppes that spread havoc in 1773–74. Yemelyan Pugachev was an army deserter who, escaping exile to Siberia, appeared in the steppes, claiming to be Peter III, Catherine's obstreperous dead husband. He gathered a large following among disaffected farmworkers and miners and declared that serfdom was abolished. His peasant army then stormed the city of Orenburg, near the Ural River, the first act in his plan of taking the throne. Thoughts of Stenka Razin of a century ago must have risen up in Catherine's mind. Pugachev burned Kazan, laid siege to Tsaritsyn, and captured Saratov before he was finally defeated by Catherine's army.* Pugachev was captured and put in a metal cage and placed on display before his public execution in Moscow. On January 21, 1775, he was beheaded, drawn, and quartered—much as Stenka Razin had been—in Bolotnaya Square. After this, Catherine no longer harbored any ideas about giving power to the people.

Another Western influence Catherine changed her mind about was Freemasonry. If it had not been brought to Russia by Peter the Great, by Catherine's reign it had certainly established itself. While Peter the Great's involvement remains debatable, most historians mark the start of Russian Freemasonry with its introduction to the country by officers in the foreign service who had encountered it abroad and brought it home with them. Its official introduction is credited to Captain John Philips of the Grand Lodge of England in 1731.[33] Membership spread in 1740 with the arrival of the flamboyant general James Keith as provincial grand master.[34]

Yet Freemasonry as a serious spiritual and ethical pursuit—and not an aristocratic old boys club—did not take root in Russia until the early years of Catherine's reign. Until then it was considered more of a sign of social status than anything else; at that time "the best Russian people," we are told, "were masons."[35] But by the 1770s attitudes toward Freemasonry had changed, both in Europe and in Russia.[36] The man most responsible for this shift in Russia was Nikolay Novikov, who is often referred to as Russia's first journalist.[37] He was a philanthropist, educationalist, and publisher and one of the leading figures in Russia's "enlightenment."

With the diminishing of the church's power and authority in the eighteenth century, Freemasonry became "the one and only spiritual movement" in Russia, at least according to Berdyaev.[38] Among

---

*Pushkin wrote a novel about him, *A Captain's Daughter.*

the masses of people religion still remained dominant, but among the growing ranks of the "enlightened" aristocracy, Freemasonry began to fill the need for an enlightened spirituality, for noble ideas and moral guidance, something the church no longer provided. And, as Berdyaev says, these early Masonic lodges were the first freely organized societies in Russia, imposed neither by the state nor the church. The unifying power here was not law or dogma but the attraction of ideas and the need for a higher vision of life. Such freedom and curiosity were something new in Russia, and the authorities soon became anxious about it. As authorities often do, they believed that left unchecked, it could soon become dangerous.

Nikolay Novikov was a product of Empress Elizabeth's passion for education. He was born in 1744 in Bronnitsky, a town near Moscow. He attended Moscow University, which was founded by the great Russian scientist Mikhail Lomonsov in 1755 under Elizabeth's direction. In 1767 Novikov had a government position, and he attended the commission Catherine had convened in hopes of reforming Russia's law along enlightened lines. Fired with the progressive ideas he had found in Catherine's Instruction, he withdrew from government and went into publishing, becoming editor of the *Moscow Gazette* and starting several satirical journals of his own, the most influential of which was *The Drone*. Novikov commented on the profoundly backward position of Russia, taking critical shots at Catherine's failure to enact any reforms, the frippery of her court, and her imitation of French ways.[39] In the beginning his cleverness, insight, and passion prompted a friendly riposte from the empress, who enjoyed a good debate. She even started her own journal in order to match wits with him. Soon, however, her response would be less good-natured.

In 1775 Novikov joined a Masonic lodge. One of the most important lodges in Russia at this time was known as the Rite of Strict Observance; it was founded in Germany in the 1750s by Baron Karl Gottlieb von Hund, and it was of a more esoteric character than the sedate brand of Freemasonry coming from England.[40] "Strict

Observance" got its name because the rite required a pledge of absolute obedience to those who were known as the "unknown superiors." These mysterious figures were high-ranking masters of a Masonic tradition that went back, Hund had claimed, to the Knights Templar of the Crusades. "Strict Observance" grew to develop higher, more esoteric degrees that involved the study of alchemy, magic, Kabbalah, and the Hermetic sciences. It attracted many among the nobility who were weary of the frivolity, superficiality, and immorality of the court and its French witticisms and sought some source of moral guidance. One of these nobles, Prince Pavel Vasilyevicth Dolgoruky, stands out. This is because he would become the great-grandfather of Helena Petrovna von Hahn, better known as Madame Blavatsky. It was discovering her great-grandfather Pavel's library at the age of fifteen, "containing hundreds of books on alchemy, magic and other occult sciences," that, Blavatsky tells us, started her on her journey in search of esoteric wisdom.[41]

Blavatsky's great-grandfather had been a military commander under Catherine the Great, and he was initiated into a Strict Observance lodge sometime in the 1770s, around the same time that Novikov was initiated. There is reason to believe that Prince Pavel joined Novikov's Lodge Latone in Moscow, and he may also have been involved in a more secret group, the Harmonia Lodge, that Novikov formed in 1781 with Ivan Schwarz, a philosophy professor at Moscow University, and that moved toward a Rosicrucian-style Freemasonry. This was a time when secret societies flourished, when semi-legendary figures such as Cagliostro and the Comte de Saint-Germain—both of whom Prince Pavel may have met—dashed across the Continent conferring initiations, and when groups like Adam Weishaupt's Bavarian Illuminati drew many from the Masonic fold into its political designs.[42] Strict Observance Masonry itself emerged from the radical subversive Masonic lodges involved in the failed Jacobite movement.[43] Blavatsky hints that her great-grandfather himself was party to some political machinations involving "the thorough metamorphosis of nearly the whole of the European map," in which Freemasonry would play an important part, and which presaged the French Revolution.[44] It was precisely these political implications of Freemasonry that would turn Catherine against it.

Novikov himself was more interested in reform than in revolution. He saw himself as an educator, spreading the Enlightenment ideas that the empress knew were true, but which she refused to turn into state policy. He did this through his newspapers and journals and also through the magazines he created for women and for children.* As Berdyaev says, the mystical side of Freemasonry interested Novikov less than its moral and social side, although other important Masonic advocates, such as Schwarz, Ivan Lopukhin, Semyon Gamaleya, and especially Alexander Fyodorovich Labzin, pursued its esoteric depths. The progressive, humanist side of Freemasonry appealed to Novikov, and it was within this milieu that the seeds of the intelligentsia of the next century would be planted.

One of the products of Novikov's activism was the *Journey from St. Petersburg to Moscow* by the critic Alexander Radishchev, which was published in 1790, but which was quickly withdrawn after Catherine read it; it was not published again until 1905. Radishchev was inspired by Novikov's writings, and his imaginary journey depicted a very real Russia that was suffering enormous social, economic, and political problems that Catherine refused to do anything about and that she in many ways exacerbated. She had the book confiscated and Radishchev arrested.[45] He was initially sentenced to death but this was changed to exile in Siberia. Some years later he committed suicide, broken by the failure of any reforms in Russia.

The atheism of the philosophes troubled Novikov, and in Freemasonry he found a spiritual belief that provided support against Enlightenment rationalism without the weight of dogma and tradition. For Novikov there should be no dissonance between religion

---

*In some ways Novikov resembles the Czech John Comenius, one of the Bohemian intellectuals who responded to the original Rosicrucian call for "universal reform" in the early seventeenth century, and who is known in central Europe as the "father of universal education."

and science, as they were two aspects of the same truth. This was an idea that inspired the original Rosicrucian movement of the early sixteenth century, out of the remnants of which many believe Freemasonry arose; it was also the central idea of Madame Blavatsky's Theosophical Society.[46] The church had lost its credibility as a source of true spirituality, and Freemasonry arose to fill the gap among the educated classes, much as the many heretical sects—which we will look at further on—did among the uneducated masses.

Unlike the philosophes, Novikov had no argument against religion; the Metropolitan Platon told Catherine that he prayed that "all over the world there may be Christians of the same sort as Novikov."[47] Novikov took pains to ensure that his Masonic beliefs in no way contradicted his Christian ones. It was through reading the "signatures" and "correspondences" between the natural and spiritual worlds, as Jacob Boehme and Emanuel Swedenborg, whose ideas informed Russian Freemasonry, had taught, that we can see the inner light that Nil Sorsky and the Hesychasts had earlier seen. In a sense, for Novikov, Freemasonry replaced Christianity as the focus of the Russian "quest for the divine truth" that Berdyaev saw as part of the Russian soul. Others saw this in it as well. That Novikov's activities were centered in Moscow and were directed against the values emanating from St. Petersburg, suggest geographic locations for the tensions polarizing the Russian soul, its desire to reach out to the world beyond its borders, and its need to feel connected to a world beyond this one. By the next century, this need for something "beyond" would become acute.

Yet the attitude toward Freemasonry was changing. The exposure of Adam Weishaupt's ambitious but never really threatening plan to overthrow the monarchies of Europe and establish a reign of reason and light through the working of the Illuminati led to a general attitude of suspicion toward all such societies, politically motivated or not.[48] When in 1784 the Bavarian government outlawed the Illuminati and all other "secret societies," a shadow fell across the activities of all Masonic groups in Europe. And when a few years later, in 1789, the French Revolution broke out, Catherine's firm hand fell across Novikov and his work.

Alarmed at the storming of the Bastille and suspicious that Freemasonry and other secret societies were responsible for it (and given Madame Blavatsky's great-grandfather's possible involvement in a proposed "thorough metamorphosis" of the "European map," that suspicion may have been justified), Catherine outlawed Freemasonry and had Novikov and other leading Masons arrested. Novikov's printing press, extensive personal library, and large stock of occult, Hermetic, alchemical, and other esoteric texts were confiscated. (One assumes Madame Blavatsky's great-grandfather escaped this purge, or at least his library did.) When Catherine died in 1796, Paul I, who had inherited the throne and was friendly to Freemasonry, released Novikov. But he was too shattered by his ordeal to carry on his work. He died in 1818, having spent the last years of his life a broken man.

But Catherine's purge was not aimed solely at Novikov. Her progressive ideas, informed by Voltaire's thoroughgoing rationalism, triggered a crackdown on anything occult. For years she had harbored the belief that the occult in general and alchemy in particular were corrupting influences in her court; she had even written a play about this, with a villain modeled on Cagliostro, whom she reportedly wanted to strangle for trying to infiltrate her court.[49] Now any sort of magical, alchemical, Hermetic, or in anywise occult practice was strictly forbidden.[50] Divination was especially outlawed; Russian subjects were not even allowed to ask about the meaning of a dream. This was a suppression of the magical side of the Russian psyche that even the church had not attempted. The only thing like it on the same scale was the Bolshevik suppression of anything that smacked of the spiritual or inner life a century later. And in both cases, the target of this suppression did not disappear but, as it had done before, merely went underground.

8

The Beautiful Soul

A Return to Childlike Innocence

The rise in popularity of Freemasonry and other mystical societies was not the only response to the decline of the church as a source of moral guidance or spiritual intensity in a Russia that was increasingly mimicking its enlightened European cousins. Along with the rise of interest in occult and esoteric teachings coming from the West, particularly Germany, and ever since the Raskol of the century before, heretical sects splintering off from the Old Believers had become a source of concern for both the church and the state. What gave these radical groups a peculiarly feverish character was the sense of the impending millennium hovering over them. Nikon's reforms, Peter the Great's emasculation of the patriarchate, and Catherine's profligate French ways—which had become de rigueur for her court—were the ever more unmistakable signs that the last days were upon the world. Those who read these signs and took them seriously knew their import and acted accordingly.

Two of the most popular and radical of the sects awaiting the apocalypse were the Khlysty and the Skoptsy, otherwise known as the Flagellants and the Mutilators. Although self-harm and castration are associated with these groups, another form of radical behavior both seem to have engaged in, and which may strike us as counterintuitive, was orgiastic communal sex. It was said that Rasputin was a member of

193

the Khlysty, although whether he was or simply came across them in his travels remains unclear. What we do know suggests that the kind of worship favored by the Khlysty and other "free love" sects, such as the Dukhobors, or "Spirit Wrestlers," would not be beyond the bounds of Russian Man.

The origins of these sects are, as is often the case in these concerns, a matter of debate and controversy, and parallels to their practices and beliefs can be found in earlier, similar sects, such as the Manichaeans of third-century Persia and the Medieval Brethren of the Free Spirit.[1] One thing these heretical teachings shared was a sense of being free from the restrictions of the church and the contempt for its laws and constraints that comes with this. They were antinomian, free from sin, and hence able to act without guilt.

The Khlysty believed that Christ returned to Earth periodically, not once in glory descending from the sky, as many depictions of the Second Coming have it, but in the body of another man. His spirit inhabits it, takes possession of it, and when that body dies, it moves on to another. This is how they understood the Resurrection, and it can be seen that it has some similarity to Hindu teachings concerning avatars, gods who are incarnated at different times in human form. According to Khlysty tradition, one of these Christs was crucified on the battlefield of Kulikovo by Dmitry of the Don.[2] Another suffered under the hands of Ivan the Terrible—which, as we've seen, may not have been too difficult to do.

Yet another appeared at the time of Nikon. Daniel Philipov was an army deserter who became a leader of the Old Believers. The divine spirit entered him one day in the form of the god Zebaoth, which is a name often given to Jehovah.[3] Philipov started his ministry in the village of Staraya, which became a site of holy pilgrimage. In Kostroma he produced a text known as the Dove Book, which became the Bible of the sect. It taught that men and women should be celibate, and that those members who are married should abandon their wives or their husbands, even their children. They abstained from drink, meat, and tobacco, avoided profanity, and lived simply. In some aspects their way of life is reminiscent of the medieval Cathars, who were linked to the eastern European Bogomils, mentioned earlier.[4]

The particular form of worship associated with the Khlysty involved flagellation, a kind of spiritual whipping, which often ended in a frenzied, Dionysian eruption of orgiastic ecstasy. The story is that they were originally called "Christy," "those who were like Christ," but this was turned to "Khlysty," "those who whip themselves" because of the similarity in sound. The idea was fundamentally the same as that which informed the Hesychast practice: to have the *experience* of God, his *gnosis,* to be filled with the "uncreated light" and awaken the divine spark slumbering within.

Philipov's followers were known to dress in white and to gather at night to dance around a fire, or sometimes a tub of water, literally whipping themselves and each other into a frenzy. Sometimes this took place in a clearing, at others in a house. Candles were lit, and the procession began. As one account has it, "As a state of dizziness was essential to the 'divine flux,' the master of ceremonies flogged any dancer whose vigour abated."[5] The dance ended with the participants falling to the floor in a fit, possessed by the Holy Spirit. And as they were no longer "themselves," they were not responsible for their actions. The candles were extinguished, and the possessed men and women coupled anonymously, enraptured in divine excess, performing what is known as a rite of *lucerna extincta* or sex in the dark. Other accounts suggest less erotic mingling and focus on the state of possession occasioned by the whipping, which was said to produce visions and prophecy.

The Skoptsy were an even more radical sect that arose out of believers who were unsatisfied with the Khlysty worship. The Khlysty set a high value on the ability to withstand pain. Tradition has it that one of their earlier leaders, Ivan Suslov, who took over after Daniel Philipov, was crucified twice in front of the Kremlin—whether by Tsar Alexis or Peter the Great is unclear—and was even flayed alive and survived.[6] The Skoptsy took the next step and advocated mutilation.

Some years after Suslov's crucifixions, an old woman, Akulina Ivanova, whom the Khlysty called the "mother of God," announced that the spirit of Christ had entered into the body of one Kondrati Selivanov.[7] Selivanov took the Khlysty message a stage further and declared that all true believers should subject themselves to mutilation. Men should be castrated, and women should have their breasts amputated or their genitals mutilated, to save them from the sin of lust. This may suggest that the Khlysty "love dances" may have been getting out of hand.

Determined to practice what he preached, at around the age of fifty, Selivanov castrated himself with a hot iron, a precedent set some centuries earlier by the early church father Origen.[8] (Some accounts have Selivanov taking part in a group ceremony.) He seems to have suffered some kind of identity crisis as well; not long after this act he began to declare that he was Peter the III, Catherine's wearisome dead husband. (To complicate matters even more, before receiving Christ's spirit, Selivanov was known as Ivanov.) We've seen that Selivanov was not the only claimant on Peter III's identity; Pugachev was one as well, as was yet another pretender to the dead tsar's right, a Serbian.*

Yet while Pugachev's pretentions led to his gruesome death, Selivanov's only brought him to a madhouse. (The Serbian apparently had some success with his imposture.[9]) Years later he was released from his asylum and was allowed to continue his ministry, which had by this time grown in numbers. As with other radical groups, such as the Cathars, there were levels of commitment among the believers.[10] Not everyone suffered what was known as the "greater seal," complete castration or amputation. For some women the loss of a nipple or even a wound would suffice; for men a cut on the penis could do, although removal of the testicles was often expected. The Skoptsy believed that Selivanov, who died in 1832 at the age of one hundred, would return

---

*The multiple pretenders to Peter III's rule echo those to the dead Dmitry during the "time of troubles."

to Earth in Irkutsk—where he lived for a time—when the number of true believers reached 144,000. This figure would be made up of an equal number of male and female virgins. This is a target they shared with another radical Christian sect, the Jehovah's Witnesses; the source of the figure for both is the Bible.[11] The Jehovah's Witnesses' presence is still felt in the world today. The Skoptsy, however, who numbered in the many thousands in the early twentieth century, are now nowhere near this number and to all intents and purposes qualify as extinct.[12]

But while the Khlysty and Skoptsy attracted many followers, mostly among the peasants—although they did make inroads into the upper classes—it was another mystical teaching that troubled Catherine's last years, one that would eventually reach the throne itself.

One form of a kind of mystical Freemasonry that had an enormous impact on Russia was Martinism. Although technically not a branch of Freemasonry, Martinism shared with it a series of grades, ceremonies, and initiations and promoted a notion of self-development that combined personal moral and ethical perfection with insight into occult secrets. Like Freemasonry, it was a chivalric esoteric order. Its influence could be felt throughout the whole of the turbulent Russian century—that is, the nineteenth century—and it was present in some form in the Russian court up to the time of the Bolsheviks, and perhaps even beyond.

Martinism gets its name from the French savant Louis Claude de Saint-Martin (1743–1803), who was known during his life as the "Unknown Philosopher." Saint-Martin was born in Amboise, France, but he got his mystical start when he met Don Martines de Pasqually de la Tour—otherwise known as Martinez Pasquales—in Bordeaux in 1767. Martinez was a follower of Swedenborg and a student of the Rosicrucian tradition, as were Nikolay Novikov and his colleagues. He was also the leader of a mystical order known as the Elect Cohens, *cohen* being the Hebrew word for priest. It is unclear if Pasquales was Spanish or Portuguese, or if he was a Jew or Catholic, but he was a serious student of esoteric knowledge, and his earnestness impressed Saint-Martin, who had until then not found a purpose in life.[13] Now Pasquales had given him one. Saint-Martin devoted himself completely to the ritual and ceremonial magic that Martinez practiced, which involved, among other techniques, forms of theurgy, a kind of magic aimed at invoking divine powers.

In 1772 Martinez left France for Port-au-Prince, where he died two years later. When the Martinists despaired at the loss of their master, Saint-Martin stepped in and assumed the role by writing the first of many books expounding his own mystical philosophy. *Of Errors and Truth* appeared in 1775. This was followed by a series of works that formed a philosophical and spiritual counterargument to the shallow rationalism of the philosophes, although Saint-Martin is much more than a mere "anti-Voltaire," as some critics have characterized him.[14] In fact, he even shared with his opponent papal opprobrium: ironically, both authors' names appear on the Vatican Index of Forbidden Books.

With the poet and painter William Blake, his younger contemporary, Saint-Martin saw that Voltaire's atheism and rationalism, which had so infected Catherine's court, were a product of what Blake called "single vision and Newton's sleep," a narrowing of consciousness that left it aware of nothing but the material world, what Blake called "the land of Ulro." Saint-Martin believed that we have arrived at this condition because of some great primal cosmic catastrophe, when we fell from our original, integral state, at one with the divine, into the world of space and time. Our task, Saint-Martin believed, was to "repair" the world, to "regenerate" our fallen selves and through this regenerate the fallen universe as well—a theme that hearkens back to ideas about the role of beauty in the redemption of the world.

Saint-Martin wrote as the "Unknown Philosopher," adopting anonymity as much for esoteric as for political reasons. But as he moved through aristocratic circles across Europe, spreading his message of the need for regeneration, Saint-Martin's identity soon became known. The theme of regeneration reached political ears in France in the years leading up to the Revolution. This was a time when Freemasonry, the spiritual teachings of Swedenborg, and the animal magnetism of the German scientist and healer Franz Anton Mesmer blended with a passionate belief in the need for immediate social change, making for a very heady brew.

Saint-Martin himself was involved with one Society of Harmony—revolutionary groups informed by Mesmer's ideas—that was attempting to decipher messages received during magnetic trances, emanating from an entity they called the "Unknown Agent," a title reminiscent of Baron Hund's "unknown superiors."[15] Yet Saint-Martin was himself a victim of the revolution, and he soon lost interest in the kind of "materialist" magic he felt grew out of Mesmer's work, which was concerned with a vital but intangible "fluid" pervading the universe that Mesmer believed he had learned to control. Saint-Martin's true interests were much more spiritual.

Man, Saint-Martin believed, had a particular mission and responsibility in the universe, and it is this focus on the peculiar task of human existence that may be his most lasting contribution to the development of Russian identity.[16] As the occult scholar and historian A. E. Waite wrote, "The message of Saint-Martin may be fitly termed the Counsel of the Exile." It is concerned with "man only, the glorious intention of his creation, with his fall, his subsequent bondage, the means of his liberation, and his return to the purpose of his being."[17] It was the riddle of our existence and its solution that led Saint-Martin to argue, contra the vision of mankind arising from the growing "scientific revolution," that we should strive to explain the world by man, and not man by the world. This, of course, is how our official science continues to try to "explain" us and our mysterious appearance here on this planet. Saint-Martin's contrary vision, which places man and his purpose—that of regeneration—at the center of things, and *not* the world in which he finds himself, would grow throughout the nineteenth century and fuel the blaze of Russian philosophy that will finally illuminate it. Unlike its older Western cousin—sceptical, cautious, and more concerned with logical and epistemological disputes—when Russian *thinking* finally comes of age, it will be unashamedly, even aggressively anthropocentric.

Saint-Martin was a reader of Jacob Boehme, the sixteenth-century Bohemian cobbler whose vision of "the signature of things," triggered by sunlight on a pewter dish, led to a series of remarkable if obscure books about the true nature of reality, couched in a difficult alchemical language, heavily influenced by Paracelsus.[18] One theme that runs through Boehme's difficult writings is that of the struggle between opposites,* the creative tension maintained between two poles of existence: one of divine light and love, the other of darkness and wrath, with human life caught precariously in the middle.[19] This theme of polarity and the potential of warring opposites to combine to produce something beyond either one, will prepare the Russian mind for the ideas that would soon come to obsess it.

WHEN CATHERINE THE Great died, one of her worst fears came to pass: her son Paul became tsar. She was convinced that he would be little more than a rerun of her despicable husband, Peter III, and by most accounts she was right. She had done everything she could to prevent this from happening, and had even written a document stating unequivocally that the throne should go to her grandson, Alexander, whom she had taken from his parents in order to rear for the job. But despite her best efforts, the disaster happened. Alexander is thought to have been aware of the document establishing him as ruler, but for some reason he failed to mention it. The first thing Paul did as tsar was get possession of the document and destroy it. He was in power—his triumph over his mother must have been sweet. But he would not enjoy it for long.

We might think that had he been treated better, Paul might have made a better tsar. Perhaps. Catherine, who disliked him from the start, kept him from the capital, setting him up in nearby Gatchina, where

---

*Berdyaev's work is deeply influenced by Boehme's dark metaphysics.

he ruled over a kind of mini-kingdom he had established on his estate. Like his father he was obsessed with Prussia and militarism, and his fastidiousness in these matters could send a man to Siberia if his buttons were not done properly. He spent most of his time devising and carrying out war games, parades, and other military extravagances, and when he came to the throne he continued to do much the same. He repealed many of his mother's policies, reestablished the right of primogeniture (its eclipse had almost cost him his tsardom), introduced harsher penalties for infringement of military rules, and changed his mind about practically every decision he made (except those involving his beloved Prussia) with a rapidity that dizzied even those few who felt some loyalty to him.

He was, however, more sympathetic to Freemasonry than his mother—it was he who freed Novikov—and he also had an audience with the Skoptsy leader Kondrati Selivanov. Selivanov informed him that he, Selivanov, was his father, that is, Peter III. To have been a witness at an interview when one madman tells another that he is really his father (who was yet another maniac) and also the reincarnated Christ, not to mention that he was proselytizing for castration at the same time, must have been something indeed. In the end, it was Paul who sent Selivanov to a madhouse. His own end followed soon enough. When reform-minded officers had had enough of Paul's bizarre behavior and indecision, they took matters into their hands and, for the good of the country, on March 23, 1801, strangled him. His son Alexander I now sat on the throne. The Russian century had begun.

ALEXANDER I GREW up in an atmosphere that was in many ways similar to that of Peter the Great's childhood. He was at court, but it was the enlightened court of Catherine, not the Byzantine court of medieval Muscovy. When the encyclopedist Denis Diderot respectfully declined Catherine the Great's request that he tutor her grandson, she secured the services of the Swiss republican Frédérik César

La Harpe instead. Alexander grew up to have an agile, open mind, and when he first took the throne at the age of twenty-four, expectations of reform were high. He was the polar opposite of Paul. He was handsome. Where Paul had the appearance of a pug, Alexander was tall, noble, and seemed to embody the qualities and character of an enlightened ruler. He was enthusiastic, with the kind of can-do attitude that informed Peter the Great and, at her best moments, Catherine the Great. He announced reforms in education, founded the creation of new schools, and worked for the training of new teachers. But his reforming zeal foundered on the same rock on which Catherine's had: the serfs.

Although the problem had increased and the pressure to solve it had grown, Alexander I saw that he could not free the serfs, and for the same reason that had stopped Catherine: the landowners would not support the move, and without them the country would collapse. So the heat on the social pressure cooker remained, and all Alexander I could do was to try to fasten the lid more securely, by affirming ever more insistently on the need for autocracy. What this amounted to was a country 90 percent of whose population were uneducated slaves, living in the Middle Ages, with a thin layer of its people aping France and doing their utmost to stay in power. Gestures toward reform that Alexander I did make were oddly reminiscent of Catherine's initial attempts. He asked his secretary Count Speransky, a Freemason, to draw up a constitution. Having to balance the tsar's insistence on absolute autocracy with an attempt to reform a barely functioning system was difficult enough. To do this without making enemies among the nobility proved practically impossible. Just as the principles in Catherine's Instruction were quietly ignored, Speransky's ideas were likewise met with a stony silence, if not outright rejection, and Speransky himself with disfavor.

It may have been with some relief, then, that Alexander I entered the struggle against Napoleon, and put these matters aside. As many had predicted, the Revolution had produced a tyrant. From 1803 until his final defeat in 1815, Napoleon Bonaparte, the "little corporal," set Europe aflame. It was a campaign that changed the face of Europe, inspired some of the greatest works of the nineteenth century—Tolstoy's *War and Peace* and Tchaikovsky's *1812 Overture,* written in celebration of the Battle of Borodino, are only two examples—and, at its end, established Russia as the greatest power on the Continent. It also led, as had happened with Catherine the Great, to Alexander I's shift from progressive reformer to defender of the status quo and upholder of tradition. The window on the West that Peter the Great had opened would now be shut to keep unwanted elements from getting in. But through cracks here and there they nonetheless did.

When Alexander marched into Paris on March 31, 1814, at the head of the coalition that had finally brought Napoleon to heel—with some help from the Russian winter—the European powers he had rallied to victory came to a sharp realization.* Backward, medieval, impossible Russia was clearly a force to be reckoned with. Its sheer size and numbers made it the most powerful nation in Europe, and other nations would now have to consider this in their dealings with her. But although the Russian bear was now looked upon with a respect that may have been lacking in the past, monarchs across the continent could nevertheless rest easier. What Alexander took upon himself to do was to single-handedly hold back the flow of progress, which to him and to the kings and queens, whose power he was determined to protect, was more like a calamitous plunge into a cataract of anarchism.

The struggle with Napoleon had driven all idea of reform out of Alexander's mind. He had exchanged the liberal and progressive views he had imbibed from his tutor and grandmother for a deep religiosity, and he was now determined to uphold the forces of autocracy, monarchy, and tradition against the corrosive influences of revolution. In

---

*Napoleon would, of course, return briefly, for his "100 days," before losing at Waterloo and finally being exiled to the remote island of St. Helena.

September 1815 Alexander ratified the treaty he had signed with Prussia and Austria that gave birth to the Holy Alliance—a name taken from the book of Daniel, which speaks of an approaching apocalypse when the reign of God will be restored. The treaty itself was written in "the name of the Most Holy and Invisible Trinity."[20] Its aim was to secure the monarchies against any uprisings and to ensure order and stability in a Christian Europe; it would, Alexander said, provide a "Christian answer" to the revolution. With hindsight we see that this was a mistake and that the energies Alexander and the others were trying to contain would sooner or later explode.

Yet we can, I think, understand why Alexander, Metternich, and Talleyrand—who drew up the alliance—were not merely "old-fashioned reactionaries who failed to grasp the lessons of history," as at least one historian suggests.[21] If we agree with Novikov, Saint-Martin, and the many others who found the philosophy behind the revolution dangerously reductive, then, while we may not agree with the draconian measures Alexander I and other monarchs took in order to stem its flow, we can see that their motivation may have been something more than mere greed for power.

There were some elements of tradition that needed to be preserved if society was not to break down, as it did following the French Revolution. These were the elements that the different mystical teachings that had sprung up were trying to satisfy.* The problem was that the opposition between the need for change and reform and the desire to hold on to what was valuable in the past had grown too great, and the polarities were moving too far apart. Perhaps this was unavoidable. The Russian people, we know, are given to extremes; for them it is, as Berdyaev tells us, either all or nothing. Compromise and middle grounds are not their forte. In fact, they are the province of the West, half measures against which the Russian soul rebels.

---

*This was precisely what William Blake was trying to do at the same time in England with his mythological epics. Blake, a political radical, was friends with Tom Paine, yet he could also chide Voltaire and Rousseau for their shallow criticism of religion.

ALEXANDER IS KNOWN to have held several audiences with Baroness Barbara Juliane von Krüdener during the campaign against Napoleon. For a time she was a trusted confidante and adviser, almost a confessor. She was a Baltic German mystic and theologian—some call her a "spiritual adventuress"—whose ideas were deeply influenced by the Moravian Church. This was an outgrowth of the work of the mystical Count Zinzendorf, who had founded his own spiritual society, the Order of the Grain of Mustard Seed, in 1723.[22] The widow of a Russian diplomat, the baroness was also a spiritualist and a follower of Swedenborg.*

The story is that the peasant prophet Adam Mueller told her that a "man from the north" would soon arise to destroy the Antichrist, which by this time meant Napoleon.[23] Krüdener looked for this man in the courts of Europe, and when she met Alexander at a soiree in Heilbronn she knew she had found him. Some historians suggest that guilt over the murder of his father may have prompted Alexander's new religious fervor, and that Krüdener took advantage of this, as they suggest many others did.[24] Whatever the case, she became for a time part of his entourage, helping him to interpret scripture and most likely influencing his decision to form the Holy Alliance.

When Alexander returned to Russia from the wars, he was a changed man. He had become paranoid, spoke ominously of the "reign of Satan," and saw secret societies rising up everywhere. As assassination plots against him were being discussed—assassination being an occupational hazard, it seems, of Russian tsars—some of Alexander's concern had its roots in reality. But like other Romanov rulers, ambivalence hamstrung Alexander. At times he was fired with great plans, but then would leave them for something else, the usual Russian switchback between sudden enthusiasm and apathy. He often spoke of abdicating and moving to Switzerland or, another option, becoming a monk. A vague hunger for some sort of spiritual peace hounded the tsar, and

---

*Oddly enough, the Moravians, like the Khlysty, were known for their erotic spirituality. At one time, Swedenborg was involved with a Moravian church in London.

Baroness von Krüdener was not the only influence upon him. Other ideas, coming from what was being called the "counter-enlightenment," reached Alexander and affected him deeply.

ALEXANDER GOLITSYN, THE tsar's conservative minister for religious affairs and education, and a friend for many years, predicted that Russia would be the birthplace of a new universal church, an idea that, as we've seen, has not entirely vanished from the Russian political consciousness. Golitsyn—whose grandson, another Alexander Golitsyn, would help Madame Blavatsky on her mystic way—had something of the unpredictable Russian character.[25] After a youth spent in debauchery and admiration of the Encyclopedists, he read the New Testament for the first time and went through a profound personal and spiritual transformation.[26] One result of this was the Russian Bible Society, which Golitsyn founded in 1813, whose mission was to combat superstition among the peasants and reveal the truth of the Gospels, something that the church seemed to have lost track of. Another was that, through Golitsyn's encouragement, the tsar read the Bible too—also for the first time—and was moved as deeply as Golitsyn had been.

Alexander began to see worldly events in terms of sacred history. The book of Revelation made a particularly strong impact on him, and Alexander read the Bible daily while making his way to the final clash with the Antichrist. The baroness had encouraged him in the belief that it was his mission to save Christendom. As one account has it, his march to do just that "resembled more an inter-confessional religious pilgrimage than a military campaign," with visits to Moravian communities, Quaker houses, and an outdoor Easter mass on the Place de la Concorde, the site of the beheading of Louis XVI, along the way.[27]

It was through Golitsyn that Alexander had a meeting with Kondrati Selivanov, whom he had released from his asylum. Golitsyn, who had made contact with the Skoptsy, set Selivanov up in a fine apartment in St. Petersburg, where he continued to preach and to prophesy, and some of his declarations reached the tsar.[28] It was through the Skoptsy that Alexander came under the influence of another female spiritual adviser, Catherine Tatarinova, the widow of a Russian colonel. She was a sort of seer who practiced a version of the Khlysty dances. She had been a member of the Skoptsy but had left and was holding religious meetings where she worked herself up into an ecstasy and delivered prophecy.[29] As with Baroness von Krüdener, for a time Alexander met with her and garnered some spiritual guidance from her pronouncements.

Golitsyn was a Freemason, as were many in the circle around Alexander, and as with Peter the Great, there is much speculation as to whether or not Alexander himself was initiated.[30] He would not have to have been, however, to have been informed with Masonic ideas: during the Napoleon campaign, Alexander encouraged Russian officers to fraternize with French Masons. One idea that was greatly discussed in Masonic circles was that of a new "universal church," something, we've seen, Golitsyn was interested in. One source of this vision was the work of a once popular but now little known Bavarian esoteric philosopher, Karl von Eckartshausen (1752–1813).

Although well known in his day, today Eckartshausen is remembered, if at all, as the author of a book that sent the notorious dark magician Aleister Crowley on his dubious path.[31] Yet the book in question, *The Cloud upon the Sanctuary* (1802), has little to do with Crowley's peculiar brand of magical philosophy. What attracted Crowley to the book was Eckartshausen's talk of an "invisible church," a "secret community of saints," at work in the world "behind the scenes," as it were. This was not, however, a secret society in the sense that the Freemasons were, nor a political one like the Illuminati, which had hijacked Freemasonry for its revolutionary purposes. One did not join this church through a strange ceremony or by undergoing trials, but through a change of heart.

In a sense, Eckartshausen's invisible church was a kind of "anti-Illuminati." It was a community of like-minded, earnest individuals who rejected the radicalism of the revolution and sought a return to the primal belief, the ur-religion that was at the foundation of all religions, an idea we came across in our encounter with the Byzantine Platonist Gemistos Plethon. This was the fundamental spiritual belief that was known to all faiths—again, an idea that was revived by Madame Blavatsky in the late nineteenth century. The followers of this religion did not meet to worship, nor did they hold to a certain creed, but all were devout nonetheless. While Alexander was drawing up his plans for the Holy Alliance, Eckartshausen's "invisible church," it seems, was very likely on his mind.

Another influence on the tsar at this time was Rodion Koshelev, a friend and associate of Golitsyn, and a Freemason (some sources suggest it was he who initiated the tsar—if he was initiated). Koshelev had been the Russian ambassador to Denmark, and during his European travels he had come into contact with Eckartshausen, Saint-Martin, and other philosophers of the mystical enlightenment.[32] It was through Koshelev that the tsar came to read both, and Koshelev also introduced him to the difficult writings of Jacob Boehme. Yet another mystical influence brought to the tsar through Golitsyn and Koshelev was the work of Franz von Baader, an interpreter of Boehme, Saint-Martin, and other works of "theosophy" in the Christian, not Blavatskian, sense.

LIKE ECKARTSHAUSEN, BAADER was born in Bavaria. He started out as a physician but left this to become a mining engineer—oddly enough a profession followed by not a few mystically minded individuals at the time.* A reading of David Hume and other philosophers of the British empirical school repelled him and sent him in the direction of Boehme, Saint-Martin, and the thirteenth-century Thuringian Christian mystic Meister Eckhart. Further reading took him deeper into mystical philosophy, and his own books, many written after he retired from his work as an engineer, present interpretations and expositions of Saint-Martin

---

*Two others of note are Swedenborg, who was an assessor of Swedish mines for many years and wrote several tracts on mineralogy, and the Hermetic German Romantic poet Friedrich von Hardenberg, better known as Novalis.

and Boehme's insights, expressed in a gnomic, aphoristic style, designed more to stimulate thought than to provide fixed answers.

One work, though, which did reach the tsar and other European rulers, was a memorandum on the need for a closer union between religion and politics that Baader drew up in 1814, in the face of the aftermath of the French Revolution.[33] Baader sent this memorandum to Alexander and to the rulers of Austria and Prussia as well, and there is little doubt that it was an important influence on the three signatories of the treaty forming the Holy Alliance.[34] Much of Baader's thought would be echoed in the unique approach to philosophy that would arise in Russia as the century moved on, especially his belief that Russia was, or could be, a "mediator" between East and West, an idea we have come upon before.[35]

Baader himself, though, never reached Russia. Invited to come to St. Petersburg by Golitsyn, Baader made the journey but was stopped at the border, arrested, and sent back. This produced angry letters to Golitsyn and the tsar.[36] One influence on Alexander I that did reach St. Petersburg, however, had a view of the union between politics and religion that was more radical, sweeping, and darker than Baader's or any others'. This was the vision of the Savoyard royalist and reactionary thinker Joseph de Maistre, whose extreme right-wing desire for a kind of papal totalitarian state is embraced today by readers of Julius Evola and by such American conservatives as Pat Buchanan.

DE MAISTRE BEGAN as a Freemason and a follower of Saint-Martin, but he soon lost patience with idealistic visions of universal brotherhood and religious tolerance and came to see the Catholic Church as the single, solitary force that could withstand the revolutionary rot. As he wrote, "Wherever an altar is found, there civilization exists." Altars were being toppled all over Europe, De Maistre declared, and it is the business of the state to erect them again and to secure them as firmly as possible.

De Maistre had a jaundiced view of human nature, the kind of benevolently cynical assessment that Dostoyevsky expressed through the figure of the Grand Inquisitor. As readers of *The Brothers Karamazov* know, the Grand Inquisitor believed that for their own good, human beings must be treated like children, shepherded so that they do not go astray. De Maistre felt the same. Like the Grand Inquisitor, he was a convinced misanthrope. He argued that, contrary to Rousseau, human beings are not naturally good, nor are they born free and later enchained by society. They are savage, selfish, wicked creatures who require strict authority for any good to come out of them. As Isaiah Berlin writes, De Maistre "emphasized the need for absolute authority, punishment, and continual repression if civilization and order were to survive."[37] He believed that we can only be saved by "being hemmed in by the terror of authority."[38] How this terror differs from that produced by the revolution that so revolted him is not clear.

This message, however, reached the tsar when De Maistre arrived in St. Petersburg in 1802 as ambassador of the king of Sardinia. He stayed for the next fifteen years, and his observations on Russian life during the Napoleonic era are captured in his *St. Petersburg Nights* (1821), a book that Tolstoy drew on when writing *War and Peace*.[39] As more than one reader has pointed out, its theme of twilight heading into darkness can be taken as a metaphor for the dimming of the Enlightenment.

Like Baader, De Maistre believed that Russia had an important part to play in European affairs; she was the savior of Europe, as she was in fact considered after the defeat of Napoleon. He became an intimate of the tsar and his morbid fascinations—he had a peculiar interest in hangmen—which led to visits to the supposedly haunted parts of Gatchina, and to the room in the Mikhailovsky Palace where Paul had been strangled.[40] It may have been De Maistre's influence that led to the "military colonies" Alexander initiated on his return from the wars, programs designed to populate uninhabited areas but which were horribly misconceived and which led to little but resentment against him from the half a million peasants forced to live in them.

IT WAS NOT long after the initial fervor over the Holy Alliance died down that the ambivalence that had always been a part of Alexander's character began to dominate him. Thoughts of abdication obsessed him, and dreams of Switzerland or a monastery crowded his mind— symbolic poles between which the entire nation was caught. His health—physical and mental—broke down. His paranoia increased, old friends now seemed enemies, and fear of plots led in 1822 to an outlaw- ing of Freemasonry. The official record was that he died of malaria in 1825 at the age of forty-eight at Taganrog, a remote port on the Sea of Azov. What he was doing there in the first place has never been ade- quately explained—it was supposedly a trip for his wife's health—nor has malaria as the cause of his death been entirely convincing; some accounts say typhus or pneumonia. A legend persists that Alexander actually faked his death and went on to live as a monk in Siberia, or possibly Palestine.[41] There are different versions of the story. In one, the tsar's coffin, when exhumed, was found to be empty. In another the body claimed to be the tsar's at the time of death was unrecogniz- able. At this point it remains a mystery. What is clear is that the next occupant of the Russian throne was determined to hold back the tide of change even more stubbornly than his predecessor. In fact, it was the first thing he did on the job.

NICHOLAS I, ALEXANDER's youngest brother, came to power through a typical Russian muddle. Alexander had left no heir, and his brother Constantine—older than Nicholas—was expected to take the throne. He, however, was in Poland, where he had married. As required, the officers of the guard had sworn their allegiance to Constantine, but then word came that he refused to accept the crown. At this, Nicholas became tsar. But when the guards were expected to now swear their allegiance to Nicholas, a reforming element within them argued that they should not, and saw him as a usurper. They were part of a movement that had begun with officers returning from the wars who had encountered liberal ideas and were ashamed at the treatment of peasants and serfs in the army. Masonic beliefs informed their sympathies and they had begun a kind of revolt against court life.[42] Now they declared their belief in the open, and called for a constitution, something they had been promised by Alexander.

On December 14, 1825, the day of Nicholas's coronation, about 3,000 officers staged a rebellion. They believed that their action would be followed by others. When it wasn't, the revolt turned into a standoff between the Decembrists—as they were called—and troops loyal to Nicholas. We can get an idea of Nicholas's character from the way he ended the stalemate: he fired artillery into the rebelling ranks. Those not killed fled and were later captured. Leaders of the rebellion were arrested, summarily tried, and executed; others were imprisoned or sent to Siberia. Thus began what one historian has called the "primitive and crushing despotism" of Nicholas I.[43]

Nicholas inherited his father's obsession with military punctiliousness and had none of his older brother Alexander's spiritual anxieties. He was impatient, obsessive, and imposing. The army was his life, and "spit and polish" was its heart. For the thirty years of his reign he did his best to run Russia like a boot camp. He was rightly known as "the gendarme of Europe." Where Alexander had pledged to maintain the rule of monarchs, Nicholas was ready to go to war in order to root out the demons of revolution. When, in 1831, a rebellion broke out in Poland—now in Russian hands—he crushed it as ruthlessly as he had the Decembrists. And when the potential for rebellion at home struck him as being all-too-ready to actualize, he took steps to ensure that it would not.

Under the banner of "Orthodoxy, Autocracy, Nationality"— guiding principles devised by his minister for education Sergei Uvarov— Nicholas instituted a system of censorship and a network of spies that harkened back to Ivan the Terrible's Oprichnina. The aim was to bring the people back to the church, to reestablish the absolute rule of the tsar, and to enforce a notion of "Russianness" that would dominate the vast empire. This was at the expense of other cultures, such as that of Ukraine, whose language and history were supressed.[44] The model for Russian identity was to be Nikolay Karamzin's *History of the Russian State* (1826) which, in its twelve volumes, sang the praises of autocracy and celebrated the deeds of its enlightened exponents.[45] Any who disagreed were quickly silenced.

One such was the critic Peter Chaadaev. In his *Philosophical Letters* (1829) Chaadaev argued that, contrary to the official account, Russia, a backward, corrupt, incompetent country, had no history to speak of and, hence, no identity. Yet it could, just possibly, have a future, if it modeled itself on Catholic Europe. He was branded insane, his *Letters* were confiscated, and he was prohibited from writing.[46] Yet Nicholas's insistence on establishing and maintaining a distinct Russian identity would in many ways fuel the resistance to his own claustrophobic aims. Because now a people that had already assimilated and adapted a number of foreign influences—French, Italian, German, Scandinavian— would seek to find themselves once more, by following the philosophical ideas of yet another foreigner.

ONE OF THE first policies Nicholas initiated in his battle against subversion was to severely limit the teaching of philosophy in Russia, if not to eliminate it entirely. During his reign he came close to doing just that, by "purging" universities of their philosophy departments. As these departments were barely up and running, we can see this as an act of intellectual infanticide.[47] Although Nicholas was successful in ousting some of the most important sources of independent thought from the academies, the horse had, by and large, already bolted from the stable. Dangerous thoughts had reached the burgeoning Russian consciousness, and they got there in the form of the philosophy of Friedrich Schelling (1775–1854).

When we think of German philosophy having an effect on Russian history, we think first of Marx. Readers with a bit of background in the history of ideas know that Marx was deeply influenced by Hegel, whom he claimed to have "stood on his head" in order to correct his ideas. But it is less widely known that the first German philosopher to have a powerful impact on Russian thought and life—an opposition that he himself sought to overcome—was Schelling. Schelling's ideas are not as well known as Marx's or Hegel's, but in recent years they have received more attention from the "alternative" community, which is open to views of reality that differ from the official "scientific" assessment, an openness that it shares with Russian thought.

Schelling was part of a group of brilliant young students at Tübingen University in the late eighteenth century that included Hegel and the poet Friedrich Hölderlin, mentioned earlier. Schelling was a child prodigy. He was initially very influential, but his work was later eclipsed and effectively forgotten with the rise of his friend and later philosophical opponent, the "world-historical" Hegel.

Schelling's ideas are complex and not easy to explain. Fundamentally they concern the relationship between consciousness and the world, a puzzle that had risen up with the triumph of Kantian idealism. Kant's follower, Johann Fichte, had come to the conclusion that nature was in some way a "projection" of the mind. Schelling found this unsatisfying, and in his *Ideas for a Philosophy of Nature* (1797) he argued instead for nature to share what we might call "equal billing" with mind. "Nature should be Mind made visible," Schelling wrote, and "Mind the invisible Nature."[48] Thus was established the fundamental polarity in Schelling's thought, a motif we have come upon already. This "dialectical tension" between opposites became the basic motor of Schelling's ideas, and one of the central themes of Romanticism, of which he was the chief philosophical proponent. As one of the professors thrown out of the academy by Nicholas's edicts taught, Schelling "expressed the dialectical thesis concerning the general connectedness of phenomena, their binary nature, and the struggle of polar opposites as the source of development."[49] In this sentence we have a great deal of Russian thought.

Romanticism grew as a response to the increasingly mechanical and reductive tendencies of the Enlightenment, specifically to its emphasis on reason and rationality as the sole agents of knowledge, and the loss of the unique individual in favor of abstract generality. It argued instead for a kind of intuitive, global knowledge that took in everything at a glance and was able to "enter into" its object of observation.[50] Schelling called this "absolute knowledge," and every poet knows what he means. We experience it in those moments when we feel a strange "communion" with nature, a feeling that our inner and outer worlds are not separated by an impassable barrier—the view of the Enlightenment—but "participate" in each other in some way we do not fully understand.

The problem with this kind of knowledge, and why it is rejected by the rationalist tradition, is that it is difficult to communicate what it reveals to someone who has not experienced it. It can only be done through symbols, metaphors, images, analogies—in other words, through art or some other creative work, not logic or deduction. And it was in the world of art and myth that Schelling's ideas had the most impact. Nevertheless, his "absolute knowledge" was a means through which some Russians sought to find their identity.

One of the outgrowths of Romanticism was nationalism, as the music of the Russian masters and that of Dvorák, Grieg, Sibelius, and other great nineteenth-century composers tells us. Romanticism argued that "every human being, country, race, institution has its own unique individual purpose," a notion informing much of the "identity politics" of our own time.[51] The idea of the "soul of the race" gained popularity against the mechanistic atomistic view of nations and societies deriving from the Enlightenment. It was an "organic" view of nations, one not based on Rousseau's idea of the "social contract" and one that the Russian people, already prone to think of "we," would find congenial. Germany saw itself as a "younger" people, not burdened with the historical weight of Rome or France, and hence with a different "purpose" than theirs, an idea that would resurface in the twentieth century. But if Germany was young, Russia was a child. The philosopher's task,

Schelling said, was to help the nation grasp its purpose and to find its place in history. As the Russians had been trying to do precisely that for some time, Schelling's ideas seemed custom-made for them.[52] The Slavophiles, who would soon try to answer the question of Russian identity, practically swallowed them whole.

ONE OF THE curious effects of Nicholas's anti-philosophy edicts was the creation of several semi-clandestine societies that met in order to discuss ideas. It was the atmosphere of repression that created the milieu in which the seeds of the *intelligentsia* would take root. The difficulties and dangers in obtaining and disseminating forbidden material created a psychic tension that gave Russian Romanticism a theatrical, dramatic character, one absolutely in keeping with its subject. The Russian tendency to take things to the limit, to favor extremes, produced an almost religious fervor around the latest insights coming from the West. Where before icons had been "windows to another world," forbidden books now became talismans, magical objects around which earnest rituals, ceremonies, and meditations revolved. Such was the case with the polymath Vladimir Fedorovich Odoevsky (1804–1869), known as the "Russian Faust."

ODOEVSKY IS LITTLE known to English readers, but he is a remarkable Russian Renaissance man whose work warrants more attention. He was a musician, critic, educationist, poet, philosopher, writer, and the author of children's stories still read today. For many years he was a librarian, and until his death was the director of the Rumyantsev Museum—in St. Petersburg and Moscow—and a senator in the Ministry of Justice. In his lifetime his work was ranked not far below that of Pushkin and Gogol and was just as popular. His most famous book, *Russian Nights* (1844), can be understood as a combination of E. T. A. Hoffmann's fantasies and Plato's dialogues (Hoffmann, too, was a music critic, and like Odoevsky, had a civic career).

As in Hoffmann's tales, an air of the occult and mystical breezes through Odoevsky's nights, and the characters engage in philosophical dialogues about the meaning of life, the purpose of art, science, and philosophy and their relation to society. Although De Maistre and Odoevsky both focus on the darkness of Russia, Odoevsky sees something of a dawn on its way; he is not a misanthrope and lacks De Maistre's savagery. Knowledge for Odoevsky was not, as it was in the West, a good in itself. True to his Faustian identity, Odoevsky emphasized the Goethean belief in the ethical constraints on knowledge, a consideration central to Russian thought. What was needed was knowledge that led us to the right way to live. What was the right way to live? A way in which the needs of the intellect and that of soul were equally met.

Odoevsky gathered around himself a circle of friends, who would meet to discuss ideas or to read from some of the German Romantic literature or philosophy that was setting their imaginations on fire; Schelling was often on the menu. Odoevsky dressed in black at these soirees and called himself "Faust," the name of the central character in *Russian Nights*. The group was known as the Lyubomudry, or "wisdom lovers." They considered themselves true philosophers, unlike the philosophes of the Enlightenment. Rodin Koshelev, who introduced Franz von Baader's work to Tsar Alexander, was in this group, as was the Slavophile Ivan Kireevsky.[53]

Some members had contact with Pushkin, the greatest writer of the time. But Pushkin's classical poise and detachment set him apart from the rising existential tension; while his style and grace were admired, he was not committed to the radical new consciousness rising up among the younger generation of poets and writers,* though he, too, was subject to official scrutiny.[54] (Sadly, in 1837 he would die in a pointless duel, an end that also came to the Romantic Mikhail Lermontov, Pushkin's successor as Russia's greatest poet, in 1841.) Odoevsky, although today

---

*Although Pushkin's poem, "The Bronze Horseman," about St. Petersburg, does set the polarity between Western progress and Russian compassion that would occupy the writers that came after him.

rightly not considered of the same rank as Pushkin, at least as a writer, was committed to the new ideas and professed his vision of a new Russia, embracing a moral idealism, tirelessly. Odoevsky asked his readers, "What should we do with our lives? How shall we live?" And most agonizingly, "What does it mean to be Russian?" the "accursed questions" that would occupy the Russian genius for the rest of the century and that still do today.[55]

Although the "wisdom lovers" disbanded following the Decembrists disaster, fearing Nicholas's reprisals against any discussion of "progressive" literature, the group was really not political. Philosophy à la Schelling was the main focus, but not all ideas coming from the West were welcome. Odoevsky's particular bêtes noires were the utilitarian philosophy of Bentham and Mill, and the "enlightened self-interest" of Adam Smith.

Such motivations as self-interest, Odoevsky claimed, were entirely foreign to the Russian soul, whose sense of moral right and social conscience were outraged by it. The fifth of his Russian Nights, "A City without Name," depicts a society in which the philosophy of self-interest leads, in the end, to its collapse. Based on the belief that the "only thing" that can "force a man not to exceed the limits of his right"—that is, not take more than his fair share—is "his own benefit," an absolutely "free market" society is created.[56] But Odoevsky shows that a society that accepts that "*benefit* is the essential motive power of all man's actions"—in the sense of personal gain, something with which, say, Ayn Rand would have agreed—"could not last long."[57] It quickly deteriorates into an "artificial life" composed solely of "mercantile operations," soulless and empty, not too dissimilar to our own.[58] It is a society without heart, and the aim of philosophy for Odoevsky and the other "lovers of wisdom" is to make sure it does not come about.

One of the central concerns of this time was the meaning of *pravda*, "truth." For readers of a certain generation, *Pravda* was the name of the official newspaper of the Communist Party; since the collapse of the USSR, it has been taken over by private enterprise. To have the official organ of the state called "Truth," was more than ironic during the Soviet years. But even in Odoevsky's day, the meaning of *pravda* was twofold. It could mean accurate knowledge, such as it is "true" that Moscow is the capital of Russia, or that the Earth revolves around the sun. But it can also mean justice, as in what is "just and right," the kind of truth usually allocated to religion, or at least to ethics, and which Plato ranked with the good and the beautiful.

Benthamite utilitarianism recognizes only the first meaning, which concerns a kind of truth that is quantifiable, that can be measured, as the standard of living in terms of material prosperity can be: "the greatest good for the greatest number." But the "lovers of truth" that grew up in opposition to Catherine's Enlightenment ways believed in and sought the other kind of truth, the moral, ethical, existential truth, which cannot be measured, only recognized and lived. It is no surprise that Nikolay Novikov used "love of truth" as a pen name, nor that the banner of Madame Blavatsky's Theosophical Society declared that "There is No Religion Higher Than Truth." Truth for them is not the same as fact.* It is something that speaks of a higher, deeper "rightness," and that comes to us through the soul, not the brain, or at least not through that part of it focused on "getting on in the world."[59] It is a truth that cannot be found through reason or calculation, but only through the kind of intuitive "absolute knowing" that the "seekers of truth" sought in Freemasonry, Martinism, Schelling, and the Romantics.

ODOEVSKY'S GENERATION BELIEVED in what they called "the beautiful soul." This was a product of German Romanticism and had its roots in the ideas of "aesthetic education" of the poet Friedrich Schiller (1759–1805).[60] As Schiller argued, the "beautiful soul" or whole human being would bring together the head and the heart, knowledge and

---

*One can, indeed, have a "love of fact." But such knowledge hoarders are collectors, not philosophers.

wisdom, truth in the sense of fact and in the sense of justice. As the psychologist Carl Jung would argue a century later, the beautiful soul, or "individuated" person, would be able to "maintain within himself a wholeness which kept his various impulses in harmony."[61] He would "pair imagination with reason" and "be lucid in both heart and mind."[62] The beautiful soul would live the union of opposites necessary to achieve a certain and impassioned grasp of the full meaning of truth. Those who pursued this path took to heart what Jung would declare decades later, that "personality is an act of the greatest courage in the face of life." The beautiful souls took up that challenge and believed that by making themselves whole, they could influence the world around them, acting as an example and inspiring others to become beautiful souls too.

It was a noble ideal and those who pursued it did so with a dedication and passion that only Russians could exhibit. But for a long-suffering people held down for years by the inertia of an incompetent and corrupt system, it seemed to some that something more than beauty was needed to change, if not to save, their world.

9

The New Men

The New Reality

The idea of a "beautiful soul" may seem foreign to our ears, but once again Dostoyevsky comes to our aid. Readers of his novels will remember that he tried at least twice to portray such a character. Once was in *The Idiot*. In the epileptic Prince Myshkin, Dostoyevsky said it was his intention to "portray a truly beautiful soul," and when we meet Myshkin for the first time, we are told about his eyes, which are "large, blue and dreamy," with something "gentle" about them.[1] Like Dostoyevsky himself—he too was epileptic—Myshkin is prone to a kind of mystical experience at the outset of a seizure, in which he sees that "all is good," a vision Dostoyevsky gives to some of his other characters; Kirilov in *The Devils* for instance. Throughout the novel, Myshkin, the idiot in question, tries to live in accordance with the high principle of love, rooted in his visions, and the plot revolves around the consequences of his doing so. As the reader can imagine, they are not always good.

Since writing *Crime and Punishment,* which gave us Raskolnikov, the "heretic," Dostoyevsky had wanted to portray a "good man," a character of moral perfection, and Myshkin was his first serious attempt at doing this. That he was not entirely satisfied with this portrayal—made up, at least according to one critic, of parts of Christ, Don Quixote, and Dickens's Mr. Pickwick—accounts for his other attempt.[2] Later, in the character of Alyosha Karamazov, he tried again. In *The Brothers Karamazov* Dostoyevsky attempted what Colin Wilson in *The Outsider* calls "the Great Synthesis," the integration of the different parts of the human psyche, body, emotions, and intellect, through the characters of the three brothers.[3] Ivan is the intellectual, the lucid rationalist who wants to return God's entrance ticket to existence because he allows the innocent to suffer. Mitya lives in the body and lacks self-control, and comes to his destiny through accepting punishment for a crime— patricide—he did not commit. Alyosha lives in his feelings and intuitions. He is studying to be a monk and is a pupil of the starets Father Zossima.

Father Zossmia was considered holy, but when he dies and his body rots like that of other men, giving off the stink of corruption, not the sweet scent of sanctity, Alyosha goes through a crisis. He has a dream in which he is at the wedding at Cana, when Jesus turns water into wine. When he wakes, he is transformed. He then leaves the vigil over the starets' body, and throws himself upon the earth, embracing it, kissing it, weeping under the night sky. The "all is good" feeling comes over him, and he feels connected to "the vault of heaven" above, "full of soft, shining stars." "There seemed to be threads from all of those innumerable worlds of God, linking his soul to them," Dostoyevsky tells us.[4] As a consequence of this experience, not only is Alyosha's faith renewed, he now has an answer to Ivan's world rejection, one not coming from the head, but from the heart. But even more significant, Alyosha decides to leave the monastery and to "sojourn in the world," rather than avoid it in a cell. He says yes to life and is determined to live by this affirmation.

It is said that Dostoyevsky based the character of Alyosha on his friend, the philosopher Vladimir Solovyov. Dostoyevsky intended to write a sequel to *The Brothers Karamazov,* about Alyosha's life during his "sojourn in the world," but he died in 1881, soon after the novel appeared, and the idea remained unrealized. That Dostoyevsky planned the new novel is clear; it was part of his project to write about a truly "good" man, to produce a positive, convincing portrayal of a life lived under the auspices of the "all is good" revelation. But whether he would have been able to write it, to achieve the goal he set himself, is another question.

It is a truism of fiction that it is easier to portray a bad character than it is to portray a good one, which is really a result of our knowing very well what we don't like, or consider "bad," but not having so clear an idea of what we do like, or consider "good." The only wholly good characters that we allow are uncomplicated heroes like the incorruptible Sherlock Holmes or Superman, until, that is, the postmodern need for neurotic superheroes took over and made even these exemplars of wholesomeness seem flawed. The good I am speaking of here is not good in a utilitarian sense, the kind that Odoevsky detested. That sort of good we have seen is easy to depict; in the century to follow, Soviet social realist writers will produce many accounts of "the common good"—quantifiable in terms of output targets and production goals—being achieved through teamwork and effort, designed to spread the Stalinist message and to commend their readers for their patriotism. But the good-in-itself, the good that we feel but cannot pin down in an explicit formula, although it runs through all the great religious and spiritual traditions of the world, is not so easily depicted without slipping into sentimentality, cliché, and a gauzy kind of earnest do-goodism that turns most readers of any discrimination away. Although Dostoyevsky gathered notes and had plans for his sequel, in a sense it may have been a blessing that he didn't live to write it. The effort may have proved too great, or the result of his efforts not worthy of the theme. This is no reflection on Dostoyevsky's powers as a novelist, but on the difficulties of the task he had set himself. The good at bottom may be simple, but such simplicity generally does not make for good fiction, which requires conflict and tension, and only after the reader experiences these can it deliver resolution.

But where Dostoyevsky faced the problem of depicting a beautiful soul that would be believable to his readers, the beautiful souls that appeared during Nicholas's harsh rule faced a greater challenge: how to live under the impossible conditions in Russia, and, even more, how to change those conditions, so that the lives of those subject to them would not be so intolerable. What the novelist tried to achieve in his imagination, the characters, which appeared in the world around him, tried to do in their lives.

As you might suspect, not many were successful, and for the same reason that many of the German Romantics, from whom these beautiful souls drew their inspiration, were crushed. The problem with the beautiful souls was that their very sensitivity, that which made them beautiful, unfits them for life. Many of them died young, as romantics like Novalis and Hoffmann did.[5] This is why Dostoyevsky's planned but unwritten sequel to the Karamazov saga would have been of crucial importance. His idea was to show a beautiful soul that could meet the demands of life and who, by doing so, could *transform* life itself, something that Dostoyevsky believed was possible. But although that book remains to be written, and that life remains to be lived, there were some at the time who tried to meet this challenge, with varying success.

IN HER BOOK *Motherland: A Philosophical History of Russia,* Lesley Chamberlain gives some examples of the beautiful souls of the day. One was the poet Dmitry Venevitinov, whom the Slavophile writer Ivan Kireevsky—a beautiful soul himself—characterized as a poet whose "every feeling is illuminated by thought, whose every thought is warmed by the heart" and "whose best song is his own life, the free development of his full and harmonious soul."[6] The novelist Ivan Turgenev wrote of the poet and philosopher Nikolay Stankevich, whose "Circle" was another influential discussion group, like Odoevsky's, that he was "full of higher truth" and that his conversation could carry others into "the realm of the Ideal." Stankevich was the son of a wealthy landowner, as many of the beautiful souls were, and a reader of Schelling and Goethe.

His smile, Turgenev said, was "extraordinarily welcoming and generous." "In his whole being . . . there was a kind of grace" and "an almost child-like naivety."[7] He believed that all of nature is "evolving toward reason," a Schellingian/Hegelian conception, and he died of consumption at the age of twenty-seven.[8]

In some ways descriptions of these beautiful souls resemble noth-ing so much as descriptions of gurus or saints, or of their followers in the 1960s and '70s, who sought salvation through a return to a childlike innocence. And in a parallel that students of that time will be sure to recognize, the failure of "flower power" and other political acts of love to change society quickly led in the late 1960s to more practical approaches, many including violence, a shift that would hap-pen more than a century earlier in Russia.[9] It was out of Stankevich's Circle that Mikhail Bakunin, the archetypal anarchist, would start his career, with the motto that "the passion for destruction is a creative passion."[10]

SOME BEAUTIFUL SOULS were less temperate than the dreamy naive personalities described here. One such was the volatile literary critic Vissarion Belinsky (1811–1848), whom Isaiah Berlin characterizes as the "original prototype" of these peculiarly Russian personalities.[11] As Berlin describes them, they are the "sincere, sometimes childish, at other times angry, champions of persecuted humanity, the saints and martyrs in the cause of the humiliated and defeated."[12] Belinsky was all of these, and he carried on a kind of one-man war against the forces of inertia weighing on his people, using the medium of literary criticism as his weapon. It may seem an odd approach to social change, but in Russia in the nineteenth century, the writer was the acknowledged conscience of the people, and what he said mattered.

Belinsky was a true Russian Man, containing within himself the usual contradictions. And as Berlin writes of him we can see the char-acter of the *yurodstvo,* or "fool for Christ," although in Belinsky's case it is less religion than morality and social conscience for which he was ready to "accept humiliation at the hands of other people." Belinsky's approach to literature was moral and ethical. The idea of "art for art's sake" appalled him, as it later did Tolstoy. For him as for other Russians, art, as we have seen, is about salvation, not satisfaction.

In many ways Belinsky is reminiscent of the early twentieth-century Viennese satirist Karl Kraus, for whom ethics and aesthetics were one. Kraus once asked how "half a man could write a whole sentence," a query with which Belinsky would have been at home and which romantics like Odoevsky, searching for an "integral" wisdom, would have appreciated.[13] For Belinsky as for Kraus, literature is the vehicle of truth, or it should be. This is truth, again, not in the factual sense but in the sense of what is right and just. Literature was the one arena in which what needed to be said could be said, and Belinsky made it his task to help along those who were saying it and to castigate those who weren't. His essays on Pushkin and Gogol helped shape the Russian literary and philosophical consciousness, and it is for this that Belinsky is often seen as the "father of the intelligentsia."

His dedication led him to some extreme views and sudden polar shifts that took him from one end of the sociopolitical spectrum to the other. He started out embracing Schelling's ideas about poetry and art as voicing the soul of a people and argued that the Russian soul was suffering under the weight of autocracy. But then an obsession with Hegel led to a determined "reconciliation with reality," given that Hegel had shown, at least to Belinsky's satisfaction, that "the real is rational and the rational is real." For Belinsky this meant that the tsar and his autocratic rule were, after all, "acting in accordance with Providence," the great unfolding of the *Weltgeist,* and the task of the writer now was to show how this must be so.[14]

Yet Belinsky soon shifted from this position to one of passionate socialism, condemning autocracy and the tsar. He wrote a damning open letter denouncing Gogol for betraying the people and himself with his *Correspondence with Friends* (1847), a selection of writings in

which the author of *Dead Souls** turns his back on his early masterpiece and extols the virtues of serfdom, the church, and autocracy,
much as Belinsky himself had done.[15] It was in fact for reading this
letter aloud in public—which, among other radical demands, called
for the freeing of the serfs—that Dostoyevsky was arrested and sentenced to death. Exile to Siberia was substituted for his execution only
at the last minute.

Like the other beautiful souls, Belinsky was concerned with the
individual and his or her right and duty to develop, to live in the right
way. But for him, how this was to be done varied wildly. Belinsky was
one of those Russian thinkers who take things to their limit. His background, unlike that of other beautiful souls, must have contributed to
this. Where many were sons of well-off landowners and had the benefits
of education, Belinsky came from a poor family and grew up in a remote
town where his father, a retired naval doctor, took to drink. Belinsky's
earnestness and single-minded devotion to literature attracted the attention of his teachers, but a spell at the University of Moscow only led to
his expulsion. From that point on he was a full-time autodidact. A play
he had written denouncing serfdom caught the attention of a critic, and
he was offered a chance to write reviews. From then on until his death
at the age of thirty-six, Belinsky used his reviews, essays, articles, and
other writings as a platform to communicate his powerful philosophical
passions, all obsessed with the urgent need for *change*.

As mentioned, this sometimes led to wildly contradictory stances.
At one point Belinksy was convinced that "the destiny of the subject, of
the individual person, is more important than the destinies of the whole
world and the health of the Chinese emperor." But he also felt that
"to render the smallest fraction of humanity happy, I believe I could

---

*In his attempt to write a sequel to *Dead Souls,* which would show the "positive" side of
the Russian people and provide exemplars of moral and ethical behavior, Gogol ran into
the same problem as Dostoyevsky and his unwritten sequel to *The Brothers Karamazov.*
Gogol did make some attempt, but the effort fell far short of expectations, and in the
end Gogol burned the manuscript.

exterminate the rest of it by fire and sword."[16] To exterminate many
human beings in order to make a few happy may seem an agreeable idea
at times, but it is not really a good mission statement, notwithstanding
that more than one utopian benefactor of humanity has embraced it. It
gives us an idea, though, of the extremes that Belinsky and other thinkers of what historians of Russia call "the remarkable decade"* (1838–48)
were capable of reaching.

A LESS VOLATILE but no less committed thinker of this time was the
essayist and moralist Alexander Herzen (1812–1870). Known as the
"father of Russian socialism," Herzen, a great friend of Belinsky, was
one of the "good men," the "outstanding personalities," that the spirit of
the time believed were needed to set examples of integrity and "truth"
for others to follow.† Herzen believed in free will and the need for the
individual to develop all sides of his personality, as a means to the right
way to live. He was a beautiful soul that had the toughness and resil-
ience needed to endure a demanding life.

Herzen was the illegitimate son of a rich landowner and a German
mother. Aside from the considerable chip it left on his shoulder, Herzen
doesn't seem to have suffered from his illegitimacy. He received an
excellent education, including German and French, but he bridled at
his father's treatment of his serfs, and his own "outsider" status led to a
scorn for the Russian social system. A reading of Schiller filled him with

---

*The phrase "the remarkable decade" comes from the critic Pavel Annenkov. His remi-
niscences of the time are collected in his literary memoirs, *The Extraordinary Decade.*
†It is interesting when considering the "good" or "remarkable" men that formed the
Russian conscience of this time, as well as the "seekers of truth" of the previous decade,
how these themes and characterizations turn up in the esoteric literature of a later generation. Madame Blavatsky in the 1870s and '80s will speak of "seekers of wisdom," and
Gurdjieff, in the next generation, will speak also of "seekers of truth" and "remarkable
men." Certainly someone can seek truth and also be remarkable in some way without
being influenced by Russian cultural history. But in the case of two esoteric thinkers
associated with Russia, one wonders.

a burning idealism, and with a friend he vowed to uphold the cause of the fallen Decembrists. Confident, eloquent, aristocratic in demeanor if not in attitude, Herzen cut a very different figure from the uncouth, rustic Belinsky. But where Belinsky's volatility gave his work a patchy character, with bursts of insight coming amid torrents of impassioned rhetoric, Herzen's more urbane and reconciling approach, full of good humor and leaning more toward reform than revolution, eventually cost him influence. As Lesley Chamberlain remarks, his "real protest was against comfortable complacency anywhere," and he was as apt to target it on the left as he was on the right.[17]

Like many others we've looked at, Herzen was first influenced by Schelling, but he was soon drawn to the utopian socialism of the French thinker Henri de Saint-Simon; in many ways he can see Herzen's life as an attempt to wed visionary idealism with the practical business of changing society. His idealism suffered a major blow in 1834, when he and others of his circle around the University of Moscow were arrested by Nicholas I's spies. Their crime was little more than discussing how Schelling's idealism could be put into practice. Eight years in exile cured Herzen of Schelling and led, as it did with others, to his reading Hegel, and to another German thinker whose works would, as his name might suggest, prove incendiary for the Russian soul. Ludwig Feuerbach (the name means "fire brook") was a materialist thinker whose ideas heavily influenced Marx. Fundamentally he argued that God was an illusion or, more positively, a projection of human desire. What Herzen took from this was the conviction that human beings had the power to change their circumstances through their own actions and that the task of the writer was to make them aware of this.

When he returned from exile Herzen fell in with the Westernizers, those of the intelligentsia who believed that in order to rise up from its ignominy Russia had to adopt Western ways and go through the same process of development as the West had, a trajectory Peter the Great had started a century earlier. Their opponents were the Slavophiles, who believed that Russia should have no truck with the West. Instead, they placed their hopes in a return to Orthodoxy and a belief in the mystical goodness of the Russian peasant. Herzen had by this time jettisoned ideas about the "peasant soul," and he had no time for Orthodoxy (neither had Belinsky). Yet his tenure with the Westernizers was brief, and he soon abandoned their liberal views for the utopian anarchism of the French political philosopher Pierre Joseph Proudhon.

In *What Is Property?* published in 1840, Proudhon coined the term *anarchy*—meaning "no" or "without government"—and created the socialist battle cry "Property is theft."[18] Mikhail Bakunin, a friend of Herzen, who emerged from the beautiful soul Stankevich's circle, started out as a conservative, but was soon converted to Proudhon's vision, and from then on voiced an "increasingly shrill call for violent change."[19] From Schelling and the need for "absolute knowledge," Bakunin had turned to the materialism and atheism of Feuerbach, Auguste Comte, and Marx. The only chance for a society of beautiful souls, Bakunin believed, was to take down the state. He identified with the rebels of the past, Pugachev and Stenka Razin, and with contemporary terrorists such as Sergei Nechayev, "perhaps the most violent and thorough revolutionary of his time."[20]

Nechayev, a man "who was fascinated by destruction for its own sake," was the model for Dostoyevsky's sociopathic terrorist Peter Verkhovensky in *The Devils*. At one point Nechayev managed to convince Bakunin that he was the envoy of an international revolutionary organization, as Verkhovensky convinces his followers in the novel. In both cases, the organization didn't exist, or if it did, Nechayev was its only member. In *The Devils* Verkhovensky plans and orders the murder of a revolutionary who had second thoughts about the revolution, or at least about Verkhovensky's ruthless approach to it. In real life, Nechayev murdered a similar backslider, and was put into the Peter and Paul fortress for it. When his followers, a group known as the People's Will, told him they could either free him or focus their attempts on assassinating Alexander II, Nicholas I's successor, Nechayev typically said ignore him and blow up the tsar. They eventually did, in 1881. By that time Bakunin was dead; he died in 1876, "a Columbus who never saw America," as Herzen wrote of him.[21]

As with Belinsky, the individual was at the heart of Herzen's thought. What he sought and advocated was a socialism devoted to "a morally and aesthetically superior way of life," that could be "freely chosen by men and women."[22] In a sense, if a soul was beautiful enough, it saw that socialism was the right way to live and chose it voluntarily.* In some ways Herzen's vision of the "right way to live" is reminiscent of Oscar Wilde's contention that the "chief advantage" of socialism would be that it would free us from the "sordid necessity of living for others," and allow us to live for, and to develop, ourselves.[23] Not in the selfish, utilitarian way that Odoevsky criticized, the way of personal "interest," but in the way of the integral thinking that had become a part of Russian philosophy, bringing the heart and mind together in the pursuit of "truth," of that which is right and just.

But this was not the same for everyone. Herzen was no leveler, and his view of society was based more on merit than equality. Although he disdained the social hierarchies of his time, he recognized that there was a difference between the peasants who needed help and those cultured, educated individuals, like himself, who wanted to help them.

ONE DIFFERENCE BETWEEN Herzen and the peasants he wanted to help was the large inheritance he received in 1846 when his father died. With it he was able to leave Russia and travel to western Europe. In 1847 he left and never returned, spending the rest of his life in self-imposed exile in France, England, and Switzerland. He wrote and founded journals, such as *Kolokol,* "The Bells," that for a time were required reading by the progressive public in Europe and Russia, where

---

*Or, conversely, that you did see socialism in this way was a sign that you were a beautiful soul.

copies were smuggled in. In England he founded the *Russian Free Press* and contributed much of its content.*

Herzen had placed his hopes on a coming social revolution, but in 1848, when the democratic upheavals in France, Germany, Italy, and Austria came to nothing but a renewal of repression with no chance of reform, he abandoned this idea. Belinsky died in the same year, and the dreams of the remarkable decade seemed to have dissipated. Herzen went through a profound personal crisis. Europe, the West, was no longer a source for inspiration or ideas for social change. The monarchies were more firmly in place than ever. But the revolutionary ideas Herzen had previously supported he now saw were false. He rejected completely the idea, based on Hegel and soon to be embraced by fervent Marxists, that the "logic of history" makes a socialist utopia inevitable, "the real is the rational," and so forth, as Belinsky had briefly believed. This meant that any present suffering and sacrifice we may endure are the price we must pay for a future liberation of which we ourselves will know nothing.

In this view, the ends justify the means, however intolerable they may be for those who sacrifice themselves to the cause. Herzen rejected this. He realized that the "well-being of society" will never be attained if "everyone makes sacrifices and nobody enjoys himself," a remark that startled the French socialist Louis Blanc, a convinced utopian.[24] Herzen believed, as Isaiah Berlin writes, that "the goal of life is life itself," and that the sacrifice of the present for a "vague and unpredictable future" eventually leads to the "destruction of all that is alone valuable in men and societies."[25] This liberal belief in the absolute value of the individual, here and now, and not as a stepping-stone to some unsurpassable future utopia, will lose much of its power as the century moves on. Through a strange irony, the utilitarianism that Odoevsky fought against was slowly becoming the mainspring of revolution.

---

*There is an English Heritage blue plaque at the site of Herzen's office on Judd Street in London, not far from the new British Library. In Herzen's time the new library did not exist, and like Marx, he would have used the old Reading Room at the British Museum.

HERZEN PLACED HIS last hopes for change in Russia on something he had rejected earlier in his career: the soul of the Russian peasant. Giving up on the West, he turned toward the ideas of the Slavophiles and in the "peasant commune" saw the source for a transformation of society. As Peter Chaadaev had argued previously, Herzen now believed that since Russia was a young country with little history to speak of, it had more possibility for a better future; it was not weighed down as Europe was with its past. His last call to arms was to the students. He praised their idealism and youthful energy and called for them to "take the message to the people," to go directly to the peasants and educate them by spreading the word of social change among them, door-to-door.

This movement of the *narodniki,* however, an 1860s and '70s version of "people power"—*narod* means "the people," or the "common folk"—did not achieve the results Herzen had hoped for and came to nothing. Many students indeed gave up their studies, their homes, and lives, in order to "teach" the peasants, and later also to learn from them, but it was little more than a children's crusade. In fact many of the peasants were scandalized by the message of the students and turned them in to the police for preaching dangerous ideas of sedition.[26] The romantic image of the natural goodness of the Russian peasant got quite a bruising. Students, filled with fervent reforming compassion, were stunned to encounter an ignorant, stubborn, and suspicious populace who loved the tsar and the church and saw their liberators as little more than troublemakers.

WE HAVE AN idea of what the Westernizers had in mind for Russia. But what did their opponents, the Slavophiles, want? Not surprisingly they themselves were not always sure, and their different ideas often conflicted with each other. But the central idea was that Russia could only be saved by a solely Russian plan, something that came out of her own people, not imported from elsewhere. They believed that Western ideas do not work in Russia. As did practically everyone else, they read Schelling and took his ideas about the "soul of the race" to heart. Many of their concerns are echoed today in the rhetoric of identity politics, just as, to some extent, the ideas of the Westernizers can be found in the arguments for globalization.

As Odoevsky and other romantics had been, the Slavophiles were repelled by the rationalism and utilitarianism of the West, but they were open to its philosophy, especially that coming out of Germany. Taking their cue from this, they saw Russia not as one nation among others, seeking to better itself through "rational self-interest," but as the carrier of a world-historical destiny. Russia was a "suprapolitical force," a kind of moral exemplar, engaged in a cosmic struggle between spiritual and material values, an idea that is not that far distant from how some in Russia see her destiny today.[27]

In his posthumously published *Sketches of Universal History*, the Slavophile Alexis Khomiakov (1804–1860) argued that history is driven by the clash between two spirits or racial souls, what he calls the Iranian (or Aryan) and the Kushite. The spirit of Iran is that of God, of inner freedom and creativity; the spirit of Kush is that of matter, force, and crude pleasure. For Khomiakov, the Slavic soul is informed with the spirit of Iran, while the West falls under the sway of Kush. Ultimately, some kind of union of the two is what is needed, with the logic of the Kushite, geared toward the material world, combining with the "supra-logical understanding of reality" that informs the spirt of Iran.[28]

Like many Slavophiles, Khomiakov was a colorful character. He was a cavalry officer, obsessed with freeing the Slavs from the Turks, and in 1828–29 he fought to that end in Bulgaria. Although he came from the landed gentry and owned an estate, his personal habits were Spartan. He traveled through Europe, read widely in German philosophy, and met Schelling. He was a poet, journalist, and playwright; a powerful opponent in debate; and also an inventor. He was not particularly successful in this last pursuit. In 1851 he brought a "silent motor" he had devised to London's Great Exhibition; unfortunately it proved more noisy than expected.[29] Against the edicts of Peter the Great he wore a beard and dressed in the old Russian style, with high boots and kaftan.[30] He was also devoutly Orthodox.

What Khomiakov believed was missing in the West was the kind of "living knowledge," a sense of the "immediate givenness" of reality, that he had absorbed from reading Schelling and which he believed resided naturally in the Slavic soul. As Herzen and Belinsky had, he reacted to Hegel's abstractions in the way that Søren Kierkegaard, his contemporary, was doing in Copenhagen, although it would not be until the early twentieth century that anyone outside of Denmark knew about this. Hegel's concepts were very good for thought, but what had they to do with life as it is lived? Kierkegaard's query led to the development of existentialism, a philosophical outlook that, as mentioned, has much in common with the kind of thinking that was emerging in Russia. For Khomiakov and other Slavophiles, it led to the notion that Russia's very backwardness could be her salvation, an idea, as noted, that began with Peter Chaadaev.

What Khomiakov sought was "a model of knowledge distinct from . . . Western theories," one that allowed for a "grasp of simple truth," without the confusion of competing ideas about the nature of reality.[31] This was a direct, intuitive, nondiscursive, immediate knowing. Like many Romantics, Khomiakov believed that we are born with an "essential knowledge" of reality, which later becomes obscured by our attempts to understand it logically. Russia had a chance, he believed, to avoid the loss of contact with the immediate world—and of its people with each other—that was the price the West had paid for its science and reason. If Russia and Russians went this route, they could achieve the kind of relation to the world and to each other that Schelling had called *Mitwissenschaft*. This is not a "knowing of" or "about" but a "knowing with," a "participatory" way of knowing, something I have written about elsewhere, and of which Goethe was a prime exemplar.[32] It is a cognitive faculty that works by synthesizing the knower and the known, bringing them together, rather than the Western analytical approach, which posits a completely "other" world that the knower must reduce to its constituent parts in order to understand. Rather than know the world from the inside, directly, as the Slav instinctively does, Western man must take it apart to "see how it ticks."

This desire for an "integral" knowledge, one not yet alienated from the world through an overemphasis on rationality and analysis, led the Slavophiles to celebrate the very backwardness from which the Westerners wanted to be free. They were the original "back to nature," "off-the-grid" eco-warriors, who wanted Russia to avoid the industrialization that was overtaking Europe. Khomiakov's Slavophile friend, Ivan Kireevsky (1806–1856), wrote that this kind of knowledge demands that we participate in it with our whole being. He also argued that it could not be achieved individually, but only within a community. Hence the Slavophile's notion of *sobornost:* which we have already encountered in the idea of *sobor,* which can mean a "gathering" but also a "cathedral," the place where the gathering occurs. With *sobernost* one joins with others freely, in a shared love of absolute values, that is, religious ones.[33] Only through a true relationship to others, and through a true integration of all our faculties—head, heart, and body—can we arrive at a true knowledge, a knowledge not only of the "facts," but of what is "right and just." Khomiakov and Kireevsky believed that by staying a step behind the West—by avoiding industrialization and the alienation it produces—Russia could remain a "beautiful and harmonious world," and so be free of the tensions that had overcome Europe.

IN A WAY, just as Nicholas I was determined to do, the Slavophiles wanted to put history on hold. They wanted to create an agrarian communal society based on the peasant communal farms, which would be held together by a shared faith and inner feeling of belonging, a unity that is usually found only in religious communities. This mystical bond of the communal soul could not be understood rationally, only experienced. As Berdyaev points out, the Slavophiles idealized the Muscovite past—much as Western Romantics had idealized the medieval "age of faith"—and saw in Ivan the Terrible's theocracy a model for the future. A wrong turn had been taken with Nikon's reforms and Peter the Great's window on the West. Moscow, not St. Petersburg, was the true heart of Russia.*

But while the Slavophiles believed that autocracy was the proper kind of government for the Russian people, they also saw that it had become corrupted, just as had happened with the church. Reform was needed. The serfs must be freed, first of all, but the Slavophiles asked for more than that. They demanded freedom of speech and more representation in the government. And they called for the dismantling of the bureaucracy that had grown up since Peter the Great and that created a barrier between the tsar and his people. But their vision of Russia went beyond solving its problems. That was only the start. Their ultimate purpose was to create a Russia that would "stand at the forefront of universal culture," whose mission was not to become "the richest or most powerful country," but the "most Christian of all human societies," one that could serve as an example to the West and whose values could even help to heal it.[34]

IN 1855 NICHOLAS I died. There was some suggestion that his death might have been a suicide. It most likely wasn't, but neither Nicholas himself nor his country could remain much longer in the state of suspended animation it had entered at the start of his reign. His death came about most likely from sheer exhaustion. Nicholas caught a cold that developed into pneumonia; his thirty-year effort to hold back time had drained him, and he succumbed. The gendarme of Europe was gone, and a thaw began to settle over "frozen Russia," not unlike that which followed the end of Stalin's era. With this came the loss of the

---

*The Westernizers in many ways looked to "democratic" Novgorod as a model for a future Russia.

supremacy that Russia had enjoyed following the defeat of Napoleon and the founding of the Holy Alliance. The clear sign of this was the trouncing it received at the hand of the Turks in the conflict in Crimea (1853–56). Incongruously, the defender of the true Christian faith met defeat at the hands of the infidel, who was supported in his effort by France and England.

How two Christian nations came to the aid of the Muslim armies at war with Holy Russia is a complicated tale. Jockeying for position among the Western powers for influence in eastern Europe was one trigger. Another cause of the conflict was that Russia felt compelled to act as the protector of the Orthodox subjects of the sultan; although it was in the hands of the Ottomans, Constantinople was still the home of many Orthodox Christians, and there were many also in Crimea.* Treaties agreed between the Ottoman Empire and the European powers obliged England and France to resist Russia. (Austria, the other third of the Holy Alliance, stayed out of the conflict, only because Russia had agreed to retreat from areas in the Danube it had captured from the Turks.) In the end, Russia suffered an ignominious defeat. But the disaster served as a wake-up call for the new tsar. After it, Alexander II saw clearly that backward, barbaric, impossible Russia had to undergo a major overhaul if it was to compete with the other nations in the world. The irony here is that the new tsar, aware of and eager to meet the needs of reform, would be the target of repeated assassination attempts, one of which would finally kill him.

WHEN ALEXANDER II (1818–1881) took the throne in March 1855 Russia was on its way to its defeat by the Turks. But a perhaps even more portentous development was taking place closer to home. Nicholas's authoritarian regime had created a mood of discontent

---

*A similar scenario informed the more recent moves of Russia into Crimea and Ukraine, that is, the supposed need to come to the aid of the Russian people living in these areas.

among the people, and his attempt to stifle dissent only made things worse. Although with his reign many long-needed reforms were actually put into place, Alexander II was a man caught, as Gurdjieff would say, between two stools. A gentle, tolerant, good-natured if irresolute soul, he grew up dominated by his overbearing militaristic father. Yet, as his uncle Alexander I had, he also grew up with more than a little liberal, humanizing influence. His mother had secured the services of the poet Vasily Zhukovsky as his tutor. Zhukovsky, the most important Russian literary figure before Pushkin, was a Romantic. He believed that poetry should offer a vision of life full of feeling, passion, and adventure, and he passed on to Alexander as much of this understanding as he could.

Zhukovsky was one of the conduits through which the works of Goethe and Schiller, and English Romantics such as Lord Byron and Sir Walter Scott, all of whom he translated, reached the Russian reading public. He was also responsible for Alexander II turning out to be what we might call an "enlightened autocrat." As did his predecessors, Alexander II did his best to maintain a firm grip on autocracy. But the humanizing influence of Zhukovsky led to his leavening his rule with much liberalism.

This resulted in reforms in education, literacy, medical care, hygiene, the prison system, railways, and in the treatment of Jews and sectarians. Alexander initiated an amnesty for political prisoners; many were released, and many exiles were returned from Siberia. The judicial system was overhauled, and the economy improved. But the central symbol of Alexander's reforms was the freeing of the serfs.

In 1861 the Emancipation Act abolished serfdom.* But in a way similar to what would happen following the abolition of slavery in the United States, the serfs were in many ways worse off being "free" than they were as part of a landowner's property. Peasants were now able to buy their own land, but the prices demanded were often much higher

---

*The United States followed in 1863, with Abraham Lincoln's Emancipation Proclamation. Great Britain had abolished slavery some years earlier, in 1833.

than what a non-serf would pay. The land available to peasants was usually of poor quality, so they were forced to work harder to get less than they would have received as serfs, while at the same time paying off an enormous debt.

In the old days, the serfs tilled all of their master's land and took from this what they needed. Now they were compelled to depend on a small patch of barely productive earth to scratch out a more precarious living than the one from which they had been "freed." In the end, neither the serfs nor their masters profited from the change. The serfs did not become a new propertied class, able to contribute to the economy; and the landowning class lost its dominance, with their lowered status only adding to the general discontent. Where before only the slaves were unhappy with their lot and threatened trouble, now the former masters were unhappy too.

With the end of serfdom and the implementation of Alexander's other reforms, as well as the deaths of Khomiakov, Kireevsky, and some of its other leaders, the Slavophile movement lost much of its punch. Many of its ideas were absorbed by a rising Pan-Slavic nationalism that took a much more aggressive attitude toward the West; although critical of the West, both Khomiakov and Kireevsky had borrowed from it selectively. Pan-Slavic ideas were also taken up by an increasingly agitated populism—the *narodniki*—that called for little less than the dismantling of the state. Reform was not enough; even the major changes that Alexander had initiated would not do. Frustration, anger, and impatience led to a rise in terrorism, directed at a tsar who, more than any other that century, had actually tried to make things better.

ANOTHER FORCE ON the rise during Alexander II's reign was the group of individuals known as the "New Men." What was new about them was that they turned to the very aspects of Western thought that had repelled Odoevsky and the beautiful souls, utilitarianism and "rational self-interest," for answers to Russia's future. Where beauty, goodness, and a poetic, "participatory" way of knowledge were the guides for the previous generation, these new men had hard, materialist science for their beacon. They were matter-of-fact and down-to-earth and had no time for souls, beautiful or otherwise.

The New Men rejected the idealism and romanticism of the previous generation, seeing it had led to nothing—Dostoyevsky makes it the object of their ridicule in *The Devils*. But they also rejected the Slavophile idea of some mysterious goodness in the peasant soul or the populist faith in the "will of the people." What was needed in order to get things done was cool, dispassionate reason and logic and the will and determination to follow these to their undeviating ends. In this way the New Men were even more Western than the Westernizers. Facts, figures, and calculations were the determinants of reality, and a strictly pragmatic approach to them was the only feasible method to bring about change.

Nikolay Chernyshevsky (1828–1889), author of the utilitarian novel *What Is to Be Done?* (1864)—written while in prison for criticizing the plight of the serfs (he was later exiled to Siberia)—was a reader and translator of Mill and Feuerbach. He and his colleagues Nikolai Dobrolyubov (1836–1861) and Dmitry Pisarev (1840–1868), both of whom were also imprisoned, rejected religion, metaphysics, and any other aspect of human life that proposed some reality other than the physical, measureable world. With Feuerbach they believed that humanity had hitherto "emptied" itself into ideas about God and heaven and that what was needed was to turn that current back into itself.

But even to speak of "humanity" was anathema for the New Men. This was an abstraction with no basis in fact.* There was no "humanity," only men and women who had immediate, earthly needs—such as food and shelter—that demanded to be fulfilled. What motivated people was the satisfaction of those needs; as Chernyshevsky wrote, hitting the Benthamite note, "all deeds, good and bad, noble and base, heroic

---

*Oddly enough, that was an insight shared by the readers of Schelling who believed in the individual "souls" of different nations and rejected the Enlightenment notion of a "universal man," a proposition the New Men would have scorned.

and craven are prompted by one cause: a man acts in the way that gives him most pleasure."[35]

What was needed was to jettison any idea that anything more than material gain and physical pleasure informed human action and then to act accordingly. The aim was, as it was with Bentham and Mill, to achieve the greatest good for the greatest number. What Chernyshevsky and his fellow New Men wanted to do was to show how rational self-interest—in other words, enlightened selfishness—can lead to the kind of communal altruistic society that is necessary for the Russian people.[36] How far they got in squaring this particular circle is debatable.

In some ways the New Men are reminiscent of the Fabian socialism of Sidney and Beatrice Webb that appeared in England a generation later. They too were social reformers who looked to graphs and statistics as guides for the improvement of human life, and who had little time for the less material needs of the soul.[37] In Chernyshevsky's hands, as in theirs, art became little more than a means of facilitating the needs of the rational state, a raison d'être it would assume aggressively during the years of Soviet socialist realism. This was something different from the claims made for it by the Romantic generation, who saw in art a way to personal and social transformation. For Chernyshevsky art serves a humble purpose as a "substitute for reality in the event of its absence"—as anti-Platonic a view of art as one could get—and as a "manual for life." Here, art is no longer concerned with our salvation, as it was in the age of the icons, but with providing us with instructions; it offers a kind of how-to booklet for efficient living. (Again, as with the Webbs, this was the central aim: no muddle, no mess, no waste.) For Chernyshevsky as for the other New Men, "reality stands higher than dreams," and what he calls "essential purpose"—feeding and clothing men and women—stands higher still.

This attitude was summed up in a saying attributed to Pisarev, who believed that "a pair of boots is higher than Shakespeare." Pisarev was much more of a cultured character than his pro-philistine remark would suggest. But the intent behind it is clear. It was obscene to fret about beauty and one's soul when people are starving. A painting never fed anyone; more often than not, not even the artist who painted it. The social order is wrong, through and through, and must be brought down. For Pisarev, "what can be broken, should be broken . . . strike right and left," a sentiment echoed in Chernyshevsky's call for a "pitiless peasant revolution" against the monarchy, which, according to one account, was "one of the main objects of his life."[38]

One of the odd repercussions of the rise of the New Men is that their faith and optimism in the power of science led, within a few years, to a vision of life that undermined the faith and optimism in practically anything. In his novel *Fathers and Sons* (1862), about the conflict between the generation of idealists and that of the New Men, Turgenev—sympathetic to, but not a fellow traveler with the radicals, a stance for which he was taken to task—popularized the term *nihilist*. Bazarov, the protagonist in the novel, denies the reality of any value other than those apprehended by science, which in effect means any value at all, given that values cannot be measured or quantified. He believes in nothing, other than the facts that science can establish. Such a "faith"—although it rejects this characterization—came to be called "positivism,"* and is most associated with the ideas of the French philosopher and founder of sociology, Auguste Comte.[39] Through yet another odd twist of fate, a philosophy based on what it considered to be absolutely "positive"—the facts of science—gave birth to a world view that believed in nothing positive at all.

Nihilism rejected anything except the realities of the physical world.†

---

*Today positivism goes under the name "scientism."

†In *The First Three Minutes*, the physicist Steven Weinberg remarks that "the more the universe seems comprehensible, the more it also seems pointless." This assessment is more or less agreed to by most of his colleagues. Nihilism in nineteenth-century Russian life and thought is a specific expression of a general assumption that has dominated modern and postmodern thought. Nietzsche made it the subject of his particular investigations, and in *Dark Star Rising: Magick and Power in the Age of Trump* I show how, through a process I call "trickle down metaphysics," the nihilism that he saw was inevitable has now reached the flatlands of everyday life, hence our age of "post truth" and "alternative facts."

There was nothing other than matter, and this meant that nothing mattered at all. Life, the universe, are meaningless, something with which our own science agrees.[40] And although, as the historian Jacques Barzun once remarked, genuine nihilists "believe in nothing and do nothing about it," and are often confused with anarchists—to whom, too, violence does not come naturally; they are "gentle trusting souls who argue for a world without government"—the nihilists who emerged among the New Men were less laid back and much more impatient.[41] Dostoyevsky gives us an account of one in *Crime and Punishment*. Its plot revolves around Raskolnikov's attempt to act as if "nothing is true," as the nihilists claim. If this is so, then we are free—"everything is permitted"—and are restrained only by our own weakness. All that is necessary is resolute action and the will to carry it out.

What Raskolnikov discovers, and what Dostoyevsky is at pains to tell us, is that this is not quite the case. Some of his contemporaries, however, disagreed. Genuine nihilists—like some of the existentialists, beatniks, hippies, punks, and slackers who followed—may have done nothing about their nihilism, or anything else, and gone unwashed, unshaven, and unkempt. But there were others who took a more active stance about their belief in nothing and about the illusions society maintains in order to give the appearance of meaning to life.

The vision of a scientific society that the new men sought had already triggered a fit of anti-utilitarian hysteria in Dostoyevsky. In his *Notes from Underground* (1864), the anonymous beetle-man declares that even if it is shown to him that all of reality could be accounted for in tables and graphs and all of his actions calculated, he would go mad on purpose, in order to have his own way, in order to express, that is, his free will, however irrational, and not be just a cog in a wheel. Hence the importance of suffering in Dostoyevsky: the very thing that the New Men want to eradicate. Where utopian socialism wants to minimize suffering, the religious view, which is Dostoyevsky's, wants to understand its meaning. For the former this is sheer obscurantism; for the latter it is the key to the transformation of life.

IN THE EVENT it wasn't the New Men who had Tsar Alexander II in their sights, but the people, or at least the populists who chose the way of violence. And while there was a movement for peaceful protest, *narodnichestvo,* it was the more radical branch of the populists that dominated the time and that brought it to its end. Narodnaya Volya, the terrorist group known as the People's Will, had little more political aim than to kill the tsar and overthrow autocracy, a goal that Alexander's ruthless suppression of the Polish uprising of 1863 only made more desirable.

Disillusioned with the serfs' emancipation, from which only the landowners seemed to profit—the state was paying them compensation for their losses—and weary of the arguments and fruitless efforts toward reform, a sudden eruption that would *change everything,* was all that the People's Will looked forward to and worked to bring about. They took as their heroes the peasant revolutionaries of earlier times, Stenka Razin and Pugachev, and contemporaries like Pyotr Tkachev, a "professional terrorist" who once called for everyone over the age of twenty-five to be "exterminated," a rather more radical gloss on the 1960s advice not to trust anyone over the age of thirty.[42] And as in those tense, expectant times, as far as the People's Will was concerned, if you were not part of the solution you were part of the problem, a seductively easy way to identify your enemy and justify striking out—as Pisarev had said "right and left"—in any direction.

Yet, aside from this central obsession, there was conflict among the aims of the intelligentsia who had made it their mission to "save the people." Even here there was uncertainty. Was it their mission to *save* the people, or to do their "will"? Were the intelligentsia there to guide the people or to act as the executors of their desires? Many of the *narodniki* who ventured out to educate the peasants came to the conclusion that the peasants themselves would not be able to effect the changes needed to improve their lot. They simply were not intelligent or motivated enough. What was needed, it seemed, were small bands of dedicated men, revolutionary "experts," who would lead the masses to their liberation. But some questioned whether it was their business to *teach* the peasants, rather than *learn* from them. Hadn't Bakunin told them to give up their classes and head to the farms? And some wondered if such training as the revolution required would not "create an arrogant elite of seekers of power" who would "give the peasants not what they asked for but what they," the elite, "thought good for them," a temptation rarely resisted by liberators of the people, either from the left or right.[43]

The need for a revolutionary elite would inform and help make successful the Bolshevik revolution. But that was in the future. At this point, the intelligentsia seemed to have been overcome by a communal guilt complex, not unlike that which seems to have appeared in many Western universities today. Like many today who feel that Western civilization is little more a system of oppression, the students, whose radical ideas led them to idealize the ignorant peasant, now began to feel a sense of guilt and shame about the very education that brought them to that point. They came to believe that they had been corrupted by the very liberal education that had revealed the inequalities of Russian life. Much like today, notions of "privilege," "elitism," and "equity" began to give them a guilty conscience.

If, as they believed, the "people" possessed a wisdom aware of values more profound than their own, what right had they to impose their ideas about what an equitable society would be like on them?[44] According to populists such as Pyotr Lavrov (1823–1900), anything that keeps individuals separate, that alienates them from others, is an obstacle that must be eliminated. This meant education, but also the self-development that Romantics like Odoevsky and the "beautiful souls" pursued. It is the will of the people that the people be one, and such barriers as culture erects among us must be taken down.

But not only this: the privileges that allow a beautiful soul to grow are paid for by the miserable lives of the poor. So far only a handful of men have enjoyed what should be available to all. As Lavrov wrote in his *Historical Letters* (1868–69), "Mankind has paid dearly so that a few thinkers sitting in their studies could discuss its progress."[45] Like today, Lavrov wanted to prick the conscience of his generation and have them take on the burden of "group guilt."* "We are responsible for the sins of our fathers," he told his contemporaries, "if we do not seek to rectify those sins." Those who do not, perpetuate them, even if their own individual actions show they are innocent: a severe moralism, to be sure. Yet while Lavrov wanted to retain a sense of individual responsibility—something that the beautiful souls he castigated embraced wholeheartedly—he was also aware that, as necessary as this is, it was not enough to bring about the changes needed. At least in the early stages, what was necessary were "vigorous, fanatical men," who will "risk everything and are prepared to sacrifice everything."[46] These were men willing to give up their own personal freedom for the good of the cause and who would act resolutely and without compunction.

As it turned out, they were not difficult to find. Where there is a People's Will, there must surely be a way.

NICHOLAS I'S REIGN, for all its suppression and paranoia, was relatively stable. Until the fatal mistake in the Crimea, the gendarme of Europe had kept a lid on the chaos bubbling within the Russian soul and barred the influences coming in waves from the West that only stirred it up. But the pendulum swings that make up so much of Russian history could not be staved off for long. When the promise of reform that awoke with Alexander's coronation did not turn into fulfillment, the frustration and disappointment that followed the emancipation of the serfs soured into something more formidable. The tsar and everything he stood for had to go. It was only a matter of time.

---

*Lavrov himself seems to have been burdened with a guilt complex. Although he had no connection with it, after one attempt on the tsar's life, he waited for the police to arrest him. He wasn't on this occasion, but later was for his activities and sentenced to exile. He later escaped, living first in France, then England.

The first attempt on Tsar Alexander II's life took place in 1866. Dmitry Karakozov, an ex-student suffering from depression, approached the tsar as he was taking his morning walk and drew a gun. Karakozov had earlier distributed a "proclamation" calling on the people of St. Petersburg to revolt. A letter he wrote to the city's governor declaring his intention to kill the tsar, whom he blamed for the people's suffering, never reached him.

Alexander was saved when a passerby grabbed Karakozov. Where his guards were at the time is unclear, but Alexander himself showed great bravery in the face of this attempt and those that followed, and reports suggest he had a "fatalistic" attitude toward death. The failed assassin was executed. All he had achieved was a new crackdown and a return to the repressions of Nicholas I. A decade of reform of varying success had ended and the bad old days of heavy-handed authority were back. This of course only prompted more outbreaks of violence and even more repression. And so the cycle continued.

The next attempt on Alexander's life was made the following year, this time in Paris, where he was attending the World's Fair. Alexander was driving in a procession with Napoleon III and the rulers of Belgium and Prussia when a Polish nationalist, Antonii Berezovski, approached the carriage. A double-barreled pistol Berezovski had designed misfired. The bullet hit a horse and the pistol exploded, shattering Berezovski's hand. Berezovski claimed he was reacting to the Alexander's suppression of the Polish uprising and wanted to free his people. His political plea was accepted in the French courts, and he escaped a death penalty, receiving life imprisonment with hard labor in New Caledonia in the South Pacific.

In April 1879 another student drew a pistol on the tsar. Alexander managed to avoid the five shots Alexander Soloviev got off before being arrested. He was hanged. Later that year the People's Will attempted to blow up a train in which the tsar was traveling. Andrei Zhelyabov, a leading figure in the group, laid a massive charge of nitroglycerin on the tracks. But when Zhelyabov pushed the plunger, nothing happened; the wire had been cut by a passing cart. He made a second attempt that was partially successful—at least the nitroglycerin exploded this time. But the tsar had changed plans at the last minute, and all that blew up was his baggage train.

The People's Will tried again in February 1880 when an explosion ripped through the dining room at the Winter Palace. The tsar was saved by the late arrival of a guest. He was not in the dining room when the blast occurred, otherwise he would have been among the many people who were killed. By this time one begins to wonder if the tsar was charmed or if the assassins were simply incompetent. But the next year they finally succeeded.

On March 1, 1881, Alexander was returning from inspecting his troops, when he decided to take an alternative route back to the palace. Zhelyabov had been found and arrested the day before, so there was reason for the tsar to feel somewhat safe. Nevertheless, some instinct suggested precaution. Zhelyabov's comrades in the People's Will, however, had the same idea, and decided to plant assailants along every possible route.

As the carriage passed one revolutionary, he tossed his explosive. The powerful blast shattered the door of the carriage and hurt one of the tsar's Cossacks and a bystander, but left Alexander unharmed. The revolutionaries hadn't counted on the carriage being bulletproof; it was a gift from Napoleon III, who had himself survived a similar attempt on his life.* But when Alexander, against the wishes of his guards, left the carriage to help the wounded man, another blast went off at his feet. The assassin was killed—the first had already been arrested—and so were twenty other people. The tsar's legs were shattered, and he was bleeding badly. He was taken to the palace on a sleigh; an hour later, surrounded by his family, he died. The People's Will had been done.

The irony is that in his pocket the tsar had a ukase, a declaration he

---

*In 1858 the Italian revolutionary Felice Orsini and two accomplices threw bombs at the carriage of Napoleon III and Empress Eugénie as they were going to the Paris opera. Several people were killed by the explosions but the emperor wasn't hurt.

had signed granting the country its first constitution.[47] He had ratified it that day but hadn't had time yet to announce it. If the people had withheld their will for a few days longer, the assassination might not have taken place and, once again, history might have been very different.

Needless to say, the assassination did not achieve what the assassins desired. Popular sentiment turned against progressive ideas, not only in their radical expression but in liberalism in general. The violence sickened many people and only strengthened the will of the aristocracy to hold on to power. Alexander III, the fallen tsar's son, who took the throne, would be as determined as Nicholas I had been to stop the clock on history. A new era of suppression and authority began, and any idea of reform became a distant memory. Nevertheless, forces had been set in motion that could not be stopped. Soon enough, Russia would be looking at the last days of the Romanovs.

10
The Silver Age
Seekers, Sages, Saints, and Sinners

On March 28, 1881, a few weeks after Alexander II's assassination, the philosopher Vladimir Solovyov gave a speech that put an end to his academic career.[1] Solovyov was a popular speaker; a series of lectures on "Godmanhood" that he had been giving for some years drew large audiences that included his friend Dostoyevsky and the novelist Leo Tolstoy. He was by most accounts considered Russia's first real philosopher, rather than a moralist or social thinker. But this did not prevent a scandal breaking out over his speech. In it Solovyov had called upon the new tsar, Alexander III, to show clemency to the murderers of his father.

In the face of the determination shown by the People's Will to kill the tsar, this was an outrageous request, and not surprisingly, it was criticized and attacked in the press. But Solovyov was serious, and in a letter he wrote to the tsar some weeks after his speech, he made his reasons clear. "The painful contemporary conditions," to which Russia was subjected, he explained, presented to the tsar, "an unprecedented opportunity" for him to show "the might of the Christian principle of supreme mercy." It would be a "great moral exploit," which would establish the tsar's moral authority upon an "unshakable foundation."[2]

The use of the word *unshakable* was, I suspect, intentional, as it was how both the old tsar and the new had expressed their support for autocracy. Solovyov was offering the new tsar another realm in which he could show unshakable determination in upholding values in which he believed—or in which he was supposed to believe, at any rate. By acting in a way that would run contrary to all natural and human reaction, the tsar could "rise to a superhuman height" and thereby demonstrate the "divine nature" of his authority. Through such an act, the tsar would exercise the "supreme spiritual might of the whole Russian Nation."[3] It was a lot to ask. And if Alexander III had risen to this challenge to act contrary to what personal revenge and political expediency demanded, his reign might have got off to a different start. But the new tsar had no intention of being a moral exemplar or of showing how truly Christian his governance could be. He wanted to show the conspirators and their supporters that he would suffer no challenge to his rule and that any act against his authority would be summarily dealt with. "In the midst of our great grief," he said during his coronation, "God's voice commands us to stand courageously at the helm of government." To do so Alexander felt compelled to "strengthen and protect" "the power and truth of autocracy" from "any encroachments."[4] And to make his point, his first act as tsar would be to hunt down and crush the radicals responsible for his father's assassination, much as Nicholas I's first act as tsar was to suppress the Decembrist uprising.

Members of the People's Will incriminated in the assassination were rounded up, arrested, and hanged. And in speeches given after the executions, Alexander III made clear that his reign would offer no toehold for reform. In a purposeful echo of Nicholas I's conservative program, Alexander III announced that his reign would be one of "Orthodoxy, Autocracy, and Narodnost," a narrower, less inclusive idea of nationality than even that which Nicholas I had had in mind. It was, in fact, a severe Russian nationalism.

With this attitude, it isn't surprising that neither Solovyov's speech nor his letter had much effect on the tsar. They did, however, mark a change in Solovyov's life. His academic career was over, and he was banned from any form of public instruction. Yet one has to admit that with Tsar Alexander III on the throne, Solovyov did not have the best material at hand with which to fashion a nation that would take its spiritual destiny seriously.

IN THE THIRTEEN years of Alexander III's short reign—he died in 1894 of kidney failure at the age of forty-nine—Russia achieved a kind of stability and managed to stay out of any major conflict, and for this Alexander was nicknamed "the peacemaker." But this relative stability—"stagnancy" would be a perhaps more accurate term for the new tsar's attempts to freeze Russia in time—was in many ways the calm before the inevitable storm. Whatever stability Alexander III achieved was very fragile.

The number of attempts on the new tsar's life matched those made against his father, and he was said to live "surrounded by policemen" at Gatchina Palace; the Winter Palace was considered unsafe. This was the beginning of an age of terrorism, the clichéd image of which is of a masked, cloaked anarchist lobbing a bomb, its fuse fizzing, at some king or prime minister.[5] The image is a cliché because it was true, and the new tsar lived in the midst of it. Lacking his father's fatalistic attitude toward death, Alexander III took inordinate precautions against his own; for one thing, everything he ate had to be prepared by his French cooks. And although the attempts on his life were not successful, Alexander III's death is, for some, indirectly linked to a rail disaster in 1888, the cause of which remains unclear.*

The disaster itself is officially recorded as an accident; the train carrying the tsar and his family was derailed, it was said, because of rotten wooden sleepers, a plausible suggestion, given the conditions of Russia's primitive railways. Yet the destruction described sounds like something

---

*One plot against Alexander III led to the arrest and execution of Alexsander Ilyich Ulyanov, brother of the revolutionary later known as Lenin.

more than an accident. His carriage was "blown to bits"; his servants lay dead and dying. And as one account has it, his daughter, unhurt by the derailment, was frightened that assassins would now come to "murder us all."[6] If the derailment was the result of an act of terror, it's understandable that the authorities would not want the public to know that it had almost worked.

The tsar's death from a failed kidney has nevertheless been traced by some researchers to this incident. The story is that when the train derailed, the tsar and his family were in the dining car. The roof collapsed and the tsar—like his forebears a large, powerful man—held it up on his shoulders while his children escaped. This exertion is said to have triggered the organ failure that in a few years would kill him. He was able to hold back history, a hereditary occupation, it seems, with the tsars of the nineteenth century, but only for a time. Soon enough it would arrive.

ALEXANDER III, HOWEVER, was a formidable block to history's advance. As a young man he did not expect to become tsar and only came in line to the throne after the early death of his older brother Nikolai. Rough, blunt, and unrefined—he liked to think of himself as a man of the people and looked the part of a *muzhik*—Alexander III grew up to have opinions rather different from his father's, rejecting his liberal ideas and attempts at reform. Practically the first thing he did upon becoming tsar was to cancel the ukase his father had signed that was to set in motion the path to a constitution. The new tsar had no intention of limiting the power of autocracy, and he had an almost obsessive hatred of representational government.

This attitude and the policies that arose from it were fashioned in no small part by the ideas of a man who came to be the éminence grise behind Alexander III's rule. This was Konstantin Petrovich Pobedonostsev (1827–1907), Alexander's tutor and the real seat of power in St. Petersburg at that time. A "bigoted and misanthropic character," Pobedonostsev had a "semi-religious faith in Russia's destiny coupled with utter contempt for the West, its ideas, and its institutions."[7] It was a view of things he did his best to make the new tsar's.

Pobedonostsev was a jurist, civil servant, and reactionary political philosopher; under Alexander's reign, he rose to the position of Chief Procurator of the Holy Synod, the secular overseer of the church, one of the most powerful positions in the government. His radically conservative vision included an assessment of human nature reminiscent of Joseph de Maistre's. For Pobedonostsev, human beings are "weak, vicious, worthless, and rebellious," and hence need a strong hand to keep them in line.[8] Given this, it is not surprising that he was nicknamed the "Grand Inquisitor."* Like Dostoyevsky's paternal despot, Pobedonostsev believed that for society to be harmonious, people's minds must be supervised and made to conform to a common belief. Unity was the goal. With Pobedonostsev directing things, Alexander III's reign was one in which the kind of harmony they desired would be put into place by royal order or by force.

In effect, this meant the Russification of Russia. Under Pobedonostsev's direction, Alexander III instituted programs designed to fashion a country of one nationality, one religion, one language, and one culture: Russian. Orthodoxy and patriotism must be cultivated by everyone, Pobedonostsev argued, from the tsar down to the lowliest peasant. Tolerance of opposing views was unacceptable. Minorities must abandon their traditional ways and accept an official "Russian way of life." Religious beliefs other than Orthodoxy were not tolerated, and in places their adherents were persecuted. There was no room for Catholics, Protestants, Old Believers, or Jews in Pobedonostsev's Russia; on Alexander's ascension to the throne, anti-Jewish riots broke out in many cities.

---

*Pobedonostsev is also thought to be the model for Senator Ableukhov in Andrei Bely's Anthroposophical novel *Petersburg*.

Languages other than Russian were banned from public use; this meant that children who spoke Ukrainian at home learned their lessons in Russian at school. Russian chauvinism was considered the proper attitude of a subject of the tsar. Anything less was suspect and reported to the Okhrana, the secret police who operated then much as Ivan the Terrible's Oprichniki had in the fourteenth century. There were also the dreaded "land captains" Alexander established—police agents in rural districts who had extraordinary powers—and who were charged with stamping out any possible disorder at the least sign of dissent. It was an era of suffocating social, cultural, and religious claustrophobia that did little to achieve the harmony it desired.

Pobedonostsev's hand was behind the tsar's manifesto on "Unshakable Autocracy." Democracy, for him, was the "dictatorship of the crowd." A constitution was unthinkable. He warned the new tsar that "flatterers will try to persuade you that, if only Russia were to be granted a 'constitution' . . . all problems would vanish. . . . This is a lie, and God forbid that a true Russian shall see the day when it becomes an accomplished fact."[9] He firmly believed that "freedom" and other Western imports simply did not work in Russia and only led to the nihilism that the New Men had advocated. Only a stern hand would prevent Russia from collapsing into anarchy, and with Pobedonostsev's help, Alexander III could provide it.

With such an agenda it isn't surprising that Solovyov's plea for clemency toward the assassins of Alexander II went unheeded and that Solovyov himself received much criticism for making it. What is surprising is that during such a repressed and intolerant time, Russia witnessed a remarkable flowering of spiritual and religious conscious-ness, of an intensity and urgency peculiar even for Russians. Combined with this was an openness to and hunger for ideas and insights of a mystical and occult character. This gave to cities like St. Petersburg a strange, hallucinatory atmosphere, a feverish, expectant air that seemed to presage *something* on its way, perhaps even the Apocalypse? It is in this milieu that we can find the start of the Silver Age.

THE SHIFT IN sentiment toward a new religious consciousness—a phrase that some of the sages of the Silver Age took to describe their own vision—had been noted by some of the New Men, who saw it as a dangerous backsliding into error and superstition. But the spiritual needs that their philosophy of material happiness denied could not be ignored for long. The utilitarianism and "rational self-interest" that were supposed to guide the people into a new era of prosperity were for some nothing less than recipes for the extermination of the soul. Under such directives the people may indeed experience higher material standards of living. But what of their inner life? What of those parts of human reality that cannot be accommodated by the "greatest good for the greatest number"? What of the spirit, which makes human beings something more than merely clever animals, which was how the Darwinian view of life, that the New Men embraced, saw us?

Dostoyevsky, we've seen, had sounded early alarm bells in *Notes from Underground* and *Crime and Punishment*. In *The Devils* he portrayed the agents of utilitarianism and "rational self-interest" as true devils or, as another translation has it, "demons." Their path of liberation led to murder and arson, and by the end of the novel, bodies are strewn here and there and an entire town is in flames. The way forward led in a different direction, and Dostoyevsky charted it in *The Brothers Karamazov*.

Dostoyevsky died just a month before Alexander II was assassinated, but in June 1880 Dostoyevsky gave a speech at the unveiling of a monument to Pushkin in St. Petersburg in which he spoke of his vision of a coming Russia, one rather different from how the New Men saw it. Dostoyevsky made clear that along with being Russia's greatest literary genius, Pushkin was important for another reason: because he embodied in his work the character of Russian *universalism*. To be truly Russian did not mean being limited to narrow ideas of nationalism, and especially not to the monolithic notions that Alexander III would soon put into practice. To be truly Russian meant being open to the world, that in the Russian soul what was most important was what was shared by all men. Pushkin was able to absorb influences from the West and make them "Russian," not by imposing Russian ideas on them or by distorting them in any way, but because as a Russian, he was big enough to embrace them and to share them with the world, to make them available to all people.*

This movement toward the universal, toward a true "brotherhood of man," began with Peter the Great and the "window" he had opened on the West. But while at first this meant that Russia had to adopt Western methods and techniques, Peter's project amounted to more than this. It was informed by purposes "grander than narrow utilitarianism," and in the end it was really aimed at a Russia able to "reconcile the contradictions of Europe" that it felt in the tension between the Slavophiles and the Westernizers. The destiny of Russia was not, as Pobedonostsev, a friend of Dostoyevsky, believed, that of "one nationality and one religion," in a narrow chauvinistic sense, but in a "pan-European universalism." This was not to be achieved by the sword nor through material riches but through the power of love and "the law of the Gospel of Christ."†

Others took up the anti-utilitarian standard. The essayist Konstantin Leontiev (1831–1891), about whom Berdyaev wrote a book, argued that the individual's moral consciousness was more important than his function in a well-run society. He was an aesthete who

---

*Pushkin's "universalism" is often seen as the Renaissance that Russia didn't have.

†Dostoyevsky published his "Pushkin Speech" in his *Diary of a Writer,* vol. 2. That Dostoyevsky himself was full of prejudices and did not always exhibit the universalism that he saw in his people is well known; Solovyov takes him to task for this in his response to his speech. In his *Diary of a Writer* we can find enough diatribes against Jews, Poles, Germans, the French, as well as other targets to make this point. Readers of the Pushkin speech today will quickly point out that Dostoyevsky once or twice mentions the "Aryan" people. Dostoyevsky could be petty, and the morbid obsessions that inform many of his characters could be found in his own personality; Tolstoy, his great contemporary, once remarked that he thought Dostoyevsky was "weak and vicious" (see Colin Wilson, *Order of Assassins*). But while this may tell us that Dostoyevsky possessed the same flaws that we all do—he would most likely say that he possessed many more—it does not necessarily undermine his belief in the need for and possibility of Russia becoming a truly Christian nation, and of its task to give this message to the world.[10]

fulminated against the dreary dullness of "rational self-interest." Yet, like many other Russian thinkers, he held contradictory views. While he extolled beauty and the free creative spirit, a few years before his death he secretly took vows and lived near the Optina Pustyn monastery. The freedoms that the West offered were for Leontiev, as they were for Pobedonostsev, really mandates to sin, and he preferred a repressive state that would funnel people's attention to things of value rather than a permissive one that would let them do what they liked. With Spengler, Leontiev held a "biological" view of history, something he shared with his countryman Nikolai Danilevsky (1822–1885). As Spengler would, Leontiev believed that the West had run its course and was rapidly declining. He believed that Russia should look to the East, and not Europe, for its future, a direction in which the Eurasianists of a later generation would also turn.

Even Tolstoy, at the height of his powers and renowned as the greatest living novelist, abandoned his art and turned to religion at this time, much as Gogol had done before him. In works like *My Confession* (1884) and *The Death of Ivan Ilych* (1886) Tolstoy confronted the meaninglessness of a life devoted to worldly success, something that he enjoyed as the author of *War and Peace* and *Anna Karenina*. In the face of death and its finality, the pursuit of fame, wealth, power, and other worldly treasures—even art—seemed absurd. Questions such as "Who am I? Why am I alive? What is the meaning of my existence?" stopped the great novelist in his tracks. His existential dread led Tolstoy to Christianity, but not that of the church—Tolstoy rejected organized religion, and Pobedonostsev in fact excommunicated him for heresy—but to an austere version of the Gospels that Tolstoy tried to live, with debatable success. His death in 1910 at the Astapovo railway station, in flight from his home, Yasnaya Polyana, can be seen as a last pilgrimage of a great soul in search of an answer to life's mystery.

But it was Solovyov who seemed to embody in one character the questing spirit of the time. The yearning that had emerged for something more than the efficiently organized society of the New Men seemed to find in him a flesh-and-blood representative, if only barely. As his friend and disciple Prince Yevgeny Trubetskoy described him, Solovyov was a "unique combination of infirmity and power, of physical helplessness and spiritual depths."[11] He was frail and "otherworldly" and to some looked like the figure on an icon, with his long hair and emaciated features. If philosophers are, as the name tells us, "lovers of wisdom," then Solovyov devoted his life wholly to this pursuit. Indeed he took it very literally, and on more than one occasion believed himself to be in the presence of the Divine Sophia herself.

VLADIMIR SOLOVYOV WAS born in Moscow on January 16, 1853, into an eminent family. His father was the author of a twenty-nine-volume history of Russia; his mother came from an old noble line that included among its members the Ukrainian sage Gregory Skovoroda (1722–1794).[12] Like a starets, Skovoroda wandered throughout Ukraine, calling on people to lead a good life and sharing his wisdom. Stories about his life impressed the young Vladimir, as did the presence of his grandfather, the Reverend Michael Solovyov, whom the boy believed was in direct communication with God. If later Solovyov did not claim so high a contact, reaching out to the divine certainly became a goal.

It was one he pursued from early on. The lives of the saints that Solovyov had learned about led to imitation; the young ascetic took to sleeping without blankets in winter, showing the lack of concern about his physical health that would last throughout his short life. What also appeared early on was a peculiarly poetic attitude toward nature and even inanimate objects.[13] Solovyov gave names to his backpack and his pencil, treating them as if they were alive. He was also said to have had prophetic dreams and visions in his childhood, something else that would carry on into his later life. He would speak with the dead in his dreams—something Rudolf Steiner also practiced—and he possessed a kind of clairvoyance: when a friend had suffered a stroke Solovyov knew of it before the news reached him.[14]

Solovyov's brilliance was soon recognized. He was a voracious reader and excelled at his studies, and at fifteen he entered the University of Moscow. At first his attention was drawn to physics and mathematics; then this switched to philosophy and theology. Like many young intellectuals, Solovyov ran the gamut of beliefs. At one point he rejected religion, gave away his icons, embraced materialism and nihilism, and was an ardent socialist. Like many Russians, Solovyov held his views passionately; at one point he firmly believed in an imminent socialist utopia that would "redeem history."[15] But a powerful experience of his youth prevented him from remaining in the atheists' camp for very long.

When Solovyov was ten years old he had his first vision of the Divine Sophia, God's Holy Wisdom. The fact that he had just been rejected by a girl he had a crush on may have triggered it, but the experience seems something more than a childhood wish-fulfillment fantasy. He tells of the encounter in his poem "Three Meetings" (1898). Sitting in church one Sunday, feeling the sting of rejection while a hymn was being sung, the young Solovyov suddenly found himself surrounded by a bright blue sky. The shimmering color entered his soul, and it seemed to radiate all around him. Then the blue seemed to weave into the figure of a woman, the Eternal Feminine of Goethe's *Faust*. She held in her hand a flower—one can't help but think of Novalis—nodded at him, smiled, then disappeared.

Solovyov would meet the Divine Sophia—for this is who he believed the woman was—on two more occasions. One was in 1874, at the British Museum in London, where he was studying Gnosticism and Indian philosophy. The other was in Egypt that same year, where he had been told to journey by Sophia herself. In Cairo he heard her voice telling him to go to the desert. He did, and no doubt the vision of the young philosopher, in frock coat and top hat, sitting on the sand, awaiting his encounter, attracted some attention. His first visitors were some Bedouins who robbed him and held him captive. Eventually they released him and Solovyov spent the night in the desert. When he awoke he saw "the earth and the circumference of the sky as if breathing with roses." The vision was, he believed, of "the first radiance of the first day of creation."[16] Again it was Sophia.

I should say here that although Sophia is at the heart of Solovyov's philosophy, and that a whole esoteric tradition, Sophiology, is dedicated to her (associated with Silver Age thinkers such as Sergei Bulgakov (1871–1944) and Father Pavel Florensky (1882–1943) and reaching back to the Gnostics of early Christianity), Solovyov's understanding of what exactly Sophia meant changed considerably over time.[17] Perhaps this is understandable, as Sophia was not a concept for Solovyov but an *experience.*

In a general sense we can say that he saw Sophia as the medium through which God reaches out to and embraces humanity and creation, and through which we and the universe can become deified, that is, like God, in whose image we have been made. Solovyov's lectures on "Godmanhood" were about precisely this: how we must become more godlike, just as, through Christ's incarnation, God became man. This was in contrast to the opposite process, in which man deifies himself *as he is,* and takes the place of God, a project that the positivism, "rational self-interest," and utilitarianism of the West had already put in motion.*

We can also see Sophia as occupying the same place in Solovyov's Christian ontology as the Anima Mundi or "soul of the world" does in Neoplatonism: as "the sympathy of all things," the presence running through all of creation linking each part to all the others.[18] Unity was very important to Solovyov, as it was to Alexander III and Pobedonostsev.[19] But the unity he imagined was not limited to one nation and it would not be achieved through chauvinistic proclamations and draconian policies.† It encompassed all of creation and would be brought about through the medium of Sophia working through all humanity on Earth.

---

*I should point out that in the official Orthodox view, Sophiology is considered heretical and is usually spoken of as "Sophianism." This, from the Orthodox perspective, sees Solovyov's Sophia as an erroneous feminine "fourth hypostatis," a heretical addition to the masculine Trinity.

†It was Pobedonostsev who in 1886 banned Solovyov from any public activities.

SOLOVYOV HAD GOT to London and the British Museum on the strength of his master's thesis, which was published in 1874 as *The Crisis of Western Philosophy*. This work earned him a position at the University of Moscow and in a very real sense established a peculiarly Russian kind of philosophy. Solovyov argued that what had precipitated Western philosophy's "crisis" was that it had lost touch with the object of its investigations, namely, reality itself. Empirical thinking, of the kind that the New Men relied on, is in the end limited to the sense data from which it makes its judgments. What it knows is not reality itself, but the impression it makes on our senses. Likewise, abstract thought of the idealist type—as in Kant—presents us with the "forms of knowledge," the mental structures in which any knowledge must come to us, but it does not give us that knowledge itself. In the first we are bound by the senses, in the other by the mind. But true philosophy, true "love of wisdom," cannot be satisfied with these and demands something more. What was that something more? It was an intuitive grasp of reality—which for Solovyov meant God—bringing together reason, the senses, and a mystical vision of unity in an immediate, direct knowing, something familiar to us through our look at Schelling.

This search for that something more made Solovyov a pilgrim. He had no regular life, no family, and no fixed abode. A cousin he fell in love with at eighteen broke off the relationship, and after that he remained alone. He ate sparingly and irregularly, lived in hotels or on the hospitality of others. At one point he considered entering a monastery but decided against it. Yet he already was on the kenotic path. Like the saints and holy men of old, he gave away what money he had, even his clothes, and enjoyed the company of all walks of life. One pleasure he did confess to was wine.* He enjoyed it because "it revealed the

---

*"But there is another and far more important reason why all of G.'s guests have to drink. . . . A great many people are passing through his hands and he is compelled to *see* them as quickly as possible." Here, in *Venture with Ideas,* Kenneth Walker, a disciple of Ouspensky, is referring to the enormous dinners Gurdjieff served at his small flat in Paris, during which large amounts of alcohol were drank.

whole man," an insight that Gurdjieff also shared, although his means of revelation, vodka, was somewhat stronger.[20] Wine also released a lighter side of Solovyov, his sense of humor, something not usually associated with philosophy. This often comes through in his writing— he is one of the few readable philosophers—appearing in the midst of syllogisms and can be found in his poetry and in his often good-natured self-deprecating remarks. Like most serious thinkers, Solovyov knew when to laugh at his seriousness.

An interest in spiritualism led to his attending séances during his stay in London. But like his countrywoman Madame Blavatsky,* he was not impressed with mediums, and like Rudolf Steiner he felt there was something wrong about these attempts to "materialize" the spirit.[21] We can in fact see this as emblematic of his later philosophy. The point wasn't to materialize spirits, but to "spiritualize" matter. One reason why Russian seekers in the Silver Age were open to Steiner's Christianized theosophy is that he and Solovyov both saw Christ's incarnation as the heart of this drama, which is worked out in human history. At this point, when God became human, the spiritualization of the world began. For Steiner and Solovyov this marked a profound change in reality, and its subsequent history has been, and will continue to be, the working out of its consequences.

WHAT THESE CONSEQUENCES amount to are what Solovyov calls the "all-unity." This is "the gathering of the universe together," a different goal than the fragmenting and atomizing of it that Western science was engaged in.[22] Through this process God enters into creation, his "other," and after dispersing himself in it, begins to reintegrate on a higher level through mankind, an evolutionary narrative shared by Hegel and Schelling. What Solovyov means by the "Universal Church,"

---

*Solovyov's brother, Vsevolod Solovyov, was in fact the author of a dubious "exposé" of Madame Blavatsky. *A Modern Priestess of Isis* (1895), however, was panned by readers such as P. D. Ouspensky and Sax Rohmer, creator of Dr. Fu Manchu.

is the "conscious unity of mankind," the living awareness of our connection with each other and the divine.[23] This is the aim of history. Through it not only mankind but the Earth itself, even the cosmos, is transfigured. As Solovyov told a correspondent, it was the "work of transforming the world."[24]

We can think of this work as a kind of theurgy, a manifestation of the holy. Just as in the Catholic Mass, through the act of transubstantiation, ordinary bread and wine is changed into the body and blood of Christ—which through "communion" makes the congregation a part of the living church—so too through the struggle to "all-unity," the mechanical universe of the New Men is transformed into the living cosmos of God.

Solovyov charts this process through different levels of "being," the mineral, vegetable, and animal worlds, up to the human. Each level enjoys a greater degree of freedom until at the human level inwardness, that is, self-consciousness appears. As Hegel did, Solovyov sees human history as the gradual unfolding of this freedom through mankind's changing religious beliefs. Primitive man saw gods everywhere, in all of nature. But this pagan polytheism is insufficient, and something in us hungers for something more profound. Rejecting simple polytheism, we arrive at the *via negativa,* the "negation" of the world as a source of reality; it is illusion. Solovyov's symbol for this stage of religious consciousness is the Buddha.* Truth, reality, can be nothing in the world, so the real truth is precisely that, "nothing," or nirvana.

Plato also rejected the world as a source of truth, but instead of Buddha's pure negation, he posited a perfect, "higher world": that of the Forms. If this world is not the true one, then *another* world must be. But while this allows us to take the *via positiva,* by positing an ideal, transcendental reality, which we can approximate by pursuing the Good, the True, and the Beautiful, this ideal realm is forever beyond

---

*Solovyov's understanding and appreciation of Buddhism was of course limited; a point critics have not shied away from pointing out.

our reach, as long as we remain in the world of space and time. We enter it only on death, an event for which Plato tells us philosophy is the preparation.

It is in the next stage, Christianity, coming out of its Judaic roots, that Solovyov believes we see the truth. Reality is not in the Buddha's "nothing," nor in Plato's Ideas, although both possess a *portion* of the truth. God is not emptiness nor the Form of Forms, but a person, a living personality. For the Jews he was Jehovah, or "I AM THAT I AM," the answer God gave to Moses when he asked him his name. But Jehovah remained remote, and at times had a dysfunctional relationship with his flock. Christianity brought God down to Earth in the person of Jesus.

With other Russian Silver Age thinkers, such as Vasily Rozanov, Dmitri Merezhkovsky, and Nikolai Fedorov, Solovyov took very seriously the corporeal aspect of Christianity, the fact that it is predicated on God's actually taking on human form, flesh and blood. Solovyov's point is that what happened with Christ's incarnation was the beginning of a process that would include all humanity and that it was Russia's historical destiny to be at its vanguard.

Throughout the 1880s Solovyov worked hard to bring about reconciliation between the Western and Eastern Churches, something not attempted since the fifteenth century. Their reunion would be the first step in establishing the Universal Christianity in which he hoped to include Protestants and Jews and eventually all mankind. All peoples and all races, Solovyov believed, are "organs of Godmanhood," serving to "unite the entire world into one living body," a vision that seems to presage the ideas of Teilhard de Chardin.[25] Solovyov even converted to Catholicism, although the extent to which this meant a rejection of Orthodoxy remains debatable; on his deathbed, he received last rites from an Orthodox priest.[26]

At this time he took the idea of establishing the kingdom of heaven on Earth quite literally. He argued for a world theocracy, with the Catholic pope as it spiritual head and the tsar as its secular ruler.

He spoke with Leo XIII about his plan and even went to the tsar, but neither was moved. Solovyov was criticized for his ideas; his friends rejected him, and for a time he had to find work with the *Messenger of Europe,* a pro-Western "positivist" journal. He was so frustrated that at one point he even considered establishing his theocracy by force, by starting a revolution, but soon dropped the idea.[27]

In his last years Solovyov came to see that his plan for a literal world theocracy was a dream, and that the kingdom of heaven on Earth would be established only through a kind of "inner apocalypse," a spiritual awakening in individual men and women, not by decree. The only theocracy worth establishing, he saw, was one that arose spontaneously in the hearts of men.

In fact, in his last work, *War, Progress, and the End of History* (1900), he argues against his earlier vision and recognizes that it has the ingredients for a nightmare, of the kind Dostoyevsky had embodied in his Grand Inquisitor, a turnaround that seems to have escaped his recent Western critics. The book consists of three conversations held by representative Russians on the fate of the world. (As a reader of Solovyov comes to recognize, three is an important number for him.) The characters discuss the meaning of history and the reality of evil, and whether, as Solovyov argues, war can be justified on the grounds of combating it—a swipe at Tolstoy's pacifism that was based on the Gospel's "resist not evil." But the most powerful part of the book is "The Story of the Antichrist," tacked on at the end.

In it Solovyov envisions the rise to world power of a superman, a kind of miracle worker, whose feats and achievements dazzle mankind and whose reign brings global peace and enormous material benefits.*

---

*Speaking of the powers of this figure, Solovyov writes: "At present we cannot . . . know the magic and mechanical technique of these prodigies"—the miracles—"but we may be sure that in two or three centuries it will advance very far from what it is now, and what will be made possible by such progress . . . is not for me to say" (*War, Progress, and the End of History,* 30).

When humanity's corporeal needs are met the world emperor engages a magician to entertain the masses with his wizardry, predicting, it seems, our own age of nonstop entertainment.[28] Finally, he achieves the kind of unity among the Christian churches—Catholic, Protestant, and Orthodox—that Solovyov had pursued, but at the price of recognizing him, not Christ, as its heart. The majority of believers are happy to agree—has he not done wonders for mankind? But the leaders of the traditional faiths, their congregations shrunken, demur, recognizing the superman for who he is. They await the true Second Coming that will end the reign of this false god. Solovyov believed they would not have to wait long.

IT HAS TO be said that the kind of unity Solovyov envisioned was limited to the Christian world, at least at this point. Throughout the book, he speaks of the threat of "Pan-Mongolism," the rise of China as a world force, the "Asiatic invasion of Europe," and his belief that a great war between East and West will take place before long.[29] This was an idea that informed the Silver Age; in Andrei Bely's *Petersburg*, the notion of a "Mongol peril" occurs repeatedly.[30] Steiner even spoke of it in some of his lectures.[31] Although Solovyov meant it literally—hence his argument in favor of actively fighting evil—we can also see it as a symbol of one part of the equation in which Russia found herself; the other, of course, was the utilitarian West. Unlike the Eurasianists of the next generation, Solovyov did not think that Russia's path lay to the East. Russia's mission was not to succumb to the blandishments of the West, nor to sink once again into the Asiatic hordes, subject to another "Mongol yoke," but to establish a "third way," different from but combining the virtues of both. It was the way of integral knowledge, synthesizing body, soul, and spirit—the senses, emotions, and mind—in one unified vision of the Absolute.

The Pan-Mongolian threat did not eventuate in the "final catastrophe" Solovyov envisioned, but other predictions he made seem more on target.* He believed that the "success" of the "Asiatic invasion" would be "greatly facilitated by the stubborn and exhaustive struggle, which some European countries will have to wage, against awakened Islam in Western Asia and in North and Central Africa."[32] Whether the rise of militant Islam in any way supports Solovyov's prophecy of a coming clash between the East and West remains to be seen, as does the significance of his warning about a figure who will "cast a glittering veil of good and truth over the mystery of utter lawlessness" characterizing the end-times.[33]

BY THE TIME Solovyov died in 1900, penniless and in the arms of his disciple, Prince Tubetskoy, the new tsar, Nicholas II (1868–1918), had been in power for six years. His coronation did not bode well for the future. On the day it took place, May 26, 1896, a stampede broke out on the Khodynka field among the hundreds of thousands of people who had come out to mark the occasion. Poor crowd control by the police was responsible, and more than two thousand people died. Yet Tsar Nicholas II's plans for the day were not affected. As Count Witte, the minister of finance and a relative of Madame Blavatsky, remarked, a gala party that had been scheduled for that evening was held as if nothing had happened. "We expected the party to be called off because of the disaster," Witte recalled, "but it took place nevertheless." The ball was opened by Nicholas II and his wife Alexandra, and the festivities carried on without a hitch.[34] It was only later that the tsar learned of what had happened. He was so horrified that he said he would retire to a monastery to pray for the victims. His advisers persuaded him not to.[35] His regret was no doubt sincere, but in many

---

*One wonders though if the immense success of Buddhism and other "Eastern imports" such as Zen, Tibetan Buddhism, yoga, meditation, and so on, in the West in the twentieth and twenty-first centuries constitutes a spiritual version of the Asiatic threat Solovyov had in mind. This, of course, is not to say that such practices and beliefs constitute an "assault" on the West, merely to recognize that they have indeed "conquered" it.

ways Nicholas was the last person Russia needed then. His singular inappropriateness as a ruler led in fact to his being the last tsar.

This terrible catastrophe of his coronation highlights the distance that had widened between the tsar and his people. The Slavophiles had blamed this remoteness on the bloated bureaucracy that had grown up since the days of Peter the Great. But they had faith that the tsar was still their "Little Father" and that he had their best interests at heart. The remoteness seemed to have settled now on the Little Father himself, and to be encouraged by the Little Mother, Tsarina Alexandra. The rift that had opened between the God-bearing, long-suffering Russian people and their benevolent ruler was quickly turning into an abyss.

Like many Romanovs before him, Nicholas II was simply not cut out for the job. Having a muscular bully of a father—he was Alexander III's eldest son—who had ingrained in him the idea that he was a weakling and failure, could not have helped, although it has to be said that Nicholas did little to contest this paternal assessment. He received a minimal military education, had few, if any, intellectual interests, and was happiest engaged in physical activity, home life, and in the pageantry of uniforms and parades. He took on the role of leader of his people as a duty; he was not enthusiastic about it and showed little aptitude for the task. He had no taste for matters of state and "was happiest in the bosom of his adoring family, a country squire by nature with no stomach for confrontation with 'historic forces.'"[36] As his father did, Nicholas believed that his authority had been granted by God, and that it was his sacred responsibility to lead Russia and her people to their destiny. What he led them to was the fall of the Romanovs and the end of the Russian Empire.

Although possessed of great charm, Nicholas was timid and avoided contact with people and had the frustrating habit of changing his mind soon after making a decision. Witte said his character was "feminine," by which he meant fickle.[37] At first, Nicholas would shower favors upon an official, complimenting him on his service; then he would grow tired of him and cast him away. In their company he was the soul of understanding; later, a minister who had been congratulated in the morning would find he had been dismissed by the afternoon. He disliked conflict and made sure there was little chance of it within his court. Nicholas "would not tolerate . . . anyone he considered more intelligent than himself or . . . with opinions different from those of his advisers," a not uncommon habit among autocrats.[38] As time went on, the number of his advisers shrank, until it amounted to one: his wife.

Soon after his coronation, Nicholas married Alix, the Princess of Hesse-Darmstadt, who would change her name to Alexandra. German by birth, she was a granddaughter of Queen Victoria and received an English education. As happens with newlyweds, the tsar and his wife were besotted with each other. While in the everyday world this could have led to a life lived "happily ever after," for Russia and her people it meant a tsar who was increasingly isolated and out of touch with reality, and a tsarina who practically ruled in his stead. More than one historian has looked at their marriage as a disastrous folie à deux. Where Nicholas was vacillating, Alexandra was neurotic. She was the dominant partner, and although Nicholas could resist her desires, in the end he gave way.

As were the tsars before him, Nicholas was religious and held the church in high esteem. But Alexandra was something of a religious fanatic. She was deeply interested in spiritualism, until a change of heart led her to see it as pernicious. The fact that spirits had given Nicholas bad advice about the disastrous Russo-Japanese War of 1904 might have had something to do with it; Nicholas had accompanied Alexandra to some séances and, among other things, had tried to make contact with his father.[39] By this time spiritualism had become very popular in Russia, carrying on the attraction it had enjoyed in America and England. As one account has it, there was no other country where spiritualism had "so great a vogue."[40] In the occult atmosphere of the Silver Age, for many it was de rigueur to speak with the dead and to pierce the veil between the worlds, and for a time the tsar and tsarina were no exceptions.

Rasputin of course is the most famous, or notorious, mystical influence in Nicholas's court, but he was not the only seer who enjoyed royal favor. For a time the tsarina came under the influence of a character named Philippe Nizier-Vachot, who was known as "Master Philippe." Philippe was a healer and mesmerist from Lyons, France, and was an associate of the great French occultist Gérard Encausse, better known as Papus. He came into contact with Alexandra in 1902, introduced to the tsarina by her friend Grand Duchess Militsa, who shared her mystical interests; she would also introduce her to Rasputin.

Philippe had hypnotic powers and was prone to prophecy. One prediction that impressed the tsarina was that she would soon give birth to a son; so far, to the tsar's chagrin, she had only produced daughters. Alexandra was so moved by Philippe's confidence that through his magnetic efforts she would produce an heir that she promptly embarked on a phantom pregnancy. Philippe's error, however, did not prevent him from achieving notable status in the Russian court. Although he had no medical degree, through Militsa's prodding, the tsar appointed him military doctor and state counselor, so he could practice undisturbed. This, however, did not secure him from hostile forces, and after the false pregnancy, the opposition to him grew too great, and the couple sent him back to France, loaded with gifts and gratitude. The failed prophecy of a son did not prevent the tsar and tsarina from corresponding with the Master until his death in 1905.

Papus, Philippe's protector, had influence in Nicholas's court too. He introduced himself to the royal couple in Paris in 1896, when they were there on a visit, by sending them a greeting on behalf of the "French Spiritualists," who encouraged Nicholas to "immortalize his Empire by its total union with Divine Providence."[41] In 1901 Papus visited Russia and met Nicholas; he returned again in 1905. On this occasion he is said to have manifested the spirit of Alexander III. The ex-tsar warned his son that he would lose his throne to a revolution. Papus is said to have told the tsar that he, Papus, could forestall this disaster as long as he was alive, a prophecy echoing one made by Rasputin. Rasputin had said that if he was killed by the peasants, all would be well; but if the aristocracy murdered him, the monarchy would fall. In 1916 Papus and Rasputin died within months of each other, Papus from tuberculosis, Rasputin at the hands of his assassins. Not long after this, the monarchy fell.

PAPUS WAS THE head of a modern Martinist order. He claimed to have been initiated into the tradition by Henri Delage, a prolific occult author who himself claimed to have been initiated into it by his grandfather, who had been an associate of the Unknown Philosopher.[42] Papus even claimed to have a notebook in which Saint-Martin copied messages received from the other planes, although its authenticity was never established.

As I point out in *Dark Star Rising*, Papus was a student of the French esotericist Joseph Alexandre Saint-Yves d'Alveydre, founder of a strange political-spiritual movement known as "synarchy." D'Alveydre's *synarchy*, which means "total government," arose in France in the explosive 1890s, the bomb-throwing decade of anarchy, and was a response to the time's apparent political chaos. In their fascinating work *The Sion Revelation*, Lynn Picknett and Clive Prince chart the strange history of synarchy—something I can only nod to here—and its influence on the modern political world.[43] D'Alveydre himself lobbied for it with Pope Leo XIII and Alexander III—rather as Solovyov had for his Universal Church—and achieved enough success to be named a chevalier of the Légion d'honneur. In the modern world, synarchy's successes have been more covert. For one thing, the Traditionalism that informs esoteric political thinkers like Julius Evola—an inspiration for Steve Bannon, the alt-right, and Alexander Dugin—emerged from synarchic soil.[44]

Papus's Martinist Order had political ambitions. One was to free Poland from tsarist rule, an idea one suspects Papus did not discuss with the tsar. Another was to dismantle the Austro-Hungarian Empire and bring about a United States of Europe.[45] World War I liberated

Poland—until the Soviets took over—and took care of Franz Joseph's empire. A United States of Europe—Winston Churchill's dream—found some reality in the European Union, which, with Brexit (the United Kingdom's exit from the EU) now seems to be disintegrating, with efforts by Steve Bannon and others helping to take it apart.[46]

Other strange figures frequented the Russian court. A woman named Daria Ossipova was believed to be inspired by God; her rantings were studied for hints of the future. The "holy fool" Mitya Koliabin, crippled with deformed limbs, spouted prophecy during his epileptic fits.[47] Militsa introduced both to Alexandra, who was still anxious to produce a son and who looked to these odd characters for help. Eastern influences were not missing at the Russian court. Nicholas's disastrous campaign against Japan was prompted by his desire for more dominance in the East, and took place during what was known as the "Great Game," the struggle between Russia and the British for influence in Tibet.

It was a time of "mystic imperialism," when visions of a Russian Asia led to engineering feats such as the Trans-Siberian Railway. Nicholas had always been fascinated with the East. In 1891 he accompanied Prince Esper Ukhtomsky on a grand tour of India. There he visited the headquarters of the Theosophical Society in Adyar; on the same trip they met Colonel Olcott, one of the society's founders, in Colombo. Ukhtomsky was a practicing Buddhist and Theosophist, and he has been suggested as the model for Prince Lubovedsky in Gurdjieff's *Meetings with Remarkable Men*.[48] Another Eastern influence on the tsar was Zhamsaran Badmaeev, who practiced Tibetan medicine.[49] Agwan Dordjieff, a Buriat Russian and later tutor to the thirteenth Dalai Lama, successfully lobbied for a Buddhist temple to be erected in St. Petersburg.[50] It was a time when, according to one account, the Russian court had become a "collective for seers, monks, and mystics."[51]

The local spiritual advisers—the church—took a dim view of these imports and decided to produce a miracle themselves. They did so by canonizing Seraphim of Sarov (1759–1833), the first starets of the early nineteenth century, the monk who started the tradition. Seraphim was a remarkable figure; a hermit, holy man, and "immobile," an account by one of his disciples describes how he saw Seraphim's body transfigured by the "uncreated light," a result of his Hesychast practice.[52] He was a healer and seer, and apparently a good choice for a saint. No sooner had he been canonized than the tsarina conceived. Nine months later, in August 1904, Tsarevitch Alexei was born. Cue Rasputin.

If the arrival of a male heir was seen as a miracle, it was not an unalloyed one. The doctors soon discovered that Alexei was a hemophiliac, an inheritance from his maternal great-grandmother, Queen Victoria.[53] Once known as the "royal disease," "Victoria's curse" brought more pain to a tsar who was already dealing with serious problems. The shattering defeat of Holy Russia by an "inferior race," the Japanese, was a blow, although the tsar seemed strangely unaffected by it. When word came of the total destruction of the Russian fleet in the Tsushima Straight in May 1905—an easy victory of modernized Japan over antiquated Russia—he remarked, "What a terrible disaster," and carried on with his tennis. Throughout the war he had sent his soldiers icons of Saint Seraphim; what they really needed were modern armaments. He was a man entirely out of touch with reality. Soon it would get in touch with him.

The disaster at Tsushima and the ongoing domestic problems led to the massacre known as Bloody Sunday. On January 9, 1905, a crowd of peaceful demonstrators led by Father Gregory Gapon decided to take their grievances directly to the tsar. Workers had begun to organize into unions, and a series of strikes broke out in St. Petersburg. Gapon, who led the Assembly of Russian Workingmen, thought that if they could only speak to the tsar, avoiding the bureaucrats, the Little Father would hear their pleas. Gapon was, in fact, supported by the police, who had begun to covertly organize workers in order to turn their dissatisfaction away from thoughts of revolution.

This was a policy known as "police socialism," and it seems that Gapon was unaware that the police had planned to use the demonstration as an opportunity to teach the people a lesson.[54] The march would "provoke" them into using force. From the revolutionaries' perspective, who by this time included many Marxists—Vladimir Lenin and Leon Trotsky among them—subsequent events, however regrettable, helped to cure the people of their fantasies about their Little Father.

The tsar would never hear Gapon's plea for "truth, justice and protection."[55] Nor would Gapon himself know how right he had been to say that having reached the end of their endurance, death would be the only alternative to "the prolongation of our intolerable sufferings." The tsar wasn't at the Winter Palace—he was with his family at Tsarskoe Selo—and when the crowd, which had grown to some thousands, reached the Narva Arch, which celebrated the victory of Holy Russia over Napoleon, they were met by armed soldiers. When they were ordered to halt and did not, a column of Cossacks rode into them. When the demonstrators regrouped, the soldiers opened fire. Workers fell. Gapon, who had led the demonstrators carrying an icon, ran, as did many others. The worst violence took place in the square before the Winter Palace. Here Grand Duke Vladimir, who was responsible for keeping order in the city, took no chances. The people needed to be rid of their constitutional fantasies. When the crowd again refused to disperse, he ordered his troops to open fire. After this, the Cossacks rode in, slashing left and right. Cannons fired along the Nevsky Prospect. How many people died remains unclear; an official account numbered 130; an unofficial account was much higher, numbering in the thousands.*

When told of the events, Nicholas asked if enough people had been killed in order to teach the demonstrators a lesson. Pobedonostsev had been his tutor and, until his death in 1907, his chief adviser. His counsel to Nicholas was the same as he had given his father. Nicholas had already declared that any hopes for a constitution or any kind of representative government were nothing but "senseless dreams" and that he would "uphold the principle of autocracy as firmly and undeviatingly" as had the last tsar.[57] Bloody Sunday was the proof.

---

*The dancer Vaslav Nijinsky tells of being caught up in the melee, and among the many people arrested that day was the sister of P. D. Ouspensky; she would eventually die in prison.[56]

The aborted revolution of 1905 that followed made a dent in this determination, but only just. Riots broke out. Peasant uprisings as in the days of Pugachev and Stenka Razin left landowners slaughtered. The crew of the battleship *Potemkin* mutinied, murdering their officers. The scene of the baby carriage on the Odessa steps in Eisenstein's film has become a symbol of the authorities' response: brutal reprisals determined to crush the revolt. In the end Nicholas agreed to sign the "October Manifesto," granting the people freedom of speech, assembly, and other civic liberties, and promising to form a body of elected representatives, the Duma. His other option, establishing a military dictatorship, foundered when Grand Duke Nicholas, whom he considered for the job, threatened to blow his brains out if forced to become dictator; he knew it would mean becoming a target for assassination.[58] Order had been restored, but not for long, and soon enough Nicholas would take away the few freedoms he had grudgingly granted.

RASPUTIN'S STORY HAS been told so often that only a brief account is needed here. He came into the tsarina's orbit in 1906, when word of a mysterious holy man and healer reached Alexandra through Grand Duchess Militsa, who had met Rasputin in Kiev the year before.[59] By this time Rasputin had earned a reputation as a starets, and his powers were thought to be little less than miraculous. More than one account seems to confirm this, and as Colin Wilson points out, although he was a peasant with strong sensual appetites, Rasputin was no charlatan or conniving power seeker; his religious beliefs were sincere and his devotion to God—if not the church—absolute.

Alexandra was desperate to hear about the holy man. The doctors had assured her that the tsarevitch would not live for very long; his illness had already claimed four lives in her family. Without the clotting agent in his blood, the slightest scratch could mean death. If Rasputin could help prevent this, he was welcome. It was a miracle that she had had Alexei, and whenever he recovered from a bruise or scratch, she believed another miracle had been granted her. The doctors could do nothing; only the will of God kept the tsarevitch alive. And only a true man of God could do his will.

Anna Vyrubova, a confidante of the tsarina, knew of Rasputin and told the Grand Duchess Militsa that it was time they were introduced. Alexei had had an accident, and the doctors were helpless. Anna sent word to Rasputin, and the pilgrim from Siberia, who was already in St. Petersburg, boarded the train for Tsarskoe Selo. When he met the tsarina Rasputin said, "Believe in the powers of my prayers. Believe in my help and your son will live." Then he put his hand on the tsarevitch's wound, told him he was a good boy and that he would be all right. Almost immediately he was.

From then until his murder a decade later, Rasputin was practically a member of the royal family. If he maintained a role as simply a faith healer, his history and that of Russia might have been different. His powers did indeed seem incredible. On one occasion, after he had been exiled from St. Petersburg and in the tsar's bad books—Nicholas was never as devoted to Rasputin as his wife was—Alexei's life was again threatened, and Rasputin was called in to save him. As soon as he was told of Alexei's condition, Rasputin started to pray, and the tsarevitch recovered, without having Rasputin in his presence. It seems he was able to heal from afar and without his patient being aware of his ministrations. But whether it was his ego, his foolishness, or simply lack of tact on the part of a peasant who suddenly found himself in the halls of power, Rasputin began to abuse his position. He suggested to the tsarina that certain advisers to the tsar should be replaced with people of his choice; sadly, Rasputin's choices tended to be bad.

This, combined with his reputation as a drunkard and satyr—Rasputin did enjoy wine, women, and song as only a Russian can—soon led to opposition to the holy man, not the least of which coming from the church. Two churchmen who were early friends in St. Petersburg, Archimandrite Theophanes and the monk Father Iliodor, turned against him. But it was the nobility in the form of Prince Yussupov that was most eager to rid the court of his influence. His hold over the tsarina was, through her power over the tsar, leading Russia into an abyss, or so they thought. Alexandra was already in disfavor with the people; World War I had been raging for two years, and as a German she was thought to favor the kaiser over her adopted country. Stories circulating of Rasputin taking the tsarina to bed could not have helped. Scandal, decadence, and hysteria—not entirely uncommon elements in the Russian court—now seemed to rule the Romanovs.

But getting rid of Rasputin was easier said than done. On December 29, 1916, the night of Rasputin's assassination, Yussupov and his accomplices had to resort to poison, bullets, beating, castration, and drowning, before the holy man from Pokrovskoe gave up the ghost. He ate and drank poisoned cake and wine and asked for more. When this didn't kill him, his assailants, panicking, resorted to a revolver. Even that wasn't enough. The life force he had poured into others put up a terrific fight. As mentioned, when his body was fished out of the frozen Neva, his hand was making the sign of the cross and there was water in his lungs, indicating that his actual death was from drowning.[60] Not long after this, as Rasputin had predicted, the monarchy fell.* Less than a year later, the tsar, tsarina, and their family were dead.

THE TEN YEARS that we can call "Rasputin's decade" passed in an atmosphere of feverish, almost morbid expectation. A spiritual frenzy seemed to grip St. Petersburg, and a passion for the occult, the mystical, the mysterious, even the satanic, raged among its artists, poets, and thinkers. We can trace the origin of this outbreak to Symbolism, the aesthetic movement that had reached Russia from France in the

---

*More than one commentator has pointed out that Rasputin's murder did not achieve what his assassins had hoped from it. It was not so much his advice that was leading Russia to a precipice as the tsarina's influence on her husband. It seems that had she been assassinated rather than the holy devil, Russia might have been pulled back from the brink.

1890s through the work of the critic A. L. Volynsky. The poet Charles Baudelaire, influenced by a reading of Swedenborg, had created an aesthetic based on the notion that the things and events of our everyday world are really symbols of a higher reality, what Swedenborg spoke of as "correspondences."[61] For Baudelaire, the poet, like the mystic or the occultist, is a reader of signs. By the time Symbolism reached St. Petersburg, signs, it seemed, were everywhere, and more than one artist and poet was determined to read them.

The leading personalities among the Russian Symbolists were the writer Dmitri Merzhkovsky (1865–1941) and his wife, the poet Zinaida Gippius (1869–1945), who are generally considered the movement's founders. Merzhkovsky was a novelist, philosopher, historian, and religious prophet; he saw the 1905 revolution as the first sign of some tremendous social and spiritual upheaval. With Gippius, he developed the idea of what he called the "new religious consciousness," an inner transformation that would bring about an outer apocalypse. They saw their work as providing a new vision and founded a journal, *Novy Put,* "New Path," to present it.

As Solovyov did, Merzhkovsky saw the world in terms of antitheses; his *Antichrist* trilogy (1895–1904) works out the dialectic of what he calls the "two truths," that of Christianity and that of paganism.[62] Merzhkovsky was another religious Russian for whom "the flesh" was a central issue, and his "Third Testament," superseding the Old and the New—and borrowed from the twelfth-century Christian prophet Joachim of Fiore—is his attempt, not entirely successful, to fuse the spiritual and the carnal worlds and so bring about a new age.

The Merzhkovskys' influence on their contemporaries was considerable, but for some, not always beneficial. Berdyaev, who knew them and who joined the Religious-Philosophical Society that Merzhkovsky founded in St. Petersburg in 1901, was not always favorably impressed. The couple took their spiritual pursuits very seriously; some might say they wore them on their sleeves. Among other things, on one occasion they made a pilgrimage to Lake Svetloyar where the Invisible

City of Kitezh lies submerged. Merzhkovsky blended speculations on sex, Atlantis, and a coming God-man in an often heady brew and, as Berdyaev remarked, seemed to live "in an atmosphere of unhealthy, self-assertive sectarian mysticism." Gippius had a mean streak and combined "a profound understanding of others" with "a capacity for inflicting pain on them." He found her "snake-like" and "entirely devoid of human warmth."[63]

Berdyaev was one of the few critical voices to be heard in this excited time; another prophet he was less than enthusiastic about was Rudolf Steiner. After hearing Steiner speak at Helsingfors (Helsinki) in 1911 he said his audience seemed like "maniacs possessed by some power beyond their control," and he was especially suspicious of a woman, Anna Mintslova, whom he called "Steiner's emissary," but whose actual connection to Steiner, if any, is unclear.[64] Mintslova struck him as evil; her influence was "absolutely negative and demonic." Berdyaev even believed she had cast a kind of spell on him, and he speaks of her mysterious disappearance, vanishing into thin air one day in Moscow while crossing the Kuznetsky Bridge.

One Symbolist who was profoundly influenced by Steiner was the novelist Andrei Bely (1880–1934). Born Boris Nikolaevich Bugaev in Moscow, he changed his name (it means "Andrew White") to avoid embarrassing his mathematician father. Bely was a voracious reader of philosophy and a follower of Solovyov. With him he believed that the West was in decline and that a new cultural epoch was about to be born in Russia (we've also seen that he agreed with Solovyov about the looming "Mongol Peril").

Bely's first novel, *The Silver Dove* (1909), spells out this thesis. In it, a poet, tired of the intelligentsia, leaves the city for the countryside and becomes involved with a mystical cult; Bely later claimed he had predicted Rasputin. Overcome by atavistic primal forces, he is forced into a blasphemous union with the "Mother of God," in an attempt to create a magical child for the new era. Bely came into Steiner's orbit in 1912 and eventually left Russia for Switzerland, to work on Steiner's

Anthroposophical temple, the Goetheanum, a remarkable work of esoteric architecture, sadly destroyed by fire in 1924. He and Steiner would
eventually fall out, and Bely would return to Russia. As mentioned,
his novel *Petersburg* is saturated with Steiner's ideas about the coming
new age, etheric bodies, the "Mongol Peril," astral journeys, and other
Anthroposophical dicta.

Bely fell under the influence of another important Symbolist,
the novelist and critic Valery Briussov (1873–1924), author of *The
Fiery Angel* (1909), a remarkable work of witchcraft and black magic;
Prokofiev based his opera of the same name on it. Briussov was a rather
different personality than Bely and the other Symbolists; a pragmatic,
somewhat superior character, he was an effective self-promoter and took
great pains to develop the "satanic" persona that he showed the world,
highlighting his Mongol features, arching eyebrows, and pointed beard.
He had an interest in spiritualism and psychic phenomena, but from a
cool, detached perspective, almost that of a connoisseur. Along with the
spiritual and mystical, Silver Age Russia had a taste for the demonic,
and Briussov was among the leading figures exemplifying what we can
call the decadent "dark side" of Symbolism.

Briussov was a man of iron discipline, and he approached his
art with the rigor of his French masters, Flaubert and Huysmans.
Fastidious, immaculately dressed, and with an eye to business, Briussov's
stern will drew him to more labile characters. One was the teenage poet
Alexander Dobrolyubov, who was a kind of Russian Arthur Rimbaud.
At seventeen he impressed Briussov with ideas about literature, but his
behavior was even more impressive. He wore only black, including fur-
lined gloves that he never removed, smoked opium, and was thrown
out of school for preaching suicide to his classmates, with some success.
Indeed, suicide was a popular pastime then, with many "suicide clubs,"
like the Black Swan, founded by the publisher Nikolai Riabushinsky,
flourishing, although how they maintained their membership is unclear.

Like Rimbaud, Dobrolyubov soon tired of poetry and abandoned
it, leaving his small, windowless room—whose black walls were covered

with satanic bric-a-brac—to go out into the world and become a religious prophet. He took to encasing himself in iron hoops and wandering through the countryside, preaching his message and gaining followers. Part of his teaching included not answering a question until a year had passed after it was asked. As Berdyaev points out, this made conversation difficult. Dobrolyubov impressed Briussov because he said he had *podvig;* as did the fabled saints of old, he had the strength to *live* his beliefs—the meaning of *podvig*—and through them, to transform life, a central aim of the Symbolists, who, in strict Russian tradition, wanted to be *saved* by their art, not merely entertained.

Bely met Briussov through the Merzhkovskys, who were promoting him as the new rising star. A changeable, unstable character—Berdyaev said it was "impossible to rely on Bely in any way whatsoever"—Bely had moved from one father figure to another (Merzhkovsky the latest) and was ready for another change. He came under Briussov's potent spell. The satanic image the older man affected awed the hypersensitive and emotional newcomer, and for a time Bely was chela to Briussov's demonic guru. But soon the two came to magical fisticuffs over a woman; the demonic triangle became the subject of Briussov's masterpiece, *The Fiery Angel,* which transports his contretemps with Bely over the unfortunate Nina Petrovskaya from pre-Bolshevik Russia to a remarkable re-creation of a magic-ridden sixteenth-century Germany.[65]

Briussov was not the only dark star on satanic St. Petersburg's horizon. The devil was in vogue, as he is from time to time. Konstantin Balmont, another important Symbolist and a protégé of Briussov, wrote a book titled *Evil Spell: A Book of Exorcisms,* arguing that dark forces were responsible for the 1905 revolution, a perspective he shared with the philosopher, economist, and priest, Sergei Bulgakov.[66] The actor Feodor Chaliapin made a career out of playing Mephistopheles in Gounod's *Faust.* The poet Lev Kobilynsky asked if Satan was not "better than a large part of the human race we try to save from him." Devilish erotica leered from the covers of magazines, Rasputin's reputation as a holy devil helping the circulation of many. One host of a suicide club proposed a special edition of a magazine devoted solely to Satan; he received more than a hundred contributions from writers and poets, eager to sign up to be the devil's spokesman. The composer and theosophist Alexander Scriabin, whose *Poem of Ecstasy, Poem of Fire,* and unfinished *Mystery* portray in musical form the evolution of human consciousness, joined the demonic ranks with his *Poem Satanic* and Ninth Piano Sonata, which he called a "black mass." The painter Mikhail Vrubel, another devotee of the satanic, spent his last years in a madhouse. Drugs, sex, transgressions of all sorts—"holy sinning"— were, of course, the rage.

Yet not all litanies to Satan were full of praise. P. D. Ouspensky rang the Dostoyevskian note when in his *Talks with a Devil* (1916) he portrayed the fallen angel as a petit bourgeois, a tedious, rather common character, "vulgarity and triviality embodied." But his voice was a lone one, and in many ways the temper of the time was more suited to the delights of perdition than the labors of making heaven on Earth, although the hell to come would arrive through trying to do precisely that.

It was not long in coming.

11

The End of Holy Russia

Power to the People

On July 17, 1918, Tsar Nicholas II, his wife Alexandra, their children, doctor, cook, and maid were executed in the cellar of a house in Ekaterinburg, a city in the Urals that at the time was, according to one account, "perhaps the most vehemently Bolshevik spot in Russia."[1] Their executioners, led by a particularly zealous overseer, did a thorough job. A White Russian army was closing in, and the Reds were concerned that it would capture Ekaterinburg and free the tsar. The fact that Ekaterinburg fell to the Whites later that month suggests their concern was justified. Nothing should be left to provide even the slightest hope of a return of the monarchy. So they took no chances. Even the family's pet spaniel was killed.

For some time the idea that one daughter, Anastasia, managed to escape, was considered a possibility, but DNA tests have since confirmed that she died along with her sisters, Ingrid Bergman's stellar performance as the amnesiac pretender in the 1956 film *Anastasia* notwithstanding. The tsar was shot, then the tsarina, the girls, the tsarevitch, and the others.* Bayonets and rifle butts finished the job. Their bodies were burned

---

*The tsarina and her daughters took longer to kill because the jewels they had sown into their dresses protected them from the first round of gunfire. This led some of their assassins to think they had supernatural protection. The bayonets disabused them of this.

with acid, then tossed down a mine shaft. Later they were retrieved and buried elsewhere. Although the remains had been located in 1976, the Soviets kept the knowledge secret; it wasn't until July 17, 1998—eighty years after their murders and seven after the collapse of the Soviet Union—that they were interred in the crypt of the Cathedral of Saints Peter and Paul in St. Petersburg. Boris Yeltsin, the first president of the fledgling Russian Federation, presided over their reburial. Now the sisters are the focus of a religious cult, the family has been canonized, and on the site of their murder stands the Church on the Blood, dedicated to "all saints resplendent in the Russian land."[2]

The abuse the corpses received suggests the kind of hysterical hatred Rasputin had provoked in his assassins. Expedient as they were, the murders were not really necessary. They served as a kind of marker, a symbol that a threshold had been crossed, and that what had been unthinkable was now the order of the day. Rasputin's body too received some posthumous attention. It was not allowed to rest in its grave in the royal park at Tsarskoe Selo, where Alexandra demanded he was buried; his wife had wanted him returned to Pokrovskoe, in Siberia, where they had lived, but her wishes were overruled. With the fall of the old regime, Bolsheviks dug up the coffin of the holy devil and burned it.[3]

Nicholas and Alexandra were not the only members of the royal family to meet a grisly fate. The day after their murders, the tsarina's sister, Grand Duchess Elizabeth,* Grand Duke Sergius Mikhailovich, along with sons of Grand Duke Constantine and Grand Duke Paul, were taken to a disused mineshaft in Alapayevsky, not far from Ekaterinburg, clubbed on the head and thrown in; only Grand Duke Sergius was shot as he attempted to resist.[4] Then dynamite was tossed in after them. Most likely the blast did not kill them and they faced a slow death from their wounds or suffocation.

This should serve as sufficient evidence of the kind of hostility and resentment that exploded with the fall of the Romanovs. As had

---

*The Grand Duchess was canonized as well, eight years before her sister.

happened in the French Revolution, even the slightest connection to the nobility, or the merest suggestion that one had profited by the old regime, was enough to warrant reprisals. Ministers were executed by the dozen; those who weren't either had the prescience to escape when they could, or threw their lot in with the Bolsheviks. "People's courts" held summary trials of individuals accused of being "counterrevolutionary." Their justice was swift and unforgiving.

In his "Letters from Russia," published in England in A. R. Orage's journal *The New Age* in 1919—the same year that Hermann Hesse published his essay on "Russian Man"—P. D. Ouspensky gave an account of what life was like with the collapse of the old regime. Ouspensky hated the Bolsheviks but had no love of the tsar—his sister was one of the victims of the 1905 revolution—and he found himself caught up in the chaos of a civil war he was trying to escape. Gurdjieff, his teacher, was doing the same, and by different routes they both wound up in Constantinople, soon to be renamed Istanbul.

Ouspensky explained to his readers that they had no idea what was really taking place in Russia and that those who had some sympathy for the "Bolshevik experiment" were especially ignorant and misinformed. What was coming into being was not the "dictatorship of the proletariat" that Marx had so confidently predicted, but the "dictatorship of the criminal element."[5] People outside of Russia, hearing of those who wished to live again "in the old way," hadn't the slightest idea what that meant. It did not mean "the re-establishment of the old regime or the oppression of the working classes" or anything along those lines, but concerned issues like "When shall we be able to buy shoe-leather again, or shaving-soap, or a box of matches?"[6] Ouspensky admitted that he himself was still alive "only because my boots and trousers . . . are still holding together."[7] When they went, he said, so would he.

Prices for the most essential items had skyrocketed; profiteering and corruption were rife, as was looting. Typhus and cholera were rampant; a fellow Gurdjieff student had already died of smallpox.[8] But the breakdown of any kind of civil order was perhaps even worse. Ouspensky tells of an interminable wait for a train at Tiflis (present-day Tbilisi) after a five-day journey from St. Petersburg. To get a seat at all was something of a miracle and required many bribes. While waiting he was witness to several shootings. Soldiers had shot someone who had stolen a few kopecks. Then they argued over whether they should have shot him or had him arrested and almost came to blows. Soon after someone else was shot, apparently another thief. Then a third shooting; this was of someone who was suspected of being a thief, but who was actually a policeman. The bodies lay on the platform and remained there. This was only one incident in a country descending into barbarity. Ouspensky remarked that at this point the soldiers and the "people" were still "comrades." But he knew that "as soon as there should be no bread and shoes, those with guns would get bread and shoes from those without guns."[9] Like many White Russians—a name given to all who weren't Bolsheviks, whether they supported the monarchy or not— Ouspensky eventually found a way to Europe and then to England, where he resettled.*

Nicholas had reached his end by way of the muddle and catastrophe that make up so much of Russia's history. The Duma he had permitted had been dissolved within months, as had the second one. Nicholas had by this time made clear that he was not really relaxing his autocracy, and he began to associate with far-right extremist groups such as the Union of the Russian People, an anti-Semitic terrorist organization much like the People's Will. The Union of the Russian People numbered among their following members of the Black Hundreds, a far-right populist movement that, since the fall of the Soviet Union, has been revived.[10] By this time the Rasputin scandal had broken and the tsarina was becoming even more unpopular. Pyotr Stolypin, who had taken over for Serge Witte as prime minister, had introduced agrarian reforms that made significant concessions to the peasants. But he had

---

*Ouspensky remarks that "Bolshevism is not a political system" and argues that it would be better understood as *pougachevchina*, an untranslatable term referring to Pugachev, the eighteenth-century rebel who caused a great deal of trouble for Catherine the Great.

also introduced policies meant to keep the lid on any dissent. Stolypin was a remarkable statesman and, like others, he tried to follow a policy of "ease up while maintaining control," allowing more freedoms while supporting the monarchy. It was not an easy task. "Stolypin's necktie"— the hangman's noose—led to many deaths. It was to be expected. According to one account, in 1907 alone, 2,543 government agents were assassinated; "Stolypin's necktie" was worn by 782 terrorists.[11] Stolypin himself became a statistic in 1911, when he was shot at a performance of Rimsky-Korsakov's opera *The Tale of Tsar Saltan* at the Kiev Opera House given especially for the tsar and his daughters.[12] Ten previous attempts to kill Stolypin had failed, although one had crippled his daughter. This one didn't.

Dmitry Borov, the Russian-Jewish radical who killed him was, as conditions would have it, simultaneously an anarchist and an agent of the Okhrana, reporting on dissident activities. He was executed even though Stolypin's wife pleaded for his life, saying his death would not cancel her husband's. Some accounts suggest that far-right elements were really behind the assassination; Stolypin had succeeded in antagonizing both the left and right, and either side would have welcomed his departure.* The far right didn't care for his taste for reform, while the far left hated him as a monarchist. It was a time when only extremes could satisfy and any voices offering a middle ground were quickly drowned out.

Another assassination, this time in Sarajevo, did not help. When Gavrilo Princip, a Bosnian Serb, Yugoslavian nationalist, and member of the Black Hand, a secret society dedicated to the overthrow of the Hapsburgs, shot Archduke Franz Ferdinand on June 28, 1914, he most likely did not think he was triggering the end of Old Europe. But when the "guns of August" starting firing soon after, initiating World War One, that is exactly what happened. Because of its alliances Russia found itself in a war with Germany and Austria-Hungary that it did not want and could not fight. The deficiencies that had led to its

---

*This was an idea Alexander Solzhenitsyn explored in his novel *August 1914* (1971).

humiliating defeat by Japan had not been rectified. Russia had soldiers, millions of them, but little else. Often they were sent into battle with rifles but no bullets; some had no rifles. The tsarina's German ancestry made her a spy in the people's eyes. Anti-German riots broke out. And when Alexandra insisted that her husband take command of the military, the end, for those who could see, was in sight.

Papus died; Rasputin was murdered, and within months of their deaths, more riots broke out, and there were increasing calls for Russia to exit a war that was doing nothing but bringing it to ruin. When his troops would no longer follow his orders to suppress the riots—some had already mutinied—Tsar Nicholas II, who had pledged to defend autocracy "firmly and undeviatingly," was finally forced to abdicate. No one wanted the throne, and in March 1917 a provisional government was formed. By the summer it was led by the moderate leftist Alexander Kerensky. But it was not the time for moderation, and in November of that year the Bolsheviks seized control.

Vladimir Lenin (1870–1924) had learned much from studying the *narodniki*. He believed in the virtue of a "revolutionary elite," a body of crack extremists, ready and willing to do what was necessary to take power and to hold it. He had trained people to do just that. So they did. As did Dostoyevsky's devils, the new men came to town. It may have been the beginning of the great People's Revolution, but it was the end of Holy Russia.

AWARE THAT A revolution in the enemy camp was awaiting its leader and how this would help in the war, Kaiser Wilhelm weaponized Lenin by sending him from Switzerland to Russia, crossing Germany in a sealed train. In April 1917 he famously arrived at the Finland Station in St. Petersburg, met by cheering crowds and a brass band.[13] He had been in exile for ten years and now he had returned. Kerensky's government had pledged to stay in the war, and this was his mistake. It is possible that the tsar might have staved off total collapse if, following Rasputin's assassination, he had made peace with Germany and withdrawn from the conflict. The fighting had quietened and the disturbances at home had, for a moment, lessened. But he and the tsarina had fallen into a kind of lethargy; Nicholas no longer bothered about going to the front and seemed to be in a state of denial. Ministers resigned left and right with no candidates to take their places. There were assassination plots against the tsarina and even talk of a coup, anything that would remove her from her position of power. Grand Duchess Marie Pavlovna, whose husband, Grand Duke Vladimir, was responsible for Bloody Sunday, said that Alexandra must be "annihilated."[14] Soon enough she would be.

VLADIMIR ILYICH ULYANOV—he took the revolutionary name Lenin in 1901—was born in Simbirsk, renamed Ulyanovsk in his honor, a city along the Volga River a few hundred miles east of Moscow. He came from the kind of cultured background he grew to despise in others. His father, a landowner, was the son of a serf; he had worked hard to become a teacher and school inspector. His mother's father was a doctor. His childhood was warm, loving, and comfortable. Lenin was a voracious reader and showed his brilliance at school early on, mastering Greek and Latin in his teens. He didn't suffer the privations we might expect from a future revolutionary and seemed destined for the life of a scholar. But he was in fact not an anomaly; his siblings grew up to become revolutionaries too. One, his brother, was executed in 1887 for his part in a plot to assassinate Alexander III. It was this, plus his father's early death, brought on by worry over losing his position—the government, as before, was growing fearful of public education and was closing down schools—that turned the bright student into a professional extremist.

As more than one historian has noted, although it is called the Bolshevik revolution, in some ways Lenin's party had little to do with it. (*Bolshevik* means "greater," although for most of the time before their takeover they were actually in the minority. *Menshevik*, the name of their opponents, means "smaller.") By the time Lenin arrived the forces in play had already been set in motion. What he was successful at was in guiding them toward his ends.[15] Lenin succeeded because he was ruthless and had narrowed his aim to an immediate and practical goal: to take power and hold it. He made promises he knew he couldn't keep. He gave promises to the people about "all that they ever dreamt of" without ever thinking if they "can or cannot be fulfilled": something practically every politician does in order to get into office.[16] Once there it didn't matter. And he stoked the fires of resentment through the crude vocabulary of accusation, defamation, and desecration, appealing to an appetite for vengeance and retribution.

Lenin had the prescience to act boldly in a time of confusion, knowing such action often carries its own warrant. Exiled from St. Petersburg as a German agent by Kerensky, he returned in disguise and in late October attended a secret meeting of the Bolshevik Central Committee, where he addressed them at length about the need to prepare for an armed takeover. They did, and on the night of November 7–8, 1917, members of Lenin's revolutionary elite arrested members of the Provisional Government and proclaimed the triumph of the new Soviet state.

From then until his death in 1924, Lenin pursued what one commentator has called a "crusade against subjectivity."[17] His goal was to eliminate the "inner world" and with it all idea of "free will," and to annihilate idealism, the belief that there is any reality other than the physical world, the brute concrete facts revealed to us through the senses.[18] The positivism that had informed the New Men of the 1870s had come back with a vengeance, this time tied to a political philosophy that denied everything that the beautiful souls who had preceded them had found meaningful in existence.

Lenin had read Marx in 1889 while in Kazan where he was studying law, and the angry prophet of the proletariat—he had died just a few years earlier—who famously stood Hegel on his head had found another devotee. Marx denied Hegel's Absolute Spirit while retaining his method, the tortuous dialectic. Now the contradictions that had propelled the unfolding of the *Weltgeist* were applied to solely material forces in order to argue that, through acquiring the means of production, the workers of the world would arrive—not immediately, but soon—at the promised Golden Age of the classless society. This was the kind of promissory note that kept the *narodniki* awake at night and that Herzen had seen the dangers of: present hardship, suffering, pain, even death in order to secure a future utopia that no one living would ever see, but that the revolutionary elite will lead the people to, for their own good. At the start of the revolution, this seemed a goal worth attaining, and in the first wave of excitement it indeed seemed attainable. As time went on, however, it receded from view.

In Isaiah Berlin's formula, we might say that Lenin was a hedgehog, one of those who knows "one big thing." Lenin's one big thing was materialism. Matter is the really real thing in existence, and the world we see when we open our eyes is the only one. It was the crudest of ontologies, but for Lenin it was the only one that would work for what he had in mind. As Joseph de Maistre and Konstantin Pobedonostsev had before him, but from the opposite side of the political fence, Lenin saw that in order to bring stability to society, people's minds must be harmonized and made to conform with a simple strong belief: too much speculation, the fantastic ideas of the God-seekers, all that wasn't good. It merely led to uncertainty, subjectivity, pursuing one's *own* vision of reality rather than humbly accepting the one we all share. That was a bourgeois pastime. It was reactionary, positively counterrevolutionary. Everything had to be made more simple. One method of achieving simplicity is to eliminate the individual, to reduce everyone to a bare commonality. A materialist philosophy, which achieves quantitative equality by jettisoning qualitative difference, is a handy tool in doing just that.

In Lenin's view, human consciousness is merely a reflection of the external world, or should I say simply "the world," as he denies the reality of an "inner" one. It possesses nothing of its own, in the same way that a mirror is blank unless something is placed in front of it. Mirrors are all the same, and if one were somehow to present something different from the others, it would merely be evidence that it was a bad or broken mirror, not that it somehow contained its own reality. Such mirrors would have to be repaired or, failing that, discarded. With Lenin in power quite a few broken mirrors found their way onto the junk pile and continued to do so throughout the entire Soviet regime.

This mirror theory of consciousness is not limited to Lenin. It is shared, oddly enough, by his bourgeois enemy, the West. It is summed up in John Locke's dictum that "there is nothing in the mind that was not first in the senses," a premise that has been accepted by mainstream Western psychology since Locke first proposed it in *An Essay on Human Understanding* (1689). Our minds are a blank, a tabula rasa, until written on by experience. What matters then is that experience.

As a good behaviorist, Lenin believed that provided the proper environment, he could inscribe the rules of an egalitarian, collective, harmonious society on the tabula rasa of his people. In this way he would be, as his successor Comrade Stalin saw himself, an "engineer of human souls," mass-producing excellent mirrors to reflect the progressive environment of the great Soviet experiment. Such optimism was a triumph of the West, where the same epistemology was at the foundation of democracy and capitalism. In both cases what is denied is the same: our inner being, our "soul," the concern, since Odoevsky, of so many Russian thinkers of the nineteenth century. For Lenin, as for progressive thinkers in the West, this was an atavism that had to be eliminated.

From Lenin's perspective all philosophy prior to his *Materialism and Empirio-Criticism* (1908)—Marx excepted—should be, as Andrei Rublev's *Spas* almost was, thrown into the fire. This work, which led to countless murders in the name of the "revolution" and destroyed an entire culture, is full of rancor and resentment, "everything you might expect from an ignorant man with a grudge against philosophy."[19] He did not argue. He poured scorn on his opponents, using vituperation and invective to achieve his purpose. His aim was to reduce reality to the barest of minimums and to apply his bargain-basement metaphysics to the great, confused mass of the Russian people. It was necessary, he believed, in order to bring some stability to the chaos. Perhaps. But reality will not submit for very long to the highly excised version of it that Lenin and those who followed him imposed on his people.

ONE OF THE first victims of Lenin's cut-rate epistemology was the church. In January 1918, with the civil war raging, Vladimir, metropolitan of Kiev—he has since been canonized—became the first priest murdered by the new regime. Bolsheviks stormed the Monastery of the Caves, dragging the monks out of their cells, stripping, and torturing them. The metropolitan was beaten and choked with the chain of his cross. He was then driven outside the monastery and shot. Vladimir is said to have blessed his executioners before he died.[20] One suspects he wouldn't be the only one to do so.

From 1917 until the collapse of the Soviet Union, the Orthodox Church in Russia "existed in a state of siege."[21] It found itself the target of a militant atheism, which was unique in history. As Timothy Ware points out, until Constantine, Rome persecuted Christians intermittently, not continuously, but was not atheist itself. But Marxist Russia was an atheist state determined to eliminate religion in any form.* It had to.[22] Marx denied the reality of spirit, of anything other than brute matter; religion, of course, was "the opium of the people." All talk of the soul, the spirit, was a cancerous outgrowth of the belief in the spurious interiority that Comrade Lenin had put in its grave, along with quite a few of its misguided believers. As Valentin Tomberg, himself a victim of the revolution, points out, for Lenin it was not a matter of doubting Christianity or religion in general, but of destroying it.[23] There is no reality other than the hard facts given us by the senses, and if you don't

---

*This is a policy that seems well in place in twenty-first century China.

see that, then, like a broken mirror, there is something wrong with you.*

There were, of course, opponents to this view. We will look at some of them shortly. But before that, we should introduce a figure who was a powerful influence on many thinkers of the Silver Age and who counted among his admirers Dostoyevsky, Tolstoy, and Solovyov, but whose ideas in many ways seem to presage the Soviet world to come. This was the visionary Nikolay Fedorovich Fedorov (1828–1903).

NIKOLAY FEDOROV IS the kind of character that could appear only in Russia. He embodies all of the extremes that make up the Russian soul. Ascetic, selfless, dedicated, authoritarian, contradictory, as the historian of Russian philosophy N. O. Lossky put it, "there can be no doubt that he was a really righteous man, an uncanonised saint," yet his worldview is rigidly totalitarian.[25] Fedorov is recognized as the leading light of the Cosmist school of Russian thought, although during his lifetime this term wasn't used, and only came into common usage fairly recently. *Cosmic,* though, certainly characterizes his thinking.

Fedorov thought on a huge scale, in terms of humanity and the entire planet, and those beyond. He thought of the notion of "spaceship earth" well before the idea was popularized in the 1960s, and took it very literally: we must learn how to unchain our planet from the sun, he believed, and use it to voyage into the cosmos. Even death was no obstacle for him. In fact we could say that it was Fedorov's "one big thing." But where religious philosophers like Solovyov saw the Christian idea of the "resurrection of the dead" in a spiritual sense, Fedorov took it quite literally. The mission of the entire human race—the "common task"—he tells us, is to resurrect our ancestors and those who came before them. Compared with this, nothing else matters.

Fedorov was the illegitimate son of Prince Pavel Gagarin, black

---

*The Soviet denial of religion even extended to their maps. During a visit to St. Petersburg—then called Leningrad—the economist E. F. Schumacher remarked that although physically visible churches were not marked on any maps of the city.[24]

sheep of a family that could trace its lineage back to the legendary Rurik. But his illegitimacy didn't seem to bother him in the way that Herzen's troubled him. From the little we know of his early life, Fedorov was on good terms with his father. His relations with his mother were not so good. When Prince Ivan Alekseevich Gargarin, Fedorov's grandfather, a leading Freemason, decided to marry off Pavel, Fedorov and his siblings were taken from their mother and moved to an estate. He saw little of her after that. This has led some commentators to remark that his early separation from his mother had a great influence on his philosophy, which, as George M. Young tells us, is extremely patriarchal and, for a Russian, uncharacteristically critical of "feminine" values.[26] Fedorov extolls the "masculine" virtues of "rigor, duty, the task, abstention, the responsibility of sons toward fathers," and attacks "the eternal temptress, the desire for trivial consumer goods . . . worldly pleasure and comfort."[27] There is little of Sophia or Damp Mother Earth in the Fedorovian scheme of things.

For people of a certain age Fedorov's animus toward "pleasure and comfort" has a familiar ring. Throughout the Soviet era, it was precisely in this way that those leading the great Marxist revolution characterized the difference between themselves and the sickly, weak, decadent democracies of the West. Even in today's Russia, although the criticism is no longer prompted by Marxist ideology, the idea that the West is wholly obsessed with consuming and comfort—the "me" society—is still strong. The source of this, in Fedorov as in Lenin—and in more contemporary advocates of this view—is the Western ego and its misguided ideas about freedom.[28] What is wrong with the West is that it believes in the "me," not the "we." That is the root of all evil. Fedorov is part of that broad current in Russian thought in which the individual does not matter, only the part he or she plays in the whole. That Fedorov did not have a "real" family may, one suspects, have something to do with his vision of uniting the entire human race into a planetary one.

Fedorov was given a good education, although in 1854 he left the lyceum he was attending without taking a degree. The story is that he got into an argument with one of the instructors and refused to complete the exiting exam. Another perhaps more pressing reason is that the uncle who was providing for his education had died, and there was no one else to pay the bills. Both are likely the case. Fedorov grew up to be stubborn, opinionated, and aware of his brilliance, and he would not hesitate to act on it.

After leaving school Fedorov led a wandering life for many years, acting as a kind of secular starets. He taught history and geography in village schools, often getting into trouble with the authorities for what they saw as his overzealousness. He regularly exceeded the duties of his office—he presaged Alexey Stakhanov by some decades—although his students apparently loved him and would remain in touch with him throughout their lives, often asking his advice before making major decisions.*

Like Solovyov and many others we've seen, Fedorov early on took the kenotic path, emptying himself of practically everything he could. He ate little, and slept, when he did, on the floor without a pillow. He continued this practice throughout his life. When, years later, working as the librarian at the famous Rumiantsev Museum in Moscow, a position he held for many years—following in the footsteps of Odoevsky—he slept on a humped-back trunk; aptly, he used a book for a pillow. His knowledge of the library was prodigious. He was said to know not only the location of each book but its entire contents; at the time, this meant about 85,000 volumes.[29] If asked for certain material, Fedorov would deliver it plus several items the visitor was unaware of and which proved necessary for his work. One story has it that when engineers about to start work on the Trans-Siberian Railway visited the museum, he was able to tell them that their maps were inaccurate. When the engineers returned from Siberia two years later, they told him he had been right.[30]

While living on the precarious income of a teacher, Fedorov gave

---

*Alexey Stakhanov was an exceptionally hard-working Soviet comrade who in 1935 was the inspiration for the Stakhanovite Movement, designed to spur fellow workers on to increased production and efficiency, something needed during the second five-year plan.

away as much of his earnings as he could; he was in fact obsessed with emptying his pockets and feared he would be found dead with a few coins in them. When a student's father fell ill, he gave all he had to help pay the medical bills. When the father died, Fedorov sold his uniform to help pay for the funeral. When he turned up at school out of uniform and dressed in his own clothes, which were little more than rags, he was lambasted by the school inspector, who demanded to know the reason for his insubordination. Fedorov refused to speak in his defense and said he would rather resign. It was only when the principal learned the truth that Fedorov was allowed to stay. He did, but not for long, and similar incidents happened in other schools.

Another incident was more serious but it led to some collateral benefit. In 1864 in Bogorodsk, a town east of Moscow, Fedorov fell in with a group of New Men, students who were charged with the utopian utilitarian views of Chernyshevsky, Dobrolyubov, and Pisarev. To call Fedorov's views "cosmic utilitarianism" would not be far wrong, although his kind of pragmatism exceeded theirs, well, astronomically. One of these New Men, Nikolai Peterson, would become Fedorov's most faithful disciple. It was also through him that Fedorov, whose views were a tad more conservative that Pobedonostsev's, was arrested for revolutionary activity.

One of the members of Peterson's circle was Dmitri Karakosov, who, we remember, made an unsuccessful attempt on the life of Tsar Alexander II, thus initiating the half century of repression that led to the revolution. During the interrogation all the members of the circle testified that Fedorov was in no way involved in the plot and that, in fact, he had done his utmost to argue the others out of their revolutionary ways. With Peterson, who received six months in jail, he had succeeded, and it was through Peterson that word of Fedorov's ideas reached some important people.

Like the starets or the wandering sages of old, Fedorov did not bother to write down his ideas, preferring speech over writing. But Peterson must have convinced him to preserve a record of his thought.

He became his amanuensis, and it was through him that not only Dostoyevsky, but Solovyov and Tolstoy would learn of his remarkable vision. Fedorov refused to publish anything, and, without him knowing, Peterson sent an article he had written that didn't mention Fedorov but which discussed his ideas to Dostoyevsky. In 1876 Dostoyevsky published some of this in his *Diary of a Writer,* with some critical remarks.[31] Sometime later Peterson sent another manuscript. This time Dostoyevsky wrote back that he was "in complete agreement with these ideas," although, as it turned out, this was not exactly the case. But Dostoyevsky was excited enough to read the manuscript to Solovyov, who was also moved by it, and felt in sympathy with it, although he too would eventually differentiate his own views from Fedorov's.

Dostoyevsky wrote back to Peterson, asking him to clarify one point. How exactly does this unnamed prophet—for Peterson had yet to name Fedorov—understand the resurrection? Does he mean it symbolically, allegorically, or literally, in the sense that the Gospels tell us? Dostoyevsky never learned the answer to his question; he died before the essay that Fedorov and Peterson worked on to answer it reached him. But it was this essay that piqued Tolstoy's interest when Peterson encountered him on a train and began to tell him of the remarkable vision of the "Moscow Socrates."

Resurrection was not an uncommon idea for Tolstoy—it was the title of his last novel—yet he would, like Dostoyevsky and Solovyov, in the end be more impressed with Fedorov the man than his ideas.[32] He visited him often at the Rumiantsev Museum and seems to have been impressed with the librarian's childlike, almost naive goodness. He was a "true Christian." Tolstoy, known for his temper, was humble before Fedorov. In his anti-art stage, he once said that all the books in the library should be burned. "People write a lot of silly things," Tolstoy grumbled. Fedorov replied "I saw many silly men in my life, but no one as silly as you."[33] Although dogmatic, Fedorov was not assertive and, like the philosopher Plotinus, he refused to have any portraits made of himself. The one we have by Leonid Pasternak—father of the poet and novelist Boris Pasternak—was made surreptitiously, with the artist hiding behind stacks of books at the library, and stealing glances at his subject.[34]

Yet for one so humble and self-effacing, Fedorov's vision is little short of Promethean and amounts to nothing less than the absolute mastery of nature, the cosmos itself, by man, driven by one central aim: the conquest of death.

DEPENDING UPON YOUR perspective, Fedorov's one big thing is either a profound and noble calling or a morbid idée fixe, prompted by the early loss of his family. For him all questions about human existence come down in the end to the question of death. In the face of it, nothing else matters. But while with a few exceptions death has been universally accepted as inescapable—something that nihilists and existentialists grimly embrace—Fedorov believed it was not so.* It was not inevitable. If the human mind put itself to the task, and if the entire race joined in, it could be conquered.

Exactly *how* it would be conquered, Fedorov couldn't say. He was no biologist or physician. But the recognition of the necessity to conquer it would drive the efforts to do so. It would establish what he called a "Psychocracy," a society in which "everyone will do his duty fully aware of the necessity of the tasks with which he is faced."[35] There would be no need for coercion, no police, no class distinction, as everyone would recognize that it was to the benefit of all that each put their efforts to the "common task." Each would find his or her proper place in the planetary work of conquering death.

That conquest would be the goal toward which the resources of the entire world would be directed. The "common task" would be the rallying point around which the diverse peoples of the globe would unite. That unity itself, for Fedorov, was both a benefit of death's defeat and

---

*George Bernard Shaw in *Back to Methuselah* (1922) proposed that death was not inevitable and would be overcome, but his view on this was very different from Fedorov's.

the source of it. Death is a process of disintegration; it is the law of entropy applied to life. But just as the body, upon death, begins to disintegrate, so too is society fragmented, fractured into a mass of competing egos, each out for its own survival. With death defeated, the selfish scramble for self-preservation would be redundant, and each could help the other in furthering the common goal.

It would start, Fedorov believed, with the first person to be purposefully resuscitated.* Then there would be others. Then, as the *necessity* of resuscitation became accepted, driven by our sense of responsibility to our ancestors—for surely, once achieving the miracle, we could not deny them its benefits—those already dead would be revived, their bodies somehow brought back to good condition. Eventually this process would continue until "whole persons could be re-created from the least trace of recovered ancestral dust," which seems a remarkable anticipation of cloning.[36] Fedorov's sense of filial duty required him to conquer death not only for one generation, but to erase its victories entirely and to recover from its cold embrace *every person who has died,* going back to the very first one.†

One has to say that it seems never to have occurred to Fedorov that the dead might not *want* to be revived, or that there may be some sphere of existence after life where our attendance is required. He certainly didn't share the feeling that his younger contemporary, the writer Leonid Andreyev, expressed in his story "Lazarus" (1908). While dead Lazarus was granted an insight into the utter futility of life; now, returned to life, all who gaze in his eyes are shattered by the same vision.[37] Fedorov's ideas may seem crude and obsessive but at least he avoided this sort of nihilism.

---

*I'm leaving out cases of "natural resuscitation," when someone declared dead "comes back to life," also those of near-death experiences. I'm not sure if Fedorov was aware of these or if they are mentioned in the literature about him.

†This does raise some questions, not only the difficult one of exactly who was the first person to die, but of who was the "first person"? Would Fedorov's project extend into our supposed animal ancestors? And what of the amoebae that preceded them?

The recovery of the "ancestral dust" needed to accomplish the common task would require some work, hence the need to get everyone on board. For one thing it would mean traveling in space, and Fedorov's ideas would influence another eccentric visionary, his fellow Cosmist, Konstantin Tsiolkovsky (1857–1935), the father of Russian space exploration. Space travel would be necessary in order to recover the particles of our ancestors, which have gone back to the stars. It would also be necessary because we would have to colonize other worlds in order to house those ancestors, once they are resuscitated. Even on Earth there was a lot to be done. The common task would draw energies from wasteful, destructive activities such as war and turn them toward this most useful goal. In the process it would overcome innumerable obstacles that have so far prevented mankind from creating a Golden Age.

In order to accomplish the task, science must master the blind forces of nature and turn them to the purposes of human life. Fedorov had none of the love of nature found among Romantics, nor was he troubled by our ecological concerns. His attitude toward nature was solely practical. It was there for man to use, a belief the Soviets shared. Nature is subject to the same forces of disintegration that condemn man to death. But man can conquer nature and transform its hostile forces into "the instruments and organs of mankind." We can begin on Earth by regulating the weather so as to improve harvests and end hunger, and by developing methods of increasing yields. Fedorov called for using solar energy as means of lessening our dependence on coal, decades ahead of our concern about renewable energies. He went further and argued that we could master the electromagnetic energy of the planet and, as mentioned, take "spaceship earth" out on cruises through the galaxy. He was nothing if not ambitious. The aim in the end was for mankind to synthesize theory and practice into a kind of rational "theurgy"— what we might call "scientific magic"—and become "the reason of the Universe."[38]

The scale of Fedorov's practical ideas, however impractical they may sound, is matched by his social vision. Everyone must contribute toward the common task. There is no room for idlers or for the pursuit of personal goals. Beautiful souls will have no time to contemplate their inner worlds, or anything else. We must all put our shoulders behind the same wheel. Stragglers will not be tolerated. The brotherhood of man, sought for since Christ, will become reality through our devotion to the work of resurrecting our ancestors. One consequence of this is that relations between the sexes will become that of brothers and sisters, not men and wives. Sex will become redundant as the selfish urge to propagate the species will die out with the rise of immortality. There will be no need to create future generations, as those living will not die. Hence the lack of the maternal in Fedorov's cosmic patriarchy (and the idea of sex as a pleasurable activity for its own sake, is, of course, an absolute nonstarter). Fedorov himself was celibate, and, aside from one unrequited affair, he had no relations with women. With the common task to bind us, there was no need. And in any case, as we are all brothers and sisters, sexual relations between us would amount to a kind of incest.

Fedorov's vision seems a kind of utilitarianism in overdrive, but he was a religious character, and there are mystical elements to his ideas that will strike us as familiar. As did Solovyov, he saw the Holy Trinity as a model for his Psychocracy. The three are separate but together, not fused into a mass, as collectivist societies are, nor fractured into competing parts, as is the individualistic West, but maintaining a unity without relinquishing difference. As the Trinity is itself impossible to comprehend rationally—it is one of the mysteries—such a society, formed around the notion of *sobernost,* sounds very desirable in theory but is very difficult to achieve in practice. As the essence of Fedorov's social thought focuses on the "unity of consciousness and action," such disparity must be overcome, as should another, more geographical one, that between East and West.[39] Fedorov was not unaware of the polarity at the heart of so much Russian thought, and in some ways we can see his answer to it as a way of his killing three birds with one stone.

Fedorov became convinced that the Pamir Mountains in Turkestan, an area separating Russia from China, would be the center of his world resurrection. It was believed to be the site of the original Garden of Eden, and Fedorov came to accept that somewhere in that desolate region the bones of Adam, the first father, were buried. Where better to begin the work of resuscitating our dead brothers and sisters? Fedorov studied ancient and modern historical documents and, as Solovyov had, he came to the conclusion that Russia's history had been guided by hidden forces, and that it was destined to "gather all the lands into one land and to make all peoples one people."[40] This was the true meaning of the Third Rome. The tsar was destined to be "the father of all living peoples," and to represent "the interests of the dead."

As the Slavophiles and others had, Fedorov believed that Russia's history was world history. The agreement in 1895 between Russia and Great Britain, granting Russia possession of the Pamirs—and thus ending, in some accounts, the Great Game—seemed to suggest as much. Why should this sacred but long-abandoned region now come under the control of the tsar, if not so that he could initiate from there the first steps in the great common task? Those steps, Fedorov believed, would return what is now wasteland to its paradisiacal glory. This could be done by establishing an observatory and cosmic research station atop one of the high peaks; from there, the particles of Adam's descendants, become so much stardust, could be detected, and new planetary homes for their reconstituted bodies could be found.[41] Thus, in the heart of Eurasia, where East meets West, the scientific mastery of nature leading to the resuscitation of the dead could begin: Fedorov's own holy trinity. The unity of the world would then be achieved at the very spot where man first stepped onto the path of disintegration and death.

Fedorov did not live to see this dream become a reality, and as yet no one has seriously taken the first steps toward accomplishing the common task. In his last years he came to see that the world was not yet ready for his vision; what he would think of today's efforts to extend life medically, our neurotic avoidance of all talk about death, and our frantic desire to maintain youth, is debatable. His own life ended in a way that seems typically Russian, rather as if Gogol had written about it in one of his strange tales. Throughout his life Fedorov went without warm clothes and he walked everywhere, like a true pilgrim. When a schoolteacher, wherever he was stationed, when he took a brief holiday, it was invariably to walk to Moscow and to use the time to study. In December 1903, during a severe freeze, friends convinced him to wear a fur coat and for once to take a cab home from the library. Most likely more to comfort them than himself, he did, and promptly came down with pneumonia and died.[42]

FOR NIKOLAI BERDYAEV, Fedorov was a "typical Russian genius."[43] Yet Berdyaev himself, equally as Russian, was a very different character. Although little read today, at least in the West, in the 1920s, '30s, and '40s, Berdyaev was one of the most widely discussed Russian philosophers, cited as one of the leading religious existentialists, along with figures like Gabriel Marcel and Berdyaev's friend and countryman Lev Shestov. During these years, while living in exile in France, Berdyaev produced a torrent of writing on a wide range of subjects—history, society, culture, politics, knowledge, creativity—in an aphoristic, at times oracular style, all related to his central obsession, what we can call his one big thing: freedom. A look at some of the titles of his books gives us an idea of his themes: *The Meaning of History* (1923), *The Destiny of Man* (1934), *Spirit and Reality* (1946).

Berdyaev is an intuitive and unsystematic thinker, rightly known as "the philosopher of freedom." But before this Berdyaev was one of the voices of the Silver Age, one pointedly aware of the inadequacies of tsarist Russia, but equally aware of the limits of the Marxist view and the dangers of Lenin's radical use of it. His autobiography, *Dream and Reality* (1950), probably the best introduction to his thought, published after his death in 1948, is one of the key documents of the time.

Berdyaev was born in Kiev in 1874 to a cultured and aristocratic family. His father was a military man who read Voltaire, and his mother was half-French with a leaning toward Catholicism. This polyglot background served him in good stead; Berdyaev grew up to have a great command of languages. Like many philosophical souls, Berdyaev was a solitary child who spent much of his time reading; by his early teens, he had read Hegel, Schopenhauer, Kant, and the works of other philosophers that he had found in his father's library, all in the original German. This precocity, however, turned him away from his father's path, and Berdyaev left military cadet school around the same time. He was to experience friction in the academic world throughout his life, and although world-renowned as a philosopher, he never took a degree. This made him something of a maverick, but with his obsession with freedom this should not come as a surprise.

At Kiev University he became interested in Marx, and it was because of this that he was arrested and expelled in 1899 for taking part in student demonstrations. He was sentenced to three years internal exile in Vologda, a city in the northwest. It was during this time that his ideas began to move away from Marx—a reading of Solovyov helped him on his way—and toward the kind of religious existentialism that would characterize his thought from then on.

Although painfully aware of the appalling social conditions of his time—he shared with earlier aristocratic rebels a sense of responsibility to rectify them—he rejected Marx's materialism and negation of the individual in favor of the collective. Berdyaev shared the Christian and Kantian belief in the absolute value of the individual person. This, however, did not make him an "individualist," as true "personalism" can only arise in the context of others, hence Berdyaev's insistence on *sobernost* as the basis of society. This "personalism" would be the cornerstone of his later philosophy of freedom, which would eventually reach into the mystical depths of Jacob Boehme's *Ungrund*, the unmanifest "irrational freedom" out of which even God himself emerges. This is Berdyaev's version of the "negative theology" that informs the *via negativa*.[44] Although the "meonic freedom" Berdyaev speaks of—from the Greek μέ ὄν (*me on*, "non being")—exceeds the political and social spheres and proceeds from dimensions of reality that Marx and Lenin would find laughable, with such ideas it would not be long before Berdyaev found himself swimming against the rising Bolshevik tide.

After his release from Vologda, Berdyaev traveled in Germany before returning to Kiev in 1904; it was then that he met and married Lydia Trusleff, his lifelong companion. The relationship was based on ideas and ideals and, according to Berdyaev, was never consummated; Berdyaev maintained a spiritual celibacy that we have seen in other Russian thinkers, such as Solovyof and Fedorov. Lydia had been one of the *narodniki* generation, trying to "educate the people," and in 1903 she had spent three months in prison for her radicalism.

On marrying they moved to St. Petersburg. Although Berdyaev was religious—he joined the Orthodox Church in 1907—he had little sympathy for organized religion and felt that, like Marx, the church tended toward authoritarianism and had little regard for individual freedom. This attitude would lead to more than a little friction. In 1914 he wrote an article in which he was highly critical of the Holy Synod for its treatment of Russian monks in Mount Athos. Their response was to charge him with blasphemy. The sentence for this offense was permanent exile in Siberia. The outbreak of World War One slowed down the court proceedings, but the thing that really saved Berdyaev was the Bolshevik revolution. This may be the one time in history when someone found guilty of blasphemy was saved from his fate because of something even more blasphemous.

By this time Berdyaev had contributed to an important anthology of ideas, *Vekhi* (1909) or "Landmarks," so called because it marked a turning point in Russian thought and the failure of the intelligentsia to keep up with the changes. It was a follow-up to an earlier collection, *Problems of Idealism* (1902). Berdyaev's contribution focused on how utilitarianism had forced out all concern with the pursuit of truth as an end in itself, in favor of truth as a means to practical ends. In this he was echoing the concerns of Romantics like Odoevsky.

For Berdyaev man is a creature of two worlds, that of spirit and that of nature. He is their "point of intersection."[45] Spirit is free and creative—one of Berdyaev's best books is the still exhilarating *The Meaning of the Creative Act* (1916), which puts the creative life as a religious practice on an equal if not higher level than the devotional one.[46] Nature is a state of slavery to necessity, and utilitarianism, which is based on the "truths" of nature, is doubly so. The only truth worth pursuing is the existential one, the "lived" truth of inner experience, precisely the sort of thing Lenin wanted to eradicate. This truth is "unnecessary," that is, it is not determined by any practical end but is a living "eruption" of freedom, a break in the "chain" (shackles?) of cause and effect. This distinction informed Berdyaev's personal life. In practical things he was always "timid, clumsy, and lacking in confidence," a result of his "non-acceptance of the world as it was given to me" and his "almost morbid weariness of the commonplace."[47] He was always "conscious of being at a distance from what is commonly called 'life.'"[48] It was something he looked at "with half-closed eyes" while holding his nose. This was not an attitude that the ultra-utilitarian Lenin would countenance for very long.

Yet for a time the "spiritual aristocrat" Berdyaev—or so he styled himself; he took great care of his appearance and was something of a dandy—was more than tolerated. Because his social and political sympathies were critical of the capitalist West, in the tradition of figures like Odoevsky, he was considered a fellow traveler, yet one the new regime needed to keep an eye on. He was allowed to continue to lecture and write and in 1919, that fateful year, he founded his own private academy, "The Free Academy of Spiritual Culture." This was fundamentally a venue for Berdyaev and those sympathetic to a spiritual view of humanity to discuss ideas and to maintain some sense of the inner world that the glorious revolution was swiftly eradicating. Yet by this time Lenin's anti-religious edicts were in effect, and the days for such gatherings were numbered.

In 1920, without a degree, Berdyaev was made a professor of philosophy at Moscow University. This token of acceptance was almost immediately countered by his arrest, this time by the Cheka, the new

Soviet secret police. He was brought to the infamous Lubyanka prison and interrogated by Felix Dzerzhinsky, head of security for the new regime. Whether out of bravery, arrogance, or naïveté, Berdyaev stood his ground, explaining to Dzershinsky why Communism was a bad idea. The story is that Dzershinsky listened politely then released Berdyaev, even providing a car to take him home. The next time he was arrested, however, the response was not so accommodating.

Berdyaev's opposition to the enforced egalitarianism being imposed on his country was a book spelling out exactly what was wrong with it. *The Philosophy of Inequality*—one of the books on Vladimir Putin's reading list—was written during the chaos of the revolution and civil war, but wasn't published until 1923, by which time Berdyaev was no longer in the country. In many ways it was a continuation of what he had written in *Vekhi*. His contribution to that collection, "Philosophical Truth and the Intelligentsia's Righteousness," had argued that the intelligentsia's passion for the "people" and the "proletariat" had become little more than idolatry.[49] Truth in the traditional sense no longer mattered; the only truths that did were those that supported the intelligentsia's attacks on the tsar and promoted their agendas. Now Berdyaev spelled out in more detail the dangers inherent in this purely functional approach to truth.

Revolutions, like the one Berdyadev was living through, emerge out of social disintegration, when a people's faith is in decline and there is a loss of "a unifying spiritual center."[50] A result of this is a kind of "possession," the kind that Dostoyevsky had made graphic in *The Devils,* an alternative translation of which is precisely *The Possessed.* The extreme elements—Lenin's professional revolutionaries—take charge, believing they are leading the way. But they are really puppets in the hands of atavistic forces, rather like those that Andrei Bely had evoked in his novel *The Silver Dove.* They are "mediums of formless elements," the Dionysian chaos at the heart of the Russian soul, that are not turned toward the future, but are "slaves of the past," tied to it by "malice, envy, and revenge," the very sentiments that Lenin's rhetoric did its best to stimulate.

Revolutions are not creative, only destructive. They can tear down outmoded structures, such as the tsarist regime, but they cannot put anything in its place, except the kind of man-god for which the New Men and their utilitarian ethos paved the way.* Technology, the child of utilitarianism, allows man to conquer nature, but in the process he is "disintegrated," made into a mere counter, a statistic, a function of the power he believes he controls. This power can create a world of material equality that, to the dispossessed, seems the only goal worth attaining. But such equality is bought at a terrific price, that of the soul, and is motivated, not by love or the sense of community given in *sobernost,* but by "resentment," the envy of the have-nots against the haves.[51]

For Berdyaev such leveling is part of the long historical process by which humanism, which began as a movement of freedom, liberating man from the constraints of a suffocating religion, turns into its opposite, an ideology responsible for totalitarian regimes, dedicated to "equality" and "the people." Yet the "equality" that these provide is in the end little more than that of slaves, equally subject to the same process of dehumanization, in which people are no longer "persons" but simply functions of the state. With Lenin's rebarbative attacks on the individual and contempt for any inner life whatsoever, the kind of "personalism" that Berdyaev advocated could not last long. Where Lenin saw human consciousness as nothing more than a reflection of the physical world, Berdyaev hearkened back to the ancient notion of the microcosm, the individual as a world unto himself, containing, not reflecting, a universe. The new Russia was not big enough for both views. One of them had to go.

OF COURSE IT was Berdyaev who left, and he was not the only one. In the fall of 1922, with the civil war over, two ships, the *Oberbürgermeister*

---

*"Revolutions have never lightened the burden of tyranny: they have only shifted it to another shoulder," George Bernard Shaw.[52]

Haken and the *Preussen,* left St. Petersburg and carried some 160 intellectuals from the victorious Soviet Republic out of Russia and across the Baltic Sea into Europe. Their port of call was Stettin, Germany (present-day Szczecin in Poland), and on board were priests, literary critics, archaeologists, journalists, historians, economists, poets, novelists, painters, mathematicians, publishers, and other figures in the arts and intellectual life of Russia that Lenin felt he couldn't outright eradicate—the international press would be too bad—but also couldn't let remain in the country.[53] There was no room in the new Russia for competing views of reality, and the people on board these ships held views very much out of step with his. The worst offenders were the philosophers; not only were their politics way out of line, their whole vision of reality was opposed to his on practically every point. They simply had to leave. So they did, and their mode of transport became known as "the philosophy steamers." It was a cultural and intellectual diaspora that would have a profound effect on both the individuals caught up in it and the country that expelled them.

Berdyaev was in good company, even if, like himself, his fellow travelers were not happy about the voyage or about the prospect of making a new life for themselves in foreign lands. They could take very little with them and so had sold most of their belongings; this meant libraries, among other things. Berdyaev's German was as good as was his French, but not all of those expelled were polyglots. Painters can paint in any language, but poets are not always so versatile, and university lecturers would also find themselves up against a linguistic wall.

But the alternative seemed even less appealing. Lenin's mission to flatten Russia's spiritual life out of existence gave no indication of letting up. If the exiles stayed they would have to submit to it or suffer the consequences. Life in an alien land seemed preferable to certain extermination, even if the land they were heading to was itself still emerging from the catastrophe of World War One. And for the prescient ones on board, as well as for those in the cities that would receive them, the prospect of another war was far from unthinkable.

Among those leaving the new Soviet Union was the religious thinker and economist Sergei Bulgakov (1871–1944), whose vision of a "Sophic economy," blending Solovyov's Sophiology with practical economics, presages in many ways our twenty-first century concern with "sustainability" and being "stewards" of the planet. As George M. Young writes, for Bulgakov, "we are the owners and managers of the cosmos, responsible under divine guidance for its survival and growth."[54]

Bulgakov came from a family of priests reaching back to the sixteenth century. His first studies were at a seminary, but he lost his faith, and at Moscow University he took up law. Like many students at the time he came under the influence of Marx, but he soon rejected his ideas. Discussions with Tolstoy and a reading of Kant led him back to the church, and Bulgakov would recount his journey from Marxism to a religious philosophy in his early work *From Marxism to Idealism* (1904).

This tension between the worldly and the spiritual would inform his belief that man, especially Russian man, was the battleground between two "kingdoms," that of heaven and that of Earth. His "Sophic economy" can be seen as an attempt to harmonize the two, so that the truth of heaven can inform the necessities of Earth. Bulgakov himself can be seen as a living example of this union. In 1907, as one of the "Legal Marxists"—politicians with a particular interpretation of Marxist theory—he was a member of the Second Duma, which was brought to a quick end by Nicholas II. In 1918 he was ordained as a priest. It was not the most propitious time to take the cloth, but by then Bulgakov had had a mystical experience that convinced him of the reality of the Divine, in much the same way as Solovyov's visitations by Sophia brought him to the same realization.

In his book *The Unfading Light* (1917) Bulgakov tells of a journey in the Caucasus when the beauty of the mountains overwhelmed him.[55] He had long grown used to seeing "in nature nothing but a dead desert under a cloak of beauty, as if it were wearing a treacherous mask."[56] But then, in sight of the snow-capped peaks, he felt a sudden ecstasy. "My soul felt glad and trembled with joyful agitation." He had known for some time that there was no God—at least that was what he was led to believe—but now that knowledge melted in the face of a living divinity.

What if the beauty invading him was not a lie, but God's own cloak—what Goethe had called God's "living raiment"?* He had been held captive by "science," "that scarecrow set up for the would-be intellectual mob . . . that spiritual pestilence of our days."[57] But now "the first day of creation" shone before his eyes, and his heart was "ready to break with bliss." The world, he saw, was not dead matter to be used by mankind for its selfish ends. It was a "theophany," God's visible manifestation; an insight that would come some years later to another Sophiologist, the French phenomenologist and esoteric philosopher Henry Corbin.[58] This theophany was not limited to the natural world. On a visit to a gallery in Dresden, Bulgakov once sat for hours before Raphael's *Sistine Madonna,* as Dostoyevsky had done years before, and reached the same conclusion as had the novelist: that beauty would save the world.[59]

Where Fedorov saw nature as so much raw material to be put to human uses—a policy that Lenin and his successor Stalin would apply ruthlessly to Russia's natural resources—Bulgakov saw the living body of the divine, with which mankind must work with "tender cooperation." "Every living organism," Bulgakov wrote, "is inextricably connected with the universe as a whole . . . and one cannot disturb so much as a grain of sand . . . without . . . disturbing the entire universe," a view with which poets as different as William Blake and T. S. Eliot would agree.[60] No five-year plan could follow such guidelines, and it's no surprise Bulgakov had to go. He was the author of many books—his last was about the Apocalypse—and he died in Paris, where he taught for many years at the Saint Sergius Orthodox Theological Institute, which he helped found in 1925, practically upon his arrival.

Another forced out was the philosopher Semyon Frank (1877–1950).

---

*Bulgakov's attitude toward nature has much in common with the "participatory epistemology" of Goethe, mentioned earlier.

Frank was born in Moscow into an Orthodox Jewish family. His father died when Frank was young, and he was brought up by his grandfather, who taught him Hebrew, and later by his stepfather, who had links to the Populists. Like Bukgakov and Berdyaev, he was early on drawn to Marx, but also like them he found himself moving away from Marxist ideas, although he maintained a belief in socialism. A pamphlet Frank wrote in 1899 led to his expulsion from the University of Moscow, and he was forced to continue his studies in Berlin. By 1901 he was back in Russia, where he was approached by the ex-Marxist liberal political editor Peter Struve, who asked him to contribute to the book *Problems of Idealism* (1902); Frank would also contribute to *Vekhi*, which Struve also edited. He worked with Struve for some years, contributing to his banned journal *Liberation*. In 1920 Struve, aware of what was coming, left Russia ahead of the pack, settling in Paris from where he worked for a time supporting the White Army's efforts.

In 1912 Frank converted to Christianity—he believed it was a natural continuation of his Judaism—and in 1916 he received his master's degree on the strength of his major work *The Object of Knowledge* (1916). Frank's fundamental idea is that logic, the sine qua non of Western philosophy, can only work because of a prior "intuition" of a prelogical "all-embracing unity."[61] In an echo of the ancient "sympathy of all things," Frank believed that every object, prior to our knowledge of it, "is in immediate contact with us," a view shared by the Anglo-American philosopher Alfred North Whitehead.[62] This unity arises not through consciousness but "through our very being." We are that unity itself, or at least a part of it, as is everything else in existence.

This is a "meta-logical" unity, one not limited to the laws of "identity, contradiction, and the excluded middle." Where logic tells us that "A = A," metalogic tells us that it must also include "non-A," an insight that informs the work that made P. D. Ouspensky's name in the West, *Tertium Organum* (1912), and would have driven Ayn Rand, an Aristotelian capitalist, up a wall.[63] Our logical grasp of experience is possible because in the act of cognition, we "wrench" the object of our knowledge out of its primal unity with the rest of existence; this cognitive separation from the "absolute" allows us to manipulate the fragments of being it splinters off, but at the expense of a true knowledge of the world as a "living being." Such "living being" cannot be grasped by logic but only by "living knowledge," which we attain in those moments—known to poets and sought by the readers of Schelling—when we not merely "contemplate" reality but "live it."[64]

In 1921 Frank joined the faculty of the University of Moscow and became involved in Berdyaev's Free Academy. In 1922 he joined Berdyaev and others on the "philosophy steamers." For a time he lived in Germany, where he was helped by his friend, the Swiss existential psychologist Ludwig Binswanger, who had been a student of C. G. Jung. But with the rise of National Socialism he had to leave for Paris, joining Berdyaev, Struve, Bulgakov, and many others, including the philosopher N. O. Lossky, whose *History of Russian Philosophy* I have drawn on throughout this book.

Not all the philosophers left on the steamers. One remarkable figure stayed behind and in the end was murdered by the Soviets during the Stalin purges of the 1930s. This was the philosopher, art historian, electrical engineer, priest, and much more Father Pavel Florensky (1882–1937), a true polymath and one of those Russian souls large enough to embrace a multitude of contradictions. As was Solovyov, Florensky was a great synthesizer; his central aim was to bring together religion and science, reason and faith. He was at home in all these spheres, and enjoyed an erudition that rivaled Fedorov's.

Florensky was as adept in marine biology as he was in geoscience, folklore, philology, astronomy, music, or electrodynamics. It was in this last capacity that, in 1918, with the victory of the Bolsheviks and the closure of theological academies, after going into seclusion during the revolution, he secured a position in the "Glavelectro," the Office of Electrical Industry, where he studied the properties of electrical fields and insulators.[65] The story is that he would wear his priest's cassock and cap to work—he had been ordained in 1911—although he had been cautioned more than once about it, and even attended the Supreme Soviet for National Economy in his holy garb. Even Trotsky was not able to get him to change his dress.[66] It was a simple gesture of his continuing faith that earned the respect of many around him, but in the end would lead to a brutal execution. Yet it was also a symbol of his desire to live in two opposing worlds and to unite them. He had a great love of God and of his country, and his patriotism—not the nationalism he has been accused of—led him to remain when it would have been safer for him to leave. We might say that his fate exemplified the fatal truth that in the new Russia, one could not serve two masters.

Florensky was born in Azerbaijan, and went to school in Tiflis (later Tibilisi). He was a younger contemporary of Stalin, who was known then as Joseph Dzhugashvili (Stalin is a concoction of the word for steel, "stal" and Lenin, hence his fame in the 1930s as the "man of steel," taking a feather from Superman's cap). Florensky's father was a Russian railway engineer who had a taste for science and literature; his Armenian mother was the daughter of a successful textile merchant. He is said to have had an "Asiatic" appearance, and Bulgakov, with whom he was great friends—there is a famous painting of the two by Mikhail Nesterov—said he looked more Egyptian than Russian. The Symbolist Andrei Bely agreed. Florensky had studied under Bely's father, the mathematician Nikolai Bugaev, at Moscow University, and Florensky was a participant in, and influence on, the many groups during the Silver Age trying to forge the "new religious consciousness," mixing with the Merezhkovskys and other God-seekers, in the febrile atmosphere of prerevolutionary Russia.

Florensky's central vision, spelled out in his most well-known book, *The Pillar and Ground of Truth* (1913), a collection of "spiritual letters," is in essence the same as that of Bulgakov and Frank: that, for all its virtues, the kind of logic associated with Western philosophy cannot lead to an understanding of true reality, which is something that always exceeds our attempts to grasp it conceptually. As did Frank, he believed that "A = A" is only half the story; it must also include "non-A" in order to obtain the whole picture.

To the logical mind this is absurd; Hegel, of course, had said much the same, but most philosophy post-Hegel, even Marx, found Hegel's brand of logic untenable. But where logic fails, images and symbols can succeed, and it was in icons, whose beauty overwhelmed Princess Olga a millennium earlier, that Florensky saw a "window onto another world," the world of "unified wholeness" that our rational intellect can only cut into lifeless pieces.

But to see this world, to look through this window, we must be in the right conditions, not in a museum, where the bright lights compete with and dim the spiritual light radiating from the icon, but, as Princess Olga did, in a church, with incense and candles and with others who also wish to peer through these doors of perception, into the realm of something like Plato's eternal Forms.[67] Timothy Leary may have popularized the idea of "set and setting" for his own faux psychedelic "mystery religion" of the 1960s, but sensitive characters like Florensky were aware of it half a century before.

Words too, can give us a glimpse of this other reality. They can act as intermediaries, messengers carrying meaning from one world to the other. This is because, for Florensky, they can move between the worlds, in both directions at once, the inner and the outer. In our rational understanding, words, "signifiers," are arbitrary sounds, associated with "meanings" through habit and convention. For us, the word *tree* is nothing like a tree. But in the true unity, beyond logic and the intellect, word and thing are one, a belief at the heart of Kabbalah and also at the center of the Hesychast practice, in which the name of God becomes a manifestation of God in the heart of the practitioner.

One can only hope that meditation on these and other mysteries sustained Florensky during the repeated arrests and persecution he was subjected to by a government to which he dedicated his considerable scientific knowledge and ability and which ultimately repaid him in 1937 with a bullet and an unmarked grave.

12

ESP in the USSR

Mind and the Masses

Not all the philosophers who left the new Soviet Union did so by steamer and under the auspices of Comrade Lenin's relocation plan. Some were aware of what was on its way and decided to leave before it was too late, fearing arrest, execution, or being trapped in a country that had descended into chaos. Some managed their escape relatively painlessly, losing only possessions or a home. The cost for others was often much higher: a family member, a friend, or a lover. And as Leslie Chamberlain tells us in *The Philosophy Steamer,* escape was often just the beginning of troubles. Starting a new life in a new land where you were not always wanted wasn't easy. Many were driven back to the land they left out of sheer desperation, having nowhere else to go. They were not always welcomed back, and the new home they found was more often than not a cell in one of the forced labor camps that would come to be known as the Gulag.

Yet other exiles did remarkably well, and their return to the new Russia—if they made it—could be under the strangest of circumstances. Consider, for example, the career of the artist and guru Nicholas Roerich (1874–1947), who left Russia cursing the Bolsheviks, became a success in America, and in the 1920s, approached the Soviets with a plan to establish a Pan-Buddhist nation in inner Asia, under the protection of Russia, the great "northern Shambhala," the name of a hidden mystical land in Tibetan Buddhist tradition.[1]*

Roerich was born in St. Petersburg into a well-off, highly cultured family. His father, a lawyer, had a great love of art, and from an early age Nicholas was surrounded by painters, musicians, poets, and writers. Another early love was for ancient Russia, a fascination that began when an archaeologist friend took him to visit some prehistoric tumuli. This love of the past stayed with Roerich throughout his life.

His artistic talent soon made itself known, and by his late teens Roerich had enrolled in the St. Petersburg Academy of the Arts. It was the start of the Silver Age, and Roerich quickly became a part of it, becoming friends with the composers Mussorgsky and Rimsky-Korsakov, and contributing sets and decorations for a performance of Rimsky-Korsakov's opera *The Maid of Pskov* (1872), about Ivan the Terrible. By this time Roerich had found a place for himself in the impresario Sergei Diaghilev's "World of Art," and had been made director of the Imperial Society for the Encouragement of the Arts. But Roerich's greatest success from the pre-Bolshevik days was in 1913, when Igor Stravinsky's raucous pagan ballet *The Rite of Spring,* choreographed and performed by Vaslav Nijinsky, premiered in Paris as part of Diaghilev's Ballets Russes and, as legend has it, caused a riot.[2]

Roerich had come up with the idea for a work about pagan Russia, and along with inspiring Stravinsky—whom World War One would maroon in Europe, never to return to Russia—he also contributed the sets, costume designs, and decorations to what is probably the most famous piece of modern music.

But Roerich also had a very strong spiritual side that came out in his many religious paintings and in his restoration work on the ancient church of Talashkino, in Smolensk, and other religious sites. Roerich's spiritual hunger was matched by that of Helena Shaposhnikov, daugh-

---

*Roerich was not the first to try to unite different Buddhist people into one nation. Space allows me only a mention of the remarkable Baron Ungern von Sternberg and his attempts to do so during the Russian Civil War.

ter of a famous architect, whom he met in 1901 and soon married. From an early age Helena had been subject to visions and strange experiences in which she felt her body to be on fire. She introduced Roerich to Eastern wisdom and especially to the work of Madame Blavatsky. Blavatsky claimed to have been guided by hidden masters in Tibet, and Helena found that she was being contacted by them too.

Roerich's new interest in the East led to some remarkable developments. One was his work on the stained glass windows in the Buddhist temple that in 1909 Agvan Dorzhiev, a Buryat monk and tutor to the thirteenth Dalai Lama, was allowed to erect in St. Petersburg. The temple was completed and opened in 1915, but its services were cut short by the revolution. At least Lenin's Bolsheviks showed that their prejudice was not only against Christianity. In 1917 they sacked the temple* and arrested Dorzhiev, who just missed execution; he eventually lived for many years under a kind of house arrest in the temple. He did not escape the Stalin purges though and died in prison in 1938.

Another result of Roerich's turn to the East is that he and Helena soon developed their own theosophical teaching, what they called "Agni Yoga," named after the Hindu god of fire. Roerich had begun his life's work of combining his artistic and spiritual pursuits in one practice. It was a combination that would produce some spectacular results.

It was from Dorzhiev that Roerich heard legends of the mysterious land of Shambhala that would eventually send him on his strange mission to form a "Sacred Union of the East," under the auspices of the fledgling Soviet state. But first he had to leave Russia. He had had premonitions of a disaster—at least some of his paintings from this time suggest as much—and when World War One erupted he knew he had been right. The revolution confirmed it, and when Roerich's doctor suggested he recuperate from a case of pneumonia in Finland, he agreed. He left calling Bolshevism "the distortion of the sacred ideas of mankind." By 1919 he was in London designing sets for Sir Thomas Beecham at

---

*The temple reopened in 1989.

Covent Garden.[3] In 1920 he was invited to exhibit his paintings in America and also to design sets for the Chicago Opera. But the Roerichs' real American success story started, as many did, in New York.*

Roerich had learned from Diaghilev how to attract patrons, and by the time he reached Manhattan, he had perfected a self-image he would project from then on. He accentuated his Mongol characters with a Fu Manchu mustache and beard and had taken to wearing Eastern garb. His reputation as a refugee and artist as well as his new persona as spiritual master was compelling, and Roerich soon found himself collecting followers. Two of them, Louis and Nettie Horch, were wealthy, and for the next decade and a half they bankrolled Roerich's projects. As Roerich explained to them and his other disciples, these had an inner and outer aspect.

The outer side was what he called *Cor Ardens* (Blazing Heart) and *Corona Mundi* (Crown of the World), names for projects within Roerich's Master Institute of United Arts. This was an association of schools for the fine arts—painting, music, architecture, drama, dance— all housed within what Roerich called the Master Building,[†] a twenty-four-story skyscraper on Manhattan's Riverside Drive that looked like a Buddhist stupa and opened for business just before the great crash of 1929.[4] It was in this aspect, as a global ambassador of the universal spiritual value of the arts, that Roerich made his biggest impact,

---

*I should point that in his excellent work, *Red Shambhala,* Andrei Znamenski seems to have got his dates a bit askew. He says that the Roerichs were unhappy in London because at the time, 1919, "there was no room for them to spread their wings to become spiritual teachers." He suggests that "the great occult celebrity Peter Ouspensky far overshadowed" them and that across the English Channel "the flamboyant George Gurdjieff" . . . was "drawing European seekers to his spiritual school." As we've seen, in 1919 Ouspensky was stuck in Ekaterinodar, at the time one of the worst places on the planet, and neither he nor Gurdjieff would wash up in Europe for another two years. Even when they did, neither Ouspensky nor Gurdjieff achieved the kind of financial success or celebrity that Roerich did, who hobnobbed with American presidents and, at one point, owned a skyscraper in Manhattan.

†It was built on the site of Horch's mansion and can be found today at 310 Riverside Drive.

getting support from figures such as Albert Einstein, Bernard Shaw, H. G. Wells, and even US presidents Herbert Hoover and Franklin Delano Roosevelt.*

But there was a secret, inner purpose behind Roerich's work, which he revealed only to his closest disciples. This was what we can call the Shambhala Project. In many Eastern traditions, Shambhala is a mysterious secret land hidden in inner Asia. It is associated with a coming new age, a time of great spirituality, peace, and harmony, and the sign of its arrival is the reappearance of the legendary Buddhist hero, Rigden-Jyepo. Roerich's plan was to go to inner Asia and to bring together Buddhists from different political states into one nation, using the myth of Shambhala as the adhesive and with himself in the starring role of Rigden-Jyepo. This would take place under the cover of an ethnographic and cultural expedition through Ladakh, the Altai Mountains, Mongolia, and other regions, which Roerich undertook between 1925 and 1929, but whose real destination was Tibet. Roerich's aim was to return the Panchen Lama, who had left Tibet after a disagreement with the Dalai Lama,† to his rightful place, believing that such a move would convince Buddhists of whatever nationality that the new age had begun.

A new Great Game had started between the British and the Soviets for influence in the region, and Roerich realized it would be to his advantage to have the Reds on his side—conveniently ignoring the many articles he had written in support of the White Army. And as Andrei Znamenski argues in *Red Shambhala* (2011), the Soviets had their own ideas about a Communist Tibet. So it was not altogether a

---

*In 1935 the Roerich Peace Pact, an international treaty designed to protect works of art and culture in times of war, was signed by President Franklin Delano Roosevelt. It was ratified by twenty-one other states and remains in effect until 2024.

†While the office of the Dalai Lama, the political leader of Tibet, is well known in the West, that of the Panchen Lama, its spiritual leader, is less so. They do not always agree. In her classic work *Magic and Mystery in Tibet,* the traveler Alexandra David-Neel tells the story of how, on departing Shigatze, "the Tashi (or Panchen) Lama left in his stead, a phantom perfectly resembling him."[5] This is known as a *tulpa.*

surprise when Roerich broke camp in China and made a side trip to Moscow en route to Shambhala.

He brought with him letters from his hidden masters for Comrade Stalin—as well as some possible intelligence about the British—and also spoke of Dorzhiev's remarks about the great "northern Shambhala," emphasizing that his work was to bring about a union of Buddhism with Communism, in order to create a great "Oriental Federation." In order to do this, he needed to get the Panchen Lama out of Mongolia and back to Tibet, and for this to happen he needed help.

Roerich's interview was with Anatoly Lunacharsky, the Soviet educational commissioner and devotee of Madame Blavatsky. After a follow-up meeting between Lunacharsky and the secret police, one Theosophist told the other to leave Moscow as quickly as possible; if he did not, he would be arrested as a spy. Lunacharsky's comrades believed that Roerich was working for the Americans and wanted to destabilize the region even more than it already was.

We can't blame the Reds. Roerich was a Russian national flying an American flag and Tibetan *thangka* over his expedition, which sported a team of Cossacks. Who *was* he working for? The British too were unsure of him and thought he was working for the Soviets. When they caught wind of his plan—not difficult to do when he was preaching it to every Buddhist from Kashmir to the Gobi Desert—they informed the Dalai Lama that it would be advantageous to prevent Roerich from entering his country. He agreed and patiently kept Roerich's party cooling their heels—and everything else—for several months at the Kam-Rong Pass, one of the coldest spots on the planet. Roerich and his team stuck it out but finally had to give up on Tibet and retreat to Sikkim, from where they eventually headed to India. Even if he had gotten into Tibet, Roerich's plan was never more than a pipe dream. When the Panchen Lama heard of it, he said that he would have nothing to do with it.

But Roerich was persistent, and a decade later he tried to initiate the new age of Shambhala again, this time with support from the United States Department of Agriculture. This attempt failed too, and when Horch, after years of funding Roerich's political designs, filed suit against him for $200,000 in unpaid loans, and also testified against him in a tax evasion suit, Roerich's dreams of Shambhala were over.[6] He remained in India, a friend of Gandhi and Nehru, until he died at the age of seventy-three at his Urusvati Research Institute in the Himalayas.

A RATHER DIFFERENT story is that of the Russian-Estonian esoteric thinker Valentin Tomberg (1900–1973), another philosophical refugee from Lenin's Russia. Where Roerich hobnobbed with celebrities and heads of state, and was a three-time Nobel Peace Prize nominee, Tomberg was for the most part practically unknown. As his editor writes, "he himself attached no significance whatever to biographical details concerning him," a modesty we have found in others in this book.[7] In fact, Tomberg had asked that his most important work, *Meditations on the Tarot* (1985), an enormous exploration of Hermetic thinking, be published anonymously and only after his death. Today it is recognized as one of the truly esoteric works of the twentieth century.

Tomberg was born in St. Petersburg to a Russian mother and an Estonian father who had some official positon in the tsarist government. By his late teens he had found his way to Theosophy and the work of Solovyov and the mystical side of the church. He was also initiated into a Martinist order of some kind. He gave up on Theosophy early on but like many others in Russia found much in the work of Rudolf Steiner. It was Steiner's positive remarks about Solovyov and his own emphasis on the importance of the "Christ event" that appealed to Tomberg.

The revolution was a catastrophe for Tomberg. Some accounts say he lost both parents and a brother. The story is told that during the chaos, Tomberg's mother ventured into the streets; Tomberg later found her and their dog, both tied to a tree, shot dead. In the event, he made his way out of Russia to Tallinn, Estonia. From here he wrote repeatedly to Steiner, in Dornach, Switzerland, which another Russian refugee, Andrei Bely, had recently left to return to the homeland. (Bely would die there, more or less forgotten, in 1934, after making strenuous efforts to portray his early mystical visions as premonitions of the coming revolution.)[8] Steiner never replied to Tomberg's letters asking to become his student, but Tomberg joined the Estonian branch of the Anthroposophical Society in 1925—the year of Steiner's death—and eventually became its secretary. But his own independent mind led to friction, and not long after he was asked to leave.

During the 1930s Tomberg wrote several articles for Anthroposophical journals. These focussed mostly on his own esoteric reading of the Gospels, the return of Christ "in the etheric"—a subtle plane of reality more spiritual than physical—and the "mission" of different nationalities and states, especially Russia, which he saw, as Steiner and Solovyov had, as the potential bearer of a new planetary culture. It was in these articles too that he spelled out the Soviet animus toward religion and Christianity in particular, its need to disparage, mock, and diminish it at every step of the triumphant march of the proletariat. It was also during this time that Tomberg went through a mystical experience that, according to him, put him in touch with the "angelic world," a privilege that did not help his relations with other Anthroposophists.

In 1938 Tomberg was in the Netherlands, working with the Dutch Resistance against the Nazis. He was again involved with Anthroposophy, but again his ideas proved too eccentric for the rank and file and he was asked to leave. (Apparently his vision was too Christocentric, even for Anthroposophists.) After the war, in Cologne he earned a degree in jurisprudence and converted to Catholicism. In 1948 he moved to England, where he worked as a translator for the BBC, monitoring Soviet broadcasts. He retired in 1960, spent the rest of his life writing, and died of a stroke while on holiday with his family in Majorca in 1973. Unlike Roerich, Tomberg had no messianic inclinations, and from what I've gathered, it would take more than the prospect of a "Sacred Union of the East" or any kind of political development, to induce him to break bread with the Soviets, who for him were by definition opposed to any interior life.[9]

IT WOULD BE a mistake, however, to think that with the Bolshevik victory, all occult, esoteric, or spiritual activities came to a halt in the new Soviet Union. Valentin Tomberg may not have been open to dealing with the Soviets, but in the early days of the revolution, some Anthroposophists did believe that their own vision of a transformed society was not entirely different from what the Bolsheviks had in mind. For a time at least, they were fellow travelers, even if, as quickly became evident, for many of them their traveling days would soon be over.

As the scholar Renata von Meydell points out, at the start of the revolution, many Russian Anthroposophists believed that they could apply Steiner's ideas to the new world that was coming into being.[10] New visions in the arts, society, and education seemed possible. In areas ranging from classes in eurythmy, Steiner's form of "cosmic dance," to the restoration of ancient monuments, Steiner's Russian followers devoted their energies and idealism to the service of the revolution. Much esoteric literature previously difficult to obtain was now available, and where before the tsar had censored public discussion of these ideas, they were now being talked about openly.

Many believed that the revolution was proof of Steiner's prediction about Russia being the birthplace of a new cultural epoch. Andrei Bely, who had a fluctuating relationship with Steiner, believed the purpose of the political revolution was to make the way clear for the spiritual one to follow. Steiner had spoken of the Bolshevik victory as a necessary "negative" revolution, to be followed by a "positive" one. This was an idea that, sans Steiner's esotericism, was embraced by the Eurasianists, some of whom, like Berdyaev, had been shipped out of Russia on the "philosophy steamers." They, too, were waiting for the first revolution to collapse, so that they could return to their homeland with a new vision for its future.

The expectations of the Eurasianists and the Anthroposophists were soon disappointed, and any chance of another revolution, spiritual or otherwise, to put the first one right quickly faded from view. In

1923 Anthroposophy was made illegal in the Soviet Union, along with all other esoteric teachings. By the end of the decade many Russian Anthroposophists had found their way into one of the many forced labor camps that, in a darkly ironic parallel, were rising up across the land in a manner not unlike the spread of Orthodoxy through the monastic movement of the thirteenth century. A new orthodoxy, it seemed, had taken its place.

Bely's belief in Anthroposophy's transformative power was an outgrowth of the Symbolist belief that through art, life itself could be changed.* This was something that his older contemporary, Alexander Scriabin, an ardent Theosophist who died before the revolution, had tried to accomplish in his monumental scores for what he called *Gesamtkunstwerk,* "total art works," an idea he took from the high priest of musical Symbolism, Richard Wagner. In the early days of the revolution, this "magical" power of art was embraced wholeheartedly, and by now reams have been written about the direct and disturbing links between aesthetics, symbolism, and political propaganda. As Bernice Glatzer Rosenthal writes, "the Bolsheviks adapted occult ideas, symbols, and techniques to political propaganda," an adaptation in keeping with the Russian tradition of absorbing outside influences and then turning them into something uniquely Russian.[11] And of course such adaptation was not limited to hammers and sickles. There is a whole subgenre of occult literature devoted to Hitler's use of magic and symbolism, and my own book, *Dark Star Rising,* is concerned with what appears to be the introduction in recent years of a new, internet-based form of "occult politics" on the far right. In a fundamental way magic and politics have a common aim: to achieve power and to use it to make changes in the world. As the transformation of Russia brought about by the revolution carried on, it seemed to many that Lenin and the Bolsheviks were doing just that.

---

*As Oscar Wilde, that arch-Symbolist, wrote in "The Decay of Lying," "Life imitates Art far more than Art imitates Life."

Symbolism is based on the power of symbols and images to reach into the psyche and through a subtle, often subliminal influence, transform it. But where Symbolism was content to evoke a strange sense of "otherness" in its audience, the revolutionaries now in charge had a more specific content in mind. They were impatient with moody, misty suggestions of another world and wanted to create one themselves, full of hard surfaces and sharp outlines, that is, a decidedly "modern" world. Although Symbolist techniques were employed in agitprop theater in the early days of the revolution, as a means of putting the right message into the audience's mind, Symbolism itself had by this time fallen to Cubo-Futurism, an ungainly union of French Cubism and Italian Futurism that had come to prominence in tandem with the Bolsheviks.* The savants of this new aesthetic were influenced by the ideas of P. D. Ouspensky about "higher space," and the "fourth dimension," and saw in mathematics, geometry, and science—which the Symbolists had avoided like the devil—ways of access to the new utopia.[12]

Yet these new prophets of the new age also fell victim to the utopia they promoted. The poet Velimir Khlebnikov, who, like Ouspensky, was obsessed with the mystery of time, wrote about the cyclical nature of history and wanted to create a new "sense free" language, zaum. Like the pilgrims of old he wandered throughout the land, carrying his poems in a pillowcase, proclaiming the millennium; he died in 1922 from exposure and malnutrition brought on by the chaos. Another poet, Vladimir Mayakovsky, put his Futurist shoulder to the revolutionary wheel until, with the clamping down on free expression and the demand to cut his poetic cloth to the increasingly severe requirements of the "common man," he shot himself in 1930.[13]

The painter Kazimir Malevich, perhaps the most successful of the new avant-garde, was, like Mayakovsky, an ardent supporter of the revolution, and he received one of its highest honors. When Lenin died in

---

*Oddly enough, this was an unusual political pairing, as Cubism found its way to Communism—via exponents such as Pablo Picasso—while Filippo Marinetti's Futurism soundly supported Mussolini's fascism.

1924 there was some talk of freezing him until, Fedorov-like, he could be resurrected. But when Lenin's body began to decompose, as did Father Zossima's, the decision was made to embalm him. Then came the question of his tomb. Malevich suggested that it should be a cube, rather than a pyramid, because that would symbolize the fourth dimension, which is beyond death, an idea with Theosophical roots.[14]

Malevich had by this time equated Lenin's passing with that of Christ, so the idea of resurrection, so much a part of Holy Russia, seems in one way to have lingered on.[15] Malevich's idea was accepted, and soon the architect Arkady Shchusev started work on Lenin's mausoleum, where the preserved body of the great leader can still be seen today.[16] Malevich, however, suffered the fate of many avant-garde or "modern" artists whose talents were used in the early days but who soon had to toe the increasingly strict party line. With Lenin's death and the rise of Stalin, abstract art of Malevich's stamp was declared "bourgeois" and anti-revolutionary. Many of Malevich's canvases were confiscated, and he was forbidden henceforth to create such works; his artistic brief now was the kind of "socialist realism" demanded by all good comrades. In this he was lucky. Like the actor Mikhail Chekhov, an advocate of Steiner's ideas who was forced to renounce them, Malevich only received a slap on the wrist.* Others were not so fortunate. The poet Osip Mandlestam died in a labor camp in 1938, and in 1940 the director Vsevolod Meyerhold, who had adapted Symbolist techniques to the new regime and was the mentor of Sergei Eisenstein, himself a devotee of a number of esoteric pursuits, was shot.[17]

Lenin may have had the last say. When Stalin died in 1953, his body was housed in Lenin's tomb, until 1961, when a message from beyond the grave came from the original Bolshevik himself. At a party meeting a female comrade announced that Lenin had come to her in a dream and told her that he was not happy sharing his cube with Stalin. The visitation was taken seriously, and Stalin was promptly reburied near

---

*Chekhov himself would leave the Soviet Union for good in 1928.

the Kremlin Wall, the move facilitated by Nikita Khrushchev's attacks on the personality cult surrounding the "man of steel."[18] What Stalin had to say about this is unknown.

IT WAS NOT only artists who informed the new Soviet world with esoteric ideas, or at least tried to. Much has been written about the religious character of the cults of Lenin and Stalin, and the revolution's promise of a new age just a bit further down the road is clearly a secular version of the apocalypse that has in many ways been the motor of Russian history. Some of the new regime, like Lev Trotsky, sticking to the letter of the Marxist law, wanted to excise the occult entirely, as nothing more than a carrier of bourgeois ideas. He targeted Anthroposophy as a particularly counterrevolutionary belief.[19] Trotsky, one of the revolution's founding fathers, would turn against Stalin, but eventually he fell victim to his purges when he was assassinated gruesomely in Mexico City in 1940, by having an ice pick slammed into his head.[20]

Yet others, equally devoted to the cause, could see where some occult or esoteric ideas could be of use to it. One was the writer Maxim Gorky (1868–1936). Where Futurists like Mayakovsky and Malevich were impatient with the Symbolist notion of some vague "other world" and wanted to make one themselves, Gorky too was not content to "seek" God, as Merezhkovsky and the other "God-seekers" had. Like a good proletariat, he was anxious to roll up his sleeves and get to work, building him from scratch.

Gorky was born Aleksey Maksimovich Peshkov but later took the pen name "Gorky," which means "bitter," a reflection on the experiences and insights of a difficult life. He had a hard childhood in a working-class family and learned the facts of life at an early age. He had hardly any schooling; a volume of his autobiographies, which many consider his masterpiece, ironically titled *My Universities* (1923), makes this clear. By the age of eight he was working to earn whatever he could, and the greatest schooling he had was the love of reading that he acquired through a cook on a Volga steamer, where he worked as a dishwasher. He was often hungry, frequently beaten, and poorly clothed, but his life as a tramp trawling through what he would later call "the lower depths"—in a play of that name—supplied him with a surplus of experience and developed the eye for detail that helped to make his reputation as an accurate chronicler of Russian life. He is a kind of combination Jack London and George Orwell of the *Down and Out in Paris and London* period, with a talent for portraying the grit and difficulties of everyday life that best comes through in his short stories.

Gorky first came into contact with revolutionary ideas through the Populists. He turned to Marx while living in St. Petersburg and soon joined the Bolsheviks, although he and Comrade Lenin did not always see eye to eye. His politics led to arrests and to several years as an exile in Europe. After he returned he criticized Lenin's tactics in gaining the Bolshevik victory until those very tactics called for his censorship. In 1921 Gorky was sent on a "medical exile" from which he did not return until 1929, when he finally settled again in Russia. As others had, he came to accept Stalin's totalitarian regime, and it remains debatable whether his death in 1936 was from natural causes or was the result of Stalin's paranoia.

Gorky was interested in occult phenomena from an early age. A reading of the philosopher Schopenhauer and the German occultist Karl du Prel convinced him of the reality of these phenomena, and a story that Nicholas Roerich tells give us an idea of what Gorky had in mind, literally. Gorky told Roerich that while in the Caucasus he met a Hindu fakir who showed him an album of "black metallic leaves." As he looked at the blank pages Gorky saw "vivid images of Indian cities" that the Hindu was making appear.[21] It was as an example of the "thought transference" from one mind to another that Gorky believed was possible and that some researchers suggest was at the root of the Socialist Realist aesthetic he came to champion.[22] Later readings in Theosophical literature, as well as in Swedenborg and the Renaissance alchemist Paracelsus, supported the idea that thoughts, rather than pale reflections of the outer world—the view promoted by Lenin—were actually "things," powerful ones. Properly concentrated and directed, they could have a real effect on the world.

Scientists in Russia before the revolution were also interested in phenomena that seemed to overturn the laws of nature, or at least suggested that those laws were incomplete and in need of reform. One difference between these efforts and similar ones in the West is that in Russia the positivist heritage remained a strong influence. This meant that many researchers, while accepting the reality of psychic phenomena, sought to anchor them in more familiar materialist explanations. An early exponent of this approach to psychical research was the Moscow psychiatrist Naum Kotik. Kotik believed that psychic phenomena had a materialist basis and could be understood as a form of radiation, what he called "N-rays," an understandable echo of the "X-rays" that had been discovered to world acclaim in 1895.

Vladimir Bekhterev, another scientist interested in what we would call parapsychology, did not think so well of Kotik's work and sought to understand psychic and related phenomena through more psychological means. He was fascinated with the phenomena of mass psychosis and had done groundbreaking research in hypnosis; for a time he had been a student of the great French savant Jean Charcot, one of the pioneers in hypnosis. Bekhterev wanted to understand how "psychological contagion" occurs, how a wave of excitement, fear, or other psychological state can quickly spread through a crowd. It seemed to operate through some agency other than rational consciousness, at some level below our ordinary awareness. Somehow a psychic state is transferred from one person to another, a phenomenon with obvious similarities to the transference of thought. How this happened was unknown, but Bekhterev believed it had nothing to do with "N-rays" or other materialist explanations.

Gorky was aware of Kotik's and Bekhterev's work, and in many ways it confirmed ideas that had fascinated him for years. The idea that a kind of psychic energy could be transmitted from one person to another featured in some of his writing, most powerfully in his novel

Confession (1916), in which a paralyzed woman is healed through the combined psychic energy of a crowd. It was this notion of somehow harnessing the mental energy of the people that informed his ideas about God-building.

God-building grew out of Feuerbach's idea that human beings should worship themselves, rather than an abstract deity that didn't exist, and it has links to the "Church of Humanity" of the nineteenth-century French philosopher Auguste Comte, the rituals, holy days, prayers, saints, and ceremonies of which Comte spelled out in *A System of Positive Politics* (1851).[23] Comte is the source of the "positivism" that informed the New Men and which, in a radically austere form, was at the heart of Lenin's rejection of anything that smacked of spirituality. God-building was a way of keeping what was "positive" about religion while jettisoning everything that was bad about it. Given that Lenin believed that there was nothing good about religion, it's no surprise he was opposed to the idea. Another opposed to building God was Berdyaev, who saw in it an expression of the self-deification that would, in his view, eventually lead to totalitarianism and dehumanization.

One of the central God-builders was Anatoly Lunacharsky (1875–1933), the Theosophist and Soviet educational commissioner who in 1925 warned Roerich of his imminent arrest. Lunacharsky was a reader of Steiner, and he was interested in the religious aspects of the revolution. In the early days of the revolutionary struggle he sided with his brother-in-law, the scientist and science-fiction writer Alexander Bogdanov, who, until the Bolshevik victory, was a rival of Lenin. Bogdanov was a believer in science as the religion of the future, and he did some apparently remarkable work on rejuvenation through blood transfusions, a challenge that his contemporary, the Russian Serge Voronof, was tackling in France through his monkey gland injections, with debatable results.[24] Through his transfusions Bogdanov apparently developed renewed vigor and improved eyesight—even his balding stopped—leading him to believe that he had achieved a victory over Fedorov's nemesis, death. Bogdanov is generally associated with the

Cosmists. Yet his miracle came to a terrible end when he exchanged blood with a student suffering from malaria. The student recovered but Bogdanov died.

Lunacharsky believed that the social and psychological dimensions of religion could be used for revolutionary purposes. Mankind has a need for ritual, symbols, and prayer, and rather than jettison these as drugs used to keep the people quiet—as Marx had maintained—they can be turned toward the cause of socialism. God in this sense is not the creator of man; rather it is the other way around. Man is on the road to creating himself, and God-building was a way of recognizing the enormous creative potential latent within mankind. Lunacharsky wanted to keep the traditional symbols and scriptures of Christianity while interpreting their message as pointing toward the socialist heaven that was on its way; in this sense, Jesus was the first Communist. This was a tactic that the Symbolist Alexander Blok had used in his poem "The Twelve" (1918), which depicts twelve Bolshevik apostles on the loose in St. Petersburg, led by their comrade, Jesus Christ.

Gorky too believed in God-building, and for him one of the materials used in his construction was the mental energy that he had come to accept through his study of psychic phenomena.* If telepathy and thought transference were real, as he believed they were, then couldn't these phenomena be harnessed and used for the revolutionary cause? The sort of subliminal communication that Symbolism had aimed at was already being used in the revolutionary theater. Shouldn't the revolution take a step further and, rather than rely on the props of the stage,

---

*H. G. Wells, Gorky's friend and a visitor to the early USSR, expressed a similar idea to God-building in his book *God, The Invisible King* (1917). Wells, a socialist and scientific atheist, had come to see that, while there is no God responsible for the universe, one is coming into being through the collective labors of mankind. As with Comte, "humanity" was the greater being transcending the individual, and while Wells rejected a personal immortality, he believed that we each survive and continue after our deaths through those who follow us. The God-builders had the same idea, although they had a more detailed liturgy for their creed than Wells, who saw the worship of his invisible King in more private terms.

implant positive ideas in the minds of the proletariat directly? The proper revolutionary thoughts could be radiated over a crowd, imbuing it with the attitudes and ideals necessary for success. As Gorky wrote, "Every year more and more thought-energy accumulates in the world, and I am convinced that this energy . . . will one day be able to effect things we cannot even imagine today."[25]

One of the things this mental energy could transmit was a feeling of power. Gorky was as aware as anyone of the inertia in the Russian soul, its tendency to Oblomovism; he had cause to write about it in some of his stories. While an Ivan the Terrible or violent uprising might have been needed in the past to get the peasants moving, through the power of thought this could be different. As Mikhail Agursky writes, according to Gorky, "A charismatic person who has a strong psychic charge can transfer that power to a weaker person and make them more active."[26]

Gorky did not know of it, but Fritz Peters, a student of Gurdjieff mentioned earlier, had an experience of precisely this. In the last days of World War Two, Peters, physically ill and a nervous wreck, visited Gurdjieff in Paris, where he had sat out the occupation. Gurdjieff told him to sit across from him and drink some coffee that he had prepared, "as hot as you can." Peters did. Then, as Gurdjieff looked at him, Peters began to feel a "strange uprising of energy," and it was "as if a violent, electric blue light" emanated out of Gurdjieff and into him.[27] Immediately Peters' exhaustion vanished. It seems Gurdjieff knew what Gorky was talking about.

Gorky believed that, eventually, the power of mind would triumph over matter and that where resistant matter rules today, there would be a universe of pure mental energy. This was an idea he shared with Bernard Shaw, who makes it the climax of his "meta-biological Pentateuch" *Back to Methuselah* (1922), a work Gorky knew, and which in a very different way, argues the victory over death that Fedorov championed. It is also not very different from the Marxist view that the materials of nature were there for man to exploit, a radically different perspective from the "Sophic economy" of Sergei Bulgakov. Yet by the 1930s and the long darkness of Stalin's rule, this idea had, as mentioned, dwindled to the kind of "positive thinking" associated with the Socialist Realism that in his last days Gorky advocated. By this time Lenin had long made clear his antipathy to God-building and those involved in his construction had laid down their tools. The insight that the mind has a power over the world that we normally do not suspect—which strikes us as liberating—had been reduced to the narrow, simplistic, and soul-numbingly "positive" message of the socialist revolution, evidence again of the strange twists we find in Russian history.

AN EVEN STRANGER twist can be found in the fascinating tale of Alexander Barchenko (1881–1938) and Gleb Bokii (1879–1937), a story involving parapsychology, Shambhala, and the Soviet secret police.[28] It seems that even the Cheka, responsible for mass arrests, torture, and the killing of hundreds of counterrevolutionaries, some of them occultists, had an interest in phenomena Lenin would have snorted at.

Depending on your sources, Alexander Barchenko was a biologist or medical school dropout, who failed to take a degree but nevertheless liked to be called "Doctor." One thing that is certain is that he had an obsession with occult and esoteric matters, which he wrote about in articles and stories. These ranged over a wide field, embracing Kabbalah, Sufism, shamanism, extrasensory perception, parapsychology, ancient civilizations, lost knowledge, synarchy, thought transference, and most prominently, Tibetan Buddhism. Like Nicholas Roerich, Barchenko was convinced of the importance of Shambhala, and he made efforts to convince others of it, such as the new Soviet authorities.

Although a true believer in the revolution, he had become uneasy at the violence that had been unleashed. Barchenko was an idealist, and the kind of terror let loose on the streets sickened him. As many found, even the slightest hint of "culture" or "education" was enough to incite hatred in the comrades, who would quickly and with impunity strike down anyone who was "different." This was not what the revolution was about, at least according to Barchenko, and when an opportunity to express his thoughts on the need for compassion and common humanity, rooted in Buddhism, arose, he took it.

The lectures he gave to sailors in St. Petersburg were so well received that Barchenko took the risk of writing to the authorities expressing his views. Specifically he pointed out the need to go to Tibet in order to discover the secrets of Shambhala, where, he believed, both teachings of compassion and ancient, lost science could be found. An expedition funded by the government would manage it. He had already traveled across much of Russia, and into Asia, in preparation for the trek.

The reply he received was an invitation to come in for questioning. This was not as bad as it sounds. The person he spoke with was interested and wanted to know more. He had even attended one of his lectures. His interrogator introduced him to another member of the secret police who had a deep interest in the occult. Soon he would meet another, even higher up in the chain of command. Barchenko began to feel that he had entered the company of kindred spirits.

Another who was interested in Barchenko's ideas was Vladimir Bekhterev. In 1920 Bekhterev invited Barchenko to join his Institute for Brain Studies. Although Bekhterev considered the revolution an example of mass hysteria, he was savvy enough to take advantage of the situation and his ideas about "positive thinking," shared by Gorky, seemed to chime with the needs of the revolution. With Gorky, Bekhterev believed that society could be changed by people focusing and concentrating their "positive thoughts" in that direction.[29] His ideas about "breeding" a new kind of person, highly disciplined and conscious of his duty to society, who would act as a kind of beacon, radiating the proper thoughts, is not that far different from the kind of moral effect the presence of the "beautiful souls" of the previous century was believed to have.

One thing Bekhterev was positive about was Barchenko's ability. In 1921 he sent him on an expedition to the Kola Peninsula in the far northwest of Russia. There Barchenko studied "mass hysteria" among the Saami people, who were subject to outbreaks of bizarre behavior, not unlike some of the activities the revolution had inspired. But Barchenko also took the opportunity to search for evidence of Hyperborea, like Shambhala, another secret land, this time tucked away near the North Pole. Barchenko was not alone in his interest in Hyperborea; the esoteric philosopher Julius Evola, a favorite of Alexander Dugin, was fascinated with the idea, as were several high-ranking Nazis who, like Barchenko and Roerich, were also interested in Shambhala.[30]

Other adventures followed. For a time Barchenko organized a commune where members combined spiritual practice with socialist ideas, and for several months he lived in Agvan Dorzhiev's temple, where he no doubt heard more about Shambhala. And when his request for funding for an expedition to Tibet was turned down by a scientific institute, he looked for other backers. Enter Gleb Bokii.

Bokii was a curious character, not one that immediately suggests a candidate for a search for Shambhala. He had worked his way up through the Bolshevik ranks, and in 1918, after the assassination of Moses Uritsky, head of the Cheka, he took his place. His first act was to order the execution of several hundred "enemies of the revolution," heightening the very Red Terror that had sickened Barchenko. The irony is that Bokii himself would soon be sickened by it too.

Like Barchenko, Bokii was an idealist, but his idealism took a somewhat different form. In his early days it meant several arrests and exiles for his political activities. Later it meant hundreds of political murders and the start of the concentration camps that would eventually become the Gulag. But when Grigory Zinoviev, Lenin's right-hand man, ordered the Red Terror to be increased and for workers to be armed so that they could mete out rough justice when, where, and to whom they saw fit, Bokii balked. The turning point came in 1921, when the Kronstadt sailors revolted, sickened, as Barchenko and Bokki were, by the terror. These were the men who led the revolution four years earlier. Now they were its enemies. Who was next?

Bokii, a top cryptographer in the secret police, had heard about Barchenko's idea about a mission to find Shambhala. Other agents within his Special Section had spoken to him about it. Like Bekhterev he was interested in ways of "conditioning" the masses so that the revolution would indeed lead to a better life. As it was, it had descended into butchery. By this time he was ready to listen to any ideas that suggested an alternative. Maybe Shambhala was real? And the kinds of mental powers that Barchenko wrote about, such as "mind reading" and "thought transference"—couldn't they help too?

In December 1924 Barchenko and Bokii met and took a liking to each other. Not long after, Bokii had arranged a meeting with his higher ups so that Barchenko could pitch his idea. Barchenko explained that there were people in Tibet who had miraculous mental powers—telepathy, thought transference, extrasensory perception—as well as other treasures and that these abilities had been scientifically proven, by Professor Bekhterev no less. An expedition to Tibet aimed at making contact with these sages and bringing back some of their knowledge would be a useful effort in the revolutionary cause. Whether it was indifference, deference to Bokii, or real interest, Felix Dzerzhinsky, who had interrogated Berdyaev a few years earlier, gave the idea his imprimatur, tasking Bokii with the job of investigating Barchenko's claims, and, if warranted, acting on them.

In the end, the Tibetan expedition, at least Barchenko's version of it, never happened. Internal intrigue and rivalries led to opposition, and there were others in the secret police who had their own ideas about penetrating "inner Asia" that were less esoteric and more politically practical than a search for ancient technology and superscience.[31] But Bokii nevertheless profited from his association with Barchenko.

For a time the esoteric medical school dropout became the cryptographer's guru. Together they studied a variety of esoteric, spiritual, occult, and mystical ideas and philosophies, and, in a special laboratory funded by the government, Barchenko was able to investigate a number of parapsychological phenomena. Barchenko—known as the "Red Merlin"—was even asked to give classes in Tibetan Buddhism and Western esotericism to others in the Special Section. As might be imagined, these were not especially successful.

Soon Bokii and Barchenko began holding private gatherings, where these ideas were discussed with kindred spirits. But Bokii, a more vital and sensual character than Barchenko, decided he wanted more. He began to hold "nature weekends" at a dacha outside Moscow, where communal gardening was done in the nude, followed by a large meal with much drink, ending in orgies of Tantric sex. Bokii was something of an eroticist, and he is reported to have had a collection of mummified penises. As Stalin, whom Bokii despised, inexorably tightened his grip on the Soviet state, word of Bokii's "free love" cult reached his superiors and he was forced to end it.

It was Stalin too who would eventually put an end to Barchenko and Bokii. The journey to Shambhala had been aborted, but Bokii had appropriated many state funds to finance several expeditions within Russia, where Barchenko met with other occultists and seekers of wisdom. But these resources were drying up, as was Bokii's prestige. By the early thirties, his Special Section was stripped down, and any exploration of psychic phenomena was now carried out by the new All Union Institute of Experimental Medicine, Bekhterev having died in 1927. By then all occult or esoteric groups had been eliminated, the only spiritual practice allowed being the worship of Stalin himself.[32] Bokii read the signs. Stalin was doing away with all the old Bolsheviks, just as Lenin had crushed the Kronstadt sailors. Who was next? Bokii had an idea. He was arrested in 1937 and after a show trial was shot.

Barchenko never gave up his belief in the usefulness of Shambhala for the revolution. Madness is perhaps a better term, because the last act in his story suggests it. After getting nowhere with other officials—Bokii had by this time broken off their contact—Barchenko, never one to think small, decided to go to the top. He'd convince Stalin himself. He didn't of course, and his attempts to reach him only attracted the attention of the secret police, at this point, the last people he should have been bothering. His efforts resulted in his arrest, also in 1937, and his implication in a "spy ring" centered on the nefarious activities of a Shambhala conspiracy, aimed at overthrowing the revolution. He was shot in 1938, along with everyone else connected in any way with his long-standing obsession.

ONE GROUP WHO did relatively well in the new regime were the Cosmists. Fedorov had long been dead—his particles still earthbound in his grave, awaiting resurrection—but one of his students carried on with several aspects of his work. And while Fedorov's projects never got far beyond his notebook, some of the designs of this protégé did actually get past the drawing board.

As mentioned, Konstantin Tsiolkovsky sat at Fedorov's feet for some years as a teenager, when he was taught by the Moscow Socrates at the Rumyantsev Museum. But although reaching out into space in order to retrieve the particles of our dead ancestors—not to mention to colonize the planets where, newly revived, they would live—was something uppermost on Fedorov's mind, Tsiolkovsky insisted that he and Fedorov never discussed space travel. This seems odd, and some historians suggest that Tsiolkovsky possessed either a faulty or selective memory. But then, Fedorov insisted on the *necessity* for space travel. Tsiolkovsky worked out how it could be done. With that to his credit, we might forgive a perhaps ungenerous need to deny his inspiration came from someone else.

Tragedy plagued Tsiolkovsky's early life. In 1867, when he was ten, scarlet fever left him deaf. Three years later his mother died. His hearing difficulty meant he couldn't take classes, so he was homeschooled. He read voraciously, having more contact with books than with human beings. Like many a Russian visionary, Tsiolkovsky grew up lonely, an outsider, who spent much of his time in his thoughts. He became fascinated with physics and mathematics and was a great reader of Jules

Verne, whose fantastic adventures always made a point of being, or at least sounding, scientifically plausible. Tsiolkovsky's early fantasies about cosmic flights, inspired by Verne, led, he tells us, to his figuring out the math that would let him, or anyone else, take them.

At sixteen he made his way to Moscow, where for three years, he came under Fedorov's protective wing. He attended lectures, using an ear trumpet, and listened to everything Fedorov had to say. Always eager to help, Fedorov taught the young genius and also provided him with a winter coat; like Fedorov himself, Tsiolkovsky was poor and went hungry most of the time. In fact, when word came to his father that Tsiolkovsky was ill and starving, his concern for his son's future compelled him to come to Moscow to take him home.

Tsiolkovsky eventually found a position teaching science at a school near Moscow. He began writing scientific papers and one, on the kinetic energy of gases, reached the ears of the great chemist Dmitry Mendeleev. Mendeleev informed Tsiolkovksy that his conclusions had already been reached, but encouraged him to carry on. A correspondence between the two led to Tsiolkovsky joining the Physio-Chemical Society. Then in 1892 Tsiolkovsky was transferred to Kaluga, an isolated town far from Moscow or any other center of learning. Tsiolkovsky would remain here for the rest of his life, his eccentricities making him an item among his neighbors. The city is now a center for a variety of scientific research projects and a place of pilgrimage for a new breed of Cosmists; since the fall of the Soviets, like many other forgotten figures, Tsiolkovsky has been rediscovered as a national hero.

Tsiolkovsky's ongoing project was to design a collapsible metal dirigible, a flexible paneled blimp that could fold up, rather like a Transformer. He created the first wind tunnel in Russia, where he studied the effects of air friction on different surfaces. His studies in aerodynamics and the models used in them would, in 1957, help put Sputnik into orbit and later inform Soviet plans to reach the moon. As early as 1903 his paper "Exploration of Cosmic Space by Means of Reaction Devices" anticipated much of what makes up rocket science today. But like many visionaries, his ideas were ahead of his time. After a decade of personal tragedies in which his son committed suicide, he lost his home and laboratory in a flood, and his daughter was arrested for political activities, Tsiolkovsky faced more disappointment at the Aeronautics Congress of 1914. Although his plans for his dirigible were foolproof, the math incontestable, and his models exemplary, no one was interested. Then the revolution came and thoughts about space travel were shelved.

Tsiolkovsky supported the revolution, but in the early Soviet days, there was not much for him to do. In 1918 he was admitted to the new Socialist Academy, a rival to the prestigious Academy of Science. He taught mathematics until 1920, when he retired. Only gradually, toward the end of the decade, was the significance of his ideas recognized. As did Barchenko and Bokii, he received some funding for research. He died in 1935 during an operation for stomach cancer.

Today Tsiolkovsky is recognized as the father of Russian space travel, and since his death he has received many honors. A crater on the dark side of the moon is named after him (his wife merits an asteroid) and in 2015 Vladimir Putin rechristened a town in his name. Yet not all of his ideas are quite as actionable as those about space flight, something that some of us may be happy about.

In 1928 Tsiolkovsky published a book, *The Will of the Universe*, in which he argued that, as the philosopher David Chalmers contends, everything in the universe is conscious in some way, a position known as "panpsychism." This notion, which goes back to the ancient Hermetic and Neoplatonic traditions and is shared by philosophers such as Henri Bergson, is not in itself particularly disturbing. But in Tsiolkovsky it is allied to ideas about cosmic colonization informed with notions of "selective breeding" under the auspices of "philosopher-kings" administrating a universal cosmic political system, rather like a galactic synarchic state. Tsiolkovsky believed in some all-pervasive cosmic intelligence, directing matters, within which human decision is negligible; we are puppets in its hands, whatever our ideas about free will.* As George M. Young points out, one thing the Cosmists all share is the urge toward some totalizing picture—the "common task"—some all-encompassing vision in which everything, from the farthest-flung galaxy to the smallest clod of earth, *must* be contained. It is the Russian "we" stretching out horizontally and vertically, and it is something within which individual freedom and choice have little place.

Another sharing this view was the mineralogist Vladimir Vernadsky (1863–1945), known as the father of geochemistry and biogeochemistry, the study of how life affects the makeup of the earth. Vernadsky, who is still little known in the West, is one of the giants of Russian science. He did well under the Soviets and received the Stalin prize in 1943. He was an adviser on their plans to make an A-bomb and promoted nuclear power as a source of energy. His support for the revolution may not have been unalloyed though. During the Civil War, Vernadsky hosted gatherings of members of the intelligentsia who, with help from Lenin, would soon be shipped out to form the émigré community of the Eurasianists. Some of his ideas would eventually inform the work of Lev Gumilev, the maverick historian and ethnogeographer who, with the fall of the USSR, enjoyed practically universal acclaim in Russia, and whose vision was absorbed into the neo-Eurasianism of Alexander Dugin.[33]

Vernadsky was born into a prestigious academic family. His father was a professor and his son, George Vernadsky, would leave Russia in 1920 and eventually immigrate to America, where he became an authority on Russian history, teaching it at Yale for many years. Before this, in

---

*There seems to be a strong tendency in the Russian psyche to deny the reality of free will. We find it in Cosmists such as Vladimir Vernadsky and Alexander Chizensky, Eurasianists like Lev Gumilev and Alexander Dugin, even in novelists such as Tolstoy who in *War and Peace* famously denies the influence of individuals—"great men"—on history. In one sense this can be seen as a reaction to the laissez-faire of the West, with everyone "free" to pursue their happiness. But for advocates of this belief who found themselves under the Soviet regime, I wonder if there isn't a sense in which they are saying, "Yes, you think you are in power and decide what is so. But you are compelled to act as you do by some power greater than even you." Is it a way, perhaps, of saying that the masters are just as imprisoned as the slaves?

Prague in the early 1920s, George Vernadsky was an important figure in the Eurasianist circle that formed there courtesy of Lenin's steamers. His father's expertise was the Earth's crust. Vernadsky Senior eventually came to see that life, including human life, can be understood as a natural outgrowth of the Earth, rather than a chance occurrence upon it. It was not an anomaly but was a product of and subject to the same cosmic laws that controlled the rest of the universe.

Vernadsky popularized the idea of the "biosphere," the coating of life that surrounds the planet, which was first put forth by the Austrian geologist Eduard Suess, who also speculated on the original prehistoric supercontinent, Gondwanaland. Vernadsky argued that the presence of life was not a fluke, as most Western scientists believed, but part of the continuous growth of the Earth. In his book *The Biosphere* (1926)—an important work for both Steve Bannon and Gurdjieffians—Vernadsky argued that the Earth could be seen as composed of three "spheres."[34] Its physical body is the "geosphere." The life that has arisen on it forms the "biosphere." And the consciousness that has appeared in human beings makes up the "noosphere," a term derived from the Greek word for mind, *nous*. And just as life has affected the conditions of the geosphere—Vernadsky was one of the first to show how primordial biological processes helped to create our atmosphere—so too is mind affecting the conditions of life. Today we would speak of the Anthropocene, but the idea is the same.

Most people aware of the term *noosphere* know it through the work of the French Catholic philosopher Teilhard de Chardin. But both De Chardin and his countryman, Éduard LeRoy, also associated with the term, attended lectures at the Sorbonne in Paris that Vernadsky gave in 1922–23, in which he discussed his ideas. De Chardin's use appeared not long after this. Debate over who coined the term first remains; what's important here is what Vernadsky meant by it.

Most of us think of the mind as a purely human terrain, in which humanity expresses its freedom and fundamental difference from the rest of nature. "My mind to me a kingdom is," as the Englishman Sir Edward

Dyer said long ago. Vernadsky tells us something different. Humanity, in Vernadsky's view, serves an absolutely natural role in the cosmic economy, rather as forests and oceans do, as a receiver and transmitter of cosmic energy; fundamentally it is no different from other natural phenomena, which have their own roles to play. This, incidentally, was an idea that Gurdjieff passed on to Ouspensky at around the same time that Vernadsky was lecturing on it to his students at Moscow University.

For Vernadsky "episodes of intense human activity are in some way connected to solar and cosmic radiations," another idea that Ouspensky learned from Gurdjieff.[35] It was also an idea that Lev Gumilev would later embrace to account for the creation of what he called *ethnoi,* large racial groups that, like forests or herds of animals, are a natural manifestation of the cosmic economy. Gumilev believed that sudden bursts of *bio-energy*—a term he borrowed from Vernadsky—coming from the stars were responsible for this. In both views, we are moved about by cosmic forces in the same way that the clouds are moved about by the wind. And just as the clouds have little say in where they are heading, so too do we have little control over our destinies.

Another Cosmist with similar ideas was the prodigy Alexander Chizhevsky (1897–1964). As a teenager Chizhevsky lived in Kaluga where he met and got to know Tsiolkovsky. A painter, poet, musician, and scientist—like other Cosmists, he was a polymath—Chizhevsky came to his life work in 1915 at the age of eighteen. He had become fascinated with sunspots, the huge dark bodies that pass across the sun's surface, and it seemed to him that there was some strange correlation between their appearance and activity on the Earth. He saw that when a large body of spots appeared in June of that year, both the aurora borealis was unusually strong and radio and telephone communication was more disturbed than usual. But what also struck him was that the fiercest battles of the war took place then too. Was there a connection?

The next year he noticed the same thing. When solar flares and the sun's magnetic storms were at their height, so was the fighting on the Galician front, where Chizhevsky was stationed. Looking back at the records, he saw a correlation between solar activity and the aborted revolution of 1905. One other correlation, involving the Bolshevik take-over, would, in the future, lead to some trouble.

In 1922 Chizhevsky's observations led to a chart he devised that showed 2,400 years of mass human activity: wars, revolutions, upris-ings, migrations, and other sudden movements from around the world. These eruptions and others corresponded exactly, he believed, to the eleven-year sunspot cycle, a period established by Rudolf Wolf and Alexander Humboldt in the nineteenth century. He had, he believed, discovered a "universal cycle of historical events," driven by the sun, or at least by its spots.[36] From the French Revolution to the outbreak of World War One, practically every major upsurge in human activity had been precipitated by a burst of solar disturbance. The correlation was so exact that Chizhevsky felt he could even predict when a similar out-break would happen. Using the sunspot cycle as a guide, Chizhevsky said things would start jumping between 1927 and 1929. They did. That period saw the establishment of António Salazar's dictatorship in Portugal, Chiang Kai-shek's capture of Peking, the march of Mussolini's fascists, the rise of National Socialism, Stalin's exiling of Trotsky, and the start of the Great Depression.

Chizhesky's work found some admirers. The economist Edward Dewey thought highly of it and used it in his own work on economic cycles. Chizhevsky believed that the direct cause of increased human activity during sunspots was the ionization of the atmosphere that was a result of the sun's magnetic waves reaching the Earth, the same cause of telephone and radio disruption. Negative ions, he recognized, act as a stimulant, the "breath of fresh air" that follows a rainstorm. Because of this he is regarded as the founder of "aero-ionization"—the study of the effect of ions on organisms—and his studies into the effect of the sun's activity on life make him the father of "heliobiology."*

---

*Oddly, Vernadsky believed that at some point, human beings will have to evolve to a stage in which they live on air and sunlight.

Yet not everyone was impressed. In 1942 Stalin grasped that if Chizhevsky was right, then it was sunspots, and not the inexorable march of the Marxist class war, that had put the Bolsheviks in power, something Chizhevsky's chart had shown. That wouldn't do, and he demanded that Chizhevsky retract his argument. By then Chizhevsky was a well-known and highly honored scientist, and he refused. One wonders if he had checked the sun that day. Stalin sent him to the Gulag for eight years, and he was treated to eight years of "rehabilitation" training after that. He was released following Stalin's death as part of the "thaw" that briefly loosened restrictions during Khrushchev's reign. As with other re-remembered Russia heroes, today he is regarded as a national treasure, with a commemorative coin struck with his image, and a Chizhevsky Science Center in Kaluga, next to the Tsiolkovsky Museum.[37]

STALIN'S REIGN SAW an occult and esoteric drought in Russia, but with his death, things started to change.[38] During the de-Stalinization and Khrushchev "thaw" of the late 1950s and early 1960s, censorship relaxed, restrictions eased, and the fear that had gripped and paralyzed the Russian psyche lessened. As was happening in the West with the "beat generation" but in a more muted way, groups of bohemians—poets, artists, writers, and other intellectuals—formed to discuss ideas that had until then been strictly taboo, a development reminiscent of the Lyubomudry (wisdom lovers) that had gathered around Vladimir Odoevsky in the nineteenth century. In this case though, the pursuit of wisdom led to some rather unusual areas.

One such group was the Iuzhinskii Circle in Moscow, which centered around the writer Yuri Mamleev (1931–2015).* Mamleev is little known in the English-speaking world; aside from his cult novel *The Sublimes* (1966), a kind of roman à clef about the group—which

---

*The name comes from the street in Moscow where Mamleev's flat, where the goup met, was, Iuzhinskii Pereulok.

has inspired contemporary Russian writers such as Vladimir Sorokin and Viktor Pelevin—hardly any of his work has been translated into English, although he has a prestigious reputation in Europe.

Transgressive might be the best way to describe Mamleev's vision. Violence, crime, sadomasochism, psychopathology, mysticism, weird sex, altered states of consciousness, and Satanism seem to inform much of his work. As one account puts it, we can see Mamleev's "metaphysical realism" as a mash-up between *A Clockwork Orange* and Yukio Mishima.[39] Mamleev himself has said that much of his inspiration came from reading Silver Age thinkers such as Solovyov and Berdyaev.

Mamleev's concerns may strike us as evidence of a morbid imagination. Yet under the repressive Soviet regime, such transgressive inclinations could carry a political force. Practically any thought outside the official party line could be understood as an act of resistance. If so, then the kinds of thoughts Mamleev and his group were thinking were positively revolutionary.

Mamleev graduated from the Moscow Institute of Forestry in 1956, then supported himself by teaching mathematics at night school.[40] His circle seems to have started when Mamleev gave readings from his work at the Lenin Library. Whoever was responsible for the library's books played a crucial role in the return of the occult to Russian consciousness. For some reason that remains unknown, the Lenin Library had a good collection of occult and esoteric literature that, until the crackdown during the later Brezhnev years, was openly available.

Mamleev made good use of the library's collection, reading everything he could about Hermeticism, the occult, parapsychology, as well as the works of Madame Blavatsky, Ouspensky, Steiner, and other esoteric thinkers, such as the Traditionalist René Guénon. One book that seems to have made a huge impact on Mamleev and his circle was Louis Pauwels and Jacques Bergier's *The Morning of the Magicians* (1960), which was published in France to a phenomenal success, soon matched by its English editions.[41] Although the book is a grab bag of occult misinformation, it is an exciting read, and many people were first introduced to characters like Aleister Crowley and Gurdjieff, as well as to the weird genre of "Nazi occultism" through it. In it, the authors describe Hitler as "Guénonism *plus* tanks."[42] While this is not exactly correct, it does give an idea of the direction that the group took after Mamleev left first the group and then Russia.

The group met at Mamleev's tiny flat, where at times up to fifty people gathered, reminiscent of the cramped get-togethers Gurdjieff hosted in his small flat in Paris during the war. It's unclear if Mamleev knew of these, although Pauwels's dubious book about Gurdjieff had been published in 1954, and Pauwels claimed to have attended some of these gatherings.[43] But Mamleev certainly knew of Gurdjieff, whose ideas were, according to reports, popular at this time.[44] In 1968 Mamleev's building was destroyed, and in 1974 Mamleev himself left Russia, the same year that saw Alexander Solzhenitsyn's arrest and deportation. But where Solzhenitsyn soon became as vocal a critic of the West as he had been of the Soviets, Mamleev liked his new homes in the United States, where he lectured on Russian literature at Cornell, and in France, where he taught Russian language and literature. As Solzhenitsyn did, with the collapse of the Soviet Union in the early 1990s, Mamleev returned. He was interviewed in the press and on television and radio; his books, which were previously available only in samizdat editions, are now bestsellers, and articles about his work appear regularly in prestigious literary journals.

When Mamleev left, proceedings were kept going by the poet Yevgeny Golovin (1938–2010) and two other important members of the circle, Geydar Dzhemal (b. 1947), a Russian Islamist, and the Gurdjieffean Vladimir Stepanov (b. 1941). By all accounts this second generation took things up a notch. Where Mamleev's gatherings were fundamentally literary, the new meetings seemed aimed at putting some of their transgressive ideas into practice. The participants believed that "Extreme experiences are needed to transcend the mediocrity of everyday life."[45] This is not an uncommon insight, and for Russians, who naturally take things to extremes, one would assume it went without saying.

Under Golovin's directions "Dionysian initiations" were performed, fuelled by large quantities of alcohol and ending in orgies aimed at transcending "everyday consciousness." Golovin was a great lover of Baudelaire and Rimbaud and gave impromptu readings of their work. His own poetry would eventually lead to collaborations with rock bands. He was also fond of mind games and "psychodrama," and led participants whom he had "zombified" in various "performances," role-playing in which they could be Knights of the Round Table or officers in the Nazi SS.[46] With Golovin and Geydar Dzhemal, the general anti-Soviet ethos of Mamleev's time became more focussed and definite, with strong leanings toward far-right politics. This can be seen as a shift from Guénon to Julius Evola, whose writings Golovin claimed to have introduced to the group.

Golovin was fascinated with alchemy, and he had come across Evola's *The Hermetic Tradition* (1931) at the Lenin Library. Where Guénon was happy to watch the West decline from a vantage point on the sidelines, Evola was eager to knock it down, a sentiment he expressed in his anti-Western diatribe, *Revolt Against the Modern World*. In this sense it would be more accurate to call Hitler "Evolism *plus* tanks," given that Evola went out of his way to ingratiate himself with the führer, after doing the same with Mussolini. It was in this milieu that Alexander Dugin found himself, literally and metaphorically. In the early 1980s, as one of Golovin's "zombies," he began his career as a postmodern political quick-change artist, moving from radical dissident to far-right fascist, with large portions of the occult helping him on his way.

Another book found in the Lenin Library was one by Ouspensky, most likely *The Fourth Way* (1957).* This was discovered by Vladimir Stepanov who, with Arkady Rovner, was a serious devotee of Gurdjieff's ideas.[47] Their interest led to Stepanov making contact with J. G. Bennett, Gurdjieff's main disciple in England—whose

---

*Strictly speaking this is not a book by Ouspensky, but a collection of his answers to questions recorded at his groups over many years.

ideas, incidentally, were combined with Vernadsky's in the design of Biosphere 2.[48] Stepanov also reached out to Idries Shah, the popular writer on Sufism whose claims to represent a legitimate tradition have been questioned.[49] In the 1960s and '70s, Shah's influence reached to respected literary figures such as the novelist Doris Lessing and the poet Robert Graves—whom Stepanov also contacted—but his reputation has suffered since his death in 1996. Shah's relationship with Bennett was curious. In *Turn Off Your Mind* I tell the story of how Shah, claiming to represent an esoteric school, talked Bennett into handing over to him his estate, Coombe Springs, where Bennett carried on the Gurdjieff work. Practically as soon as he did, Shah sold it.[50]

ODDLY ENOUGH, WHILE an underground occult scene was kept alive by groups like the Iuzhinskii Circle and other such gatherings, the state from which these "underground men" were hiding was itself descending into occult waters. Or at least into dark depths of parapsychology. And where Golovin's and Mamleev's occult excursions were aimed at somehow escaping the conformity of the Soviet state, the magic that had official sanction had something else in mind. It was something more like a return to the pre-Stalin belief that, if such things are possible, shouldn't we figure out how they work and put that knowledge to use?

In 1971 Sheila Ostrander and Lynn Schroeder's book *Psychic Discoveries Behind the Iron Curtain* appeared and informed its readers of the widespread interest in parapsychology in the Soviet Union, and how the Russian government was investing in its research. Although the United States had been aware of Soviet interest in this area since the mid-1960s, as the psychic Uri Geller writes, the book most likely "helped energize" similar research in America.[51] The Cold War had taken an inward turn, and the idea of "psychic warfare," involving an "inner space race," usually left to science fiction, took on a dark reality. By now there are several shelves' worth of books devoted to informing the public of the "secret" research into psychic abilities carried on by the Russians and Americans, involving remote viewing, telepathy, precognition, telekinesis, and other paranormal abilities, and drawing on the services of famous psychics, like Geller. According to many reports, these investigations continue today.

Probably the most famous and influential discovery revealed by Ostrander and Schroeder was the work of Semyon Davidovich Kirlian. Kirlian, an electrician from Krasnodar, seemed to have come upon a way to photograph the "aura" of living things, including humans, the invisible energy field that, according to Theosophists and other occultists, surrounds the body.[52] By the mid '70s, photographs of leaves, hands, flowers, and other objects, surrounded by or emitting flares and sparks of some strange energy, had become world famous, and experiments made elsewhere confirmed the effect.[53] More in line with the possible military use of psychic abilities were the investigations into the strange powers of Nina Kulagina, a housewife and ex-member of a Red Army tank regiment. Kulagina claimed to be able to move objects at a distance, through thought alone, an ability known as telekinesis. She was apparently able to move small objects—matchsticks, tennis balls, a salt shaker—but also to be able to affect organic matter as well. She is reported to have stopped a frog's heart and to have induced an increased heartbeat in a human subject. Though skeptics tried repeatedly to prove her a fraud, the jury remains out on her authenticity.

Accounts of the work of the great Russian physiologist Leonid Vasiliev who conducted secret parapsychological experiments during Stalin's regime, and the psychic Wolf Messing, whose powers even Stalin feared, as well as many others let readers know that, while on the surface the world of Brezhnev, the Cold War, and the arms race was "occult free," down below something else was going on.[54] There was. But throughout the dark years of the 1970s and '80s, when superpowers sought psychic powers for their superspies, did anyone suspect that the return of Holy Russia was at hand?

13

The Return of Holy Russia?

The Occult Revival

The collapse of the Soviet Union in 1991 brought democracy and a free-market economy to what had been a stagnant Communist state. Leonid Brezhnev's glacier-like reign, from 1964 until his death in 1982, had turned Khrushchev's thaw into another ice age. Ironically, the only thing heating up during this time was the Cold War, with both Russia and the United States holding the planet for ransom as they enlarged their nuclear arsenals according to the dictates of the policy of "mutually assured destruction," aptly abbreviated as MAD. This suggested that the only way to ensure global peace was for the two superpowers to hold loaded pistols to each other's head, cocked and ready to fire. The fact that the rest of the world might suffer when they blew each other's brains out was a factor of "collateral damage" that was somehow accounted for in the calculations of militarists. And although at the time of writing, a postmodern, positive-thinking US president—see *Dark Star Rising* for the details—has announced that America is abandoning a treaty with Russia that has inhibited the development of nuclear weapons for more than thirty years, we can, I think, still look back with grateful wonder at the fact that we did manage to get through that time without a nuclear incident.[1] Whether this will be so in the future is, it seems, another story.[2]

The efforts of Mikhail Gorbachev, the USSR's last leader, in the service of glasnost (more open government) and perestroika (economic reform) in the late 1980s paved the way for the end of the Soviet empire. Its demise was hailed in Western countries as a tremendous break-through, although not everyone in Russia was happy about it. Indeed, in 1993, hard-line old school Soviets staged a coup, attempting, like some tsars of old, to hold back history and keep the revolution going. They were not successful; yet strangely, at least for Westerners, in the excitement and uncertainty that followed, nostalgia for the good old days under Soviet rule soon set in. And in more recent times Vladimir Putin, the second president of the new Russian nation—for the first time in its history Russia is not an empire, at least not yet—has declared that the collapse of the Soviet Union was "the greatest political catas-trophe of the twentieth century." He also said that if he could bring it back, he would.[3] As I point out in *Dark Star Rising*, his activities in Crimea and Ukraine seem to be motivated by a desire to do just that.

Others were of a different mind about the end of the USSR. Some, like the American political scientist Francis Fukuyama, claimed that the collapse of Soviet power—evidenced in the collapse of the Berlin Wall in 1989—signaled the "end of history," at least from a Hegelian point of view. What Fukuyama meant was that with the end of the Cold War and the spread of liberal democracy, Western civilization had tri-umphed and was increasing its influence around the world. Hegel saw the movement of history as the progressive embodiment of freedom in the social and political worlds. With the global concern for human rights and democracy, and the concomitant spread of a free-market economy, Fukuyama believed that Hegel's vision had become a reality and that the *Weltgeist* or "world spirit" informing human action had reached its goal.* The liberalizing of the planet was at hand, Fukuyama argued, a

---

*Fukuyama got much of the inspiration for his book from the work of Alexander Kojève, a Russian-born French philosopher whose influential *Introduction to the Reading of Hegel: Lectures on the Phenomenology of Spirit* (1947) combined Hegel, Marx, Nietzsche, and Heidegger in an often heady brew. Kojève was also a statesman and was influential in the foundation of the European Union.

development that was applauded by many but did not go down well with some individuals. One such was Alexander Dugin, who saw Fukuyama's "end of history" as a carte blanche given to the forces of "globalization." According to Dugin, their only interest was in securing a larger market for their needless, soul-destroying commodities, a point he makes with vehemence if not clarity in his book *The Fourth Political Theory* (2009).[4]

This blessing, however, soon became a curse, when it became clear that these Western values, with which Russia had had a love-hate relationship at least since Peter the Great, were not "taking" as well or as easily as all had hoped they would. As one historian remarked, the ideals of "freedom, democracy, and a market economy have been planted among a people with a very different past history, facing a bewildering host of present problems."[5] The "democratic experiment" that took place in Russia in the 1990s had "greater potential for building a better world" than had been appreciated. But there was also equal potential for "more continuing damage that we have generally realized."[6]

By the late 1990s the realization that the collapsed Soviet structures could not withstand the "democratic experiment," and that the resulting vacuum had given birth to anarchy, was unavoidable. As more than one commentator has remarked, the West Russia was resembling was more like the American Wild West than any country run according to "rational self-interest." Political gangsterism became the order of the day. Police authority was gutted by corruption. Private security firms ruled. Government services collapsed. Organized crime prospered. The powerful and wealthy sliced up the corpse of the Soviet empire, creating little kingdoms for themselves, as the original tribes of Kievan Rus' had done a millennium earlier. It was the rise of the oligarchs. And when the ruble collapsed in 1998, any pretence of stability and normality went out the window.

It was the kind of chaos with which Russians, sadly, were not unfamiliar, and that usually led to the appearance of a strong man to bring things to order. It did. In 2000, with a landslide victory, ex-KGB operative Vladimir Putin assumed the post of president of Russia—the second such—a position he has occupied, with a short break as prime minister, ever since.

The collapse of the Soviet Union brought something else to the Russian people, or rather it revived a question that had plagued them throughout their history but which was supposed to have been answered through the great Soviet experiment: the question of their identity. If we're no longer Communists or Marxists, then what does it mean to be Russian? We have seen that Russians have been asking themselves this question for quite some time. But when a world is collapsing around you, the need to know who you are seems even more pressing.

One way to answer this question is to ask, "Who have we been?" Since the loosening of restrictions under Gorbachev, Russians have been rediscovering everything that had been *zapreshchano,* "forbidden" under the Soviet regime. In many ways this has amounted to an "occult revival," which has been going on in Russia for some time now, and which is itself part of a larger reawakening of a spiritual consciousness that had been arrested and held in a kind of metaphysical Gulag for most of the last century. As one observer of this esoteric renaissance remarks, "Today's occult revival should be seen . . . as the result of seven decades of the forceful suppression of metaphysical thought in Russia."[7]

Seventy years of repression is quite a lot. Small wonder then that this occult revival often seems like much more of a flood. There is even some suggestion that New Age spirituality played a part in the USSR going under, although in the end free-market capitalism really did the trick.

THROUGHOUT THE 1970s and '80s, Michael Murphy, one of the founders of the famous Esalen Institute on California's Big Sur coast, directed an exchange program between the United States and the USSR that at different points involved the CIA, KGB, and FBI. Esalen began in 1962, when Murphy and Richard Price (who died in 1985) wanted to put into practice Aldous Huxley's ideas about discovering and harnessing "human potential." The result was a retreat in a beautiful

natural setting, where a variety of "alternative" philosophies and practices were eagerly explored, everything from Eastern religions, yoga,
alternative medicine, and altered states of consciousness, to shamanism and the spiritual aspects of psychedelic drugs, with much else in
between. Practically every big name in the alternative world at the time
held seminars or gave courses at Esalen—Joseph Campbell, Abraham
Maslow, R. D. Laing, Colin Wilson, Stanislav Grof, Fritz Perls, and
Huxley himself, to name only a few—and it earned a reputation as a
kind of "hot tub think tank." In a way we can say it is where the New
Age went through a water birth.

When Murphy began his dialogue, he was amazed to discover in
Russia the same kind of people he was meeting at Esalen: "dowsers,
yogis, shamans" and other explorers of inner worlds.[8] Their presence
seemed so ubiquitous that Murphy summed it up by saying that "if you
scratch a Russian, you'll find a mystic," an insight that readers of this
book might well agree with. Murphy even experimented with sending
telepathic messages from the California coast to Karl Nikolaiev, a psychic in Russia, with substantial success, part of the "ESPionage" scene
of the 1970s. One later product of the Esalen exchange program was
the "space bridge" of 1982, when direct satellite communication was
established between US and Russian citizens, outside official channels.
Another was the Esalen-Lindisfarne Library of Russian Philosophy,
some of whose titles I have used in writing this book. But perhaps the
most remarkable result was the visit to America made in 1989 by Boris
Yeltsin, soon to be Russia's first elected president.

Yeltsin, a reformer and critic of Gorbachev—whom Esalen
supported—didn't make it to the hot tubs, but during his two-week
tour he did visit the Statue of Liberty, the New York Stock Exchange,
the Lyndon B. Johnson Space Center in Texas, had a chat with President
George H. W. Bush, and visited the ex-president Ronald Reagan in his
hospital room, where he was recovering from neurosurgery. According
to reports, Yeltsin, known for his drinking, was drunk most of the time,
and was apparently deep in his cups when visiting the White House.[9]

But the most moving experience for him was an unscheduled stop at an "average" American supermarket. All his life Yeltsin had heard that the supposed bounty of American life was simply window dressing, propaganda for capitalism. Now he wanted to see for himself.

He did. According to Jeffrey Kripal in his history of Esalen, when Yeltsin walked into a supermarket somewhere in Texas, he was "flabbergasted by a profusion of carefully arranged and beautifully lit fruits, vegetables, meats, cheeses, frozen entrées, and canned goods too numerous to count."[10] He was already amazed that there wasn't a line of people outside waiting to get in, which was business as usual in Russia. And that the shelves weren't half-empty—standard back home—but overflowing was more than he could believe. It took some work to convince him that this wasn't planned or that any other supermarket would look exactly the same. When he recovered from his awe—rather like Princess Olga at her first glimpse of Constantinople—Yeltsin declared that, "Communism has been lying to us. I'm going to get Gorbachev. Communism needs to be destroyed."[11] When he returned to Russia, he resigned from the Politburo, something no one had done before. By 1991 Gorbachev too had resigned, the USSR had been dissolved, and Yeltsin had become the first president of the newly formed Russian Federation. Not bad for what has been called "hot tub diplomacy."

YELTSIN WAS ALREADY determined to destroy communism, or at least Gorbachev, before his visit, and it was the cornucopia of an American supermarket that set him off, not a mystical experience. Yet, a few years later, when he was dissolving the Soviet Union, the KGB suspected that those opposing Yeltsin were using "psi generators" in order to undermine his health.[12] Yeltsin's health was bad—his drinking didn't help—but the new regime took no chances. Yeltsin was treated by Djuna Davitashivili, one of Russia's top psychic healers, and he had "psychic scanners" installed in his office in order to prevent bugging, both electronic or telepathic.[13]

That such parapsychological protection reached the upper echelons of Russian government tells us that the occult revival of post-Soviet Russia was not simply a matter of popular culture or a fad. As Birgit Menzel writes, "the fascination with esoteric, supernatural, and non-orthodox spirituality . . . in post-Soviet Russia can be found on all levels of intellectual and artistic life, including the sciences and politics."[14] It was across the board, and had as much to do with recovering a Russian identity as it did with recovering the lost knowledge that the various newly recovered occult traditions had to offer.

ONE SOURCE OF knowledge that was made available practically immediately was the work of the Silver Age sages. Interest in this had been building up for some time. As James Scanlan writes, "even before *perestroika* began there was a significant body of literature having to do with the previously scorned Russian philosophers."[15] By the late 1980s, writers and thinkers who had been forbidden by the Soviets were enjoying a remarkable revival. This included classics such as Gogol, Tolstoy, and Dostoyevsky, much of whose work was difficult to come by if it could be found at all.* But those who really profited by the end of censorship were figures like Berdyaev, Solovyov, Sergei Bulgakov, Pavel Florensky, the Symbolists, the Cosmists, and thinkers in the esoteric tradition, such as Steiner, Blavatsky, Ouspensky, Gurdjieff, Roerich, Guénon, and others.

Books that had previously been banned were published in huge editions—a common practice in Russia apparently—and met with equal sales. Occult and esoteric ideas exerted a kind of magnetic attraction on the culture at large, drawing everything to them. Or, conversely, their emanations, rather like that of some radioactive material, penetrated

---

*In his autobiography *Dreaming to Some Purpose* Colin Wilson tells the story of visiting Leningrad (now St. Petersburg again) in 1960 and having difficulty locating where Dostoyevsky lived. His Intourist guide "strongly discouraged us from trying to find Dostoyevsky's house" and told Wilson and his wife that "Dostoyevsky was no longer read."

everything, casting a glow or sheen about it. As one critic writes, "It is almost impossible to understand contemporary Russian literature without being equipped with an encyclopaedia of the occult."[16] And what was happening in the humanities was also reaching out into practically all areas of Russian life. Numerous conferences on topics ranging from shamanic healing to life extension, transpersonal psychology, and bio-energy mushroomed in the wake of the occult flood that hit the post-Soviet world. Universities offered courses on "cosmic consciousness," UFOs, alternative medicine, and other aspects of the supernatural that would have led to a stint in the Gulag just decades before. We could almost say it was an occult revolution.

But it wasn't only the heroes of the Silver Age that the search for a new Russian identity revived. The look back before the Soviets in some cases reached much further, to a pre-Christian Russia. One of the first and most popular manifestations of the Russian spiritual renaissance is what is known as the Slavic Native Faith.[17] This is a "modern" pagan religion* that claims to synthesize in a new form the beliefs of the pre-Christian Slavs, the gods and goddesses that Prince Vladimir tossed into the Dnieper when he accepted Christianity. We have seen how, although Russia became holy, the earlier pagan religions never really completely died out, and how, through the power of *dvoeverie* or "double belief," ancient ideas and practices could exist side by side with or incorporated into the new Christian ones. Practitioners of the Slavic Native Faith claim that throughout Russia's history, there was a secret, hidden tradition of the ancient ways that was kept alive, and which now, with the end of the Soviets, can come out into the open. They also claim that Christianity was a disaster for the Slavs, and that only now they are recovering from its influence.

Understandably they are not approved of by the church, which itself has gone through a remarkable recovery, from being an outlawed bourgeois practice to becoming a "defining characteristic of Russian

---

*There is a return to the ancient pagan ways in Poland as well.

identity," a development applauded both by the Kremlin and its occasional geopolitical adviser, Alexander Dugin.[18]

Adherents of the Slavic Native Faith see their tradition rather how some practitioners of Wicca see theirs, as a modern expression of an ancient belief. But whether the claims to a continuation of a hidden tradition hold up or not, what is clear is that there seems to be a strong revival of a kind of Slavophile thought with the return of the ancient ways. This movement to revitalize the "historical beliefs of the Slavs" identifies itself as an "ethnic religion," and it is a faith in which ethnicity and identity play central roles, even reaching into politics.[19] Its pantheism and polytheism can be found in other native beliefs. But along with the gods, nature spirits, and ancestor worship that make up what is called "Rodnovery," there is also a strong emphasis on the collective over the individual, and the patriarchal ethos of the movement includes a great deal of what is called "ethnic nationalism." For many in search of a new Russian identity, this revival makes a strong offer, and it is an expression of the feeling that any answer to the Russian question must come from Russia itself. For others it is fundamentally a return to the Slavic Romanticism of the nineteenth century and, as such, provides no real advance over the limitations that movement encountered.

Another more straightforwardly modern religion emerging from post-Soviet Russia, one making no claims on any hidden tradition—indeed, it is based on a work of fiction—is "Anastasianism."[20] This has nothing to do with the Romanov daughter who supposedly got away from her family's executioners. This Anastasia is a character in a novel of the same name that is the first in a series of best-selling books about the mystical powers of the "ringing cedars of Russia," Siberian trees with apparently remarkable spiritual abilities. The book first appeared in 1996 and has by now sold "10 million copies without any advertising except word of mouth," at least according to the official website.[21] Other reports put the figure at 20 million with translation into twenty languages.[22] The phenomenon isn't limited to Russia; the fastest-growing spread of the belief is taking place in the United States. Russia may or may not have interfered with American elections, but it seems to be making great headway in exporting its new religious movements.

THE RINGING CEDARS movement began in 1995, when the entrepreneur and writer Vladimir Megre took a trip to Siberia. There he underwent a series of strange mystical experiences that were somehow linked to the sacred "ringing" Siberian cedar trees, which are apparently actually a species of pine. He also met the woman Anastasia, who lived in the taiga, the Siberian "snow forest," and who can be seen as a female Russian Don Juan to Megre's Carlos Castaneda. He spent three days with her during which she taught him the secrets of the trees and also expounded her ideas about the need for mankind to return to nature. Although there is some debate over whether or not "Anastasianism" can be seen as a branch of the Slavic Native Faith, for many there are enough points of overlap to make the distinction academic.

Megre was prepared for his encounter with Anastasia, whose name is linked to "resurrection," and whose teaching involves ideas of a coming new age to supplant our current dark one. He had grown up amid nature in a small village where he was looked after by his grandmother, who was a healer. After he heard Anastasia speak about the need to raise children in the midst of nature, in a self-sustaining home, growing one's own food and returning in one's mind to the early "Vedic" period of human history, when we were altogether closer to the gods, he accepted her challenge to write a book about it. He gave up his career and without a ruble in his pocket—not usual for writers at any time but especially so for one in Russia in the late 1990s—he went to Moscow and wrote the first in his series of now global spiritual blockbusters. Along with branches in the US, the cedars are ringing very clearly in other Slavic countries, such as Poland, but also in lands more far afield, such as Asia and Australia.

But it is not only a return to the pagan past and the bosom of Damp Mother Earth that has been triggered by the occult revival.

Dreams of unbelievable futures have also arisen, with mankind conquering nature, defeating death, and venturing out into galactic space in order to colonize the universe.* The Cosmists have made a comeback. In fact we could say that the times have caught up with them.[23] Not only in the sense that space exploration has been part of the modern world—at least since Konstantin Tsiolkovsky's calculations helped put Sputnik in orbit in 1957, followed by Laika, the first dog in space—but also very contemporary ideas about "transhumanism," artificial intelligence, downloading consciousness onto a computer so that we could "live forever," and other popular futuristic scenarios seem pretty much in keeping with the "transcendence through science" that Fedorov and his followers promoted as the "common task."[24] And it is apt that along with the honors posthumously bestowed on Tsiolkovsky and Alexander Chizhevsky, an N. F. Fedorov Museum and Library opened in Moscow in 1993.[25]

Throughout the 1980s interest in Fedorov's work was kept alive by the scholar Svetlana Semenova, who oversaw publication of Fedorov's writings, and, with her daughter, saw the establishment of the museum. Conferences on Fedorov and other Cosmists and related thinkers, academic papers, and even holidays—Vernadsky's birthday, Astronomy Day, and the anniversary of Yuri Gagarin's first cosmic flight—help to keep the ideas of the philosopher of the common task alive in the new Russia.[26] At the Institute for Scientific Research in Cosmic Anthropoecology, in Novosibirsk, Siberia, experiments with, and research into, parapsychology from a Cosmist perspective have been pursued since the early 1990s, with a special emphasis on exploring the possibilities of Vernadsky's noosphere.[27] Some of these possibilities have

---

*In some ways we can see the return of ancient pagan beliefs and the revival of futurist visions in post-Soviet Russia as an example of the historian Arnold Toynbee's dictum that when faced with a "time of troubles," a people respond in two stereotypical ways: by retreating into the past or leaping into the future. That examples of "archaism" and "futurism" can be found in the West as well, suggests that our current "time of troubles" is a global phenomenon.

even reached the political sphere, or at least an eccentric though no less troubling area of it.

In 2016 President Putin made a surprise move, removing Sergei Ivanov, a long-term supporter and associate, from the office of chief of staff and replacing him with his relatively unknown deputy chief of staff Anton Vaino.[28] Exactly why Putin made this switch is unclear, but one thing that quickly became known about Vaino was that he was the co-author of a strange, apparently unreadable paper titled "The Capitalization of the Future." What this "pseudo-scientific text" written in a "blend of quasi-mystical language and academic jargon" introduces is what Vaino calls the "nooscope."[29] This is supposed to be some odd device that enables one to "read the noosphere," that coating of mind and consciousness that Vladimir Vernadsky saw as a "natural" product of the planet, just as clouds and trees are.

The noosphere is the "collective consciousness" of the human race, and the nooscope will allow those who possess it to be able to "read" this collective consciousness and detect trends in it, to, as it were, see in advance what the planet is thinking.

Vaino's statements about his discovery are about as difficult to decipher as the nooscope itself—he never quite tells us exactly what it is or how it works. But at a more mundane level, what he seems to be talking about amounts to the kind of data gathering and analysis that organizations such as Cambridge Analytica—influential in Trump's victory and the UK's Brexit referendum—have been up to. According to Vaino, information on our various "smart cards" and "smart phones" about ourselves and habits is fed into the global databank and those with nooscopic savvy can read the signs and profit by them.

While this sounds like business as usual in the information age, remarks like these from Vaino give a somewhat darker character to what we have become inured to: his nooscope will be used in the service of "some kind of all-embracing system of government that has to be enforced by top officials."[30] That for more than a decade, Vladislav Surkov, Putin's PR man throughout the 2000s, created a "virtual reality" that was fed to the Russian people via television, newspapers, and other media, having little to do with "actual reality," gives us an idea of the kind of power those who possess the nooscope or something like it, can wield.[31] In recent times Facebook—which provided the information that Cambridge Analytica analyzed—has faced growing demands to clean house and protect its users' information. This may be a sign that the nooscope is not quite yet the all-seeing eye it is claimed to be.[32]

ONE EFFECT OF the collapse of the Soviet system is that many figures who had been villains of the old regime—counterrevolutionaries, spies, saboteurs, or whatever Stalin's paranoia painted them as—were now seen as heroes and were celebrated accordingly. One such was the maverick historian and ethnographer Lev Gumilev, who is considered both a Eurasianist and Cosmist. Gumilev's odd career ranged from Gulag resident throughout the 1930s, '40s, and '50s—with a brief stint outside during WWII—to rediscovered national genius in the late 1980s until his death in 1992.

Gumilev was the son of the Silver Age poets Anna Akhmatova and Nikolai Gumilev, and as many children did during the Red Terror, he lost his father to the Cheka, who shot him in 1921, when Lev was nine. From about the age of twenty to his mid-forties, Gumilev spent time at some of the worst places on the planet: the White Sea Baltic Canal labor camp, another one at Norilsk, within the Arctic Circle, then in Kazakhstan and Siberia. He was released for good in 1956, during the Khrushchev thaw, but it wasn't until the late 1980s, with glasnost and perestroika, that his luck changed. At that point, his books and ideas about the formation of ethnic groups and the force, "passionarity," that holds them together, and his great love, the life of the ancient people of the steppes, the Mongols and Tartars, became hugely popular and influential.

As I show in *Dark Star Rising,* for a few years, Gumilev enjoyed the kind of success and influence that he could only have dreamed of during his imprisonment, and which most writers never see, even when free. His books, previously banned and unavailable, became bestsellers, and were mandatory reading in universities. His vocabulary—*ethnoi, passionarity, complementarity,* and other terms unknown in the West—dominated historical and ethnological discourse. A postage stamp in his honor appeared in Kazakhstan, where a university is named after him.[33]

Like Vernadsky, Tsiolkovsky, Chizhevsky, and others, Gumilev too denies human free will. Our actions are really determined by planetary and cosmic forces, bursts of "bioenergy" coming from the stars that motivate us rather than our conscious decisions.* Oddly, in his—and its—last days, Gumilev became an outspoken supporter of the Soviet system that had murdered his father and had imprisoned him for decades. Some have seen in this an example of the so-called Stockholm syndrome, in which captives identify with their captors. But one wonders if his years of imprisonment informed to some degree Gumilev's ideas about our lack of free will. The thought that although I am in prison, my fellows outside, who believe they are free, really are not, may have provided some dark comfort during Gumilev's days in the Gulag.

ANOTHER POST-SOVIET HERO to emerge from a Soviet prison took a rather different view of humanity and its place in the world. There is little spirituality in Gumilev, who belongs to the "positivist" school of thought; he believed he could measure *passionarity,* the force that drove the Mongols across the steppes and into Europe, in the same way we can electricity or magnetism.[35] This was not the case with Daniil Andreyev (1906–1959).

Daniil Andreyev was the only son of the nihilist writer Leonid Andreyev, whose ideas about the resurrection of the dead, we've seen,

---

*As mentioned, this was something Gurdjieff said, except he laid greater emphasis on the moon.[34]

were rather different from those of Fedorov.[36] His father's dim view of life was no doubt confirmed at Daniil's birth. His mother died soon after having Daniil. His father was so crushed by this that he refused to have anything to do with his son, whose presence reminded him of his wife and whose birth he believed was responsible for her death. Daniil was given to his mother's sister to bring up; she did, with help from his maternal grandparents, in a home that received many distinguished visitors, such as the composer and Theosophist Scriabin and the actor and singer Chaliapin. In 1917 Leonid Andreyev left Russia and his son to the Bolsheviks, whom he despised. He moved to newly independent Finland, where he remained until his death in 1919.

Leonid Andreyev was a successful writer, and his friend, Gorky, stood as Daniil's godfather. Daniil too showed literary skill early on, writing poems and stories of a mystical character, and he later admitted that he hated his father's work because of its pessimism. Yet this literary inheritance worked against him after the revolution. Like many others, Daniil was denied access to university because of his non-proletarian background. His studies stopped when he left the literary course he followed through his teens. It was around this time that he began to support himself as a graphic artist, leaving his evenings free to write. One effort was a novel titled *Sinners,* which he did not complete and which, with most of his other early works, was confiscated and destroyed by the Soviets.

In 1942 Daniil was conscripted into the Red Army, where he served as a noncombatant. He was among the medical orderlies who helped carry supplies across frozen Lake Ladoga during the siege of Leningrad. He also helped bury bodies, over whose graves he said prayers; through the efforts of a friend he had returned to the church in 1921. Saying prayers for fallen comrades was a risky practice, even during the Great Patriotic War. But Daniil's faith in spiritual powers would help sustain him through what was to come.

In 1947 he was arrested by the MVD, or Ministry of Internal Affairs. He was charged with writing anti-Soviet propaganda; the evidence for this was his novel *Wanderers of the Night,* a kind of spiritual testament. But even worse was the charge of plotting to assassinate Stalin, fabricated out of nothing but Stalin's paranoia. For this both Daniil and his second wife, Alla, were sentenced to twenty-five years in prison. Daniil spent most of his sentence, which was reduced to ten years during the Khrushchev thaw, in the Vladimir Central Prison, Russia's largest. There, in 1954, he suffered a heart attack, a sign of the heart condition that would eventually kill him. In 1957 he and Alla were released; they had had no contact with each other for ten years. In 1959, just two years after his release, Daniil died.

During his time in the Vladimir Prison, Daniil experienced a series of mystical visions, and he had communication with spirit "voices," some of whom he claimed were those of Dostoyevsky, Blok, and Lermontov. They served for him the same function that first Virgil and then Beatrice did for Dante during the inspiration that became *The Divine Comedy,* a comparison that for some is more than apt. (It may come as no surprise that the highest place in Andreyev's heaven is reserved for Russia's great writers.) But it was not only the spirits of Russia's great poets that spoke to him. Russia's soul itself did, and also that of other nations.

In Daniil's case the voices guided him through a series of strange inner landscapes and other worlds, the meaning of which he tried to capture in his remarkable and baffling mystical work *Roza Mir* or "The Rose of the World." This huge spiritual visionary text, which aims to integrate not only all of Russian history but also that of the world and those beyond, was written on tiny scraps of paper that Daniil had to hide from his captors, a subterfuge Solzhenitsyn's *Gulag Archipelago* also had to endure.[37] It was only during the last years of his imprisonment that he was allowed decent writing paper.

Copies of Andreyev's work first circulated in *samizdat* in the 1970s. Then in 1989 excerpts from it were published in the magazine *Novy Mir,* or "New World." In 1991 it was finally released in book form, and in 1997 it was published in an English translation as part of the Esalen-Lindisfarne Library of Russian Philosophy.

"The Rose of the World" is not an easy work to summarize. According to some readers, *Roza Mir* is "considered the greatest mystical revelation since the Gospels."[38] Andreyev himself has been compared to Tolstoy, Milton, Goethe, and, as mentioned, Dante, with whose mystic rose Andreyev's own has much in common; both reach from Hell to Paradise.[39] This praise may seem exaggerated, and readers of *Roza Mir* must decide for themselves. But it is clear that Andreyev's work is in the tradition of much of Russian thought. It seeks a universal spirituality through the union of all religions, speaks of the unique spiritual destiny of Russia—her potential as the first "post-historical" nation—and affirms the need to synthesize science, the arts, politics, and religion into one all-embracing system of knowledge. All this is in service of transforming the world.

In different forms—in Solovyov, Fedorov, and others—we have seen these themes appear time and again. It is that urge in the Russian soul for a "total" picture, embracing everything in the world, from the smallest to the grandest, and in Andreyev's case, it involves worlds beyond. We can say it is a vision of the eternal Sophia found in the dark pits of hell.

Any brief account of Andreyev's "Rose of the World" will certainly not do justice to its richness, depth, and imaginative power. As one reader puts it, it offers a "hierarchical system of worlds, visible and invisible." The petals of Andreyev's rose are formed by the different churches, and within this spiritual bloom, contrary beliefs can find harmony. That is the point. The priest, the artist, the politician, even the scientist are all part of one life, and each must find his or her meaning within the whole. This is one reason why readers of different backgrounds can find a place for themselves here and feel that Andreyev is speaking to them.

Another visionary poet who comes to mind in reading the work is William Blake. Like Blake, Andreyev creates his own mythology, and inhabits it with strange entities and landscapes. Another work I am reminded of is the remarkable gnostic novel *A Voyage to Arcturus* (1920) by the Scot David Lindsay. Both Blake's and Lindsay's vision were so individual yet universal and so powerful that they had to resort to creating their own universes to house it. Andreyev does the same. Along the way he creates a new vocabulary, coining neologisms in order to communicate his vision, rather as Gurdjieff did in his own mythological masterpiece *Beelzebub's Tales to His Grandson* (1950).

There are names for concepts, such as "Bramfatura," which means the different levels of materiality found in planets and stars. The Bramfatura of our Earth is called "Shadanakar"; as in the gnostic tradition, it is made up of numerous "planes of matter," of less or greater density, each inhabited by its own demons. "Nauna" is the name of Russia's feminine essence. "Iarosvet" is a demi-urge, who, according to Andreyev, first appears in Russian history in the tenth century. "Velga" is a feminine demon. "Gartungr" is the principle of evil on Earth, and he hails from the lower levels of Shadanakar. "Zventa-Svetana" is the masculine feminine essence, rather like Jung's idea of the "anima." The "Zhrugirs" are the demons of the state, whom we assume Andreyev got to know quite well during his years in the Vladimir Prison. The "Stikhiali" are nature spirits, elementals that live in the wind, trees, snow, rivers, and other natural settings. Like the Slavic Native Faith and Anastasianism, Andreyev places great emphasis on the need to return to nature, to learn to live with it rather than master it, as the Soviets tried to do, with debatable results. As a child Andreyev liked to look at the stars, and an early piece of writing of his was about journeying to other worlds, a fantasy shared by more than one Russian visionary.

There is a great deal of struggle and conflict in Andreyev's world, just as can be found in Blake's and David Lindsay's. So, for example, Gartungr, the principle of evil, is engaged in a perpetual battle with the Planetary Logos. The Russian demi-urge Iarosvet was supposed to wed Nauna, the communal soul of Russia, but he was prevented from doing this by Velga, the lascivious feminine demon, who is on a par with Lilith and Kali. Their separation continued until the nineteenth century, but since then there has been the possibility of their reunion.

The work of Russians today, of all mankind in fact, is to help bring that about. It is a version of the balancing act between eros and logos—love and reason, intuition and intellect, nature and spirit—that has occupied Russian thinkers since the time of Odoevsky and his "lovers of truth" in the early nineteenth century, which suggests that Andreyev's spiritual chronology may just be right.

At the heart of *Roza Mir* is what we can call the "feminization" of the world, the shift from masculine power to feminine love, symbolized in the image of Sophia. It is not a question of one replacing the other, but of both uniting in a mystical marriage, the *hieros gamos* or "sacred union" of mythology, or the *coniunctio oppositorum* of alchemy. In the end, this will lead to a new universal church and state, a modern theocracy informed with the warmth of Sophia, and not the judgments of a harsh God.

But as Solovyov saw, the ideal universal theocracy of the future has the very real potential of turning into a spiritual dictatorship. As in many Russian future histories, the Antichrist and Apocalypse play a central role in Andreyev's prophecy of things to come. Sophia, the Eternal Feminine, has the potential of becoming little more than a temptress, and a sign of the arrival of the Antichrist is the loosening of restrictions and constraints on sex, with the mystical marriage turning into a global love cult. What Andreyev may have thought of the strange sexual world of today, where permissiveness and a new puritanism seem to exist side by side, we don't know. But of sightings of the Antichrist in Russia in recent times, there is no dearth.[40] And that sightings of Jesus are also not lacking suggests that the dramatis personae of the end-times may indeed be waiting in the wings.[41]

ONE SILVER AGE sage who has found a new readership within Putin's new Russia we have yet to mention. One of the passengers on the philosophy steamer taking Berdyaev and others into exile was the political philosopher Ivan Ilyin (1883–1954). Along with Berdyaev and

Solovyov, Ilyin was one of the philosophers whom President Putin urged his regional governors to read at the annual meeting of United Russia in 2014. Of the three, Ilyin is the most political, and his views about Russia and its place in the world have had the most influence on Putin. It is also true that of the three, Ilyin's philosophy comes closest to warranting the kind of censure that critics like David Brooks and others have expressed. He has been called "the most controversial of Russia's forgotten philosophers," attracting epithets ranging from "Russian patriot" to "Russian Christian fascist."[42] The fact that for many, including Putin himself, he is "Putin's philosopher," suggests that, whatever we may think of them, his ideas deserve our attention.

Ilyin was born in Moscow into an aristocratic family that claimed descent from the Rurikid line. From early on he seemed to have a sense that there was something wrong with the world. As other religious idealists did, he recognized that it was fallen and in dire need of redemption. Things had been good in the garden, but since then it's been downhill, a view he shared with Traditionalist thinkers such as Guénon and Evola. His perspective was not unlike that of Joseph de Maistre or Konstantin Pobedonostsev, advisers to Alexander I and III, respectively. All three saw history as one long catastrophe—a view not limited to conservative thinkers—and human beings as inherently bad and in need of guidance. "There never was a good moment in history," Ilyin said, and "there is no intrinsic good in people." Small wonder that his politics often sounds like an argument for Dostoyevsky's Grand Inquisitor.

Ilyin did not always feel this way. While studying law at Moscow University—1901 to 1906—he was a follower of Kant, and believed with the sage of Konigsberg in the power of reason to illuminate the "categorical imperative" of morality. This led to Ilyin's lifelong theme, what he called "legal consciousness." This is fundamentally an individual's recognition of the need for and validity of the "rule of law." Once this enlightenment has been achieved, individuals could govern themselves; there would be no need for coercion. Oddly, this is a view embraced by anarchists, whose politics are generally far from Ilyin's, which are much more of an authoritarian synarchist stamp.

Ilyin's notion of "legal consciousness" is rather like the idea that the "beautiful souls" of the nineteenth century would adopt socialism voluntarily, because they recognized that it was the "right" way to live. Ilyin was soon disabused of this optimistic moonshine and, as generally happens with bruised romanticism, he turned in a very different direction.

After human reality proved unwieldy—the 1905 revolution was, for him, evidence of this—through a reading of Hegel, an analysis under Freud, and studies with the philosopher Edmund Husserl,* founder of phenomenology, from which existentialism sprang, Ilyin gradually adopted a rather different view.[43] "Legal consciousness" would indeed lead to self-government, and in some individuals this has been achieved. But the great mass of humanity is incapable of this and for their own good must be guided on the right path by higher men. These are individuals dedicated to truth who can set an example that those they shepherd may never meet but which will inspire their efforts nonetheless.

In this sense the government, for Ilyin, serves in the political sphere the same function as the church does in the spiritual one. In fact, the two should work together, as they did during the best times in Russia's history, or at least in the less catastrophic ones. Here Ilyin echoes the "symphony" that church and state performed for a time during the reign of Ivan the Terrible, or which was heard played with transforming beauty in lost Constantinople. What had happened in Russia and would lead to the revolution, Ilyin argued, was that the ruling class ignored their responsibilities, abused their position, and drifted further away from the people, a complaint first voiced by the Slavophiles. The ruling class had been negligent in its duties. If the Grand Inquisitor needed a cue, this was it.

Such a view was of course at odds with that of Lenin, whom Ilyin despised and saw as a "Pugachev with a university degree," although Lenin too saw the need for a "revolutionary elite" to guide the "people"

---

*Another Russian student of Husserl's was Lev Shestov.

to their "liberation." Both in different ways also saw the legitimacy of the use of violence for political purposes; Ilyin wrote a book about it and took Tolstoy to task for his ethos of nonresistance, a criticism he shared with Solovyov who does the same in *War, Progress, and the End of History*.[44] Both saw the need for a temporary dictatorship, a strong hand to steer the people through the chaos that was an inevitable product of social collapse, although as Ouspensky saw, the "dictatorship of the proletariat" quickly became that of the "criminal element." And both also saw the need for a government that ran through the entire society, from top to bottom, leaving little room for individual choice or decision. The only difference was that for Lenin the revolution and the coming classless society—arriving soon—were the ideals holding the otherwise anarchic people together. For Ilyin it was something different.

For James Scanlan, Ilyin "directly continued the Russian religious-philosophical tradition," and his utopian dream differed from that of the Marxists by being one of a "transfigured holy Russia of the future." He was firmly committed to Orthodoxy and had more than a streak of the Slavophile in him. His view of Russia as an "organic being," and not a nation in the Western sense, but an "extra-historical" mystical unity, smacks of Schelling and anticipates Spengler's ideas about the "biological" character of civilizations, and is taken up today by neo-Eurasianists.

Unity was central to Ilyin's political and social views. As with so many Russian thinkers, for him individuals on their own are nothing; they can only be "free" within the embrace of a community. Here they can find themselves by finding their true place among their fellows. Although he was critical of Nicholas II, Ilyin was a monarchist and believed in the paternal role of the tsar as the "Little Father" of his people. He falls under the "patriarchal" line of Russian philosophy, with figures like Fedorov and the "fathers" of the Slavic Native faith; there is little of Sophia in Ilyin's thought, although his belief in the "Russianness" of Russian soil suggests some connection to Damp Mother Earth. And although his elusive ideal is the "legal consciousness" that will voluntarily recognize the rule of law, like the Slavophiles he accepted the need for autocracy and its arbitrary expression of power, and engaged in more than one flight of Hegelian dialectics in order to reconcile the two.

Ilyin approved of the February revolution, but he was a fierce opponent of the Bolsheviks, and between 1918 and 1922 he was arrested by the Cheka six times. At his last arrest he was sentenced to death, but this was commuted to exile, Lenin himself intervening on his behalf, out of respect for a formidable enemy. This is how Ilyin found himself aboard the *Haken* with Berdyaev and other rejected philosophers on their way to the West. But while Berdyaev moved more and more toward his antinomian and anarchic intuitions of freedom, which, fundamentally, went deeper than politics, Ilyin found ideological and historical comfort in the rise first of Mussolini, then Hitler. This was a stint of spiritual-political fellow traveling that paralleled a similar path taken by his contemporary Julius Evola. For both, fascism and Nazism were heroic ventures, spiritual resistance movements defending the values of tradition against the rot of Western democracy and the rise of atheistic communism. They were organic, unified cultures fighting against the mechanized, atomized societies of the West and the mass leveling of the Bolsheviks.

What Ilyin appreciated about Mussolini was the idea of the "great man," the hero, who rises above mediocrity and impresses his will and resolve on his world and culture. This, of course, was the opposite view of Tolstoy, whose long historical passages in *War and Peace*—which many readers skip to get back to the story—argue against this idea. Napoleons do not impress their will upon history; history tosses them up and moves them here and there like a cork upon the waves. Ilyin appreciated the corporatist character of fascism, the "place" it gave everyone according to their function in society—like a cell in an organism—but in the end he found Mussolini's fascism wanting, just as Evola did. The Nazis seemed a better bet, another idea he shared with Evola.[45]

When Ilyin disembarked from the *Haken* he landed in Berlin, and from 1922 to 1934 he taught there at the Russian Scientific Institute.

He also became the central ideologue of the émigré White Russian anti-Bolshevik resistance and later claimed with apparently some satisfaction that the Nazi animus toward Jews was informed at least in part by the tenets of "Judeobolshevism," the idea that the Bolsheviks were somehow a Jewish phenomenon, a belief rampant among the Whites.* Aside from the fact that Marx was Jewish (and of course Trotsky) there is little factual support for this idea, as there is for an earlier incarnation of Russian anti-Semitic paranoia, which unfortunately has infected some of its best minds.[46] This was the *Protocols of the Elders of Zion,* the Russian forgery "exposing" a Jewish plot to dominate the world, which garnered some important readers when it appeared in 1905, and still befuddles minds today. One of its later readers was Hitler, and when he came to power he made it required reading throughout Germany. Another fan was Evola.

Ilyin was happy when Hitler became chancellor in 1933.[47] As many did during the "dirty thirties," he saw National Socialism as the only power in Europe able to stop the spread of communism. In 1934 he wrote to Hitler, expressing his belief that only he could save the world from the Bolsheviks.[48] I am not sure if he received a reply, and naturally Hitler agreed, but like many who in the early days of the Third Reich believed something positive might come from it, Ilyin was soon disappointed.† If nothing else Hitler's view of the Slavs as subhuman (*Untermenschen*) could not have helped, and the Molotov-Ribbentrop Pact of 1939 between Hitler and Stalin soon made clear that sworn spiritual enemies could nevertheless shake hands when political expediency demanded it, a piece of realpolitik that confused leftists as well, and redrew the map of eastern Europe.

Articles Ilyin wrote criticizing the anti-Semitism he seemed to have applauded caught the authorities' attention.[49] He was brought in for questioning and when requested to modify his views so that they were

---

*Most notably Alexander Solzhenitsyn
†This number included figures as far afield as C. G. Jung and the English writer Wyndham Lewis.

gleichgeschaltet—"conformed" to Nazi ideology—he refused.* He had shown the same integrity when confronting the Cheka, and his moral forthrightness had made him a kind of superhero among the émigrés, tolerating no compromise on ideals. Lenin saved him from execution the first time. Here he was removed from his position, banned from employment, and threatened with incarceration in a concentration camp. In 1938, with help from the composer Sergei Rachmaninov, who had left Russia in 1918, Ilyin escaped from Germany and went to Switzerland, where he would remain for the rest of his life.[50]

There he wrote a series of articles, which, more than anything else has helped in his resurrection today. As in Germany he was banned from working and publishing. In a preecho of the fugitive *samizdat* press that would begin to sprout with the death of Stalin, Ilyin mimeographed his short essays and distributed them by hand to his steadily shrinking circle of readers. By the time of his death in 1954 he was forgotten by what remained of the émigré community for whom he was a conscience, and by the soulless regime that had exiled them. Today he is a central if controversial figure in the Russian search for identity, with assessments ranging from an "implacable enemy of totalitarian systems" who nevertheless celebrated Hitler to "twentieth-century version of Old Testament prophet," a persona he shares with Solzhenitsyn.[51]

Ilyin may have remained forgotten but for one of the articles making up *Nashi Zadachi,* "Our Tasks." This is a collection of the mimeographed essays Ilyin produced in the 1940s and '50s, and which were first published in book form in 1956. More recently Vladimir Putin put them on his governors' reading list. One piece, "What the Dismemberment of Russia Means for the World," written in 1950, predicts what will follow the collapse of the Soviet Union, a breakdown that Ilyin, and the Eurasianists, with whom he had common cause, knew was inevitable, if long in coming. The essay languished in obscurity for

---

*I can't help but point out that this is another similarity with Evola, who also came to reject the "crude biological" racism of the Nazis, in favor of his own more sophisticated "spiritual racism."

decades, but in 1990 the journal *Kuban* republished it along with other excerpts from "Our Tasks." The timing couldn't have been better. What Ilyin had predicted would happen seemed to his newfound readers to be taking place right around them.

Ilyin feared what he called the "Balkanization of Russia," its breaking up into smaller, separate bodies, which for an organic unity like itself, was really a kind of "dissection" or even "vivisection." Ilyin predicted that under the pretext of "self-determination," "freedom," "independence," and other democratic shibboleths, Western powers would cut up Damp Mother Russia and parcel her out as new individual nations, neutralizing her as a power, and gaining greater influence in her now lost lands. (He is often seen as a proponent of "Russophobia," the belief that the West fears Russia and will do all it can to destroy her, a notion not unknown today.) One very important part of Russia's organic unity for Ilyin was Ukraine, the original lost kingdom, the heart and soul of its people. According to his prophecy, Russia itself would soon be lost too.

By the early 1990s, what Ilyin had seen forty years earlier had come to pass. The Soviet Union had collapsed. Ukraine, the lost kingdom, had found itself, as had other former member states of the USSR. The West beckoned with offers of aid and assistance and promises of free-market economies. It was, as Francis Fukuyama saw, the end of history. And Ilyin had also been correct about what would follow in its wake: chaos. And what would Russia need to reestablish order and unity—temporarily, of course, until the "rule of law" could be established? A hero, a strong man, a figure outside history, who would step in and seize the reins of power and restore control through a temporary "national dictatorship."

Does this sound like anyone to you?

In 2005 ex-KGB agent turned Russian president Vladimir Putin had Ilyin's remains moved from Switzerland and reinterred in the Donskoy Monastery in Moscow. That same year saw Ilyin's name and ideas appear in Putin's speeches to the Federal Assembly and in his interviews with the press. Vladislav Surkov, spin doctor supreme, by then at the controls of the Virtual Reality Russia he was directing for Putin, echoed the president, inserting Ilyin into his mix of government-managed media. Dmitry Medvedev, leader of United Russia and soon to be Putin's stand-in for a presidential term, began recommending Ilyin's works—by then published in huge volumes—to young readers. Everyone seemed to be dropping Ilyin's name, including senior figures in the newly restored church. In 2006 Michigan State University, which had housed Ilyin's papers since 1963, sent them to Moscow. And Ilyinmania continued. In 2015 a two-and-a-half-hour film documentary about President Putin's achievements in office—saving the nation from chaos within and aggression without—devoted a six-minute segment to Ilyin and his ideas. The year before, asked by a delegation of history teachers and students to name his favorite Russian historian, Putin without hesitation said Ilyin.[52] This was the same year that his required reading assignment reached his governors.

Putin has strong views on history, and he isn't afraid of expressing them or of putting them into action. As you might expect, they are not shared by everyone. For the historian Mark Galeotti, Putin's view of history has more to do with creating a new Russian myth than with historical fact, a preference not uncommon among Russia's leaders, or those of other nations if truth be told. For him, Putin has "pushed not only the creation, but the standard imposition of a 'new Russian history,' curated to maximize political advantage to the regime."[53] As evidence of this he points to the "Russia—My History" ongoing multimedia installation on view in Moscow's VDNKh exhibition park.[54] It is a celebration of Russia's greatness; her heroic achievements, her glorious past, and her traditional values; her unity, faith, patriotism, capacity for suffering (Gumilev's "passionarity"), and need for a strong leader. Also included is patriotic and nationalist rhetoric explaining how the recent contretemps in Crimea and Ukraine are part of this stirring story. Films depicting similar virtues are also promoted widely by the government, and the statue of Prince Vladimir of Kiev, which Putin had erected just outside the Kremlin, tells us that like Ilyin, he sees Ukraine as unquestionably part of Russia.

Orwell warned about the consequences of a nation's historical narrative falling into the hands of a dictator, and in Russian history this has happened often enough. We've seen how the chronicles have been shaped in favor of some players—or at least we recognize that there is sufficient reason to suspect that they have—and how under the Soviets such historical revision was business as usual. But in the world of mass infotainment, post-truth, and shrinking attention spans, the ability to rewrite history according to one's needs is greatly facilitated. And if, as Putin does, you also have a say over what is being taught in the classrooms, you have a good chance of being successful.

In 2013 Putin called for a single textbook teaching a single history of Russia—the heroic one he prefers—to be made mandatory in schools, citing a need to end academic squabbles over the details and also taking advantage of an opportunity to set his own regime firmly within the standard Russian narrative.[55] The need for a strong, renewed Russian identity is more pressing in today's Russia, he believes, than is a finicky academic fastidiousness over facts. Ilyin believed in the notion of the "noble lie," or more generously, the myth necessary to unite a people and move them to greatness, something he shared with the American political philosopher Leo Strauss and the French socialist George Sorrel. Putin seems to be taking that insight seriously, and it is one that seems to be shared by other "patriotic" leaders in Europe.[56] Ilyin foresaw a time when "Russia will rise from disintegration and humiliation and begin an epoch of new development and greatness."[57] Putin it seems is determined that this resurgence will arrive under his watch.

Religion is also an important topic for Putin, as it was for Ilyin. In May 2016 he made a pilgrimage to Mount Athos, an event televised by the billionaire turned Orthodox nationalist Konstantin Malofeev on his Tsargrad TV channel, a slightly less vulgar Russian version of Fox News with a focus on religion. According to one analyst, Putin was treated as a "visiting Byzantine Emperor."[58] In 2017 he visited the newly restored New Jerusalem Monastery outside Moscow, much of which had been destroyed by the Nazis. The political aspect of a strong leader with a strong faith has not escaped him, something that the thinly veiled Third Rome references in speeches validating his annexation of Crimea seem to suggest.[59]

More chilling perhaps, given the Russia penchant for apocalypse, were the nuclear exercises Putin conducted seemingly in tandem with pronouncements on the end-times coming from Patriarch Kirill, bishop of Moscow. Kirill warned that "One must be blind not to see the approach of the terrible moment of history about which the Apostle and Evangelist John the Theologian spoke in his Revelation."[60] In a perhaps unconscious nod to Francis Fukuyama, the patriarch warned of the danger of "slipping into the abyss and the end of history." What comes as the fulfillment of the liberal dream for some appears as an eschatological nightmare for others. And while we are all well advised not to be alarmists, a look at Russian history does not dispel the suspicion that in it, nightmares sometimes come true, or that for some even, Russia itself *is* "history as nightmare."[61]

In recent times however, this reconnection with Holy Russia has hit some speed bumps, and so the apocalypse might just be put on hold for a spell. In early 2019 Bartholomew I of Constantinople, "first among equals of Orthodox clerics," granted independence to the Ukrainian Orthodox Church, which had previously been under the rule of Moscow.[62] This did not go down well with Putin, who invariably puts "Ukraine" in quotation marks in his speeches, to highlight its "supposed" independence from the motherland. The establishment of an independent Ukrainian church is, for him, an act of political and religious heresy. Putin, however, is ready to go it alone, and he seems to be receiving support from agencies that the church itself brands satanic.

Soon after the Ukrainian church secession, media around the world reported on a coven of Russian witches who gathered together in support of the president, forming a "circle of power" in order to "make the world better off through Russia."[63] Wearing black robes and hoods, and clutching a book of spells, the witches and warlocks called on the "primordial power" to cast all those who hate Russia "into the abyss," and for the coming days to "open the gates of happiness" to Russia.[64] Included in Russia's foes was President Trump, who has already been the focus of a "binding spell" that American witches have been directing against him for some time.[65] The American witches themselves have come under spiritual fire by Christian evangelists who believe Trump has God on his side, a support many Russians feel he shares with their own president. If this isn't magical politics, I don't know what is.

Yet witches or no, Putin has unmistakably assumed the moral high ground in the new cold war that for some is much more a clash of civilizations than a spate of old-school saber rattling. In his presidential address of 2013, he declared that "we know that there are more and more people in the world who support our position on defending traditional values that have made up the spiritual and moral foundation of civilization in every nation for thousands of years: the values of traditional families, real human life, including religious life, not only material existence"—always the province of the West—"but also spirituality, the values of humanism and global diversity."[66] Putin admitted that this was a "conservative position." But he drew on a Silver Age sage to defend it, although this time it was Berdyaev, not Ilyin, who helped him out. The point of conservatism, Berdyaev, the spiritual anarchist, said, was that it did not prevent movement "forward and upward," but was a safeguard against a movement "backward and downward, into chaotic darkness and a return to a primitive state."[67]

Who knows more about "chaotic darkness and a return to a primitive state" than Russian Man? Whatever we may think of it, at least from Putin's perspective, Holy Russia is making a comeback.

A Third Way?

A Different Way of Knowing

I began this book with a look at some prophecies and predictions made in the early twentieth century about the possibility of a new cultural epoch, a new development in the evolution of human consciousness, appearing in Russia at that time. Rudolf Steiner made some of these predictions. Oswald Spengler made others. And, as we've seen, voices within Russia itself suggesting similar developments were not scarce. In fact, if there is one theme appearing throughout the tumultuous series of events we've come to understand as Russian history, it is what the *meaning* of that history could be.

Most Western historians laugh at such an idea, considering it the height of presumption. But then most thinkers in the West jettisoned the idea of any meaning to life or existence in any form long ago, considering it a throwback to religious superstition. Yet it was against precisely this presumption that Russian philosophy, with its emphasis on meaning, arose, a point I will return to shortly.

All nations consider their past and their future, and their citizens devote some thought at some time to what their place in the history of the world may be, whether they are proud of this or find it laughable. Only the dullest minds take each day as it comes, without a thought to where they are going or of what they have left behind. Such thought about one's country's place in history can lead to the most brazen nationalism. Or, perhaps less often, to a humble appreciation of the contribution, of whatever stature, that one's homeland has made to the story of who we are on this planet and where we might be going.

As we've seen, for Russians this is no small matter. There is something peculiarly intense and obsessive about Russia's search for identity. Practically all the historians and cultural commentators I have looked at have said so. Strangely, no matter how easily recognizable Russians may be throughout the world—it may be my prejudice, but I have the impression that they usually stand out—they themselves seem to have trouble in knowing who they are. Perhaps this is because they have been so many things: Slavs, Vikings, Mongols, wannabe Westerners, the God-bearing people, and dogmatic Marxists, to name a few. And here they are, once again, faced with this question.

Again, I am not sure and could be wrong, but I do not know if the people of another nation have had to absorb so many different past identities and have felt so pressing a need to find one that fits. But then, as we've seen, Russian Man is so large, open, contradictory, and accommodating that perhaps no other people have the capacity for this.

Hermann Hesse's essays on *The Brothers Karamazov,* in which he talks about the peculiarities of Russian Man and what these may mean for the West, his "glimpse into chaos" I write about in chapter 1, appeared in 1919. As I write this now, it is late winter 2019. The passing of a century provides a neat reason to reflect on what Hesse's insights might mean for us today, not to mention also a felicitous way to bring this book around full circle. And, if we allow for a certain liberty in chronology, this is not the only centennial worth mentioning. The first volume of Spengler's *Decline of the West,* in which he too speaks of the future of Russia, was published in 1918. Of course, the Bolshevik revolution began in 1917, and was over in 1922, with the end of the civil war and the establishment of the Soviet Union. It was also in 1922 that the philosophy steamers left St. Petersburg—by then Petrograd and on its way to becoming Leningrad—carrying their freight of Silver Age philosophers to the West. Barring apocalyptic expectations, 2022 is only a few years away. So there seems sufficient reason to ask, now, a hundred years on, what this can mean for us in the early twenty-first century, as we find ourselves passing through our own "time of troubles," one not limited to a single nation, but, according to most reports, involving the entire world.

The initial impetus for this book came from writing my previous one, *Dark Star Rising.* There, among other things, I explored the effect of the "Eurasia meme" promoted by Alexander Dugin and others, on contemporary events. From this I was led to the recognition that in their search for their identity, the idea of Holy Russia seemed increasingly appealing to many Russians, not the least of whom was their president, Vladimir Putin. From there I discovered that Putin had some interesting tastes in reading and that in speeches and interviews he referred to some Russian philosophers whose work I knew—Berdyaev and Solovyov—and some I didn't: Ilyin. This surprised me. But then Julius Evola was turning up in the *New York Times,* in connection with Steve Bannon and Putin, so perhaps I shouldn't have been surprised at all.

I then discovered that Western critics, who might be expected to be suspicious of Putin's "must read" list, made remarks about Russian philosophy that struck me as curious and to some degree inaccurate, or at least rather odd. I had been reading Berdyaev for many years and had written about his still powerful early work, *The Meaning of the Creative Act,* in a book of my own.[1] I was less familiar with Solovyov, but I refer to him in that book too,* and had written about his book *The Meaning of Love* in an article years earlier.[2]

My own love of Russian literature and thought began many years before, in the late 1970s, when a reading of Colin Wilson's *The Outsider* inspired me to read Dostoyevsky, to whose work Wilson devoted many pages. I have fond memories of crossing cobblestoned Second Avenue

---

*I should perhaps point out that I know Russian literature and thought only through translation. I neither read nor speak Russian, a fact that most likely has dawned on readers of this book who do.

in New York's East Village, with paperback copies of *Crime and Punishment* or *The Devils* stuffed into my overcoat pocket, as I made my way to the Kiev Coffee Shop, or the Veselka, or, on occasion, farther east to the Odessa on Avenue A. With a bowl of borscht and a hunk of challah bread I could be Raskolnikov or Kirilov for an hour or so. Later I took on Tolstoy, became acquainted with Berdyaev and his friend, Lev Shestov, and found my way—again via Wilson—to less-known figures like Mikhail Artsybashev, whose *Sanine* made a splash in 1907, and Leonid Andreyev, who I mention in this book. Many years later, in *A Dark Muse* (2005) I wrote about the Silver Age and the work of Andrei Bely, and contributed an afterword to a new edition of Valery Briussov's *The Fiery Angel*. I have also written biographies of P. D. Ouspensky and Madame Blavatsky.

So much for credentials.

The question I asked myself, and which got this book going, went something like this. Whether Putin is reading these thinkers or not—and as far as I can tell it seems he really does read them—what matters is what they have to say, no? Or, to put it another way, the fact that he does read them shouldn't put us off from doing the same, if, that is, we are really interested in knowing what they have to say, and are not satisfied with accepting the assessments of critics whose view of their ideas will be, perhaps understandably, skewed by their view of Putin.

All this is of course predicated on the idea that these thinkers of the Silver Age, and other Russian philosophers, *do* have something to say that we in the West should hear. I believe they do, but not for the reasons Putin does, or those his critics believe he does. In one sense it doesn't matter if Putin reads them or not, and I will leave the deciphering of his intentions in doing so to others. But I am glad that he has reminded me of them and that he has brought the question of what they, and Russian thinking in general, have to offer us to my attention. The point of this book is to bring it to its readers.

Putin may be name-dropping these philosophers in order to give his regime some philosophical and spiritual gravitas, or as support for his promotion of Russia as not a new nation—one not yet thirty years old—but a new civilization. Of the three thinkers he refers to, it strikes me that only one, Ilyin, is really on the same page as he is in this regard. We've seen that in the end Solovyov had doubts about some actual historical theocracy—his concern about the Antichrist tells us this—and came to believe that only an "inner apocalypse," a change in spiritual orientation, in *consciousness,* could help mankind out of its predicament.

Berdyaev, too, had no use for a political answer to our existential challenge. In *The Russian Idea* he is critical of the Third Rome myth, and although his love of Russia is evident on every page he wrote, he also had no use for nationalism and was often scathing about the Slavophiles. Both knew the West had much to offer, but both also knew that Russia had much to offer the West.

It was clear what the West had to offer Russia. We've seen the efforts that rulers like Peter the Great and Catherine the Great made in order to get it. Lucid, clear logic; reason, rationality, and order; a practical efficiency that would pull Russia out of the Middle Ages; a society based on Enlightenment ideas and liberal reforms that would, in principle, lead to a better life for her people. In a word: *modernity.* But what did Russia have that the West could use? Or, to put it another way, what did Russia have that the West lacked?

The answer to that question, I believe, is that Russia had something that it took from the West, and that *the West didn't want.* What was that? To answer this, I think we have to go back to Friedrich Schelling and his notion of "absolute knowledge" that I look at in chapter 8.

What is important here, I think, is not the conclusions Schelling drew from this knowledge, although, of course, they warrant close study. It is the kind or *way* of knowing he speaks of that concerns us. It is a radically different way of knowing providing a very different kind of knowledge than that with which the West is familiar, although of course it had many proponents in the West and can be traced back to its earliest thinkers.[3] As Schelling said, it was a *Mittwissenschaft,* a "knowing with," an immediate, direct, unreflective knowing, what in the Western esoteric tradition is known as *gnosis*. It was an intelligence not of the head alone, but, as I show in *Lost Knowledge of the Imagination* (2017), also of the heart. And if there is one thing Russians have, it is heart.

This is a way of knowing that "participates" with the object of its knowledge. It enters into it rather than remaining at the surface, which is how our usual way of knowing approaches things, from outside.* As Berdyaev says, our usual way of knowing "objectifies" what it knows, turns it into an "object," a thing, amenable to our manipulation. Nothing is spared this basilisk stare, and what troubled Berdyaev and many other thinkers and poets and artists since the rise of such "objectification" as the dominant mode of knowing the world, was that the human was falling prey to it too.

The very power of the rational mind that made us the master of the world, in terms of our ability to manipulate and control it, was also in danger of undermining our experience of ourselves as free, living beings. By placing ourselves under the microscope of the analytical mind we found out what made us tick, and in the process reduced ourselves to mere cogs in the wheel of a cosmic machine. This, we remember, was the state of affairs that drove Dostoyevsky's "underground man" to declare that he would go insane on purpose in order to deny this, in order to show that he was "free." While this commitment to freedom is daring, one hopes we can find a better vehicle for it than madness.

What Russian thought had to give to the West was the urgent recognition that such a view of reality was unsupportable, a realization that many in the West, from William Blake on, shared. What it also had to give was the belief in the possibility of a way of knowing reality, of "being in the world," that did not result in this disastrous split between our inner and outer experience, between the visions and values that make life meaningful, and a clockwork universe that is oblivious of them. Between, that is, the head and the heart.

---

*This is, of course, how Henri Bergson describes what he calls "intuition." He even refers to it as providing an "absolute knowledge." Bergson, of course, is not the only Western thinker to have recognized this.[4]

This was the "all is good" revelation that Dostoyevsky experienced, the moments, as I write earlier in this book, "when we feel a strange 'communion' with nature, a feeling that our inner and outer worlds are not separated by an impassable barrier—the view of the Enlightenment—but 'participate' in each other in some way we do not fully understand." Call this mysticism if you like; it is nonetheless a part of human reality, as much as its opposite, our usual sense of being separated from the world, is.

Russian philosophy seems strange to Westerners—a point Lesley Chamberlain is at pains to make—because it begins with the premise that such moments tell us something that is true about the world and ourselves. They are not anomalies to be explained in terms of our usual way of knowing, which is how most Western thinkers approach them. That they are difficult to translate into the language of philosophy is no argument against them. Practically anything worth saying in philosophy suffers from the same drawback. The meaning such moments reveal cannot be reduced to a neat syllogism, but it can be evoked through the determined attempt to grasp it. This can lead to a knowledge that is an experience, that is, a gnosis. It is a living knowledge and it is the reality of this, I believe, that Russian thought tried to keep alive.

Before the philosophy steamers sent them off to a Europe that often didn't want them, the Silver Age sages believed that they could offer a way that was different from either the increasingly mechanized and reductive West, or the mystical, amorphous East. It was a way that combined these two, yet transcended both in a new, "third way." To be sure, the idea of a "third way" got a lot of mileage and appears in different ways in thinkers like Solovyov, Berdyaev, and Ilyin. I am using it here solely in the sense of a way of knowing and participating with the world that does not reduce it to merely raw material for human consumption, nor reduces humanity to merely a part of nature, a clever animal, but animal nonetheless. It is a way that reveals our profound connection to the world—it is geared more toward the "Sophic economy" of Sergei Bulgakov than Fedorov's "common task"—without sacrificing our separation from it, the self-consciousness that sets us apart from our fellow creatures, that which makes us *in* the world but not totally *of* it.[5] It is a way in which the "all is good" revelation is not an end point, but the start of a deeper exploration of the mystery of existence.

This mystery was ever-present to souls like Dostoyevsky, Solovyov, Berdyaev, and others. The sight of it had grown dim in the West. Its vision had become limited to only that which was illuminated by the rational mind, the utilitarian ego, what Blake called "single vision and Newton's sleep." To borrow from Blake, Russian thought wanted to clean the West's "doors of perception," so that it could see with another light as well. This was the "uncreated light" that the Hesychasts sought in order to know God's energies. It was the light of truth that people like Odoevsky and his "wisdom lovers" caught sight of in their Romantic revels. It was the light that made the plight of the serfs glaring and made the need for their misery to end unmistakable.

Hesse had recognized the need for this illumination, and he believed he saw a possible means of achieving it. His glimpse into chaos offered by *The Brothers Karamazov* had suggested to him that "perhaps a combination of Ivan and Alyosha would result in that higher more fruitful conception which must form the foundation of the coming new age."[6] He continues: "Then will the unconscious no longer be the devil but rather the god-devil, the demi-urge, he who always was and out of whom all things emerge." Ivan is the intellectual brother who wants to return God's entrance ticket to life because he cannot accept its suffering. Alyosha is the monk who has the "all is good" revelation following the crisis of Father Zossima's death. Their union, or something like it,* was something Hesse himself tried to bring about in his novel *Narcissus and Goldmund* (1930) and other works. It is one that we, in our postmodern world, sorely need to achieve.[7]

The Silver Age philosophers had an idea of this but their message

---

*It is a union that involves the harmonizing of our two cerebral hemispheres, as well as our two cultural traditions, the mainstream Western intellectual stream and its hidden, esoteric counterpart, an argument I make in *The Secret Teachers of the Western World.*

was cut short by the forces of history. The Russia they loved no longer existed, and its new rulers did not want them. The lands they were exiled to were not receptive to their message either. Some, like Berdyaev, kept sending out the warning, writing book after book, but although respected and acknowledged, his influence was minimal at best. The fact that a century later we are faced with the same challenge says as much. Recent events suggest that the unconscious remains a devil, at least in the sense that we have yet to assimilate it and the "other" way of knowing associated with it. The consequence of this is that the "irrational" forces the conscious rational Western mind would like to ignore have appeared on center stage and seem in many ways to be running the show. Hence the return of a kind of occultism in postmodern politics, a development I look at elsewhere.

The return of Holy Russia is not the answer. But a return to the ideas that the philosophers of the Silver Age and their predecessors tried to convey to a world that was not yet ready for them may help point us in the direction of one.

LONDON, FEBRUARY 2019

Acknowledgments

Many people helped to make this book possible. I'd like to thank my old editor, Mitch Horowitz, for putting me in touch with Jon Graham, who commissioned it. As is often the case, my thanks go to the staff of the British Library and to that of my local source, Camden's Swiss Cottage Library; I hope my many requests for material stored in their reserve stock section have not prejudiced them against me. Many thanks also go to David Jones and the staff of *New Dawn* magazine, who supplied me with a wealth of material, only a fraction of which I was able to use. I would also like to thank Victoria Nelson for alerting me to sightings of contemporary *Oprichniki*. Writing a book is always a challenge and doing so while undergoing a personal crisis is doubly difficult. I'd like to thank the friends who helped me through a very dark time: Ray Grasse, Helene Arts, Malcolm Rushton, James Hamilton, Lisa Jane Persky, and my sons, Max and Joshua. But my deepest thanks is reserved for my arctic flower and Sherpa, Anja Fløde Bjørlo, who gave me more than she knows. That our paths had to divide is more painful than I can say.

Notes

Introduction. Welcome to the Silver Age

1. Tomberg, *Russian Spirituality and Other Essays,* 67–68.
2. See Lachman, *In Search of P. D. Ouspensky,* 63–75.
3. https://wn.rsarchive.org/Lectures/19150615p0.html. This is the transcript of a later lecture series, "Preparing for the Sixth Epoch," given in Düsseldorf, Germany, on June 19, 1915. Steiner's remarks about Russia in it echo those of his earlier lecture.
4. See Lachman, *Rudolf Steiner: An Introduction to His Life and Work,* 169–75.
5. https://nationalpost.com/news/putins-heroes.
6. http://favobooks.com/politicians/86-vladimir-putin-reads.html.
7. www.nytimes.com/2014/03/04/opinion/brooks-putin-cant-stop.html.
8. www.washingtonpost.com/news/monkey-cage/wp/2014/03/02/how-putins -worldview-may-be-shaping-his-response-in-crimea/?utm_term=.86240e1cc25a.
9. http://harvardpolitics.com/culture/using-dostoyevsky-understand-vladimir -putins-aggression.
10. Quoted in Billington, *The Icon and the Axe,* 58.
11. Smoley, *Inner Christianity,* 27.
12. Billington, *The Icon and the Axe.*
13. This was recognized by the Esalen Institute and Lindisfarne Press, who in the 1990s collaborated in reprinting English translations of works by Nikolai Berdyaev, Vladimir Solovyov, and other important figures from the Silver Age in their Library of Russian Philosophy. See Berdyaev, *The Russian Idea,* 287.
14. Chamberlain, *Motherland,* 251.

1. Russian Man

1. Hesse, *My Belief,* 71.

2. Hesse, *My Belief,* 71.

3. Hesse, *My Belief,* 74.

4. He speaks of it clearly in his *Tagebuch* for 1920–21, where he writes; "I can't really say whether I, with my attempt to find freedom and immersion in chaos, am not just as dangerous, just as destructive as the patriots and the retroverts. I demand of myself that I go back beyond the pairs of opposites and accept chaos." In *Turn Off Your Mind: The Mystic Sixties and the Dark Side of the Age of Aquarius,* I argue that in many ways the various "revolutions" of the 1960s—including the "occult revival" of that decade— corroborated Hesse's concern about a coming age dominated by "Russian man." See *Turn Off Your Mind,* 127–30.

5. Hesse, *My Belief,* 73.

6. Hesse, *My Belief,* 73.

7. Spengler, *The Decline of the West,* 2:295, n. 1.

8. Spengler, *The Decline of the West,* 2:295, n. 1.

9. Spengler, *The Decline of the West,* 1:201, n. 2.

10. Spengler, *The Decline of the West,* 1:201, n. 2.

11. Spengler, *The Decline of the West,* 2:296.

12. Spengler, *The Decline of the West,* 2:278.

13. Spengler, *The Decline of the West,* 2:194.

14. Spengler, *The Decline of the West,* 2:194, 196.

15. www.edgarcayce.org/about-us/blog/blog-posts/out-of-russia-will -come-hope.

16. www.edgarcayce.org/about-us/blog/blog-posts/out-of-russia-will -come-hope.

17. www.light-weaver.com/LW-old/destiny/dest1027.html.

18. www.light-weaver.com/LW-old/destiny/dest1027.html.

19. Wilson, *Rasputin and the Fall of the Romanovs,* 17.

20. Berdyaev, *The Russian Idea,* 21.

21. Berdyaev, *The Russian Idea,* 21.

22. Young, *The Russian Cosmists,* 24.

23. Young, *The Russian Cosmists,* 24.

24. Lawrence, *The Seven Pillars of Wisdom,* quoted in Wilson, *The Outsider,* 93.

25. Ouspensky, *A New Model of the Universe,* 422.

26. www.freeclassicebooks.com/P.G.%20Wodehouse/The%20Clicking%20 of%20Cuthbert.pdf, 16.

27. See my afterword to Briussov, *The Fiery Angel.*

28. Hendry, *The Sacred Threshold,* 33.

29. Berdyaev, *The Russian Idea,* 96.

30. Dostoyevsky, *The Brothers Karamazov,* 273.

31. George Steiner, *Tolstoy or Dostoevsky,* 208.

32. First published in an English translation in 1918, its Russian publication was earlier than this and predates Yevegny Zamyatin's *We,* generally considered the first modern dystopia, which was first published in an English translation in 1924. The first edition available in the Soviet Union was published in 1988. See https://archive.org/details/republicofsouthe00bryuiala.

33. Lachman, *Madame Blavatsky: The Mother of Modern Spirituality,* 5.

34. Rudolf Steiner, *Spiritualism, Madame Blavatsky, and Theosophy,* 157–58.

35. Berdyaev, *The Russian Idea,* 23.

36. https://humanism.org.uk/campaigns/successful-campaigns/atheist-bus -campaign/.

37. Berdyaev, *The Russian Idea,* 24.

38. Wilson, *The Occult,* 379.

39. See Lachman, *In Search of P. D. Ouspensky,* 83.

40. See introduction by Gary Lachman in Gurdjieff, *Meetings with Remarkable Men,* xviii.

41. Peters, *My Journey with a Mystic,* 215–19. This is an edition of Peters's *Boyhood with Gurdjieff* and *Gurdjieff Remembered* bound together; the story originally appeared in *Gurdjieff Remembered.*

42. Fülöp-Miller, *Rasputin: The Holy Devil.*

43. Shukman, *Rasputin,* 13.

44. Shukman, *Rasputin,* 15.

45. Wilson, *Rasputin and the Fall of the Romanovs,* 190.

46. Berdyaev, *The Russian Idea,* 24.

47. See Lachman, *The Secret Teachers of the Western World,* 124–30.

48. Billington, *The Face of Russia,* 21.

2. Motherland

1. Billington, *Russia in Search of Itself,* ix.

2. Gogol, *Dead Souls,* 259.

3. Longworth, *Russia's Empires*, x–xvii.

4. Berdyaev, *The Russian Ideal*, 21.

5. Clover, *Black Wind, White Snow*, 122.

6. Berdyaev, *The Russian Ideal*, 21.

7. Billington, *The Face of Russia*, 21.

8. Ascherson, *Black Sea*, 41.

9. Gogol, *Dead Souls*, 258.

10. Longworth, *Russia's Empires*, 5.

11. Longworth, *Russia's Empires*, 6.

12. Billington, *The Face of Russia*, 21.

13. Billington, *The Face of Russia*, 10.

14. Longworth, *Russia's Empires*, 10.

15. Gooch, *Cities of Dreams*, 8–18.

16. Billington, *The Face of Russia*, 51.

17. J. G. Bennet's introduction in Ouspensky, *Talks with a Devil*, 1.

18. Lachman, *The Secret Teachers of the Western World*, 191–92.

19. See my interview with Nikita Petrov for MeaningofLife TV: www.youtube .com/watch?v=JkGxPw4AJ5M.

20. Anderson, *The Face of Glory*, 69–70.

21. Longworth, *Russia's Empires*, 12; Gooch, *Cities of Dreams*, 137–38.

22. Billington, *The Face of Russia*, 51.

23. Ascherson, *Black Sea*, 24.

24. Wilson, *A Criminal History of Mankind*, 240–41.

25. Billington, *The Face of Russia*, 22.

26. Lachman, *Dark Star Rising*, 172.

27. Toynbee, *A Study of History*, 238.

28. www.ancient-origins.net/myths-legends/viking-berserkers-fierce-warriors -or-drug-fuelled-madmen-001472.

29. Wilson, *A Criminal History of Mankind*, 271.

30. Foote and Wilson, *The Viking Achievement*, 220.

31. Haywood, *Encyclopaedia of the Viking Age*, 162.

32. Longworth, *Russia's Empires*, 24.

33. Koestler in *Bricks to Babel*, 308.

34. Koestler, *Bricks to Babel*, 308.

35. Koestler, *Bricks to Babel*, 309.

36. Hamilton, *Koestler; A Biography*, 363.

37. Haywood, *Encyclopaedia of the Viking Age*, 111.

38. www.telegraph.co.uk/news/worldnews/europe/russia/3072167/Jewish-city -feared-by-Stalin-is-rediscovered.html.

39. Foote and Wilson, *The Viking Achievement,* 28.

40. Foote and Wilson, *The Viking Achievement,* 45.

41. Haywood, *Encyclopaedia of the Viking Age,* 198.

42. Billington, *The Face of Russia,* 3.

43. Haywood, *Encyclopaedia of the Viking Age,* 162.

44. Herrin, *Byzantium,* 137.

45. Longworth, *Russia's Empires,* 29.

46. Wilson, *A Criminal History of Mankind,* 261.

47. Herrin, *Byzantium,* 141.

3. Beauty Will Save the World

1. Herrin, *Byzantium,* 9.

2. Herrin, *Byzantium,* 9.

3. Wells, *A Short History Of the World,* 189.

4. Billington, *The Face of Russia,* 4.

5. Yeats, *The Collected Poems of W. B. Yeats,* 193.

6. In Raine, *Defending Ancient Springs,* 78.

7. Raine, *Defending Ancient Springs,* 131.

8. Herrin, *Byzantium,* 55.

9. Norwich, *A Short History of Byzantium,* 65.

10. Norwich, *A Short History of Byzantium,* 65.

11. Spengler, *The Decline of the West,* 1:200.

12. Spengler, *The Decline of the West,* 1:200.

13. Yeats, *The Collected Poems of W. B. Yeats,* 193.

14. Herrin, *Byzantium,* 179.

15. Yeats, *The Collected Poems of W. B. Yeats,* 194.

16. Ware, *The Orthodox Church,* 38.

17. Ware, *The Orthodox Church,* 38.

18. Ware, *The Orthodox Church,* 40.

19. Ware, *The Orthodox Church,* 39.

20. Ware, *The Orthodox Church,* 33.

21. Ware, *The Orthodox Church,* 34.

22. Herrin, *Byzantium,* 51.

23. Billington, *The Face of Russia,* 18.

24. Billington, *The Face of Russia*, 18.

25. Billington, *The Face of Russia*, 36.

26. https://mikedashhistory.com/2014/12/16/the-fayum-mummy-portraits.

27. Ware, *The Orthodox Church*, 32.

28. Ware, *The Orthodox Church*, 32.

29. Billington, *The Face of Russia*, 66.

30. Spengler, *The Decline of the West*, 1:44.

31. George Steiner, *Martin Heidegger*, 22–24. This distinction would hold during the rediscovery of the classical world that we call the Renaissance. As I point out in *The Quest for Hermes Trismegistus*, two kinds of humanism arose then, one based on Latin roots, the other on Greek, 157–60.

32. Lachman, *The Secret Teachers of the Western World*, 184–85.

33. Norwich, *A Short History of Byzantium*, 196.

4. The Lost Kingdom

1. Longworth, *Russia's Empires*, 37–38.

2. Billington, *The Icon and the Axe*, 6.

3. Billington, *The Icon and the Axe*, 6.

4. Norwich, *A Short History of Byzantium*, 210.

5. Norwich, *A Short History of Byzantium*, 208.

6. Ascherson, *Black Sea*, 41.

7. Ware, *The Orthodox Church*, 76.

8. Ware, *The Orthodox Church*, 78.

9. Plokhy, *Lost Kingdom: A History of Russian Nationalism from Ivan the Great to Vladimir Putin*, vii.

10. Plokhy, *Lost Kingdom: A History of Russian Nationalism from Ivan the Great to Vladimir Putin*, viii.

11. Billington, *The Icon and the Axe*, 5.

12. Billington, *The Icon and the Axe*, 7.

13. https://oca.org/saints/lives/2016/08/17/102310-venerable-alypius-the-iconographer-of-the-kiev-near-caves.

14. https://oca.org/saints/lives/2008/05/03/101282-icon-of-the-mother-of-god-of-sven.

15. Haustein-Bartsch, *Icons*, 20.

16. Haustein-Bartsch, *Icons*, 6.

17. Haustein-Bartsch, *Icons*, 6.

18. Haustein-Bartsch, *Icons,* 6.

19. Haustein-Bartsch, *Icons,* 11.

20. Billingsworth, *The Icon and the Axe,* 11; Longworth, *Russia's Empires,* 40.

5. From Mongols to Muscovy

1. Wilson, *A Criminal History of Mankind,* 306.

2. Billington, *The Icon and the Axe,* 13. But see Vernadsky, *A History of Russia,* 8.

3. See Khodakavsky, *Wooden Church Architecture of the Russian North,* 5–6; Billington, *The Icon and the Axe,* 125.

4. Vernadsky, *A History of Russia,* 91.

5. Billington, *The Face of Russia,* 44.

6. See Lachman, *The Secret Teachers of the Western World,* 37–38.

7. Vernadsky, *A History of Russia,* 94.

8. Billington, *The Face of Russia,* 43.

9. www.art-abode.com/emergence-russian-avant-garde-kazimir-malevich.

10. Haustein-Bartsch, *Icons,* 78.

11. www.rusicon.ru/eng/centre/press/revival.htm; and www.rbth.com/society /2014/10/11/conversing_with_god_but_not_for_everyone_the_revival _of_icon_painting_40535.html; and www.orthodoxartsjournal.org /contemporary-iconographers-russia.

12. Longworth, *Russia's Empires,* 57.

13. Norwich, *A Short History of Byzantium,* 304–5.

14. Norwich, *A Short History of Byzantium,* 350.

15. Vernadsky, *A History of Russia,* 91.

16. Billington, *The Face of Russia,* 56–57.

17. Longworth, *Russia's Empires,* 48; Billington, *The Icon and the Axe,* 48.

6. A Terrible Time of Troubles

1. Vernadsky, *A History of Russia,* 90–91.

2. For more see Lachman, *The Quest for Hermes Trismegistus,* 11–12.

3. Billington, *The Icon and the Axe,* 57.

4. Plokhy, *Lost Kingdom,* 20

5. Billington, *The Icon and the Axe,* 59.

6. Plokhy, *Lost Kingdom,* 23.

7. Plokhy, *Lost Kingdom,* 8–9.

8. Plokhy, *Lost Kingdom,* 9–10.

9. Dvornik, *The Slavs in European History and Civilization,* 367.

10. Longworth, *Russia's Empires,* 76.

11. Longworth, *Russia's Empires,* 76.

12. Longworth, *Russia's Empires,* 76.

13. Plokhy, *Lost Kingdom,* 14.

14. www.rbth.com/multimedia/pictures/2016/03/23/vladimir-monomakh
    -russian-ballsitic-missile-submarine_578287.

15. Plokhy, *The Lost Kingdom,* 14–15.

16. Billington, *The Icon and the Axe,* 59.

17. Billington, *The Icon and the Axe,* 86.

18. Billington, *The Icon and the Axe,* 86.

19. Billington, *The Icon and the Axe,* 86.

20. Borrero, *Russia: A Reference Guide from the Renaissance to the Present,*
    177.

21. Corinthians 1:18.

22. Berdyaev, *The Russian Idea,* 26.

23. Billington, *The Icon and the Axe,* 63.

24. Billington, *The Icon and the Axe,* 63.

25. Berdyaev, *The Russian Idea,* 25.

26. Wilson, *A Criminal History of Mankind,* 401.

27. Wilson, *A Criminal History of Mankind,* 401.

28. Longworth, *Russia's Empires,* 89–90.

29. Wilson, *Rasputin and the Fall of the Romanovs,* 59.

30. Longworth, *Russia's Empires,* 87.

31. Billington, *The Icon and the Axe,* 65.

32. Lachman, *In Search of P. D. Ouspensky,* 273.

33. Plokhy, *Lost Kingdom,* 15.

34. Wilson, *Rasputin and the Fall of the Romanovs,* 60.

35. www.nytimes.com/1988/02/14/books/the-prince-and-his-czar-letters-from
    -exile.html.

36. Rowland, *Medieval Russian Culture,* 172.

37. Longworth, *Russia's Empires,* 100.

38. Plokhy, *Lost Kingdom,* 17.

39. Ryan, "Magic and Divination: Old Russian Sources," 47.

40. Wilson, *Rasputin and the Fall of the Romanovs,* 61.

41. www.orthodoxchristianbooks.com/articles/555/ivan-terrible-saint-or
-sinner/; and www.theguardian.com/world/2016/aug/02/russian-orthodox
-church-head-backs-ivan-the-terrible-sculpture.

42. www.telegraph.co.uk/news/worldnews/europe/russia/1421276/Crusade-to
-make-Rasputin-a-saint-splits-church.html.

43. Ryan "Magic and Divination Old Russian Sources," 46.

7. A Window on the West

1. Lachman, *The Dedalus Book of Literary Suicides,* 19.

2. Billington, *The Icon and the Axe,* 131.

3. Ryan, "Magic and Divination: Old Russian Sources," 42.

4. Ryan, "Magic and Divination: Old Russian Sources," 42.

5. Ware, *The Orthodox Church,* 107.

6. Ware, *The Orthodox Church,* 106.

7. Plokhy, *Lost Kingdom,* 29.

8. Billington, *The Face of Russia,* color insert.

9. Plohky, *Lost Kingdom,* 41.

10. The *popovtsy* and *bezpopovtsy,* "with priests" and "without priests," respectively.

11. Billington, *The Icon and the Axe,* 134.

12. Berdyaev, *The Russian Idea,* 30.

13. Billington, *The Icon and the Axe,* 155.

14. Vernadsky, *A History of Russia,* 136.

15. Vernadsky, *A History of Russia,* 138.

16. See Lachman, *Madame Blavatsky: The Mother of Modern Spirituality,* 32.

17. Billington, *The Face of Russia,* 73.

18. An interesting look at Peter the Great and Freemasonry can be found here:
www.academia.edu/449346/A_Mason-Tsar_Freemasonry_and
_Fraternalism_at_the_Court_of_Peter_the_Great.

19. Collis, *The Petrine Instauration,* 32. Whether Wren was a Mason or not
remains a controversial point. An idea of the debate can be found here:
https://skirret.com/archive/misc/misc-w/wassirchristorpherwrenamason
.html, and here www.masonicdictionary.com/wren1.html, although these
are merely examples.

20. Ridley, *The Freemasons,* 133.

21. Ridley, *The Freemasons,* 133.

22. Lincoln, *Sunlight at Midnight,* 54.

23. Collis, *The Petrine Instauration,* 32.

24. Collis, *The Petrine Instauration,* 32.

25. Gogol, *The Diary of a Madman and Selected Stories,* 111; For Biely and Steiner, see Lachman, *A Dark Muse,* 212–219.

26. Lincoln, *Sunlight at Midnight,* 1.

27. Billington, *The Face of Russia,* 84.

28. Lachman, *Madame Blavatsky,* 19.

29. Wilson, *Rasputin and the Fall of the Romanovs,* 64.

30. Billington, *The Face of Russia,* 90.

31. Billington, *The Face of Russia,* 90.

32. Vernadsky, *A History of Russia,* 172.

33. Carlson, "Fashionable Occultism," 144.

34. Billington, *The Icon and the Axe,* 246.

35. Berdyaev, *The Russian Idea,* 35.

36. Lachman, *The Secret Teachers of the Western World,* 315–16.

37. Billington, *The Icon and the Axe,* 247.

38. Billington, *The Icon and the Axe,* 247.

39. Billington, *The Icon and the Axe,* 242.

40. Lachman, *The Dedalus Book of Literary Suicides,* 50–52.

41. Blavatsky, *H.P.B. Speaks,* vol. II, 63.

42. Goodrick-Clarke, *Helena Blavatsky,* 3.

43. Lachman, *The Dedalus Book of Literary Suicides,* 50–52.

44. Lachman, *Madame Blavatsky,* 20.

45. Berdyaev, *The Russian Idea,* 36.

46. Chamberlain, *Motherland,* 17.

47. Lachman, *The Dedalus Book of Literary Suicides,* 47.

48. Lachman, *The Dedalus Book of Literary Suicides,* 47.

49. Lachman, *A Dark Muse,* 49–52.

50. www.ritmanlibrary.com/2012/11/the-petersburg-crucible-alchemy-and-the -russian-nobility-in-catherine-the-greats-russia.

8. The Beautiful Soul

1. Wilson, *Rasputin and the Fall of the Romanovs,* 37, 39.

2. https://archive.org/stream/russiandissenter10cony/russiandissenter10cony _djvu.txt.

3. North, *A History of the Church from Pentecost to Present,* 463.

4. Lachman, *The Secret Teachers of the Western World,* 190–97.

5. Quoted in Wilson, *Rasputin and the Fall of the Romanovs,* 38.

6. www.atlasobscura.com/articles/the-curious-story-of-wierszalin-a-belarussian -prophets-1930s-forest-utopia.

7. Wilson, *Rasputin and the Fall of the Romanovs,* 40.

8. Lachman, *The Secret Teachers of the Western World,* 127.

9. Wilson, *Rasputin and the Fall of the Romanovs,* 41.

10. Lachman, *The Secret Teachers of the Western World,* 192.

11. Revelation 7:1–8 and 14:1–5.

12. www.rbth.com/politics_and_society/2016/08/25/the-skoptsy-the-story-of -the-russian-sect-that-maimed-for-its-beliefs_624175.

13. See Lachman, *A Dark Muse: A History of the Occult,* 30–34.

14. Billington, *The Icon and the Axe,* 255.

15. Lachman, *The Dedalus Book of Literary Suicides,* 87.

16. For more on Saint-Martin's philosophy see Lachman, *The Caretakers of the Cosmos,* 157–61.

17. Waite, *The Life of Louis Claude de Saint-Martin,* 113.

18. Lachman, *The Secret Teachers of the Western World,* 288–93.

19. See Berdyaev's introduction to Boehme's *Six Theosophic Points and Other Writings.*

20. http://courses.lumenlearning.com/boundless-worldhistory/Chapter /napoleons-defeat.

21. Wilson, *A Criminal History of Mankind,* 444.

22. Lachman, *The Dedalus Book of Literary Suicides,* 54–56; Lachman, *The Dedalus Book of Literary Suicides,* 56–62.

23. Troubetskoy, *Imperial Legend,* 70.

24. Troubetskoy, *Imperial Legend,* 70.

25. Lachman, *Madame Blavatsky,* 28.

26. Billington, *The Icon and the Axe,* 281.

27. Billington, *The Icon and the Axe,* 283.

28. Troubetskoy, *Imperial Legend,* 69.

29. Troubetskoy, *Imperial Legend,* 69.

30. Troubetskoy, *Imperial Legend,* 69.

31. Lachman, *Aleister Crowley,* 51–52.

32. Johnson, *The Masters Revealed,* 24.

33. Billington, *The Icon and the Axe,* 283.

34. Faivre, *Access to Western Esotericism,* 84. For more on Franz von Baader, whom I can only mention here, see also Faivre, 113–34.

35. Berdyaev, *The Russian Idea*, 70.

36. Berdyaev, *The Russian Idea*, 70.

37. Berlin, *Russian Thinkers*, 57.

38. Berlin, *The Crooked Timber of Humanity*, 118.

39. Berlin, *Russian Thinkers*, 57.

40. http://berlin.wolf.ox.ac.uk/lists/nachlass/maistre.pdf; Billington, *The Icon and the Axe*, 274.

41. Wilson, *Rasputin and the Fall of the Romanovs*, 66.

42. Berdyaev, *The Russian Idea*, 41.

43. Berlin, *Russian Thinkers*, xvii.

44. See Plokhy, *Lost Kingdom*.

45. Berlin, *Russian Thinkers*, 159.

46. Chamberlain, *Motherland*, 16.

47. Chamberlain, *Motherland*, 7.

48. Schelling, quoted in Bubner, *German Idealist Philosophy*, 209.

49. Chamberlain, *Motherland*, 11.

50. Such knowledge is the subject of my book *Lost Knowledge of the Imagination*.

51. Berlin, *Russian Thinkers*, 119.

52. See Billington, *Russia in Search of Itself*.

53. Odoevsky, *Russian Nights*, 8.

54. See Gibian, *The Portable Nineteenth-Century Russian Reader*, 8–22.

55. www.prospectmagazine.co.uk/magazine/whatisrussia.

56. Odoevsky, *Russian Nights*, 103.

57. Odoevsky, *Russian Nights*, 103.

58. Odoevsky, *Russian Nights*, 112.

59. In *Lost Knowledge of the Imagination* and *The Secret Teachers of the Western World*, I show how the kind of knowledge associated with this form of truth is linked to the right brain.

60. Schiller, *On the Aesthetic Education of Man*.

61. Chamberlain, *Motherland*, 36.

62. Chamberlain, *Motherland*, 36.

9. The New Men

1. Dostoyevsky, *The Idiot*, 3.

2. George Steiner, *Tolstoy or Dostoevsky*, 152.

3. Wilson, *The Outsider*, 203.

4. Dostoyevsky, *The Brothers Karamazov*, 380–81.

5. See Lachman, *A Dark Muse*, 73–84.

6. Chamberlain, *Motherland*, 34.

7. Chamberlain, *Motherland*, 34.

8. Lossky, *History of Russian Philosophy*, 52.

9. Lachman, *Turn Off Your Mind*, 357–60.

10. Lossky, *History of Russian Philosophy*, 60.

11. Berlin, *Russian Thinkers*, 152.

12. Berlin, *Russian Thinkers*, 152.

13. Quoted in Heller, *In the Age of Prose*, 102.

14. Lossky, *History of Russian Philosophy*, 53.

15. Lossky, *History of Russian Philosophy*, 53.

16. This is the overall title Isaiah Berlin gives to the four essays covering the origin of the Russian intelligentsia in his *Russian Thinkers*, 114–209.

17. Chamberlain, *Motherland*, 27.

18. Wilson, *A Criminal History of Mankind*, 518.

19. Chamberlain, *Motherland*, 65.

20. Wilson, *Order of Assassins*, 172.

21. Wilson, *A Criminal History of Mankind*, 519.

22. Wilson, *A Criminal History of Mankind*, 519.

23. Wilde, "The Soul of Man under Socialism," 19.

24. Berlin, *Russian Thinkers*, 194.

25. Berlin, *Russian Thinkers*, 194.

26. Chamberlain, *Motherland*, 68.

27. Billington, *Russia in Search of Itself*, 12.

28. Lossky, *History of Russian Philosophy*, 40.

29. Chamberlain, *Motherland*, 38.

30. Lossky, *History of Russian Philosophy*, 32.

31. Chamberlain, *Motherland*, 40.

32. See Lachman, *The Secret Teachers of the Western World*; Lachman, *Lost Knowledge of the Imagination*.

33. Lossky, *History of Russian Philosophy*, 41.

34. Lossky, *History of Russian Philosophy*, 40.

35. Quoted in Chamberlain, *Motherland*, 49.

36. Chamberlain, *Motherland*, 51.

37. MacKenzie and MacKenzie, *The Fabians*, 60.

38. MacKenzie and MacKenzie, *The Fabians*, 60–61.

39. See Lachman, *Lost Knowledge of the Imagination,* 17–24.

40. Weinberg, *The First Three Minutes,* 154; Lachman, *Dark Star Rising.*

41. Barzun, *From Dawn to Decadence,* 630.

42. Berlin, *Russian Thinkers,* 214; Chamberlain, *Motherland,* 67.

43. Berlin, *Russian Thinkers,* 214–15.

44. Berlin, *Russian Thinkers,* 216.

45. Chamberlain, *Motherland,* 70.

46. Quoted in Chamberlain, *Motherland,* 73.

47. Zouboff, introduction to Solovyov, *Lectures on Godmanhood,* 31.

10. The Silver Age

1. Solovyov, *Lectures on Godmanhood,* 12.

2. Solovyov, *Lectures on Godmanhood,* 13.

3. Solovyov, *Lectures on Godmanhood,* 14.

4. Quoted in Floyd, *Russia in Revolt,* 5.

5. Wilson, *A Criminal History of Mankind,* 518.

6. Wilson, *Rasputin and the Fall of the Romanovs,* 70.

7. Floyd, *Russia in Revolt,* 6.

8. Berlin, *Russian Thinkers,* 67.

9. Floyd, *Russia in Revolt,* 6.

10. https://pages.uoregon.edu/kimball/DstF.Puw.lct.htm#DstF.Puw.lct; Dostoyevsky, *Diary of a Writer,* vol. 2; Wilson, *Order of Assassins,* 165.

11. Lossky, *History of Russian Philosophy,* 88.

12. Solovyov, *Lectures on Godmanhood,* 9.

13. Lossky, *History of Russian Philosophy,* 83.

14. Lossky, *History of Russian Philosophy,* 91.

15. Lossky, *History of Russian Philosophy,* 10.

16. Lossky, *History of Russian Philosophy,* 12.

17. Lossky, *History of Russian Philosophy,* 63.

18. Lachman, *The Secret Teachers of the Western World,* 145–50.

19. Solovyov, *Lectures on Godmanhood,* 27.

20. Walker, *Venture with Ideas,* 141.

21. See Lachman, *Madame Blavatsky,* 301, n. 21.

22. Solovyov, *The Justification of the Good,* 190.

23. Solovyov, *The Justification of the Good,* vii.

24. Solovyov, *The Meaning of Love,* 15.

25. Lossky, *History of Russian Philosophy*, 120.

26. Solovyov, *Lectures on Godmanhood*, 28.

27. Solovyov, *Lectures on Godmanhood*, 27.

28. Solovyov, *War, Progress, and the End of History*, xxx.

29. Solovyov, *War, Progress, and the End of History*, xxx.

30. Bely was not alone in his concern. M. P. Shiel wrote of it in *The Yellow Peril* (1898), Jack London in *The Unparalleled Invasion* (1910), and also the Polish avant-garde polymath Witkacy in his unclassifiable work *Insatiability* (1927).

31. Bely, *Petersburg*, xix.

32. Solovyov, *War, Progress, and the End of History*, xxxi–xxxii.

33. Solovyov, *War, Progress, and the End of History*, xxxii.

34. Floyd, *Russia in Revolt*, 11.

35. Wilson, *Rasputin and the Fall of the Romanovs*, 58.

36. Shukman, *Rasputin*, 6.

37. Floyd, *Russia in Revolt*, 6.

38. Floyd, *Russia in Revolt*, 6.

39. Wilson, *Rasputin and the Fall of the Romanovs*, 87.

40. https://archive.org/details/courtofrussiann01hodguoft/page/n7.

41. Webb, *The Occult Establishment*, 168.

42. Dubois, *Fulcanelli and the Alchemical Revival*, 11.

43. Picknett and Prince, *The Sion Revelation*.

44. Lachman, *Lost Knowledge of the Imagination*, 109–17.

45. Picknett and Prince, *The Sion Revelation*, 368.

46. www.bloomberg.com/news/articles/2018-09-19/bannon-seeks-european-upset-with-appeal-to-eu-s-populist-forces.

47. Perry, *Gurdjieff in the Light of Tradition*, 21.

48. Webb, *The Harmonious Circle*, 58.

49. Perry, *Gurdjieff in the Light of Tradition*, 21.

50. Webb, *The Harmonious Circle*, 57.

51. Meyer and Brysac, *Tournament of Shadows*, 242.

52. Ware, *The Orthodox Church*, 115–16.

53. https://blogs.scientificamerican.com/observations/queen-victorias-curse-new-dna-evidence-solves-medical-and-murder-mysteries.

54. Floyd, *Russia in Revolt*, 55.

55. Floyd, *Russia in Revolt*, 58.

56. Floyd, *Russia in Revolt*, 64; Wilson, *Rasputin and the Fall of the Romanovs*, 82; Lachman, *In Search of P. D. Ouspensky*, 32–33.

57. Lachman, *In Search of P. D. Ouspensky*, 5.

58. Wilson, *Rasputin and the Fall of the Romanovs*, 84.

59. Shukman, *Rasputin*, 25.

60. Shukman, *Rasputin*, 104.

61. See my essay, "The Spiritual Detective: How Baudelaire Invented Symbolism by way of Swedenborg, E. T. A. Hoffmann, and Edgar Allan Poe" in McNeilly ed. *Philosophy, Literature, Mysticism: Essays of the Thought and Influence of Emanuel Swedenborg.*

62. Merzhkovsky's "Tolstoy and Dostoyevsky" (1901), for example, is the first work of criticism to pair the two Russian masters in a polarity that has by now become widely accepted; George Steiner, *Tolstoy or Dostoevsky*, 322.

63. Berdyaev, *Dream and Reality*, 144–45.

64. Berdyaev, *Dream and Reality*, 192–94.

65. Readers can find more about this affair in my afterword to Valery Briussov, *The Fiery Angel*, 393–411.

66. Lossky, *History of Russian Philosophy*, 199.

11. The End of Holy Russia

1. Quoted in Wilson, *Rasputin and the Fall of the Romanovs*.

2. www.atlasobscura.com/places/the-church-on-the-blood-yekaterinburg-russia; and www.telegraph.co.uk/news/worldnews/1353012/Romanovs-move-from -tsardom-to-sainthood.html.

3. Shukman, *Rasputin*, 106.

4. www.rt.com/russia/442902-romanov-anniversary-elizabeth-kremlin.

5. Ouspensky, *Letters from Russia 1919*, 3.

6. Ouspensky, *Letters from Russia 1919*, 1.

7. Ouspensky, *Letters from Russia 1919*, 6.

8. Lachman, *In Search of P. D. Ouspensky*, 167.

9. Ouspensky, *Letters from Russia 1919*, 21.

10. Laqueur, *Black Hundred*, 16–17.

11. Lossky, *History of Russian Philosophy*, 173.

12. Longworth, *Russia's Empires*, 232.

13. See Edmund Wilson's classic account *To the Finland Station* (1940).

14. Wilson, *Rasputin and the Fall of the Romanovs*, 196.

15. Berdyaev, *The Russian Idea*, 223.

16. Ouspensky, *Letters from Russia 1919*, 19.

17. Chamberlain, *Motherland,* 190.

18. Chamberlain, *Motherland,* 189.

19. Chamberlain, *Motherland,* 190.

20. Ware, *The Orthodox Church,* 121.

21. Ware, *The Orthodox Church,* 140.

22. www.nytimes.com/2018/12/16/world/asia/xinjiang-china-forced-labor -camps-uighurs.html.

23. Tomberg, *Russian Spirituality and Other Essays,* 127.

24. Schumacher, *A Guide for the Perplexed,* 1.

25. Lossky, *History of Russian Philosophy,* 75.

26. Young, *The Russian Cosmists,* 52.

27. Young, *The Russian Cosmists,* 52.

28. See Lachman, *Dark Star Rising,* 178–79.

29. Young, *The Russian Cosmists,* 69.

30. Lossky, *History of Russian Philosophy,* 75.

31. Dostoyevsky, *Diary of a Writer,* 1:246–47.

32. Tolstoy, *Resurrection* (1899).

33. Lossky, *History of Russian Philosophy,* 76.

34. Lossky, *History of Russian Philosophy,* 76.

35. Lossky, *History of Russian Philosophy,* 77.

36. Young, *The Russian Cosmists,* 49.

37. www.online-literature.com/leonid-andreyev/1479.

38. Lossky, *History of Russian Philosophy,* 76.

39. Lossky, *History of Russian Philosophy,* 77.

40. Young, *The Russian Cosmists,* 73.

41. Young, *The Russian Cosmists,* 73.

42. Lossky, *History of Russian Philosophy,* 76.

43. Berdyaev, *The Russian Idea,* 223.

44. Lossky, *History of Russian Philosophy,* 235.

45. Berdyaev, *Dream and Reality,* 20.

46. I discuss this in *The Caretakers of the Cosmos.*

47. Berdyaev, *Dream and Reality,* 20.

48. Berdyaev, *Dream and Reality,* 24.

49. Lossky, *History of Russian Philosophy,* 173.

50. Lossky, *History of Russian Philosophy,* 243.

51. Bernard Shaw, *The Revolutionist's Handbook,* at www.bartleby.com/157/5.html.

52. Shaw, *The Revolutionist's Handbook,* 246.

53. For a full and fascinating account of this expulsion see Leslie Chamberlain's *The Philosophy Steamer: Lenin and the Exile of the Intelligentsia*.

54. Young, *The Russian Cosmists*, 119.

55. Some translations have the title *The Undying Light*.

56. Quoted in Lossky, *History of Russian Philosophy*, 194.

57. Lossky, *History of Russian Philosophy*, 194.

58. Corbin, *The Voyage and the Messenger*, xxxii–xxxiii.

59. Young, *The Russian Cosmists*, 108.

60. Quoted in Young, *The Russian Cosmists*, 111; William Blake: "A Robin Redbreast in a Cage / Puts all Heaven in a Rage," from "Auguries of Innocence"; T. S. Eliot "Do I dare / Disturb the universe?" from "The Love Song of J. Alfred Prufrock."

61. Lossky, *History of Russian Philosophy*, 267.

62. Whitehead, *Essays in Science and Philosophy*, 72–74.

63. Ouspensky, *Tertium Organum*, 223–24.

64. Lossky, *History of Russian Philosophy*, 268.

65. Lossky, *History of Russian Philosophy*, 176.

66. Young, *The Russian Cosmists*, 130.

67. Young, *The Russian Cosmists*, 123.

12. ESP in the USSR

1. I tell this story at greater length in *Politics and the Occult*, 142–53.

2. Illies, *1913 The Year Before the Storm*, 121–23.

3. Znamenski, *Red Shambhala*, 162.

4. www.therestisnoise.com/2014/04/the-roerich-cornerstone.html.

5. David-Neel, *Magic and Mystery in Tibet*, 94.

6. For Roerich's second attempt at the Shambhala Revolution, see *Politics and the Occult*.

7. Robert Powell in Tomberg, *Lazarus Come Forth!* vi.

8. Gutkin, "The Magic of Words," 242 n.48.

9. Tomberg, *Russian Spirituality and Other Essays*, 168–72.

10. Von Meydell, "Anthroposophy in Russia," 158.

11. Rosenthal, *The Occult in Russian and Soviet Culture*, 1.

12. Lachman, *In Search of P. D. Ouspensky*, 63–66.

13. Lachman, *The Dedalus Book of Literary Suicides*, 125.

14. Rosenthal, *The Occult in Russian and Soviet Culture*, 405–6.

15. https://blogs.bl.uk/european/2017/06/the-death-of-lenin.html.

16. https://edition.cnn.com/travel/article/lenin-mausoleum-moscow/index.html.

17. See Lövgren, "Sergei Eisenstein's Gnostic Circle," 273–98.

18. Rosenthal, *The Occult in Russian and Soviet Culture,* 413; see also https://www.history.com/this-day-in-history/stalins-body-removed-from-lenins-tomb.

19. Rosenthal, *The Occult in Russian and Soviet Culture,* 25.

20. www.historytoday.com/richard-cavendish/leon-trotsky-assassinated-mexico.

21. Roerich, *Altai-Himalaya,* 24.

22. See Agursky, "An Occult Source of Socialist Realism," 247–72.

23. Wilson, *Below the Iceberg,* 94–96.

24. www.atlasobscura.com/articles/the-true-story-of-dr-voronoffs-plan-to-use-monkey-testicles-to-make-us-immortal.

25. Quoted in Hagemeister, "Russian Cosmism in the 1920s and Today," 194.

26. Agursky, "An Occult Source of Socialist Realism," 265.

27. Peters, *Gurdjieff Remembered,* in *My Journey with a Mystic,* 251.

28. I am indebted to Andrei Znamenski's *Red Shambhala* (2011) for this account.

29. For a more contemporary expression of "positive thinking" in politics, see Lachman, *Dark Star Rising,* 25–49.

30. See Evola, *Revolt against the Modern World;* see also Hale, *Himmler's Crusade.*

31. This was an idea, in fact, that T. Lopsang Rampa used to great success in his book *The Cave of the Ancients* (1963), part of series of very imaginative adventures set in the Himalayas.

32. Rosenthal, *The Occult in Russian and Soviet Culture,* 407–8.

33. Lachman, *Dark Star Rising,* 160–65.

34. For Vernadsky's, Bannon's, and Gurdjieff's links to Biosphere 2, see Lachman, *Dark Star Rising,* 163–64.

35. Clover, *Black Wind, White Snow,* 211; Ouspensky, *In Search of the Miraculous,* 24–26.

36. Playfair and Hill, *The Cycles of Heaven,* 277.

37. Lachman, "As Above, So Below: Are Cosmic Forces at Work on Earth?" 11–18.

38. An interesting take on this development can be found in Armando Iannucci's 2017 film, *The Death of Stalin.*

39. www.rbth.com/literature/2014/04/14/meet_yuri_mamleev_insanity_murder_and_sexual_depravity_on_the_quest_for_35879.html.

40. For much of this section I am indebted to Maureen Laruelle's fascinating paper "The Iuzhinskii Circle: Far-Right Metaphysics in the Soviet Underground and its Legacy Today," at www.academia.edu/24268164/_The_Iuzhinskii _Circle_Far-Right_Metaphysics_in_the_Soviet_Underground_and_Its _Legacy_Today_The_Russian_Review_74_2015_563_580 published in *The Russian Review* 74 (2015): 563–80. I have to mention that on p. 566 Ms. Laruelle mistakenly claims that in 1909, P. D. Ouspensky "theorized" about Gurdjieff's ideas in his book *The Fourth Dimension,* published that year. Ouspensky did not meet Gurdjieff until 1915 and did not publish anything about him in his lifetime. His account of his years with Gurdjieff, *In Search of the Miraculous,* was published after his death in 1947; see Lachman, *In Search of P. D. Ouspensky.*

41. See my *Turn Off Your Mind,* 13–38, for an account of the book's impact on the 1960s "occult revival."

42. Pauwels and Bergier, *The Morning of the Magicians,* 180.

43. Pauwels, *Gurdjieff.*

44. https://traditionalistblog.blogspot.com/2007/03/russian-traditionalism -started-with.html.

45. Laurelle, "The Iuzhinskii Circle," 566.

46. Clover, *Black Wind, White Snow,* 157.

47. https://traditionalistblog.blogspot.com/2007/03/russian-traditionalism -started-with.html.

48. Lachman, *Dark Star Rising,* 164.

49. www.gurdjiefflegacy.org/40articles/neosufism.htm.

50. Lachman, *Turn Off Your Mind,* 235–36.

51. Ostrander and Schroeder, *Psychic Discoveries,* xiii; also www.atlasobscura .com/articles/how-a-famed-new-age-retreat-center-helped-end-the-cold-war.

52. Ostrander and Schroeder, *Psychic Discoveries,* 164–65.

53. Wilson, *Mysteries,* 388–90.

54. Ostrander and Schroeder, *Psychic Discoveries,* 6–7, 379.

13. The Return of Holy Russia?

1. www.nbcnews.com/politics/politics-news/u-s-suspends-nuclear-treaty-russia -plans-pull-out-6-n965751.

2. www.bbc.co.uk/news/world-europe-46458604.

3. www.washingtonpost.com/news/worldviews/wp/2018/03/03/putin-says

-he-wishes-he-could-change-the-collapse-of-the-soviet-union-many-russians
-agree/?utm_term=.041a56cddfd7.

4. Lachman, *Dark Star Rising,* 175–76.

5. Billington, *Russia in Search of Itself,* xii.

6. Billington, *Russia in Search of Itself,* xii.

7. Menzel, introduction to *The New Age of Russia,* 14.

8. www.atlasobscura.com/articles/how-a-famed-new-age-retreat-center
-helped-end-the-cold-war.

9. www.atlasobscura.com/articles/how-a-famed-new-age-retreat-center-helped
-end-the-cold-war.

10. Kripal, *Esalen,* 396.

11. www.atlasobscura.com/articles/how-a-famed-new-age-retreat-center-helped
-end-the-cold-war.

12. Ostrander and Schroeder, *Psychic Discoveries,* 332.

13. Ostrander and Schroeder, *Psychic Discoveries,* 332.

14. Menzel, *The New Age of Russia,* 13.

15. Scanlan, *Russian Thought After Communism,* 6.

16. Menzel, *The New Age of Russia,* 13.

17. https://culture.pl/en/article/roots-revival-how-slavic-faith-returned-to-poland.

18. https://edition.cnn.com/2017/03/30/europe/russian-orthodox-church
-resurgence/index.html.

19. https://brewminate.com/the-native-faith-religious-nationalism-in-slavic
-neo-paganism.

20. www.slavorum.org/bizarre-spiritual-movement-ringing-cedars-anastasianism
-is-a-religion-based-on-a-novel.

21. www.ringingcedars.com.

22. https://vmegre.com/en/events/39457.

23. See Lachman, *The Secret Teachers of the Western World,* 463–64.

24. www.telegraph.co.uk/culture/hay-festival/11627328/Humans-could
-download-brains-on-to-a-computer-and-live-forever.html.

25. Young, *The Russian Cosmists,* 219.

26. Young, *The Russian Cosmists,* 222.

27. Young, *The Russian Cosmists,* 225.

28. https://abcnews.go.com/International/putins-chief-staff-claims
-invented-nooscope-study-collective/story?id=41429546.

29. https://abcnews.go.com/International/putins-chief-staff-claims-invented
-nooscope-study-collective/story?id=41429546. 30. https://www.theguardian

.com/politics/2017/feb/26/robert-mercer-breitbart-war-on-media-steve-banon -donald-trump-nigel-farage.

31. Lachman, *Dark Star Rising,* 138–44; readers can find an outline of Gumilev's ideas here: https://motherboard.vice.com/en_us/article/mg9vvn /how-our-likes-helped-trump-win.

32. Laruelle, *An Ideology of Empire,* 10.

33. See Ouspensky, *In Search of the Miraculous,* 24–26, 85–86.

34. Lachman, *Dark Star Rising,* 162–63.

35. Lachman, *Dark Star Rising,* chapter 11.

36. http://content.time.com/time/arts/article/0,8599,1829150,00.html.

37. Epstein, "Daniil Andreev and the Mysticism of Femininity," 330.

38. Epstein, "Daniil Andreev and the Mysticism of Femininity," 328.

39. https://uk.news.yahoo.com/smartphones-paving-way-antichrist-says -180822244.html.

40. http://woked.co/man-second-coming-of-jesus-following.

41. www.nybooks.com/daily/2018/03/16/ivan-ilyin-putins-philosopher -of-russian-fascism.

42. See Walter Benjamin's "Theses on the Philosophy of History," *Illuminations,* 249, in which he famously compares history to "one single catastrophe which keeps piling wreckage upon wreckage."

43. Again, Walter Benjamin, an unorthodox Marxist to be sure, expresses a similar view to Ilyin's. See his "Critique of Violence" in *Reflections.*

44. For Evola and Mussolini and Hitler, see Lachman, *Dark Star Rising,* 125–30.

45. www.nybooks.com/daily/2018/03/16/ivan-ilyin-putins-philosopher -of-russian-fascism.

46. www.nytimes.com/1985/11/13/books/solzhenitsyn-and-anti-semitism-a -new-debate.html.

47. www.nytimes.com/1985/11/13/books/solzhenitsyn-and-anti-semitism-a -new-debate.html.

48. Chamberlain, *The Philosophy Steamer,* 257.

49. Lachman, *Dark Star Rising,* 127–29.

50. Chamberlain, *The Philosophy Steamer,* 257.

51. Chamberlain, *The Philosophy Steamer,* 257; Scanlan, *Russian Thought After Communism,* 168.

52. See www.nybooks.com/daily/2018/03/16/ivan-ilyin-putins-philosopher -of-russian-fascism/ and http://www.openculture.com/2018/06/an-introduction

-to-ivan-ilyin.html and https://www.foreignaffairs.com/articles /russian-federation/2015-09-20/putins-philosopher.

53. www.opendemocracy.net/mark-galeotti/education-in-putin-s-russia-isn-t -about-history-but-scripture.

54. http://vdnh.ru/events/vystavki.

55. www.rbth.com/society.

56. www.nytimes.com/2016/11/10/arts/design/museum-of-the-second-world -war-in-poland-debate.html.

57. www.huffingtonpost.com/nathan-gardels/putin-g-8_b_4912108.html.

58. Shaun Kenney, www.academia.edu/37635783/Putins_Political_Philosophers _Neo-Orthodoxy_Identitarianism_and_the_Russian_Federation ?auto=download.

59. www.politico.com/magazine/story/2014/03/new-cold-war-russia-104954.

60. https://observer.com/2017/11/russia-conducts-nuclear-exercises-amid -orthodox-end-times-talk.

61. Wilson, *Rasputin and the Fall of the Romanovs,* 58.

62. https://catholicherald.co.uk/news/2019/01/08/ecumenical-patriarch -recognizes-independence-of-orthodox-church-of-ukraine.

63. www.themoscowtimes.com/2019/02/06/russian-witches-cast-spells -in-putins-support-video-a64420.

64. www.dailymail.co.uk/news/article-6674431/Coven-Russian-witches -perform-circle-power-ritual-Moscow-support-President-Putin.html.

65. www.bbc.co.uk/news/world-us-canada-39090334.

66. http://en.kremlin.ru/events/president/news/19825.

67. http://en.kremlin.ru/events/president/news/19825.

Epilogue. A Third Way?

1. Lachman, *The Caretakers of the Cosmos,* 108–11.

2. Lachman, "From Russia with Love," 54–59.

3. Lachman, *Lost Knowledge of the Imagination,* 21–26.

4. Bergson, *An Introduction to Metaphysics,* 1.

5. Lachman, *The Caretakers of the Cosmos,* 222–24.

6. Hesse, *My Belief,* 81.

7. See Lachman, *The Secret Teachers of the Western World,* 463–64.

Bibliography

Agursky, Mikhail. "An Occult Source of Socialist Realism." In Rosenthal, *The Occult in Russian and Soviet Culture*, 247–72. Ithaca, N.Y.: Cornell University Press, 1997.

Anderson, William. *The Face of Glory*. London: Bloomsbury, 1996.

Annenkov, Pavel. *The Extraordinary Decade*. Ann Arbor: University of Michigan Press, 1981.

Ascherson, Neal. *Black Sea*. London: Vintage Books, 2015.

Barzun, Jacques. *From Dawn to Decadence*. New York: HarperCollins, 2000.

Bely, Andrei. *Petersburg*. London: Penguin Books, 1995.

Benjamin, Walter. "Critique of Violence." In *Reflections*. New York: Harcourt Brace Jovanovich, 1978.

———. "Theses on the Philosophy of History." In *Illuminations*. London: Fontana Press, 1992.

Berdyaev, Nikolai. *Dream and Reality*. London: Geoffrey Bles, 1950.

———. *The Russian Idea*. Hudson, N.Y.: Lindisfarne Press, 1992.

Bergson, Henri. *An Introduction to Metaphysics*. Translated by T. E. Hulme. New York: G. P. Putnam's Sons, 1912.

Berlin, Isaiah. *The Crooked Timber of Humanity*. London: Pimlico, 2003.

———. *Russian Thinkers*. London: Penguin Books, 1979.

Billington, James H. *The Face of Russia*. New York: TV Books, 1998.

———. *The Icon and the Axe*. New York: Vintage Books, 1970.

———. *Russia in Search of Itself*. Washington, D.C.: Woodrow Wilson Center Press, 2004.

Blavatsky, Helena Petrovna. *H.P.B. Speaks*. Vol. 2. Edited by C. Jinarajadasa. Adyar: Theosophical Publishing House, 1951.

Boehme, Jacob. *Six Theosophic Points and Other Writings.* Ann Arbor: University of Michigan Press, 1958.

Borrero, Mauricio. *Russia: A Reference Guide from the Renaissance to the Present.* New York: Facts on File, 2004.

Briussov, Valery. *The Fiery Angel.* Translated by Ivor Montagu and Sergei Nalbandov. Sawtry, UK: Dedalus Books, 2005.

Bubner, Rüdiger, ed. *German Idealist Philosophy.* London: Penguin Books, 1997.

Carlson, Maria. "Fashionable Occultism: Spiritualism, Theosophy, Freemasonry, and Hermeticism in Fin-de-Siècle Russia." In Rosenthal, *The Occult in Russian and Soviet Culture,* 135–152. Ithaca, N.Y.: Cornell University Press, 1997.

Chamberlain, Leslie. *Motherland.* New York: Overlook Press, 2007.

———. *The Philosophy Steamer: Lenin and the Exile of the Intelligentsia.* London: Atlantic Books, 2006.

Clover, Charles. *Black Wind, White Snow: The Rise of Russia's New Nationalism.* London: Yale University Press, 2016.

Collis, Robert. *The Petrine Instauration: Religion, Esotericism and Science at the Court of Peter the Great.* Leiden, Netherlands: Brill, 2001.

Corbin, Henry. *The Voyage and the Messenger.* Berkeley, Cal.: North Atlantic Books, 1998.

David-Neel, Alexandra. *Magic and Mystery in Tibet.* London: Souvenir Press, 2009.

Dostoyevsky, Fyodor. *The Brothers Karamazov.* Translated by Constance Garnett. New York: Modern Library, n.d.

———. *Diary of a Writer.* Vol 2. London: Cassel and Company, 1949.

———. *The Idiot.* Translated by Constance Garnett. New York: Modern Library, 1962.

Dubois, Geneviéve. *Fulcanelli and the Alchemical Revival.* Rochester, Vt.: Destiny Books, 2006.

Dvornik, Francis. *The Slavs in European History and Civilization.* New Brunswick, N.J.: Rutgers University Press, 1962.

Epstein, Mikhail. "Daniil Andreev and the Mysticism of Femininity." In Rosenthal, *The Occult in Russian and Soviet Culture,* 325–56. Ithaca, N.Y.: Cornell University Press, 1997.

Evola, Julius. *Revolt against the Modern World.* Translated by Guido Stucco. Rochester, Vt.: Inner Traditions, 1995.

Faivre, Antoine. *Access to Western Esotericism.* Albany: State University of New York Press, 1994.

Floyd, David. *Russia in Revolt.* London: Macdonald and Company, 1969.

Foote, P. G., and D. M. Wilson. *The Viking Achievement.* London: Sidgwick and Jackson, 1979.

Fülöp-Miller, René. *Rasputin: The Holy Devil.* New York: Garden City Publishing Co., 1928.

Gibian, George, ed. *The Portable Nineteenth-Century Russian Reader.* New York: Penguin, 1993.

Gogol, Nikolai. *Dead Souls.* Translated by David Magarshack. London: Penguin Books, 1961.

———. *The Diary of a Madman and Selected Stories.* Translated by Ronal Wilks. London: Penguin Books, 2005.

Gooch, Stan. *Cities of Dreams.* London: Aulis Books, 1995.

Goodrick-Clarke, Nicholas, ed. *Helena Blavatsky.* Western Esoteric Masters Series. Berkeley, Cal.: North Atlantic Books, 2004.

Gurdjieff, G. I. *Meetings with Remarkable Men.* Introduction by Gary Lachman. London: Penguin Modern Classics, 2015.

Gutkin, Irina. "The Magic of Words: Symbolism, Futurism, Socialist Realism." In Rosenthal, *The Occult in Russian and Soviet Culture,* 225–46. Ithaca, N.Y.: Cornell University Press, 1997.

Hagemeister, Michael. "Russian Cosmism in the 1920s and Today." In Rosenthal, *The Occult in Russian and Soviet Culture,* 185–202. Ithaca, N.Y.: Cornell University Press, 1997.

Hale, Christopher. *Himmler's Crusade.* Hoboken: John Wiley and Sons, 2005.

Hamilton, Iain. *Koestler: A Biography.* London: Secker & Warburg, 1982.

Haustein-Bartsch, Eva. *Icons.* London: Taschen, n.d.

Haywood, John. *Encyclopaedia of the Viking Age.* London: Thames and Hudson, 2000.

Heller, Erich. *In the Age of Prose.* Cambridge: Cambridge University Press, 1984.

Hendry, J. F. *The Sacred Threshold: A Life of Rilke.* Manchester, UK: Carcanet Press, 1983.

Herrin, Judith. *Byzantium.* London: Penguin Books, 2008.

Hesse, Hermann. *My Belief.* London: Jonathan Cape, 1976.

Illies, Florian. *1913: The Year before the Storm.* London: Clerkenwell Press, 2013.

Ilyin, Ivan. *On Resisting Evil with Force.* Berlin: Privately published, 1925.

Johnson, K. Paul. *The Masters Revealed: Madame Blavatsky and the Myth of the Great White Lodge.* Albany: State University of New York Press, 1994.

Khodakavsky, Evgeny. *Wooden Church Architecture of the Russian North.* London: Routledge, 2015.

Koestler, Arthur. *Bricks to Babel*. New York: Random House, 1980.

Kripal, Jeffrey. *Esalen: America and the Religion of No Religion*. Chicago: University of Chicago Press, 2008.

Lachman, Gary. *A Dark Muse: A History of the Occult*. New York: Thunder's Mouth Press, 2005.

———. *Aleister Crowley: Magick, Rock and Roll, and the Wickedest Man in the World*. New York: Tarcher Perigee, 2014.

———. "As Above, So Below: Are Cosmic Forces at Work on Earth?" *New Dawn* 12, no. 3 (special issue): 11–18.

———. *The Caretakers of the Cosmos*. Edinburgh: Floris Books, 2013.

———. *Dark Star Rising: Magic and Power in the Age of Trump*. London: Penguin Publishing, 2018.

———. *The Dedalus Book of Literary Suicides: Dead Letters*. Sawtry, UK: Dedalus Books, 2008.

———. "From Russia with Love." *Gnosis*, no. 43. (Spring 1997): 54–59.

———. *In Search of P. D. Ouspensky*. Wheaton, Ill.: Quest Books, 2006.

———. *Lost Knowledge of the Imagination*. Edinburgh: Floris Books, 2017.

———. *Madame Blavatsky: The Mother of Modern Spirituality*. New York: Tarcher Penguin, 2012.

———. *Politics and the Occult: The Left, the Right, and the Radically Unseen*. Wheaton, Ill.: Quest Books, 2008.

———. *The Quest for Hermes Trismegistus*. Wheaton, Ill.: Quest Books, 2011.

———. *Rudolf Steiner: An Introduction to His Life and Work*. New York: Tarcher/Penguin, 2007.

———. *The Secret Teachers of the Western World*. New York: Tarcher Penguin, 2015.

———. "The Spiritual Detective: How Baudelaire Invented Symbolism by Way of Swedenborg, E. T. A. Hoffmann, and Edgar Allan Poe." In Stephen McNeilly, ed. *Philosophy, Literature, Mysticism: Essays on the Thought and Influence of Emanuel Swedenborg*. London: The Swedenborg Society, 2013.

———. *Turn Off Your Mind: The Mystic Sixties and the Dark Side of the Age of Aquarius*. New York: Disinformation Co., 2003.

Laqueur, Walter. *Black Hundred*. New York: HarperCollins, 1993.

Laruelle, Marlene. *An Ideology of Empire*. Baltimore: Johns Hopkins University Press, 2008.

———. "The Iuzhinskii Circle: Far-Right Metaphysics in the Soviet Underground and its Legacy Today." *The Russian Review* 74 (2015): 563–80.

Lawrence, T. E. *The Seven Pillars of Wisdom*. Harmondsworth, England: Penguin Books, 1979.

Lincoln, W. Bruce. *Sunlight at Midnight: St. Petersburg and the Rise of Modern Russia*. Oxford, UK: Perseus Books, 2001.

Longworth, Philip. *Russia's Empires*. London: John Murray, 2006.

Lossky, N. O. *History of Russian Philosophy*. London: George Allen and Unwin, Ltd., 1952.

Lövgren, Håkan. "Sergei Eisenstein's Gnostic Circle." In Rosenthal, *The Occult in Russian and Soviet Culture*, 273–98. Ithaca, N.Y.: Cornell University Press, 1997.

MacKenzie, Norman, and Jeanne MacKenzie. *The Fabians*. New York: Simon & Schuster, 1977.

Menzel, Birgit. Introduction to *The New Age of Russia,* edited by Michael Hagermeister, Birgit Menzel, and Bernice Glatzer Rosenthal. Munich-Berlin: Verlag Otto Sagner, 2012.

Merzhkovsky, Dimitry. "Tolstoy and Dostoyevsky." *Mir iskusstva,* 1901.

Meyer, Karl, and Shareen Brysac. *Tournament of Shadows*. London: Little, Brown and Co., 2001.

North, James B. *A History of the Church from Pentecost to Present*. Joplin: College Press Publishing Company, 1991.

Norwich, John Julius. *A Short History of Byzantium*. London: Penguin Books, 1997, 2013.

Odoevsky, Vladimir Fedorovich. *Russian Nights*. Translated by Ralph E. Matlaw. Evanston, Ill.: Northwestern University Press, 1997.

Ostrander, Sheila, and Lynn Schroeder. *Psychic Discoveries: The Iron Curtain Lifted*. London: Souvenir Press, 1999.

Ouspensky, P. D. *In Search of the Miraculous*. New York: Harcourt, Brace, 1949.

———. *Letters from Russia 1919*. London: Penguin Books, 1991.

———. *A New Model of the Universe*. New York: Alfred A. Knopf, 1969.

———. *Talks with a Devil*. New York: Alfred A. Knopf, 1973.

———. *Tertium Organum*. New York: Alfred A. Knopf, 1981.

Pauwels, Louis. *Gurdjieff.* New York: Weiser, 1972.

Pauwels, Louis, and Jacques Bergier. *The Morning of the Magicians*. New York: Dorset Press, 1988.

Perry, Whitall N. *Gurdjieff in the Light of Tradition*. Bedfont, Middlesex, UK: Perennial Books, 1978.

Peters, Fritz. *My Journey with a Mystic*. Laguna: Tale Weaver Press, 1986.

Picknett, Lynn, and Clive Prince. *The Sion Revelation*. London: Time Warner Books, 2006.

Playfair, Guy Lyon, and Scott Hill. *The Cycles of Heaven*. London: Souvenir Press, 1978.

Plokhy, Serhii. *Lost Kingdom: A History of Russian Nationalism from Ivan the Great to Vladimir Putin*. London: Allen Lane, 2017.

Raine, Kathleen. *Defending Ancient Springs*. West Stockbridge, Mass.: Lindisfarne Press, 1985.

Rampa, T. Lopsang. *The Cave of the Ancients*. New York: Ballantine Books, 1963.

Roerich, Nicholas. *Altai-Himalaya*. Kempton, Ill.: Adventures Unlimited Press, 2001.

Rowland, Daniel Bruce. *Medieval Russian Culture*. Berkeley: University of California Press, 1994.

Ridley, Jasper. *The Freemasons*. London: Robinson, 1999.

Rosenthal, Bernice Glatzer, ed. *The Occult in Russian and Soviet Culture*. Ithaca, N.Y.: Cornell University Press, 1997.

Ryan, W. F. "Magic and Divination: Old Russian Sources." In Rosenthal, *The Occult in Russian and Soviet Culture*, 35–58. Ithaca, N.Y.: Cornell University Press, 1997.

Scanlan James., ed. *Russian Thought after Communism*. Armonk, N.Y.: M. E. Sharpe, 1994.

Schelling, Friedrich Wilhelm Joseph von. *Ideas for a Philosophy of Nature*. In *German Idealist Philosophy*, edited by Rüdiger Bubner. London: Penguin Books, 1997.

Schiller, Friedrich. *On The Aesthetic Education of Man*. New York: Fredrick Ungar Publishing, 1971.

Schumacher, E. F. *A Guide for the Perplexed*. New York: Harper and Row, 1977.

Shaw, George Bernard. *Back to Methuselah*. New York: Brentano's, 1922.

———. [John Tanner, pseud.]. *The Revolutionist's Handbook and Pocket Companion* https://www.bartleby.com/157/5.html.

Shukman, Harold. *Rasputin*. Stroud, UK: Sutton Publishing, 1997.

Smoley, Richard. *Inner Christianity*. Boston: Shambhala, 2002.

Solovyov, Vladimir. *The Justification of the Good*. Translated by Boris Jakim. London: Constable and Company, 1918.

———. *Lectures on Godmanhood*. Translated by Peter Zouboff. London: Denis Dobson Ltd., 1948.

———. *The Crisis of Western Philosophy*. West Stockbridge, Mass.: Lindisfarne Press, 1996.

———. *The Meaning of Love.* West Stockbridge, Mass.: Lindisfarne Press, 1985.

———. *War, Progress, and the End of History.* London: University of London Press, 1915.

Solzhenitsyn, Alexander. *August 1914.* Translated by Michael Glenny. New York: Farrar, Straus, and Giroux, 1971.

Sorokin, Vladimir. *Day of the Oprichnik.* Translated by Jamey Gambrell. New York: Farrar, Strauss, Giroux, 2006.

Spengler, Oswald. *The Decline of the West.* Vol. 1. Translated by Charles Francis Atkinson. New York: Alfred A. Knopf, 1937.

Steiner, George. *Martin Heidegger.* Chicago: University of Chicago Press, 1987.

———. *Tolstoy or Dostoevsky.* London: Faber and Faber, 1980.

Steiner, Rudolf. *Spiritualism, Madame Blavatsky, and Theosophy.* Great Barrington, Mass.: Anthroposophic Press, 2001.

Tolstoy, Leo. *Resurrection.* Translated by Louise Maude. New York: Dodd Mead, 1890.

Tomberg, Valentin. *Lazarus Come Forth!* Translated by Robert Powell and James Morgante. Great Barrington, Mass.: Lindisfarne Books, 2006.

———. *Russian Spirituality and Other Essays.* San Rafael, Cal.: LogoSophia, 2010.

Toynbee, Arnold. *A Study of History.* Abridged edition. London: Oxford University Press, 1972.

Troubetskoy, Alexis S. *Imperial Legend: The Mysterious Disappearance of Tsar Alexander I.* New York: Arcade Publishing, 2013.

Vernadsky, George. *A History of Russia.* New Haven: Yale University Press, 1944.

Von Meydell, Renata. "Anthroposophy in Russia." In Rosenthal, *The Occult in Russian and Soviet Culture,* 153–167. Ithaca, N.Y.: Cornell University Press, 1997.

Waite, A. E. *The Life of Louis Claude de Saint-Martin.* London: Philip Wellby, 1901.

Walker, Kenneth. *Venture with Ideas.* New York: Weiser, 1972.

Ware, Timothy. *The Orthodox Church.* London: Penguin Books, 2015.

Webb, James. *The Harmonious Circle.* New York: G. P. Putnam's Sons, 1980.

———. *The Occult Establishment.* La Salle, Ill.: Open Court, 1976.

Weinberg, Steven. *The First Three Minutes.* New York: Basic Books, 1993.

Wells, H. G. *God the Invisible King.* London: Cassell, 1917.

———. *A Short History of the World.* London: Penguin Books, 2006.

Whitehead, Alfred North. *Essays in Science and Philosophy*. London: Rider, 1948.

Wilde, Oscar. "The Decay of Lying." *The Complete Writings of Oscar Wilde*. New York: The Nottingham Society, 1909.

———. "The Soul of Man under Socialism." In *De Profundis and Other Writings*. London: Penguin Books, 1986.

Wilson, Colin. *Below the Iceberg*. San Bernardino, Cal.: The Borgo Press, 1998.

———. *A Criminal History of Mankind*. New York: G. P. Putnam's Sons, 1984.

———. *Dreaming to Some Purpose*. London: Century, 2004.

———. *Mysteries*. London: Watkins Publishing, 2006.

———. *The Occult*. New York: Random House, 1971.

———. *Order of Assassins*. Frogmore, UK: Panther Books, 1975.

———. *The Outsider*. New York: Penguin Random House, 2016.

———. *Rasputin and the Fall of the Romanovs*. New York: Farrar, Strauss and Co., 1964.

Wilson, Edmund. *To The Finland Station*. New York: Doubleday and Co., 1940.

Yeats, W. B. *The Collected Poems of W. B. Yeats*. New York: Macmillan, 1989.

Young, George M. *The Russian Cosmists*. Oxford: Oxford University Press, 2012.

Znamenski, Andrei. *Red Shambhala*. Wheaton, Ill.: Quest Books, 2011.

Zouboff, Peter. Introduction to *Lectures on Godmanhood,* by Vladimir Solovyov. London: Denis Dobson Ltd., 1948.

Index

"absolute knowledge," 215, 230
aero-ionization, 348
Ahmed, Khan, 135–36
Aleksei, 131–32
Alexander I
  about, 201–2
  ambivalence, 205
  appearance, 202
  Baader and, 208–9
  death of, 211
  de Maistre and, 209–11
  Golitsyn and, 206–7
  Holy Alliance and, 204
  Koshelev and, 208
  Napoleon and, 202–3
  preserving tradition and, 204
  return after wars, 205
  serfs and, 202
  shift to status quo, 203
  von Krüdener and, 205, 206
Alexander II
  about, 239
  assassination of, 250, 251
  attempts on life of, 248
  end of serfdom and, 239–40, 247
  New Men and, 240–45
  People's Will and, 245

  taking of throne, 238–39
  Zhukovsky and, 239
Alexander III
  attempts on life of, 253
  as block to history's advance,
    254
  death of, 253, 254
  Pobedonostsev and, 254–56
  precautions, 253
  reform and, 252
  reign as short, 253
  Solovyov and, 251–52, 253, 256
  taking the throne, 250
  "Unshakable Autocracy," 256
Alexander Nevsky, 115–17, 139
Alexandra, 271, 277–79, 285, 286
"all-unity," 264
Alyosha (character), 26, 222, 392
Alypius, 95–96
Anastasianism, 363–64
Andreyev, Daniil
  about, 368–69
  arrest, 369–70
  concepts, 372
  prophecy, 373
  Roza Mir, 370–71, 373
  spirit "voices," 370

struggle and conflict, 372–73
vision, 371–72
in Vladimir Prison, 370
Anima Mundi, 262
Anthroposophy, 326–28
Antony, Saint, 94–95
apocalyptic temperament, 150
art, beauty and, 75, 76
Avvakum, 169, 170, 171

Baader, Franz von, 208–9, 217
Bailey, Alice, 22–23
Bakunin, Mikhail, 230–31
"Balkanization of Russia," 380
Barchenko, Alexander
  about, 337
  Bokii and, 339–41
  interrogation of, 338
  "mass hysteria," 339
  as "Red Merlin," 341
  revolution and, 337–38
  Shambhala belief, 341
  Tibetan expedition and, 340
Batu Khan, 106, 107, 116–17
beautiful souls
  about, 219–20
  characteristics of, 220
  descriptions of, 225
  Dostoyevsky depiction of, 221,
    223–24
  examples of, 224
beauty, 75, 76, 84, 90, 93, 107
Bekhterev, Vladimir, 333, 338–39
Belinsky, Vissarion, 225–27, 228, 229,
  231, 232, 328
Bely, Andrei, 281–82, 283, 310
Berdyaev, Nikolai, 5–6, 11, 25, 30, 38,
  172, 188, 236
  about, 306–7

absolute value of the individual and,
  307
as critical voice, 281
departure from Russia, 311–12
enforced egalitarianism, 310
The Free Academy of Spiritual
  Culture, 309
as intuitive and unsystematic
  thinker, 306
"Landmarks," 308
leveling, 311
lifelong companion, 308
man as creature of two worlds and,
  308–9
nature and, 309
"negative theology," 307
on our usual way of knowing, 390
professor of philosophy, 309–10
The Russia Idea, 25, 389
as "spiritual aristocrat," 309
Billington, James H., 34, 38–39, 55,
  65, 75, 93, 149, 153
bioenergy, 362, 368
"biosphere," 346
Biosphere 2, 353
Blavatsky, Helena Petrovna, 1–2,
  27–29, 189, 191, 192, 219
"Bloody Anna," 183–84
Bloody Sunday, 275–76, 291
Bokii, Gleb, 339–41
Bolshevik experiment, 8, 13, 38, 287
Bonaparte, Napoleon, 202–3, 205,
  210, 238
Borov, Dmitry, 289
Briussov, Valery, 282, 283
Brothers Karamazov, The
  (Dostoyevsky), 16, 34, 210, 222,
  257, 386, 392
Bruce, James, 179

Bulgakov, Sergei, 313–14, 317, 391–92
Byzantines, 57–58, 65, 71, 85–86, 90, 107, 139–40
Byzantium "New Rome," 64–66, 68, 70–72, 78, 128, 138

Catherine I, 183
Catherine the Great
  about, 182, 185
  death of, 200
  Freemasonry and, 187, 192
  Instruction of Catherine the Great and, 186, 188
  Ivan VI and, 183–84
  Novikov and, 191
  Pugachev rebellion and, 186–87
  purge of, 192
  Radishchev and, 190
  serfs and, 186
  son Alexander, 201–2
  Western ideas and, 185–86
Chaadaev, Peter, 213
Chamberlain, Lesley, 224, 229, 319, 391
Chernyshevsky, Nikolay, 24, 241, 242–43
Chizhevsky, Alexander, 347–49
Christianity
  Constantine and, 62, 63, 64
  corporeal aspect of, 266
  as disaster for the Slavs, 362
  Freemasonry as replacing, 191
  iconography and, 76
  monasticism in, 94–95
  as new state creed, 63
  Olga and, 69
  Orthodox, 2, 10, 11, 56, 383
Church of the Holy Wisdom, 66–67, 112–13, 140–41
Cimmerians, 46

Cold War, 353, 354, 355–56
common task, 301, 304, 305, 391
Comte, Auguste, 230, 243, 334
Constantine, 61–64, 67
Constantine VII, 70, 71, 72
Constantinople, 10–11, 38, 49, 53, 56–58, 64–69, 89–98, 129
Constantius I Chlorus, 61
"cosmic consciousness," 362
"cosmic dance," 327
Cosmists, 342–49, 361, 365
Cossack revolt, 174–75
Council of Florence and Ferrara, 78, 141, 142
Creation, 100
Crime and Punishment (Dostoyevsky), 26, 170, 221, 244, 257, 388
Crisis of Western Philosophy, The (Solovyov), 263
Crucifixion and Ascension, 100–101

Damp Mother Earth, 39–40, 42, 44–45, 99, 116, 364, 376
Dark Star Rising, 8, 9, 13
de Maistre, Joseph, 209–11, 255, 293
Devils, The (Dostoyevsky), 25, 221, 230, 241, 257, 310, 388
"dialectical tension," 214
Diocletian, 60–61, 62
"Dionysian initiations," 352
Dionysius, 81, 82, 83
Divine Sophia, 260, 261–62
Dmitry, 132–34
Dobrolyubov, Alexander, 241, 282–83
domovyk (deities of the household), 44
Dorzhiev, Agvan, 321
Dostoyevsky, Fyodor, 5, 6, 16, 20–21, 26–27
  "all is good" and, 391

beautiful souls and, 221, 223–24
death of, 257
"good man" and, 221, 223
importance of suffering and, 244
Peterson and, 300
planned Karamazov sequel, 224
duality, 43
Dugin, Alexander, 9, 38, 273, 339, 345, 387

Eckartshausen, Karl von, 207–8
Elizabeth, 183–84
encaustic, 76
Eurasia, 8, 9, 10, 13
exiles, 319
existentialism, 14

Fedorov, Nikolai
about, 296–97
"common task," 301, 304, 391
cosmic patriarchy, 304
education, 297–98
giving away earnings, 298–99
kenotic path, 298
large-scale thinking, 296
nature as raw material and, 314
with New Men, 299
"one big thing," 296, 301
Pamir Mountains and, 304–5
Peterson and, 299–300
pleasure and comfort and, 297
"Psychocracy," 301
recovery of "ancestral dust," 303
scale of ideas, 303–4
solar energy and, 303
Tolstoy and, 300
vision, 301
wandering life, 298
"feminization," 373

Feodor III, 174–75
fiction, truism of, 223
Florensky, Father Pavel, 12, 316–18
Frank, Semyon, 314–16, 317–18
Freemasonry
attitude toward, as changing, 191
Catherine the Great and, 187, 192
as "enlightened aristocracy," 188
Golitsyn and, 207
Martinism and, 197
Novikov and, 188–89
Paul sympathy towards, 201
Peter the Great and, 12, 178–79
popularity of, 193
as replacing Christianity, 191
"Strict Observance," 188–89
taking root in Russia, 187
Fukuyama, Francis, 356–57, 380, 383

Gapon, Father Gregory, 275–76
Geller, Uri, 353–54
Gemistos, George, 138–39
Genghis Khan, 105–6, 110, 111, 112
Gesamtkunstwerk ("total art works"), 328
Gippius, Zinaida, 280, 281
God
creationist view, 82
as everywhere, 124
existence of, 29
knowing, by emptying ourselves, 33
Solovyov and, 263
God-building
defined, 334
ending of, 337
Gorky and, 335–37
Lenin and, 334, 337
Lunacharsky and, 334–35
in recognizing creative potential, 335

Godunov, Boris, 162–63, 165, 166
Gogol, Nikolai, 37, 216, 226, 259,
    305–6
Golden Gate of Kiev, 93–94
Golitsyn, Alexander, 206–8
Golovin, Yevgeny, 351–53
Gorbachev, Mikhail, 355–56
Gorky, Maxim, 331–33, 335–36
Grand Inquisitor, 210, 255, 267,
    374–75
Great Schism, 78–79
"Great Synthesis," 222
Gregory of Palamas, 123–24
Gumilev, Lev, 8–9, 367–68
Gurdjieff, G. I., 30–31, 239, 274, 336,
    347

Hagia Sophia, 67–68, 112, 140–41
Hegel, 214, 226, 232, 235, 292, 318,
    356
heliobiology, 348
Herzen, Alexander
    about, 228–29
    influences, 229
    inheritance, 231
    "peasant soul" and, 230
    "right way to live," 231
    social revolution and, 232
    soul of the Russian peasant and, 233
    "well-being of society," 232
    with Westernizers, 229–30
Hesse, Hermann, 16–18, 19, 21, 150,
    287, 386, 392
Hesychasts, 33, 83, 95, 121–24,
    151–53, 191, 195, 275
"higher space," 329
Holy Alliance, 204, 208, 211
"holy fools." See yurodstvo
"holy pictures," 76

Holy Russia
    end of serfdom and, 285–318
    "God-bearing" people of, 42
    justification of idea of, 169–70
    as making a comeback, 10
    Muslim armies at war with, 238
    Putin and, 384
    reconnection with, 383
    return to, 393
    shattering defeat of, 275
Holy Spirit, 79, 82, 195
Holy Trinity, 79, 81
"human potential," 358

iconoclasm, 74–75, 76–77
iconography, 75–77
icons
    defined, 76
    first Russian, 95–96
    holy, 96–97
    as "meditations in color," 99
    miraculous powers of, 97–98
    as part of worship, 77
    as "pointer to eternal reality," 99
    as a promise, 98–99
    spreading knowledge through, 74
    transcendental beauty of, 90
    universal language of, 84
    as "windows on another world," 12,
        76, 216
Idiot, The (Dostoyevsky), 16, 72, 221
Igor, 57–58, 69, 103
Ilyin, Ivan
    about, 6, 373–75
    articles, 378–79
    February revolution and, 377
    Hitler and, 378
    "legal consciousness," 375, 376
    as monarchist, 376

Mussolini and, 377
"Our Tasks," 379–80
as political thinker, 5
unity and, 376
view of government, 375–76
"inner stillness," 119
Instruction of Catherine the Great,
    186, 188
"integral" knowledge, 236
"invisible church," 207–8
Invisible City of Kitezh, 107
Iuzhinskii Circle, 349–53
Ivan I, 129–32
Ivan III, 134, 140, 142, 143–45, 153
Ivan IV ("the Terrible")
    about, 153–54
    in Alexandrova, 159
    Anastasia's death and, 158
    coming to power, 154–55
    as cruel and ruthless, 154, 158–59
    daughter-in-law miscarriage and,
        161–62
    death of, 162
    early years of rule, 157
    killing son, 162
    long-term aim, 145
    Oprichnina, 212
    police state, 160
    reforms, 157
    as Right Man, 160
    as Russian man, 158
    tutoring by monks, 156

Jehovah's Witnesses, 197
"Judeobolshevism," 378
Justinian, 66–67

Karakozov, Dmitry, 248
Karamzin, Nikolay, 213

Khazars, 50–51, 52, 57
Khlysty, 193–95, 196–97, 207
Khomiakov, Alexis, 234–36
Khrushchev, Nikita, 331, 349
Kiev, 55–57, 92, 93–95, 104–5, 107–8
Kievan Rus,' 37, 39, 92, 93, 101, 103,
    106, 118
Kirlian, Semyon Davidovich, 354
knowledge
    absolute, 215, 230
    "integral," 236
    living, 316
    participatory, 235
    spreading through icons, 74
Koestler, Arthur, 51–52
Koshelev, Rodion, 208, 217
Kotik, Naum, 333
Kraus, Karl, 226
Krüdener, Barbara Juliane von, 205,
    206
Kulagina, Nina, 354

Lavrov, Pyotr, 246–71
"Law and Grace," 102
"Legal Marxists," 313
Lenin, Vladimir
    about, 291–92
    bold actions, 292
    Bolshevik revolution and, 291–92
    "crusade against subjectivity," 292
    death of, 329–30
    flattening spiritual life and, 312
    God-building and, 337
    as good behaviorist, 294
    "inner world" elimination, 292
    knowing "one big thing," 293
    Marx and, 292–93
    mirror theory of consciousness,
        293–94

murder of metropolitan of Kiev, 295
philosophy and, 294–95
religion and, 334
relocation plan, 319
revolution and classless society and,
376
"revolutionary elite," 290
view of human consciousness,
293
Lenin Library, 352
Leontiev, Konstantin, 258–59
leshie (wood spirits), 44
life, meaninglessness of, 259
"living knowledge," 235
Locke, John, 294
lost kingdom, 91, 92
"lovers of truth," 219
Lunacharsky, Anatoly, 334–35

Malevich, Kasimir, 77, 329–30
Mamleev, Yuri, 349–51
Martinism, 197–200
Marx, Karl, 214, 230, 287, 292, 295,
307, 313, 318
Mary, as God-bearer, 96–97
Mehmed II, 140, 141
Merzhkovsky, Dmitri, 280–81
mirror theory of consciousness,
293–94
modernity, 389
Monastery of the Holy Trinity,
120–21, 127
monasticism, 94–95, 121–25
"Mongol peril," 268
Mongols
church role and, 118
hierarchy, 117
history's depiction of, 110
impact of, 112

Kiev and, 106–8, 109
missionary work under, 119
pagan beliefs of, 111
religion and, 112
Russian northern expansion, 118–19
Russian psyche and, 37
Tengri and, 111
"Mongol yoke," 12, 268
Monomakh, Vladimir, 147–48
Monomakh's cap, 148
Moscow
Aleksei and, 132
founding of, 129
as holy city, 141–42
Ivan I and, 131
Ivan III and, 144
loss of holy city and, 141
Mamai and, 133
as new Byzantium, 143
opening gates, 134
Petr move to, 131
"sophistication and self-discipline"
and, 144
struggle for prominence, 129–30
as Third Rome, 142–43, 170
Muscovite empire, 37–38, 143–47,
156, 175
Myshkin (character), 72, 221
"mystic imperialism," 274

Napoleon, 202–3, 205, 210, 238
narodniki, 233
nationalism, 215
Nechayev, Sergei, 230
negative theology, 122
Neoplatonism, 79–80
New Age spirituality, 358
New Men
about, 240–41

enlightened selfishness and, 242
Fedorov with, 299
nihilists, 243–44
positivism, 292
reality and, 242
rejection of idealism, 241, 243
repercussions of rise of, 243
science as beacon, 241
Nicholas I
    about, 212
    battle against subversion, 213
    censorship and spies and, 212–13
    coming to power, 211–12
    death of, 237
    "primitive and crushing despotism
        of," 212
    reign, as stable, 247
    semi-clandestine societies, 216
Nicholas II
    about, 270–71
    Alexandra and, 271, 275, 285, 286
    autocracy defense and, 290
    coronation catastrophe, 269–70
    execution of, 285–86
    grand tour of India, 274
    "Master Philippe" and, 272
    as not cut out to be tsar, 270
    "October Manifesto," 277
    Papus and, 272–73
    Pobedonostsev and, 276
    Russo-Japanese War of 1904 and,
        271
Nietzsche, 16
nihilism, 243–44
Nikon
    about, 167
    Alexis and, 168–69, 173
    Avvakum and, 169, 170, 171
    campaign, 169

as a "great sun," 169
    megalomania, 172–73
    reforms, 170–71
    as Right Man, 168
    secular power, 171–72
    sovereign power, 171
    stripping of patriarchal vestments,
        173
    as via positiva, 168
Nizier-Vachot, Philippe, 272
noosphere, 346, 366
Nordau, Max, 16, 19
Notes from Underground
    (Dostoyevsky), 244, 257
Novgorod, 38, 52–56, 93, 105, 112–15
Novikov, Nikolay, 187, 188, 190–91,
    192

"October Manifesto," 277
Odoevsky, Vladimir Fedorovich,
    216–19, 223, 231, 232, 246
Old Believers, 170–71, 172, 175, 193,
    255
Olearius, Adam, 98
Oleg, 57–58, 74, 104
Olga
    about, 58
    approaching New Rome, 68
    baptism, 72–73
    building of churches, 84
    in Byzantium, 69–72
    Christianity and, 69
    conversion, 73, 74
    mission, 83–84
    return to Kiev, 74, 77
    way of affirmation and, 83
"one big thing," 293, 296, 301
Oprichniki, 160–61, 162, 256
Orage, A. R., 287

Orthodox Christianity, 2, 10, 11, 56, 295
Orthodox consciousness, 138
Ouspensky, P. D., 30, 31, 77, 284, 287–88, 315, 329, 352

pagan people, 11–12
"panpsychism," 344–45
Papus, 272–74, 290
Paul (tsar), 200–201, 202, 210
People's Will, 245, 247, 248, 252, 288
Petchersky Lavra (Monastery of the Caves), 94–95
Peter III, 184–85, 196, 200, 201
Peterson, Nikolai, 299–300
Peter the Great
    arrival on the throne, 175–76
    as "can-do" character, 176
    Catherine I and, 182–83
    changes in Russian life, 180
    childhood, 177
    crush of rebellion, 176
    Freemasonry and, 12, 178–79
    "Grand Embassy," 178
    Great Northern War and, 182
    monk requirements and, 180
    physical characteristics of, 178
    Russian seaport and, 177–78
    St. Petersburg and, 180–82
    success, 178
    Western Enlightenment and, 179
    "window" opened by, 258
Philaret, 166–67, 173
Philip II, 160–61
Philipov, Daniel, 194–95
Philotheus, 146–47, 148
Pisarev, Dmitry, 241, 242–43
Plato, 79–80, 138, 139, 216, 219, 265–66, 318

Pobedonostsev, Konstantin Petrovich, 254–56, 259, 276
"polarity and transcendence," 43
"police socialism," 275
political gangsterism, 357
polyovyk, 44
positivism, 292
"prayer of the heart," 123
Proclus, 80, 81
"Psychocracy," 301
Pugachev rebellion, 186–87
Pushkin, 163, 216–18, 226, 239, 257–58
Putin, Vladimir, 5–10, 13, 92, 357–58, 366, 374, 380–83, 387

Radishchev, Alexander, 190
Rasputin, 31–32, 193–94, 272–73, 277–79, 286, 290
"Rasputin's decade," 279
Rastrelli, Bartolomeo, 184
Razin, Stenka, 173–74
Red Terror, 4, 8, 127, 339, 367
religious colonization, 125
Religious-Philosophical Society, 280
"remarkable decade, the," 228
resurrection, 300
"right way to live," 231
Ringing Cedars movement, 364–67
Roerich, Nicholas
    about, 320
    Dorzhiev and, 321
    dreams of Shambhala and, 324–25
    as exile, 319–25
    Gorky and, 332
    inner purpose, 323
    interest in the East, 321
    letters for Stalin, 324
    outer side, 322–23

self-image, 322

spiritual side, 320–21

Tibet and, 324

Romanov, Alexis, 167–71, 173

Romanov, Feodor, 165–66

Romanov, Michael, 164–66

Romanov empire, 37, 163, 286–87

Romanticism, 215, 216

Rosicrucian movement, 191

Rublev, Andrei, 126–27

Rurik dynasty, 53–54

rusalki (mermaids), 44

Russia

  as country of extremes, 36–59

  as nation of "traditional values,"
    9–10

  promise of future synthesis, 21–22

  as troika, 37

Russian character, 3, 24, 26–27, 41,
  206

"Russian Faust," 216–19

Russian history, 37, 38, 55, 382

"Russian idea," 7, 8, 29

Russian identity

  development of, 199

  model for, 213

  new, search for, 362–63

  question of, 36, 55, 180, 216

  recovering, 361

  renewed, need for, 382

  search for, 386

  St. Petersburg as symbol, 181

"Russian justice," 101

Russian literature, 20–29, 31–33

Russian Man

  Belinsky as, 225

  as beyond good and evil, 19

  contradictions, 39, 158

  defined, 15, 18

  glimpse into chaos as, 18

  "underground man," 27, 353, 390

  as "unshaped material," 20

Russian people, 4, 11–12, 26

Russian philosophy, 13

Russian psyche

  duality of, 117

  free will and, 345

  Khrushchev "thaw" and, 349

  Kievan Rus' and, 91

  magical side of, suppression of, 192

  Mongols and, 37

  Peter the Great and, 177

  Tartar yoke and, 110

Russian soul, 3, 11, 25, 29, 218

Russian universalism, 257–58

Russification of Russia, 255

Russo-Japanese War of 1904, 271

Saint-Martin, Louis Claude de

  about, 197–98

  as "anti-Voltaire," 198

  Baader and, 208–9

  beliefs, 198, 199–200

  Jacob Boehme and, 200

  Society of Harmony and, 199

  as "Unknown Philosopher," 198

Sankt Pieter Swedes, 181

Sarmatians, 46–47

Satan, litanies to, 282–83

Schelling, Friedrich, 213–14, 215, 216,
  217, 229, 389

Schiller, Friedrich, 219–20

Scriabin, Alexander, 284

Scythians, 46, 47, 48

sedentary character, 24

Selivanov, Kondrati, 196–97

Seraphim of Sarov, 274–75

serfdom, end of, 239–40, 247

Sergius of Radonezh, Saint, 120–21, 124, 133, 159
Shambhala, 320–25, 337–42
Silver Age
　art and, 75
　cultural epoch, 3–4
　defined, 2
　demonic and, 282–83
　ideas, return to, 393
　incompatibility with iron regime, 4–5
　"Mongol peril" and, 268
　new religious consciousness, 257
　poets and artists of, 77
　sages of, 5–6, 7–8, 13–14, 391–93
　start of, 256
"Six Wings, The," 149
Skoptsy, 193, 195–97, 207
Slavic Native Faith, 362, 363, 364, 372, 376
Slavophiles, 233–37, 258, 270, 305, 363
Society of Harmony, 199
Solovyov, Vladimir
　about, 260–61
　Alexander III and, 251–53
　"all-unity," 264
　Antichrist and, 389
　characteristics of, 260
　childhood, 261
　death of, 269
　Divine Sophia and, 261–62
　as embodying spirit of the time, 259–60
　God and, 263
　last years, 267
　levels of "being," 265

people as "organs of Godmanhood," 266
plea for clemency, 251–53, 256
predictions, 268–69
Putin suggestion and, 5, 6
search for something more, 263
spiritualism and, 264
"Universal Church," 264–65
vision of unity, 264–65, 268
Sorsky, Nil, 151–52, 153, 171, 191
"soul of the race," 215
Soviet Union, 38, 351, 353, 355–56, 358, 379–80
"space bridge," 359
Spengler, Oswald, 17, 20–21, 28, 78, 259, 386
spirit, obsession with, 30
spiritualism, 264, 271, 282
Stalin, Joseph, 330–31, 337, 341, 349
Stankevich, Nikolay, 224
Steiner, Rudolf, 1–4, 6, 13–14, 26–27, 260, 281, 327
Stepanov, Vladimir, 352–53
Stephen of Novgorod, 127–28
Stephen of Perm, Saint, 119
Stolypin, Pyotr, 288–89
St. Petersburg, 55, 180–82, 184
"Strict Observance," 188–89
Stylites, 150
Svyatoslav I, 83–84, 85–86, 87
Symbolism, 279–81, 282, 328–29, 335, 361

Tale of the Princes of Vladimir, 147
Tartar yoke, 37, 109–10, 130–31, 133–35, 144, 148
Temujin, 105–6
Tengriism, 110

"theology of light," 81
theosis, 125–26
Theosophical Society, 27, 29, 191, 219, 274
Third Rome, 142–43, 170, 305, 383
third way, 21–22, 43, 385–93
Tolstoy, Leo, 75, 203, 210, 226, 251, 259, 300
Tomberg, Valentin, 325–27
"transhumanism," 365
Trans-Siberian Railway, 274, 298
Trotsky, Lev, 317, 331, 348, 378
"truth," 218–19, 235, 276
Tsiolkovsky, Konstantin
    about, 342–43
    collapsible metal dirigible and, 343–44
    as father of Russian space travel, 303, 344
    at Fedorov's feet, 303, 342
    "panpsychism," 344–45
    revolution and, 344

Ukraine, 39–40, 41, 356, 380
Ulyanov, Vladimir Ilyich. *See* Lenin, Vladimir
"uncreated light," 122, 124
"underground man," 27, 353, 390
Union of the Russian People, 288
universalism, Russian, 257–58
"Unshakable Autocracy," 256
utilitarianism, 13, 219, 232, 240, 257–58, 299, 308–9, 311

Vaino, Anton, 366
Vandals, 47–48

Varangians, 53–54, 55–56, 163
Vasilii II, 136, 137
Vasilii III, 145–46, 154
Vasilii IV, 155, 163
Venevitinov, Dmitry, 224
Vernadsky, Vladimir, 345–47
Vikings, 38, 48–50, 53–54, 56–57
Vladimir
    about, 86
    baptism, 89, 91, 92
    Basil II and, 87, 88–89
    code of law enforcement, 90–91
    emissaries, 86–87
    Putin praise of, 92–93
    warriors, baptism of, 90
    worship of pagan deities, 90
Volotsky, Joseph, 152–53, 156

War and Peace (Tolstoy), 203, 210, 259, 377
way of affirmation, 82, 83
way of negation, 82–83
Wilson, Colin, 23, 28–30, 48, 63, 154, 158, 222, 387
"windows on another world," 12, 76, 216
"wisdom lovers," 218

Yaroslav the Wise, 93–94, 101–3, 112, 113, 143, 155
Yeltsin, Boris, 359–60
yurodstvo, 28, 150, 225, 32.95

Zhukovsky, Vasily, 239
Zoroastrianism, 43
Zossima, Father (character), 34, 222, 330, 392

About the Author

Max Jones-Lachman

Gary Lachman is the author of many books on the links between consciousness, culture, and the Western esoteric tradition, including *Dark Star Rising: Magick and Power in the Age of Trump, Lost Knowledge of the Imagination, Beyond the Robot: The Life and Work of Colin Wilson,* and *The Secret Teachers of the Western World.* He writes for several journals in the US, UK, and Europe, lectures around the world, and his work has been translated into more than a dozen languages. In a former life he was a founding member of the pop group Blondie and in 2006 was inducted into the Rock and Roll Hall of Fame. Before moving to London in 1996 and becoming a full-time writer, Lachman studied philosophy, managed a metaphysical book shop, taught English literature, and was Science Writer for UCLA. He is an adjunct professor of Transformative Studies at the California Institute of Integral Studies. He can be reached at

www.garylachman.co.uk
www.facebook.com/GVLachman
twitter.com/GaryLachman